The Democratic Theory of Michael Oakeshott

British Idealist Studies Series
1: Oakeshott

imprint-academic.com/idealists

The Democratic Theory of Michael Oakeshott

Discourse, Contingency, and 'The Politics of Conversation'

Michael Minch

imprint-academic.com

Published in the UK by Imprint Academic
PO Box 200, Exeter EX5 5YX, UK

Published in the USA by Imprint Academic
Philosophy Documentation Center
PO Box 7147, Charlottesville, VA 22906-7147, USA

ISBN 9 781845 40152 8

A CIP catalogue record for this book is available from the
British Library and US Library of Congress

imprint-academic.com/idealists

Contents

Acknowledgments

The following persons have given me immeasurable support and assistance. These contributions were, in nearly all cases, moral and emotional in nature, rather than intellectual in kind. For this reason, it was all the more important. My gratitude, then, must be expressed here to Danna Burns Minch, Peter Diamond, Tom McClenahan, Clifton Sanders, Suzanne Bratcher, Cindy and Scott Smith, Scott Abbott, Brian Birch, Chris Weigel, Laurie Whitt, Chandran Kukathas, and Noël O'Sullivan. Special thanks to Ben Rankin for proofreading this book, and preparing its Index. His help in this regard was incalculable. Thanks also to Cathryn Thayne for help with the bibliography. Of course, all errors in this book are mine alone.

I dedicate this book to my children, Bethany Marie and Dane Michael. May they come to know a more democratic future, and therefore, a more just and peaceable world.

Chapter 1

Introduction

This book offers a description, explanation, and evaluation of Michael Oakeshott's democratic theory. He was not a democratic theorist as such, but as a twentieth-century English political theorist for whom liberal theory held deep importance, his thought often engaged democratic theory implicitly, and many times did so explicitly. Fortuitously, my project penetrates two renewals. The first is the revitalization of interest in Oakeshott, and the second is the renewal of democratic theory which began in the 1980s. In respect to this latter renewal, I will engage the deliberative turn in democratic theory. These revivals create the context for this new look at Oakeshott. To state the matter as a problem, one might say that in light of new and fecund democratic theory, it is a problem for political theory if one of the most important political theorists of the twentieth century is left out of the discourse *insofar* as he has something relevant to say about deliberative democracy. It is of no small importance that almost all the work in democratic theory being done these days is of the deliberative/discursive kind, or responses to it. That is, deliberative theory is driving the agenda of democratic theory. I argue that Oakeshott does indeed have something relevant to say which is applicable to this democratic theory.

I will say some new things about Oakeshott, but not, in a direct way, too much about democratic theory. It is the argument I will put forward about conceptual relationships between his thought and deliberative democracy which will provide new ways of understanding him. I will not be making new claims about deliberative theory; this project's purpose will be to see new things about Oakeshott as he is understood in respect to such theory. My argument will be that his theory of "civil association", in particular, found in *On Human Conduct*, but not unrelated to his other texts, finds certain compatibilities with the deliberative turn. Insofar as this is the case, reading him in this way brings his thought to new light. It makes some contribution to how he can be understood. Although I will consider Oakeshott's political theory up to *On Human Conduct* in respect to how it sheds light on his understanding and evaluation of democracy, it is his theorization of civil association in and the argument of *On Human Conduct* which will be of most interest.

His work before *On Human Conduct* makes some reference to democracy. In "The Masses in Representative Democracy", he is critical of "popular government" because he sees it as fitting "mass man".[1] "Popular government" in this essay looks much like rationalism in, for example, "Rationalism in Politics",[2] and what becomes "enterprise association" and *universitas* in *On Human Conduct*, because it is defined by the substantive engagements and interests it promotes.[3] Unsurprisingly, Oakeshott understands democracy proper as parliamentary or representative democracy, and sees it as a superlative expression of the individuality that is so important to the liberal tradition, both morally and politically. He writes approvingly of democracy as the disappearing of the ruling class,[4] he thinks that "education must serve democracy",[5] and he notes that if "the English manner of politics is to be planted elsewhere in the world, it is perhaps appropriate that it should first be abridged into something called 'democracy' … ".[6] In some of his earliest essays he argues that democratic theory stands in contrast to rationalism and is, rather, based on skepticism.[7] In "The Rule of Law", published late in his career, he writes that what the rule of law "requires for determining the *jus* of a law is not a set of abstract criteria but an appropriately argumentative form of discourse in which to deliberate the matter; that is, a form of moral discourse … ".[8] The fullest theorization of democracy comes, however, I argue, in *On Human Conduct*.

Oakeshott's civil association is a nonfoundational, noninstrumental, nonpurposive, and radically contingent association, and therefore, as such, its content is not predetermined by its members: this is to say, that although a political association has "content", for example, rules or laws, incentives and disincentives, and purposes of various kinds (e.g., public safety); that content need not be of any particular *kind* in Oakeshott's civil association. It is entirely up to the association's members to determine the content of their association. If civil association is as nonpurposive and contingent as I will argue Oakeshott theorizes it, then such an association

---

1   "The Masses in Representative Democracy" (1961) can be found in *Rationalism in Politics and Other Essays* (Indianapolis: Liberty Press, 1991), 363–83.

2   "Rationalism in Politics" (1947) also in *Rationalism in Politics and Other Essays*, 5–42.

3   Paul Franco, *The Political Philosophy of Michael Oakeshott* (New Haven: Yale University Press, 1990), 155.

4   In the 1949 essay, "The Universities", in *The Voice of Liberal Learning* (Indianapolis: Liberty Fund, 2001), 120.

5   These words belong to Timothy Fuller, from his Foreword to Oakeshott's collection of essays published as *The Voice of Liberal Learning* (viii). Fuller's comment relates to a general argument made by Oakeshott throughout these essays and his views about learning, education, and the proper role of the university.

6   In the 1951 essay "Political Education", *The Voice of Liberal Learning*, 171; also published in *Rationalism in Politics and Other Essays*, 43–69.

7   See, e.g., "Scientific Politics" and "The Customer is Never Wrong" in *Religion, Politics and the Moral Life*, edited by Timothy Fuller (New Haven: Yale University Press, 1993), 116–7.

8   "The Rule of Law" in *On History and Other Essays* (Indianapolis: Liberty Fund, 1999), 156.

leaves an open space for deliberative politics. Further, I will argue that because Oakeshott so highly valued individuality, freedom, "self-enactment", and concomitantly, was deeply concerned about forces and structures (especially the state) that infringed such individuality, freedom, and self-enactment; deliberative democracy is not only compatible with civil association, but that civil association, at least in some respects, *is* democracy that needs and promotes discourse. That is, deliberative democracy and civil association have theoretical congruous interconnections and overlaps. Oakeshott specifies a number of "postulates" which constitute human conduct, which, in turn, constitutes the basis for the civil condition and civil association. One of the postulates he theorizes is, in fact, deliberation.[9] About the civil condition he theorizes as normative and the politics it sustains, he writes,

> As a deliberative and an argumentative engagement directed to reaching conclusions sustained by reasons designed to persuade others of their cogency, politics is identifiable not in terms of persons, places, or occasions, but only in respect of a focus of attention and a subject of discourse. The conditions of *respublica* ... may allow for the election or appointment of certain persons to devote themselves to political deliberation and negotiation ... [but] there is nothing in the engagement itself to suggest a profession and much to eloquently deny it ... . Political deliberation is, of course, conditional upon the postulates of human conduct and of moral and civil association ... .[10]

Although I will interrogate Oakeshott rather thoroughly in respect to his career-long political theory, I can only use the work of representative figures to define deliberative democratic theory. The literature is far too substantial to do otherwise. I will consider the work of John Rawls, Jürgen Habermas, John Dryzek, and Amy Gutmann and Dennis Thompson for this purpose. Gutmann and Thompson have coauthored their important work on deliberative democracy, so they will naturally be treated as one source. Between these four perspectives, I will engage much of the most important work in deliberative theory.

This book contributes to Oakeshott studies in that it considers his work in a new light and adds to our understanding of his political theory, and his theories of political activity, morality, and mostly, civil association. Of course, for those interested in deliberative democracy, new considerations of Oakeshott's civil association may shed light into that literature too, especially in respect to his treatment of moral practice. Again however, this book is meant to offer insight into Oakeshott, and the modest contribution to democratic theory will be secondary and derivative of the effort to see Oakeshott in a new way. This project thus follows well-worn paths insofar as work which warrants consideration over time is routinely

---

9   OHC (New York: Oxford University Press, 1996), 44–46.
10   *OHC*, 165, 173. *"Respublica"* names, for Oakeshott, "the comprehensive conditions of [civil] association", *OHC*, 108.

scrutinized from various angles and perspectives, so that new conceptual connections can be made, new directions for further exploration suggested, new questions raised, and perhaps, even, old or new questions answered.[11]

Oakeshott is interested, most fundamentally in the problematic of human conduct. His exploration of this matter leads him quickly and directly to the perennial question of how human beings conduct themselves in respect to one another and how they cooperate. His political theory, especially as guided by the book which reflects "his thoughts [put] together", *On Human Conduct*, develops from consideration of human association and moves to political association.[12] His political theory holds as fundamental the radical agency, individuality, freedom, and contingency of human beings. He theorizes a way for persons to live in association which is intrinsically moral and at the same time, legal, contingent, and nonpurposive. This is, he writes, "civil association", and in the third and final essay of *On Human Conduct*, he turns to the use of a term from medieval Roman private law, *societas*, to signify civil association as it is theorized and insofar as it is approximated in concrete terms as an historical state.[13]

Briefly, then, the connections between Oakeshott's theory and the deliberative turn that I argue are meaningful and, as such, contribute to Oakeshott studies are as follows. I begin with the matter of contingency. Several scholars have noted the radically contingent nature of Oakeshott's theory of political activity and civil association.[14] It should also be mentioned that Mapel and others understand the meaning of contingency in

---

11   In respect to Oakeshott, he has been studied, for example, from the perspective of his understanding and treatment of Hobbes, and of history, his defense of modernity, his scepticism and critique of the Enlightenment, his conception of philosophical understanding, and his conception of political activity. See respectively, Ian Tregenza *Michael Oakeshott on Hobbes: A Study in the Renewal of Philosophical Ideas* (2003); Luke O'Sullivan, *Oakeshott on History* (2003); Efraim Podoksik, *In Defence of Modernity: Vision and Philosophy in Michael Oakeshott* (2003); Roy Tseng, *The Sceptical Idealist: Michael Oakeshott as a Critic of the Enlightenment* (2003); Kenneth B. McIntyre, *The Limits of Political Theory: Oakeshott's Philosophy of Civil Association* (2004); and Suvi Soininen, *From a "Necessary Evil" to an Art of Contingency: Michael Oakeshott's Conception of Political Activity* (2005). All books published by Imprint Academic, Exeter, UK.

12   Michael Oakeshott, *On Human Conduct*, vii. He writes, "The themes explored here have been with me nearly as long as I remember, but I have left the task of putting my thoughts together almost too late … ".

13   Civil association and *societas* are "ideal characters", much like Weber's ideal types, which are theorized as opposite to "enterprise association" and *univerisitas*.

14   Ian Tregenza writes, "… it is difficult to avoid the conclusion many commentators have pointed to regarding his [Oakeshott's] preference for this type of association on account of its privileging a contingent, historic disposition to cultivate individuality". In *Michael Oakeshott on Hobbes* (Imprint Academic, 2003), 215. See, most notably, David Mapel, "Civil Association and the Idea of Contingency", *Political Theory*, Vol. 18, No. 3 (August 1990); and "Purpose and Politics: Can There be a Non-Instrumental Civil Association?", *Political Science Reviewer* 21 (Spring 1992); Terry Nardin, *The Philosophy of Michael Oakeshott* (University Park: The Pennsylvania State University Press, 2001); Efraim Podoksik, *In Defence of Modernity: Vision and Philosophy in Michael Oakeshott* (Imprint Academic, 2003); and Suvi Soininen, *From a "Necessary Evil" to an Art of Contingency: Michael Oakeshott's Conception of Political Activity* (Imprint

Oakeshott as nearly synonymous with "nonpurposive" and "noninstrumental". They are right in doing so, as Oakeshott himself uses these terms in synonymous and nearly synonymous ways, as these terms are so interconnected as to often be nearly indistinguishable.

As I wrote above, if Oakeshott's theorization of political activity in general, and civil association in particular, is as contingent as it is widely interpreted, then *one of the ways* association and politics can be expressed is through deliberation. Benjamin Barber, among others, sees this, writing that Oakeshott "envisions the political order as *defined by* rules rather than ends, by processes rather than substance, by common deliberation rather than common action … ".[15] Mapel puts it this way: "Oakeshott's view of authority is compatible with a wide variety of political arrangements, including … participatory democracy … it is a mistake to think of civil association as a competitor with participatory democracy".[16] Barber, Mapel (and others, as we will see) must be correct in their interpretation of Oakeshott at this point. Oakeshott is at pains to do two things that bear directly on the question of the compatibility of democratic deliberation on the one hand, and with political activity and civil association on the other.

First, over the course of many years, in one form or another, he waged a philosophical war against what he famously termed "Rationalism", and what comes to be known in *On Human Conduct* as enterprise association and *universitas*. His fundamental commitment to robust agency, individuality, freedom, and self-enactment, and the concomitant limited state such values often imply (and he certainly thought they implied), lead to the space and freedom for citizens ("*cives*" in *On Human Conduct*) to engage in the processes of their own choosing. Further, not only are citizens theorized as having such normative freedom, but we would be caught short, seeing an incompleteness in an Oakeshottian civil association in which citizens obediently followed the dictates of others, and lived homogenized, submissive lives. While in some sense Oakshottian citizens *could* choose this for themselves, one can hardly imagine Oakeshott approving of such a choice, or finding it plausible that persons *would* choose it for themselves. Mere products and servants of rationalistic institutions, structures, and customs do not befit the citizens he theorizes as those who live properly in civil association. Oakeshott was a constant

---

Academic, 2005). A polyvalent, complexified, or nuanced conception of contingency leads to the inclusion of Timothy Fuller, "The Poetics of the Civil Life" in Jesse Norman, ed., *The Achievement of Michael Oakeshott* (London: Gerard Duckworth, 1993), 67–81; Glenn Worthington, "Michael Oakeshott on Life: Waiting with Godot", *History of Political Thought*, 16, 1 (Spring 1995)105–19; David Walsh, *The Growth of the Liberal Soul* (Columbia: The University of Missouri Press, 1997), 56–70; and Wendell John Coats, Jr., "Michael Oakeshott and the Poetic Character of Human Activity" in *Political Theory and Practice: Eight Essays on a Theme* (Selinsgrove, PA: Susquehanna University Press, 2003), 101–11.

15   Benjamin Barber, *The Conquest of Politics: Liberal Philosophy in Democratic Times* (Princeton: Princeton University Press, 1988), 155 (italics are mine).

16   Mapel, "Civil Association and the Idea of Contingency", 405.

critic of states that sought or exercised more control over individuals than he thought consistent with the individuality and freedom he saw as the high achievement of Western civilization. If what he meant by Rationalism, enterprise association, and *universitas* is a detriment to the best kinds of human lives and association, it follows that democratic means to diminish such detriment might easily be an allowable feature of political activity and civil association.

John Dryzek makes much the same point, in stronger form, when he writes that "Instrumental rationality is antidemocratic ... [it] represses individuals".[17] He argues that contemporary heirs to Aristotle such as Arendt, Gadamer, MacIntyre, and Habermas have as a common aim the resurrection of "authentic and reasonable discourse" and that such discourse "has been eroded over the centuries by instrumental rationality manifested in hierarchy, administration, and technocracy ... ".[18] Dryzek is a deliberative theorist influenced by both critical theory and liberal theory, but from the critical theory side, he notes that it is "chary of overly precise specification" and that critical theorists are "profoundly suspicious of the contemporary state" and that they renounce "instrumental manipulation of social conditions, even in pursuit of manifestly desirable ends". It follows, then, that discourse is valuable in "the public space between individuals and the state".[19]

This sounds much like an Oakeshottian warning against Rationalism and *universitas*, the rationalist state. If Dryzek is correct, then some relation exists between "authentic and reasonable discourse" and discursive democracy on the one hand; and the diminishment of "instrumental rationality", or what Oakeshott called Rationalism, on the other. Dryzek adds that Habermas also worries about the destructive invasion of "unrelenting instrumental rationality" into the "lifeworld" (Habermas's term for human relationships outside of politics, similar, but not identical, in meaning to civil society).[20] As I argue below, Habermas's theorization of deliberative democracy, like that of Dryzek, is, in part, seen as a necessary response to this rationalism.

---

17   John S. Dryzek, *Discursive Democracy: Politics, Policy, and Political Science* (New York: Cambridge University Press, 1999), 5.

18   *Ibid.*, 14.

19   *Ibid.*, 40. Similarly, and sounding Oakshottian again, Dryzek adds "it is the authority claimed by expertise that leads rationality to confront, corrupt, and perhaps even destroy democracy", 218. In articulating the same idea, Oakeshott might say that "popular government", rationalism, and "the politics of faith" threaten "representative democracy". See Oakeshott, *The Politics of Faith and the Politics of Scepticism*, edited by Timothy Fuller (New Haven: Yale University Press, 1996). Cf. Christopher Lasch, "Conversation and "The Civic Arts" in *The Revolt of the Elites and the Betrayal of Democracy* (New York: Norton, 1995).

20   Habermas uses the term *zweckrationalitat* to signify the concept Dryzek refers to as instrumental rationality.

Second, Oakeshott did not merely define and attack Rationalism, enterprise association, and *universitas*;[21] he also constructed a positive theory of human association that, as Barber and Mapel recognize, has built-in features which are entirely coherent as connected to deliberative democracy. I have already touched on the possibility of nonpurposiveness, noninstrumentality, and contingency as allowing deliberative democracy; but it can be added that there is something about these phenomena (and note that they move between nearly synonymous and synonymous meanings) that may *call for* discourse, and therefore, deliberation. Free individuals who live in contingency would rather straightforwardly be free to engage other such citizens in discussion about political and associational matters, just as they would be free to engage fellow associate about other matters. Not only would they be free to do so if their political association reflected their status as free individuals who have authentic agency, but the very terms of their agency might call for discursive engagement because such terms would be considered most fitting to such agents. Here, I think Oakeshott's sensibility of *conversation* to be helpful. Rorty refers to Oakeshott's theorization of *societas* as against *universitas*, as "a band of fellow eccentrics collaborating for purposes of mutual protection rather than as a band of fellow spirits united by a common goal".[22] It is the idea of collaboration, discourse, deliberation, or conversation that Rorty (as with Barber, et al.) also identifies as central to Oakeshott's civil association and *societas* that I think constitutes some measure of raw material for building a bridge between Oakeshott and deliberative democracy. His essay "The Voice of Poetry in the Conversation of Mankind" contributes to a kind of *gestalt* that Fuller and Coats have also recognized in Oakeshott.[23] While this essay is about the voice of poetry, it is also about *conversation* among modes of discourse and understanding; that is, it is also about the value of conversation. I have so far suggested that Oakeshott's theorization and use of the concepts of nonpurposiveness, noninstrumentality, contingency, Rationalism, and conversation suggest connections to discourse and deliberation (rationalism does so in a negative way; the other conceptions do so positively). Another dimension of Oakeshott's theory relevant to discourse and deliberative democracy is his understanding of morality and moral practice.

---

21 Oakeshott did not "attack" enterprise association and *universitas* with the unconditional vivacity he reserved for Rationalism. As "ideal characters" they did not do the concrete damage done by rationalism. Further, he recognized that all societies and states can only be a mixture of civil association and enterprise association, *societas* and *universitas*.

22 Richard Rorty, *Contingency, Irony, and Solidarity* (New York: Cambridge University Press, 1993), 59.

23 "The Voice of Poetry in the Conversation of Mankind" (1959), in *Rationalism in Politics and Other Essays*, 488–541. Recall that Fuller writes of the extension of poetic and conversational character to civil life, and Coats writes of its extension to human activity; in Fuller, "The Poetics of the Civil Life" and Coats, "Michael Oakeshott and the Poetic Character of Human Activity", *op. cit.*

Amy Gutmann and Dennis Thompson begin their influential book, *Democracy and Disagreement* by maintaining that,

> Of the challenges that American democracy faces today, none is more formidable than the problem of moral disagreement. Neither the theory nor the practice of democratic politics has so far found an adequate way to cope with conflicts about fundamental values. We address the challenge of moral disagreement here by developing a conception of democracy that secures a central place for moral discussion in political life.
>
> Along with a growing number of other political theorists, we call this conception deliberative democracy ... although the idea has a long history, it is still in search of a theory.[24]

Below I argue that Oakeshott's moral theory is of singular importance within his theory of civil association. In *On Human Conduct* he argues that civil association *is* moral association, that is, that it is essentially and inextricably moral in character. If civil association not only allows for deliberative democracy, but if deliberative democratic politics *fits* civil association, then Oakeshott's theorization of morality must comport with, if not promote and necessitate, deliberative practices and/or structures. As Gutmann and Thompson indicate, deliberative theory is quite concerned with moral problems and moral discourse; and quite often such theory develops in response to various impasses and conflicts in moral discourse. A basic feature of the problematic is how to take morality seriously without treating it reductively; that is, how can we deal with moral disagreement seriously without reducing our conversations and commitments (cultural, political, and legal) to mere prescriptions and admonitions, dividing society into winners and losers? How can we maintain liberal values of individuality, freedom, and plurality without obfuscating or obliterating the importance of moral convictions and discourse?

The nonpurposive, noninstrumental, contingent, and adverbial nature of morality, as Oakeshott theorizes it, allows for and encourages discourse; and at the same time, because morality is intrinsic to our humanity and, therefore, to all human association, it is of irreducible importance. Morality is not, for Oakeshott, a sphere, dimension, or arena of human existence; rather, it is intrinsic to and inseparable from all aspects of human existence. We cannot but act morally (which does not necessarily mean doing the right thing), because we are essentially moral beings. Since civil association is moral association, is constituted by moral practice, the discursive practices in such association must conform — normatively — to moral practice.

This inherent connection between morality and civil association is one of the reasons Chantal Mouffe is drawn to Oakeshott. She argues that what

---

24 Amy Gutmann and Dennis Thompson, *Democracy and Disagreement* (Cambridge: Belknap/Harvard, 1997), 1.

we need is a mode of political association which, without postulating the existence of a substantive common good, nevertheless,

> implies the idea of commonality, or an ethico-political bond that cre-
> ates a linkage among participants in the association, allowing us to
> speak of a political "community" even if not in the strong sense. In
> other words, what we are for is a way to accommodate the distinctions
> between public and private, morality and politics which have been the
> great contribution of liberalism to modern democracy, without
> renouncing the ethical nature of political association.
>
>   I consider that ... the reflections on civil association proposed by
> Michael Oakeshott in *On Human Conduct* can be very illuminating for
> such a purpose.[25]

Mouffe agrees with Mapel that civil association creates a wide space for a variety of political forms which can include deliberative democracy. She is concerned to point out that although Oakeshott makes conservative use of the distinction between *societas* and *universitas*, that the distinction need not be conservative.[26] There is no need, for our purposes, however, to negotiate the question of conservative or radical uses to which Oakeshott can be put. Discourse and deliberation are neither "conservative" or "radical" in an essential or direct sense. It is important to see, however, that for Oakeshott, political discourse is intrinsically related to morality, as my quote from "The Rule of Law" above implies.

Insofar as Oakeshott values agency, individuality, freedom, self-enactment, and at least the latter three are moral phenomena, then it is the way that civil association makes space for this aspect of our moral lives that may be of most importance in respect to the connection between the moral practice intrinsic to civil association and discursive practices in deliberative democracy. This insight is rightly shared with Mouffe, by Mapel and Walsh.[27] Lawrence Cahoone agrees that the moral character of civil association inherently promotes certain moral features in our politics. He writes that the "goal-less endurance" of conservatism (which Oakeshott called civil association) requires that conservative government "must as far as possible preserve life and prevent misery".[28] Further, glossing Oakeshott, he adds,

> Society as civil is society understood as a moral association of free
> members ... . In a land-locked paraphrase of Oakeshott, civil society
> and culture engage in a kind of dance which has no end outside itself.

---

25 Chantal Mouffe, "Democratic Citizenship and the Political Community", in Mouffe, ed.,
    Dimensions of Radical Democracy: Pluralism, Citizenship, and Democracy (London: Verso, 1992),
    231–32. This chapter is also found in Chantal Mouffe, *The Return of the Political* (London: Verso,
    1993), 59–73.

26 *Dimensions of Radical Democracy*, 234.

27 David Walsh, *The Growth of the Liberal Soul* (Columbia: University of Missouri Press, 1997),
    56–69.

28 Lawrence E. Cahoone, *Civil Society: The Conservative Meaning of Liberal Politics* (Malden, MA:
    Blackwell, 2002), 131.

> But dancing, when it is well-done, often kindles hopes whose realiza-
> tion would end the dance. The point, however, is to keep dancing.[29]

The hopes, one hardly need add, are moral in nature. That is, civil association (which Cahoone sees as civil society) is not only inherently moral but,
as such, generates moral practice signified by moral hope.

There is scarcely a need to demonstrate the deep concern that motivates
deliberative theorists in respect to how morality is diminished insofar as
democracy is limited. My quote of Gutmann and Thompson is merely a
representation of this fact. We will see how clear this is when considering
the theories not only of Gutmann and Thompson, but Rawls, Dryzek, and
Habermas. As I will show, Oakeshott's civil association democratizes
morality in that he disassociates morality from hierarchy, specialization,
and rule-bound behavior. He sees morality as woven into the warp and
woof of everyday life and our human agency, individuality, and freedom
as primary dimensions of this morality. If political association is to bear
the proper reflection of human conduct, it too will embody moral practice
and as such promote freedom and other moral commitments. I argue
below that civil association does just this and, in this way, connects to
certain commitments pervasive in deliberative theorists.

It is customary, of course, to stake out one's position over against contending positions in an introductory chapter such as this, and to make
one's argument against alternative arguments in the pages that follow. I
write, however, primarily against a void, against inattention more than
against contending views. I am unaware of any argument that Oakeshott
theorizes discourse out of politics, or that deliberation violates his theory
of political activity or civil association. However, there is one carefully
made argument about the *limits* of Oakeshott's theory to which I must
respond. Steven Gerencser's "A Democratic Oakeshott?" is a detailed
account of Oakeshott's understanding of authority. Gerencser argues that
Oakeshott places authority beyond the reach of critical deliberation,
although he also admits of what appear to be conflicting views in
Oakeshott's work about this question. In sum, he finds Oakeshott to be
neither "directly amenable to the participatory or radical democrat, or …
directly inimical".[30]

I think that Oakeshott is more amenable to deliberative democracy than
does Gerencser, and I certainly think civil association leads to deeper

---

29   *Ibid.*, 263. Those familiar with Oakeshott will recognize Cahoone's allusion to this famous
     passage: "In political activity, then, men sail a boundless and bottomless sea; there is neither
     harbour for shelter nor floor for anchorage, neither starting-place nor appointed destination.
     The enterprise is to keep afloat on an even keel; the sea is both friend and enemy; and the
     seamanship consists in using the resources of a traditional manner of behaviour in order to
     make a friend of every hostile occasion." In "Political Education", *Rationalism in Politics*, 60.

30   Steven Anthony Gerencser, "A Democratic Oakeshott?" in *Political Research Quarterly*, 52, 4
     (December 1999), 864. This essay holds much in common with the last chapter of Gerencser's
     book, "Oakeshott, Dissent, and Democracy", in *The Skeptic's Oakeshott* (New York: St. Martin's
     Press, 2000).

democratic sensibilities and structures than any Oakeshott demands or assumes. After a critical reading of Gerencser, I seek to demonstrate in what respects his argument is incorrect.

Even democratic theorists most committed to deliberative and participatory structures argue about where boundaries are to be found that either invite or seal off deliberation. Everything cannot always be subject to change; all agree that boundaries exist and in some respects, in some places, deliberation stops in even the most democratic of political associations. For Gerencser, Oakeshott disallows deliberation about the basic structure of authority but invites deliberation about all political matters in question, after the basic rules of authority are established. He imports the conceptions of "consensus", "conflict", and "antagonism" into Oakeshott's theory mistakenly and thereby constructs an argument which is in some respects incoherent and in other respects too simple. I will argue that if Gerencser's argument is correct, Oakeshott's theories of authority and politics are grossly incoherent and confusing. My project, then, interrogates Gerencser as well as offers an argument to this (relatively) unattended void.

The inattention is not absolute, of course, because Mapel, Mouffe, and Gerencser have turned their attention to the relationship between Oakeshott and deliberative, or participatory, democracy.[31] Mapel and Mouffe have offered brief essays that gesture in the direction of Oakeshott's compatibility with deliberative democracy, and while I think their suggestions are correct, there still exists the need for a sustained and thorough argument as to why. Gerencser takes account of Mapel and Mouffe and offers a more constrained account of Oakeshott, but his argument is also insufficient to adequately address the question of in what respects and for what reasons Oakeshott's theory is able to be integrated with deliberative democratic theory and vice versa. My project here goes beyond Mapel, Mouffe, and Gerencser in its comprehensive account of Oakeshott and its careful account of deliberative democratic theory. I would add that others have also suggested that Oakeshott and forms of democracy beyond representation are compatible. John Wallach notes Oakeshott's view that politics is "attending to arrangements", and writes that he sees Oakeshott as endorsing politics that are conversational—a "free-flowing, open-ended, tolerant exchange of views—as proper for the

---

31 This sentence should not be read to indicate that I take deliberative and participatory democracy to be synonymous, for they are not. Mapel, Mouffe, and Gerencser, however, do not distinguish between these terms when they use them. Nonetheless, nothing is at stake in respect to this book in using the terms "participatory" and "deliberative" in roughly synonymous ways. A different project could call for the parsing of differences (in brief, deliberation is one kind of participation).

community's moral and political deliberations".[32] Richard Flathman holds a view of Oakeshott as welcoming self-enacting, discursive democratic practices, deeply liberal and self-making. He gives much more attention to Oakeshott than does Wallach or Rorty. Fred Dallmayr makes much use of Oakeshott in ways that are congruent with Flathman's use.[33]

In the second chapter I interrogate Oakeshott's work prior to *On Human Conduct* in respect to his consideration of democracy. I will give attention to, for example, "The Authority of the State", "The Masses in Representative Democracy", "The Political Economy of Freedom", and "The Voice of Poetry in the Conversation of Mankind";[34] but all of his work relevant to democracy will be considered. As I indicated above, this last essay concerns conversation, and I will argue that it forecasts a nascent communicative ideal which prefigures Habermas and which later deliberative theorists echo and extend. I will also consider his thought regarding what he calls "the individual manqué", "the anti-individual", "the politics of faith", and "Rationalism".[35] These interrelated conceptions emerge in important ways in *On Human Conduct* as enterprise association and *universitas*, and they prevent, diminish, erode, or violate democracy in various ways. In this chapter, then, I provide a survey of Oakeshott's work up to the text that he saw as his *magnum opus*.

The third chapter turns to consideration of *On Human Conduct* and of civil association in particular. "The Rule of Law" will also be briefly considered, as it was written late and fits comfortably with *On Human Conduct*. Here I explain civil association and its relationship to *societas* and to the several postulates that constitute both human conduct and the civil condition (including the postulate of "deliberation"), which make civil association coherent. I also describe, explain, and analyze Oakeshott's

---

32   John R. Wallach, "Liberals, Communitarians, and the Tasks of Political Theory", *Political Theory*, 15, 4 (December 1987), 599. Oakeshott's characterization of politics as attending to arrangements is found in his "Political Education" in *Rationalism in Politics*. Wallach also notes "The Voice of Poetry in the Conversation of Mankind", as influencing his interpretation of Oakeshott.

33   Richard E. Flathman, *Reflections of a Would-Be Anarchist: Ideals and Institutions of Liberalism* (Minneapolis: University of Minnesota Press, 1998). He uses Oakeshott throughout the book, but see especially 71–77; *The Practice of Political Authority: Authority and the Authoritative* (Chicago: The University of Chicago Press, 1980); and *Willful Liberalism: Voluntarism and Individuality in Political Theory and Practice* (Ithaca: Cornell University Press, 1992). Fred Dallmayr, *Polis and Praxis: Exercises in Contemporary Political Theory* (Cambridge: MIT Press, 1984). Dallmayr explicitly ties Oakeshott to deliberative theory in pp. 190–223. In short, Rorty, Wallach, Flathman, and Dallmayr hold similar views of Oakeshott's democratic capacities.

34   "The Authority of the State" (1929) appears in *Religion, Politics and the Moral Life*; the three latter essays are in *Rationalism in Politics*.

35   The conceptions of individuality wrongly conceived and gone bad, as well as that of rationalism appear, for the most part, in *Rationalism in Politics*. The "politics of faith" lacks the proper measure of skepticism. It is theorized in *The Politics of Faith and the Politics of Scepticism*, edited by Timothy Fuller (New Haven: Yale University Press, 1996). Note that Oakeshott capitalizes Rationalism in the essays concerned with this conception in *Rationalism in Politics*. I have elected not to capitalize the word when I use it, but it is not a typographical error when it is found capitalized inside of quotes of, or references to, texts by Oakeshott.

conception of "moral practice" and morality. I explain why he sees civil association *as* moral practice, how "civil association *is* moral association". Here I put flesh on Mouffe's thought that Oakeshott provides a theory of political association which "although it does not postulate the existence of a substantive common good, [it] nevertheless implies ... an ethico-political bond that creates a linkage among participants in the association ... ". I show how and why Oakeshott contrasts the morality of individuality with the "morality" of the "anti-individual". Describing and analyzing his moral theory will go a long way toward the demonstration of its affinities with and connections to deliberative democracy.

In the fourth chapter I describe, summarize, and explain the deliberative democratic theory to which my project refers. As I have written, this is a considerable volume of literature, so I will use some of its most important proponents to represent what I mean by deliberative theory. Rawls, Habermas, Dryzek, and Gutmann and Thompson are without qualification important, if not essential, deliberative theorists. Rawls and Gutmann and Thompson speak to democratic theory using, primarily, liberal resources. Habermas and Dryzek approach democratic theory primarily from critical theory. Using the work of these five people is more than sufficient in respect to describing and analyzing deliberative democracy; and for the reader familiar with democratic theory, my use of these theorists makes immediate sense. It is not my task to argue for deliberative democratic theory, to mediate all specific and nuanced differences between alternative conceptions, or to critique deliberative theory. It is my task to report on what deliberative democratic theory is.[36]

The final chapter summarizes the work which precedes it and concludes the argument, which will have already been unfolding, that while Oakeshott is not simply an early and undiscovered deliberative democratic theorist, important parts of his political theory comport with deliberative theory. This is particularly, and most importantly, true in respect to his theory of civil association. Rorty, Wallach, Flathman, and Dallmayr offer small gestures in this direction; Mapel, Mouffe, and Gerencser engage Oakeshott more firmly in regard to this question. My project, however, offers a comprehensive and sustained exploration of in what respects Oakeshott's theory overlaps and agrees with deliberative democracy.

I have stated that the goal is to cast light on Oakeshott and contribute to the Oakeshott literature, but perhaps just a bit more can be said in this regard. I began with a mention of the renewal in Oakeshott studies, that this renewal means that there are things yet to learn about Oakeshott, and

---

36 I will treat the terms "deliberative"/"deliberate" and "discursive"/"discourse" in roughly synonymous ways. Clearly these terms do not mean exactly the same thing (e.g., persons can engage in discourse without deliberating); but I mean to communicate that no technical or theoretical distinction in respect to democratic theory hangs on the difference in terms, as I use them here.

applying his thought to a new area of inquiry, at least in principle, is a viable pursuit. This book will elucidate an entire topic and field of study in respect to Oakeshott, which up to the present has been largely ignored in respect to him. That is, his understanding of democracy and democratic theory will receive just the comprehensive treatment that is missing.[37] Democratic theory is too important a field of inquiry to be left alone in the thought of an important political theorist, if he has, in fact, offered a contribution to that field. I argue, of course, that Oakeshott does just this.

Oakeshott is widely argued to have presented one of the most interesting and original theories of *liberal* association and politics in the twentieth century.[38] It is no accident that the key elements of Oakshott's liberal theory are those which either implicitly or explicitly constitute his (underdeveloped) democratic theory. His contingent, nonpurposive, noninstrumental, and adverbial civil association, which promotes and privileges agency, individuality, freedom, and self-enactment, is an association which must make space for plurality and diversity.[39] These postulates naturally and logically lead to some forms of democracy, as Oakeshott, of course, recognized.[40] Curiously, however, while his liberal theory has received considerable attention, it has been insufficiently connected to democratic theory. My project is concerned with the relationship between liberal and democratic theory in Oakeshott, explicating the connections between them. That is, insofar as I am concerned with his democratic theory, I must address the postulates of his liberal theory.

Civil association penetrates, then, liberal and democratic theory; but Oakeshott's theory of morality — so crucial to civil association — is itself woefully unattended. An explication of in what respects civil association penetrates democratic theory will, of necessity, explicate the moral theory intrinsic to civil association. Thus, another contribution made here is a

---

37   Rorty, Cahoone, Wallach, Flathman, Dallmayr, Mapel, Mouffe, and Gerencser all make their observations and arguments entirely, or almost entirely, in respect to civil association.

38   For example, Flathman, Walsh, Dallmayr, *op. cit.* ; D. Thomas, Review of *On Human Conduct* in *Mind*, 86, 453–56; Wendell John Coats, Jr., "Michael Oakeshott as Liberal Theorist", *Canadian Journal of Political Science*, 18, 773–87; Paul Franco, "Michael Oakeshott as Liberal Theorist", *Political Theory*, 18, 3 (August 1990); *The Political Philosophy of Michael Oakeshott*; and *Michael Oakeshott: An Introduction* (New Haven: Yale University Press, 2004); John Gray, *Liberalisms: Essays in Political Philosophy* (London: Routledge, 1989), 199–217; and *Post-Liberalism: Studies in Political Thought* (London: Routledge, 1993), 40–7; N. O'Sullivan, "In the Perspective of Western Thought", in *The Achievement of Michael Oakeshott*, ed. Jesse Norman (London: Duckworth, 1993), 106; and D. Manning, "The Philosophical Foundations of Liberal Ideology", *Journal of Political Ideologies*, 2 (1997), 137–58.

39   As Chandran Kukathas writes, "the central insight of classical liberalism is that human goals, practices, ways of life, are plural and not capable of being brought under control in a single harmonious whole". In "What's the Big Idea?" (his review of John Gray's *Isaiah Berlin*) in *Reason* online. I am here uncontroversially identifying Oakeshott's liberalism with "classical liberalism".

40   Franco writes that the postulates of civil association just simply are, *as such*, postulates of liberal democracy. That is, he sees civil association as Oakeshott's theory of "liberal democracy". In *Michael Oakeshott: An Introduction*, 22.

serious consideration of this undervalued aspect of Oakehott's theory. What virtues, if any, are necessary for democracy? What moral values, if any, does democracy promote? Is there an intrinsic relationship between morality and democracy, and if so, what is it? What relationship exists between liberal theory, liberal values, and democracy? These questions, and others like them, are of great concern to recent democratic theory, and Oakeshott's work, especially his theory of civil association, casts light into the discourse around these questions. His democratic theory is worth investigating on its own merits, his moral theory is worth investigating on its own merits as well. His moral theory is interrogated here because it is intrinsic and crucial to his theory of civil association, and civil association is the primary nexus between his work and democratic theory. Since deliberative theory is pervasively concerned about moral issues (especially disagreement about moral views), insofar as civil association helps us to negotiate moral questions democratically, it contributes to the discourse surrounding this problematic.

Lastly, while I have stated that this project is about contributing to the Oakeshott literature, it cannot help but make some contribution, however modest, to the democratic theory literature as well. Those reading in democratic theory may be drawn to Oakeshott as they explore questions of, for example, authority or morality. They may find new insight or nuance in Oakeshott, or find the conceptual apparatus to push questions in new or deeper directions. Again, it is not my task to say new things about deliberative theory, but saying new things about Oakeshott will bring some contours of new understanding to democratic theory, if only in a derivative manner. These are the dimensions of this study, all of which will be brought to relationship with one another in its culminating and final chapter.

Chapter Two

Before On Human Conduct

I now undertake an investigation of Oakeshott's conceptions of political philosophy, political activity, and political discourse; the state, authority and law; liberalism, individuality, and anti-individuality; skepticism; rationalism and ideology; contingency; and, of course, democracy, as these themes are presented in his work before *On Human Conduct*. I am interested in these matters just to the extent that they bear relationships to democracy and democratic theory, and as they either allow or disallow deliberative democracy. One will not find Oakeshott building a theory of deliberative democracy, as such, but will encounter him explicating a political theory. The question for our consideration is whether or not his political theory, at this stage in his career, comports, overall, with deliberative democratic theory. The way to answer that question is an exploration in what particular ways important features of his political theory allows, welcomes, disallows, or refuses deliberative theory. After an analysis of the relevant particulars, I will be in a position to draw broader conclusions. It makes sense to begin the interrogation with a consideration of Oakeshott's writing about democracy itself. What did he have to say about democracy in his work before *On Human Conduct*? To begin, note that I will investigate Oakeshott's work in roughly chronological order, "roughly" only because the order cannot in all cases be known with precision, and more importantly, I will not want to present a wooden record, void of appropriate details and nuance; but let various claims touch upon other claims that come from other writings published at different times. I will (roughly) cycle through texts chronologically over and again until we have considered all the relevant work appropriate to each theme.

Democracy

George Feaver writes that "Michael Oakeshott had a good deal to say about democracy". He adds that his "insights and asides about the character of democracy" became "uttered in an idiom that was exploratory, tentative or ironic, rather than definitive in tone". Further, "his many important insights about democratic regimes have been ignored, misunderstood, or plainly misrepresented."[1] Later in his essay, Feaver writes that Oakeshott's "life-long interest in democracy... usually appeared as the shadowy background of his wider philosophical essaying into the character of government and politics in modern Europe."[2]

My view is that Feaver's conclusions are, for the most part, accurate. In terms of his written work, Oakeshott has offered less than one might have hoped. Nevertheless, I think he has written sufficiently so as to warrant an investigation into his thought about democracy, although implicit conclusions will be at least as important as consideration of explicit statements. Feaver is certainly right that Oakeshott's voice regarding democracy is often exploratory, tentative, ironic, or "shadowy"; and I think Oakeshott's insights about democracy have been ignored more than misunderstood or misrepresented. Feaver is also correct in noting that "Oakeshott sought not a rejection of Representative Democracy, but a radical restatement of its principles",[3] as I endeavor to demonstrate below. The philosophical and political "principles" that support democracy will be seen as this project unfolds, but certainly Oakeshott rejected platonic ideals about democracy (as with all other matters), and his appreciation for democracy is profoundly contingent.[4] Characteristically, he valued democracy "not as an approximation to some 'ideally' democratic system of government, but as an instrument of remarkable refinement and responsiveness, thrown up in the course of our political history, [and] capable of digesting the enterprises of zealots".[5]

In 1939 Oakeshott published the anthology, *The Social and Political Doctrines of Contemporary Europe*. Its chapters concern Representative Democracy as well as Catholicism, Communism, Fascism, and National Socialism. He writes about "representative democracy" in his Introduction in order to explain certain editorial decisions he has made, and his relevant comments can be briefly summarized. He claims that the philosophy that supports representative democracy is more substantial than that which is foundational to "some" of the other doctrines. It is easy to conclude that he thinks Fascism, Communism, and National Socialism to have inferior philosophical foundations; but in any case, the important

---

1   George Feaver, "Regimes of Liberty: Michael Oakeshott on Representative Democracy", in Corey Abel and Timothy Fuller, eds., *The Intellectual Legacy of Michael Oakeshott* (Imprint Academic, 2005), 133.

2   *Ibid.*, 155.

3   *Ibid.*, 136.

4   My reference to "platonic ideals of democracy" cannot mean, of course, ideas of democracy held by Plato. Clearly Plato was far from a democrat. I mean to focus attention on the matter of Plato's "forms" or "ideals", i.e., those perfect instances or entities of everything. Oakeshott rejects the notion of perfect "forms" or "ideals" of anything, including, then, of course, democracy.

5   Michael Oakeshott, "Introduction" to Reginald Bassett, *The Essentials of Parliamentary Democracy*, 2d ed. (London: Frank Cass, 1964), xxi–xxiv; in Feaver, 150.

thing to note is that while he sees democracy (if I may at this juncture abbreviate his term) as more philosophically astute and solid than the alternative doctrines, it is nevertheless "not a philosophy which anyone could accept nowadays without a radical restatement which has yet to be provided".[6]

It is interesting that Oakeshott thinks these two things simultaneously: first, that the philosophical foundations of democracy are superior to other doctrines (excepting, perhaps, Catholicism), and that these philosophical foundations stand in need of radical restatement. In this light, I can simply note that the material he includes as representative of contemporary European democratic "doctrine" is, I think, unsurprising. It includes Mill, Tocqueville, Paine, Lincoln, and T.H. Green; and he refers to this representative democratic "doctrine" as "simple-minded".[7] These texts endorse conventional representative and liberal notions. Of course, for my purposes, I wish Oakeshott had made the effort to contribute something of his own along the lines of the "radical restatement" he thinks necessary. Nonetheless, his mere claim that such a restatement is necessary, communicates that conventional representative and liberal notions, at least as he knew them in 1939, were unsatisfactory; and therefore, there is a forward -looking orientation he evinces.

Importantly, he notes that taking representative democracy to be only a method of government is an "untenable view", and that it should be understood as related intrinsically to conceptions of the nature of society and of the individual,[8] echoed later in "The Authority of the State" and *On Human Conduct*. One is, then, reminded of the book's title, one that takes these "doctrines" to be at once social and political. This, too, is a forward-looking idea insofar as later and more recent democratic theory (and civil society theory as well, incidentally) eschews simple compartmentalizing among "government", "society", "state", "economy", and so on; *and* this is particularly true among deliberative theorists. Oakeshott intimates that there is something forward-looking about the rejection of democracy as merely a method of government and the conception of it in broader terms. For the claim he makes in this regard is accompanied by the qualifier, "we need not trespass into the future".[9] Oakeshott writes that the other doctrines cannot be understood apart from democracy and that they are, in differing ways, reactions to democracy. He also claims that because of democracy's strengths, they all find it necessary to make compromises

---

6   Michael Oakeshott, ed., *The Social and Political Doctrines of Contemporary Europe* (Cambridge: Cambridge University Press, 1939), xvi. He adds that it "is by no means either a complete or a satisfactory expression as it stands" and that "it is impossible to make of it [as it now stands] an entirely coherent doctrine", xviii.

7   *Ibid.*

8   *Ibid.*

9   *Ibid.*

with it; so, in one degree or another, democratic doctrine "lives on" in the other doctrines.[10] We should note, of course, that his claim is about "doctrine", not about actual democratic practice.

While I have stated that the material he chooses for this chapter is unsurprising and conventional, this does not mean that Oakeshott had an easy time determining which texts to use. He writes that he, in fact, had a difficult time in deciding this matter. What he wanted to do, he tells us, is to convey what he takes to be its "central principles", summarized in this way, that "society must not be so unified as to abolish vital and valuable differences, nor so extravagantly diversified as to make an intelligently co-ordinated and civilized social life impossible, and that the imposition of a universal plan of life on a society is at once stupid and immoral ... ".[11] Here one readily sees his identification of democracy with liberalism. Indeed, he writes that he chose the title "Representative Democracy" as a matter of convenience. He rejects "Liberal Democracy" as the chapter's title only because he does not want the doctrine he seeks to represent to be "confused with the crude and negative individualism which is apt to be associated with Liberalism". Nonetheless, he continues, the doctrine of democracy he intends to represent "is a Liberal doctrine". Although he uses the word "doctrine" throughout the book, in respect to democracy, it is less a doctrine, and more a "tradition and a tendency than a well-knit doctrine". It is, therefore, superior to the alternatives because it "has shown itself capable of changing without perishing in the process, and has the advantage ... of belonging to a long and impressive tradition of thought".[12] This conception of democracy as a tradition shows up in his later work as well. For example, he writes that British democracy "is not an abstract idea. It is a way of living and a manner of politics which first began to emerge in the middle ages".[13] Here, then, in one of his earliest writings, Oakeshott endorses a liberal and representative democracy, while at the same time he sees incoherence in its philosophical foundations and need for further and better democratic theory.

One other brief claim about liberal democracy made in *The Social and Political Doctrines of Contemporary Europe* is relevant to my inquiry. He states that liberal democracy contains a "moral ideal" which is "the plausible ethics of productivity". He finds Fascism's critique on this point "far too acute to be merely ignored" and writes, "the attack on the moral ideal of Liberal Democracy is, I think, well-founded; that was always the

---

10   *Ibid.*, xvii.

11   *Ibid.*, xix. Suvi Soininen correctly finds in this passage a declaration against "power politics", which is "a foe of diversity and individuality." See her *From a "Necessary Evil" to the Art of Contingency: Michael Oakeshott's Conception of Political Activity* (Charlottesville, VA: Imprint Academic, 2005), 89.

12   *Ibid.*, xvii–xviii.

13   Michael Oakeshott, "Contemporary British Politics", *The Cambridge Journal* 1 (1947– 48), 489.

weakest part of the doctrine."[14] One need not engage Oakeshott here on the question of in what respects or to what degree his characterization of liberal democracy is accurate. It is simply a fact that liberalism grew hand-in-hand with the rise of commercial societies and the free market. Further, the connection between individualism, autonomy, and the market was seen as a moral ideal to many (or the connection was seen as a phenomenon that emerged from a moral ideal). In any case, it is of import that Oakeshott sees this matter as the single most problematic aspect of "liberal democracy." I think the term "liberal" alone, leaving democracy aside, would make the claim more accurate and convincing, for his critique is, properly speaking, against liberalism, not democracy. More specifically, his critique is against liberalism just to the extent that it promotes an "ethics of productivity", an economic form of rationalism; indeed it is against what many mean when speaking of captialism.[15] This critique of liberal democracy is also forward-looking insofar as more recent democratic theorists, and again, especially radical, participatory, and deliberative theorists, would strongly agree. Indeed, the materialistic, market-driven, consumer-oriented, individualistic "ethics of productivity" that Oakeshott denounces is a profound detriment to democracy in the view of virtually all recent democratic theorists.

Oakeshott's "Scientific Politics", (1947) is a review of Hans Morgenthau's 1946 *Scientific Man Versus Power Politics*. Morgenthau undertakes an analysis of "scientific" politics and the "science" of politics, which allows Oakeshott to introduce, lightly, his conception of Rationalism, which he develops later. In his reflections on the relationship between rationalism and parliamentary government (now putting his own thought forward rather than summarizing Morgenthau), Oakeshott writes that "parliamentary government and rationalistic politics do not belong in the same tradition and do not, in fact go together ... [and] that the institutions of parliamentary government sprang from the least rationalistic period of our politics ... ".[16] A fuller meaning cannot be gained as to what he means until I investigate rationalism, but for now, one can notice the simple claim that Oakeshott sees rationalism and parliamentary government as unrelated and perhaps hostile to one another. Indeed, he also writes that an "illusion is entertained" when "Englishmen ... speak of 'democratic planning' ... [thinking it to be] ''democratic' because they believe (not from the history and experience of their own society but on the word of a set of ignorant foreigners) that 'democracy' and scientific politics sprang from

---

14 *Social and Political Doctrines*, xx, xxi.

15 His comments here anticipate his 1958 Harvard Lectures in which he writes against "The Political Theory of Collectivism", and the "Productivist" version of collectivism. These lectures will be discussed below.

16 Oakeshott, *Religion, Politics and the Moral Life*, 109.

the same root".[17] Again one encounters his rejection of the concept of an idealistic (as well as related rationalistic) foundation for democracy. One should also notice that he slips easily from writing of parliamentary government to writing of "so-called 'democratic' theory". In this respect too, rationalism is at a great distance: "The root of so-called 'democratic' theory is not rationalist optimism about the perfectibility of human society, but scepticism about the possibility of such perfection".[18] A fuller account of this meaning awaits one's consideration of skepticism, but it is clear that Oakeshott sees parliamentary government and (whatever might be meant by at least some conceptions of) democratic theory as distant from or even hostile to rationalism and, on the other hand, intrinsically related to skepticism.

One can only speculate as to Oakeshott's language here of "so-called 'democratic' theory". His cynical, pessimistic, or ironic tone cannot be missed. Perhaps an exhaustive historical report of the use of "democratic theory" in the political theory contemporary to Oakeshott would clarify sufficiently what his tone signifies. However, I suggest that one knows enough of Oakeshott and the goings-on in the world and the world of political theory in 1947 to surmise the reason for this tone. As is well known, Oakeshott is wary, to say the least, about ambitious plans to spread anything, including a kind of rationalist-infused and insufficiently humble and skeptical "democracy". If, in the immediate post-war period, there were legions of enthusiasts, builders of dreams, and social planners, he was cautious of their motivations and their efforts. I will show this below when I explore rationalism, skepticism, and more. Insofar as democratic theory had the character of missionary zeal or Bentham-like construction, Oakeshott was disapproving and worried. For in such misconstrued conceptions of political activity, both human conduct and political activity are misunderstood; and outcomes are often regrettable if not straightforwardly dangerous. Oakeshott's life spanned nearly all of the twentieth century, and he was therefore schooled by so-called "democratic" "socialist" dreams which became hostile and even murderous to the liberal values he cherished, let alone to countless human lives. Soininen notes that in Great Britain during this time,

> the future of democratic institutions was often considered to be under threat by political thinkers. The act of voting as means of ensuring democracy was questioned; the connection between democracy and representation was itself refuted, [and a] ... certain amount of elitism as regards politics was not unusual at the time, and Oakeshott's views are reflective of this general mood.[19]

---

17   *Ibid.*
18   *Ibid.*
19   Soininen, 101.

Of course, it remains to be said that because one is cautious, cynical, or even contemptuous of some others" "so-called 'democratic' theory", this does not mean one is dismissive or cynical about democracy or democratic theory altogether.[20] I have already shown briefly, and will show more, that Oakeshott values (at least his own understanding of) democracy quite highly.

Around 1948 Oakeshott wrote a short essay entitled "The Voice of Conversation in the Education of Mankind". In it he argues for an intrinsic relationship between conversation and politics, normatively understood, in the modern age. He writes,

> Moreover, this approximation of politics to conversation is, I think, the gist and meaning of democracy. Democratic politics has been perverted and brought into disrepute by being misidentified with the rule of the people, the government of the majority, the propagation of a dogmatic faith and the pursuit of a manner of living to be imposed equally upon all men. It is, in fact, the politics of the man of conversation. And how it came about may be understood in a brief abridgment of our history ... politics, alone among the subjects of discourse, belongs solely to the realm of conversation: dogmatic intelligence was met by conversational intelligence, and what we now call "politics" is the byproduct of this encounter .... At its lowest, democracy appeared as a device for talking out the dogmatic reformers; at its highest, it is the politics of conversation.[21]

There is little need to elaborate upon this passage. It is profoundly anticipatory, and all but prophetic in relation to the recent deliberative turn in democratic theory. Here Oakeshott rejects the very narrow and distorted views of democracy now widely rejected, while he valorizes the essence of democracy as conversation, or discourse. Indeed, in this essay, he sees this essential fact of democracy as animating "an abridgment of our history". Oakeshott is rhapsodic as he writes about "whoever he was" who first brought this meaning of democracy to us; for "he was certainly a second Prometheus for whom the world waited for salvation from the fire that the first had poured into the belly of the race. At least, he was the first democrat; and his gift was the gift of oil and wine, the power to neutralize this [previous, Middle Age] ideological rage".[22]

---

20 Luke O'Sullivan makes a quite similar observation when he writes that Oakeshott "was entirely typical in pronouncing the death of liberalism in the 1930s. A mood of disillusion, even despair, had followed the disappointment of hopes for a more peaceable world and a better society after 1918. The depression, the collapse of the post-war democratic regimes and the rise of Fascism, National Socialism and Communism, all contributed to what Oakeshott saw as the widespread revolt against the legacy of Locke and 'so-called Victorianism.'" In *Oakeshott on History* (Imprint Academic, 2003), 57. Cf. related remarks in Debra Candreva, *The Enemies of Perfection: Oakeshott, Plato, and the Critique of Rationalism* (New York: Lexington Books, 2005), 24.

21 Michael Oakeshott, *What is History? And Other Essays*, Luke O'Sullivan, ed. (Imprint Academic, 2004), 194–95.

22 *Ibid.*, 195.

In 1955 Oakeshott wrote an essay entitled "Conduct and Ideology in Politics" which fits nicely with the conception of democracy in the essay just discussed. Here, he makes the argument that political conceptions such as liberty, liberalism, socialism, communism, justice, and of course, democracy, are not concepts like "table". When one assumes that such concepts have "*real* meanings" in a platonic, rationalist sense, one has made a mistake.[23] He writes that words like "democracy" do not have "fixed meanings [or] correspond to specific present or ideal objects". Therefore, he adds, one cannot "begin" as a "Democrat", rather it is a "disposition" one "can acquire". He continues to argue that words like "democracy" are "abstract statements of characteristics observed in conduct", and if "democracy" means anything, "it means a set of principles which set out in short-hand certain complicated ways of behaving".[24]

I write that his thought about democracy in the 1955 essay corresponds well with his thoughts in the 1948 essay because the contingency argued in the latter seems to be rationally consonant with the focus on conversation in the earlier one. That is, if discourse constitutes an enterprise, that enterprise will be subject to the contingency of discourse. Where discourse leads, the very constitution of the enterprise follows just insofar as the enterprise is constituted by the discourse. In short, if democracy is radically ("radically", as in "at the root") discursive, as Oakeshott claims, then it is radically contingent as well. This may be the case in relation to the extent that discourse is not contained in some fashion, such that any number of matters are off the table for discussion. Insofar as discourse is limited, it follows that contingency may be lessened, although it can never be entirely absent. Soininen makes much the same point when she writes, that the "openness to conversation refers to the contingency of politics ... "[25]

In his 1955 response to Walter Lippmann's book *The Public Philosophy*, Oakeshott sees Lippmann as offering a view of the virtues and vices of contemporary politics or "liberal democracy". Again he places these two words in quotation marks, just as he had "democratic" theory above. This kind of bracketing of terms is not uncommon in Oakeshott because he is fastidious with language and an insightful observer in respect to how words are used and abused, how their meanings are fluid and malleable. Indeed, he gives up on various terms, seeing their meanings as so effusive or distorted that they become useless. One can see the culmination of this attitude in *On Human Conduct* where he makes use of medieval terms in place of modern and contemporary words in an explicit effort to shake loose of meanings he wants to avoid. Here, then, I take the placement of

---

23   Michael Oakeshott, "Conduct and Ideology in Politics", in *ibid.*, 249.
24   *Ibid.*, 250–53.
25   Soininen, 103.

"liberal democracy" in quotation marks not to signify cynicism or irony, but an acknowledgment of a certain meaning, to which he is not hostile.[26]

The concern here is with liberal democracy, and the interesting matter for our purposes is that while Lippmann is pessimistic about the prospects of "liberal-democratic government", Oakeshott thinks such gloom to be "exaggerated and misplaced".[27] He thinks that Lippmann expects too much, and that liberal democracy depends upon "acquired habits of moderation". Whereas Lippmann sees the desired result of liberal democracy to be "*definitive* peace and order", this, for Oakeshott, is to "judge it by an inappropriate standard".[28] He thinks that the "partners" who constitute liberal democratic government are "held in check" by their "courage and integrity", as well as their "common human vices". What holds demagoguery at bay is a matter of moral qualities, and also pride, indifference, and even laziness.[29] Oakeshott here sees liberal democracy as a viable, workable way of conducting governmental affairs. Fortunately, both our virtues and our vices conspire to make this so. It is not that liberal democratic office holders, structures, or institutions are incorruptible — far from it; but more importantly, this kind of political association works sufficiently so as to negate the need for pessimism. Whatever its problems, there are clearly no better alternatives as far as Oakeshott is concerned.

Oakeshott goes on to comment on the relationship between liberal democracy and free speech (because Morgenthau discusses the two liberal democratic institutions of property and free speech in explaining his view of politics). He argues that liberal democracy values free speech not in order to discover or perpetuate any great "one" truth but because of the belief that "politics are not concerned with this sort of 'truth' at all". For,

> Jacobinism is politics where "truth" as opposed to "error" is sought, and consequently in which speech is recognized as argument and is permitted, but only until "truth" appears. Liberal democracy is, on the other hand, sceptical politics, in which "truth" appears not as the opposite of "error" but merely as the opposite of "lies", and in which utterance is largely free because it is recognized not as argument but as conversation.[30]

Again, one sees the connection between liberal democracy and skepticism, but a new element is introduced as well: the idea of open-ended,

26   I am here, of course, claiming one function of quotations marks quite different than another. It is odd, that quotation marks do two very different things: lock meaning into place, or call meaning into question. Hopefully, the context allows the reader to know what function the writer intends.

27   *Ibid.*, "The Customer Is Never Wrong", 113.

28   *Ibid.*, 113–14. The emphasis on "definitive" is mine, because it is worth observing that his claim is not that liberal democracy can have no positive effect in promoting peace or order. Indeed, one will see as this study unfolds, he does think this very thing.

29   *Ibid.*, 115.

30   *Ibid.*, 116–17. Cf. my opening remarks in this section about Oakeshott's rejection of platonic ideals, his embrace of contingency, and again, the quote from his Introduction to Bassett.

pluralistic, nonfoundational conversation. Oakeshott is obviously not here using the term "argument" in the philosophical sense, but as a way to signify the goal and purpose of agreement, i.e., argument being a means to come to agreement and discover truth. In contrast to this nonskeptical understanding, he sees liberal democracy as valuing conversation that need not come to agreement, especially agreement on "truth" as opposed to "error." It is clear that this constituent part of liberal democracy, as Oakeshott sees it, is not unlike the pluralistic and hermeneutical considerations and valuations made by several deliberative democratic theorists. It shares, at the very least, a sensibility with the nonfoundational, contingent, postmodern, hermeneutical premises that undergirds various deliberative theories (e.g., that of Habermas and Dryzek). It also clearly shares in classical liberal theory, as noted in Chapter One.[31]

In 1957, Oakeshott wrote a short review of Spearman's *Democracy in England*, and his remarks can be coalesced as follows:

> The word "democracy" comes to us dishevelled and unsteady from so many *liasons tripotages* that a writer .... does well to consider ... how he proposes to use it ... . The opportunity for confusion is large, and escape requires luck as well as cunning ... . In these circumstances Mrs Spearman is disposed to shift her ground a little, to distinguish among these emergencies ... entailments ... divergencies ... [and] dangers ... This is an honest and commendable move ... round this ambiguous and unmanageable concept "democracy". ... "Democracy" by design is not forbidden an appearance, but in the main it is recognized to be a by-product of other choices, of circumstance and of chance ... . This is not a "Whiggish" success-story of "democracy": it is a story in which vicissitudes are recognized as the stuff and not the hindrances of change.[32]

The basic idea here, of course, is that democracy is and can be used in any number of ways, and that the varying conceptions are often ambiguous, confusing, and unhelpful.[33] Again, however, one notices his endorsement of the idea that democracy is not the result of "design", but rather of entirely contingent matters, indeed of "vicissitudes". In fact, what he writes here of democracy is almost verbatim what he will write of civil association much later. Further, it is to be noticed how Oakeshott's continuous insistence on the contingent nature of democracy fits perfectly with the notion that its essence is conversation, a connection I sought to identify above in respect to his essays "The Voice of Conversation in the Education

---

31   Recall Kukathas's words, "the central insight of classical liberalism is that human goals, practices, ways of life, are plural and not capable of being brought under control in a single harmonious whole" in the first chapter.

32   Michael Oakeshott, "Democracy in England", in O'Sullivan, ed., 279–82.

33   Cf. Oakeshott's similar comment in his "The Idea of "Character" in Modern Politics", in O'Sullivan, ed., 276; and in his "Political Thought as a Subject of Historical Enquiry", 414, in the same volume. O'Sullivan agrees that this observation about the conception(s) of democracy was central to Oakeshott's reflection. See his Introduction in *What is History?* 20–21.

of Mankind" and "Conduct and Ideology in Politics". If democracy is, at
its deepest, discourse, then it is also chameleon-like, and not necessarily in
any pejorative sense. It is in good measure discourse that would allow for
democracy as the "by-product of ... circumstance and chance" just as it is
such contingency that compels conversation. This robust contingency and
discourse are just what was missing in the Middle Ages, according to
Oakeshott, and they are what allowed democracy to emerge in modernity.

The Politics of Faith and the Politics of Scepticism will be considered in
greater detail below in respect to skepticism, but here I can briefly note a
few explicit comments Oakeshott makes in respect to democracy. In the
Introduction Oakeshott discusses the fluid and malleable nature of political terms that I mentioned above. Among those terms which have
acquired a "complexity of meaning" is "democracy".[34] Of course this is an
entirely ordinary claim, but I mention it here as it will be helpful to keep in
mind. I have already shown a kind of cynical or ironic tone in respect to at
least some (unspecified) version of democratic theory, and I have already
demonstrated his embrace of democracy. Additional nuances in respect to
democracy will continue to be seen in the literature interrogated below.

When writing of the politics of faith, he notes that to regard it as "the
faithful consort of something called 'democracy' is altogether to misun-
derstand it".[35] I have already shown this approach, the *via negativa* of
claims as to what democracy is *not*. Just as Oakeshott claims that democracy is unrelated and hostile to rationalism and the effort to discover
"truth" opposed to "error", so he also sees democracy as unrelated and
hostile to "the politics of faith". The natural and obvious reading of this
book makes clear that the placement of "democracy" in quotation marks in
this passage is meant to stress the separation between it and the politics of
faith.

What, however, is meant by the "politics of faith"? This phrase describes
one end of a dialectic, the other end being "the politics of scepticism". Like
civil association and enterprise association, and *societas* and *universitas*, the
dialectical pairs introduced in *On Human Conduct*, "faith" and "scepticism" in this early text identify different ways of understanding and
undertaking political association and governance. As with these later concepts, "faith" and "scepticism" exist not in pure and isolated forms, but in
relation to the other; and all governments have been and continue to be a
mixture of such faith and skepticism. Indeed, he thinks that the politics of
skepticism had dominated political thought and conduct until modernity,
and that the politics of faith have dominated for the last 150 years. A

---

34 Oakeshott, *The Politics of Faith and the Politics of Scepticism*, 9; cf. 14 where he writes of a "*double entendre* in 'democracy'". It is more accurate, however, to admit of several ways democracy has been and is understood, as he does in *The Politics of Faith and the Politics of Scepticism* where he confesses that a "complexity of meaning" obtains to "democracy".

35 *Ibid.*, 56–66.

proper balance, however, must be found; a purity without balance is to be avoided. "Faith" has nothing to do with religious, theological, or metaphysical faith.[36] It is faith in the power of human reason and effort, especially as applied through government. It is political Pelagianism. The politics of faith, then, connect with the similar and related conceptions of rationalism, anti-individualism, enterprise association, and *universitas* which I will consider below. Timothy Fuller writes:

> If the politics of faith overestimates the possibilities for human action, the politics of scepticism will underestimate or fail to recognize them. Neither the politics of faith nor the politics of scepticism comprehend the whole of politics … . Thus politics, in Oakeshott's now famous formulation, is "the pursuit of intimations" … . The advantage of the sceptic is the modest one that the sceptic may make fewer mistakes by not forgetting that politics cannot ever transcend the pursuit of intimations … . This, then, is an essay against political excess and the barbarism of perverted order. It is an assessment of the politics and doctrines of the twentieth century which have produced many graveyards of orderliness.[37]

Fuller is right in indicating that Oakeshott sees an advantage in skepticism. This is in keeping with his preference for liberal values, individualism, civil association, and *societas* as over against their dialectical partners (or enemies, as the case may be). More will be said about the politics of faith and skepticism below, but this introduction is sufficient at present.

In keeping with his earlier comments about the "double entendre" and the "complexity of meaning" of democracy, in the conclusion to this book, Oakeshott returns to a reflection on this theme. He again notes that the word "democracy" is "a manifold word, referring to two different *sets* of ideas" (emphasis, mine). It refers to both the authorization, constitution, and institutions of government and also to "the activity of governing turned in a certain direction".[38] In the mode of the politics of faith, of governing "in a certain direction", democracy is superior to monarchy because it "generates more power". In the mode of skepticism, democracy is superior because it is better at controlling government and protecting the community against various pursuits of government. Because democracy can be variously understood, to "merely defend or to attack 'democracy' is a

---

36 Indeed, on Oakeshott's understanding of religious faith, the politics of faith signifies phenomena quite different, incommensurate, or even opposed to religious faith.

37 *The Politics of Faith and the Politics of Scepticism*, xviii, xx (Editor's Introduction). The reference to Oakeshott's claim that politics is the "pursuit of intimations", comes from his essay "Political Education", found in *Rationalism in Politics*. I quote Fuller at this length to buttress my earlier claim that Oakeshott's cynical or ironic tone about "so- called 'democracy' " must be understood in the context of, to use Fuller's words, "barbarism", "perverted order", and "graveyards of orderliness", that sometimes all too often, and tragically, had the word "democracy" attached to them in the twentieth century.

38 *Ibid.*, 130–31.

meaningless activity."[39] Using this text from *The Politics of Faith and the Politics of Scepticism* and others, Soininen rightly concludes that Oakeshott "assigns authority instrumental value in a democracy as a counterforce of governmental power."[40] I will demonstrate this more clearly below in my consideration of the state, authority, and law.

Oakeshott touches upon a topic in the Conclusion of this book which is of central importance to my project. He writes that politics

> is a conversation between diverse interests, in which activities that circumstantially limit one another are saved from violent collision; and here, words which have within them a little latitude of meaning (words, indeed, which have a continuous range of meaning in which the extreme meanings are mediated to one another) may sometimes serve our turn better than a scientific vocabulary designed to exclude all doubleness ... . Consider, for example, the word "democracy". It is a manifold word ... .[41]

Here I focus not on the polyvalent meaning of democracy, but on the notion that politics is discursive, "a conversation between diverse interests". As he considers how conversation gives richer understanding to our vocabulary, he is led to put forward "democracy" as an example of his argument. Democracy, then, is here tied to the enriching of understanding that conversation brings and, concomitantly, tied to the essence of politics. Of course, this matter of the relationship between politics and discourse will be explored below.

Although Oakeshott can appear at times as an elitist and has been charged by some as such, one should note that democracy, on his understanding, cuts against elitism. He admits into the discussion and the sharing of political power those who are not professional political actors (let alone political philosophers). In his 1949 essay "The Universities", he writes that democracy has "multifarious implications" involving among other things, "the disappearance of anything in the ruling class: any man may find himself among those who control the available power".[42] Oakeshott also writes, in an approving manner, of the "mixture of amateurism and professionalism" in political activity.[43] The anti-elitism of democracy in Oakeshott's view will culminate (as do so many other

---

39 *Ibid.*, 131–32. Although Oakeshott here refers to democracy as related to two differing modes of governance, one should not forget that he earlier rejected the notion of democracy as merely a mode of government and he again rejects the simple equivalence of democracy and government in his "The Masses in Representative Democracy" (see below).

40 Soininen, 111–12.

41 *The Politics of Faith and the Politics of Scepticism*, 130–31.

42 Michael Oakeshott, *The Voice of Liberal Learning*, Timothy Fuller, ed. (Indianapolis: Liberty Fund, 2001), 120.

43 In "The Study of 'Politics' in a University", *Rationalism in Politics and Other Essays*, 207. Cf. Soininen, 169–70.

strands of his thinking) in *On Human Conduct*, where, for example, he will write:

> As a deliberative and an argumentative engagement directed to reaching conclusions sustained by reasons designed to persuade others of their cogency, politics is identifiable not in terms of persons ... but only in respect of a focus of attention and a subject of discourse. The conditions of *respublica* ... may allow for the election or appointment of certain persons to devote themselves to political deliberation and negotiation; but although some will be better equipped to do it than others, there is nothing in the engagement itself to suggest a profession and much to deny it.[44]

To venture into *On Human Conduct* is to get ahead of myself, however. Democracy, as I have shown so far, then, refers to a multiplicity of meanings as used by various persons, communities, traditions, governments, and narratives (and the word is used in multivalent ways by those who use it without precision). Oakeshott is surely right about this observation; indeed as I have noted above, I think several meanings can be identified beyond those he acknowledges. If it is the case that "democracy" is understood in various ways, then one may endorse certain meanings while disagreeing with others. This is just what Oakeshott does. I quite well imagine that deep or deliberative democrats disagree that the word "democracy" as it is ubiquitously used in popular discourse, very often stands for what they mean when they use the word. I have also demonstrated that Oakeshott ties democracy to political activity and discourse.

Oakeshott's 1962 essay, "The Masses in Representative Democracy" is about the masses — actually about a character he names "mass man" — much more than about democracy; therefore his explicit remarks about democracy made here can also be briefly summarized. As he has earlier, Oakeshott disallows the idea that democracy names a simple conception or historical fact. He writes that representative democracy should be understood neither as an approximation of an ideal manner of government nor as "a modification of a manner of government" but that it "is simply what emerged in Western Europe where the impact of the aspirations of individuality upon medieval institutions of government was greatest".[45] Unfortunately, what Oakeshott means by "a modification of a manner of government" is unclear. That is, if he is denying that a government cannot be "modified" so as to be more democratic, then it is unclear if democracy can mean anything at all, and he has no reason to endorse representative democracy (because making a government more representative

---

44   *OHC*, 165.
45   Oakeshott, "The Masses in Representative Democracy", in *Rationalism in Politics*, 368. This essay was first published as "Die Massen in der repräsentative Demokratie", in *Masse und Demokratie*, ed. by A. Hunold (Erlenbach-Zürich und Stuttgart, Rentsch, 1957). Cf, e.g., his comment about the contingency of democracy above (note 5) from his Introduction to Bassett's *The Essentials of Parliamentary Democracy*.

would not be recognized as a democratic good). However this does not seem to be his claim. What he seems to mean is that democracy does not reduce to "a modification of a manner of government", there is far more to democracy than this. Oakeshott echoes his earlier claim that democracy is more a tradition and a tendency than a doctrine and that it is not merely a "method of government." Yet, although it is not *merely* a "method of government", he did write earlier that "democracy" may best be used when referring to "a certain manner of collecting together, or constituting or authorizing a government".[46] He also writes that "democracy" is a word which, among its other meanings, stands for "conditions in relation to what governments *do...* ".[47]

It is clear that Oakeshott sees not only an intrinsic relationship between individuality and democracy but that the latter grew out of the former. In "The Masses in Representative Democracy", he notes, for example, that "the intimations of individuality" manifest themselves in government as rights, duties, and authority and that the laws created are "favourable to the interests of individuality". In fact, "it provides the detail of what became a well-understood condition of human circumstance, commonly denoted by the word 'freedom.'" This manner of governing (although, recall that democracy does not simply reduce to governance) reached its climax in the " 'parliamentary' government which emerged in England and elsewhere in the late eighteenth and early nineteenth centuries". Indeed, individuality, for Oakeshott, emerges as "the pre-eminent event in modern European history". [48]It also becomes clear that individuality and freedom have a close, if not intrinsic, relationship (helping to make democracy and freedom related in an inherent way). In short, "The Masses in Representative Democracy" is an essay about "mass man", the "anti-individual", and the "individual *manqué*" and then also about individuality, but it is *therefore* derivatively and briefly about democracy too.[49]

In summary, I have shown that Oakeshott gives some attention to democracy in the earlier part of his career. It is clear that he values what he calls representative democracy, and would be happy to call liberal democracy if only he could be assured "liberal" would not be misunderstood. It is also clear that he understands democracy to be multivalent, and thus to extend in meaning beyond any given form of government. He is aware

---

46   Michael Oakeshott, "Current Ideas about Government", in O'Sullivan, ed., 285.

47   Michael Oakeshott, "The Idea of 'Character' in Interpretation of Modern Politics", in *ibid.*, 270.

48   *Rationalism in Politics*, 368–69, 370.

49   Oakeshott's concern about the "mass man" and the "anti-individual" was forecast in a 1951 review of E.H. Carr's book *The New Society*. In this review, Oakeshott quotes Carr's reference to "mass democracy" with characteristic distaste, which borders on mockery. He asks "is there not something a little disingenuous or sloppy in saying that the great problem is that of 'reconciling democracy with planning for socialism' and 'adapting to the mass civilization of the twentieth century the conceptions of democracy found in earlier highly individualistic periods of history'?" In O'Sullivan, ed., 226–27.

that conventional conceptions of democracy are insufficient and that a "radical restatement" of democracy is needed.[50] I have also demonstrated that whatever shortcomings he thinks obtain to conventional understandings of democracy, he thinks they are more philosophically justified than the political alternatives.[51] Lastly, he sees democracy as the result of contingencies and "vicissitudes", rather than the result of platonic ideals, rationalism, or "design". In keeping with all these convictions about democracy, he thinks that conversation is at its core. Luke O'Sullivan writes that for Oakeshott, " 'liberalism' and 'democracy' were shorthand expressions for complex historic forms of public life".[52] This is another accurate description, in keeping with Feaver's and my own judgment. While he certainly gives no sustained or detailed analysis of, or argument for, a theory of democracy, he writes enough for these conclusions to be drawn. Most relevant to this project is the affirmation that nothing he writes about democracy disallows or opposes premises which are fundamental to the deliberative democratic literature overall. Indeed, as I have shown, he gestures, and at times, more than gestures, toward conceptions of democracy wholly in keeping with the deliberative turn.

Before moving to the other considerations of this chapter, I will quite briefly summarize conclusions on Oakeshott's early thought about democracy by Feaver and Soininen. As I indicated above, while I disagree with Feaver that "Oakeshott had a good deal to say about democracy", I recognize, of course, the simple problem here of identifying what "a good deal" means. In any case, Feaver goes through some of the material discussed above and draws conclusions similar to those here. Indeed, I would add that in respect to the literature reviewed up to this point, interpretation is a minimal and easy task, as it seems that what Oakeshott wrote about democracy explicitly seems quite clear. It is worth noting that Feaver agrees with the argument I will elaborate in the next chapter: that Oakeshott's "preferred sense of democracy is ultimately linked to the attributes of non-purposive, "civil association".[53]

Feaver notes that only in Oakeshott's lifetime did liberal democracy gain its "historically unprecedented ascendancy", and therefore his intellectual

---

50   In 1966 W.H. Greenleaf wrote that Oakeshott "is not a 'democrat' in the naive, modern sense of the term, an adherent to the current ideological cant; though the traditional British way of attending to political arrangements is quite another matter and has all his devotion." In W.H. Greenleaf, *Oakeshott's Philosophical Politics* (New York: Barnes and Noble, 1966), 86. This comment is congruent with those made by Luke O'Sullivan, Debra Candreva, and me. It underscores the conclusion that Oakeshott both embraced democracy of a certain kind, while at the same time finding any number of other conceptualizations of it to be insufficient or problematic (if not dangerous). It also implies that he thought improvements were possible in respect to democratic theory.

51   Although it is not clear whether he thinks Catholicism might be equally or more philosophically coherent.

52   In Luke O'Sullivan, ed., Introduction, 18.

53   In Abel and Fuller, eds., 148.

biography matches his consideration of democracy. He concludes that for Oakeshott, democracy means

> sustaining in rising generations of associates an understanding of the proper office of government ... . The practices of representative democracy are a legacy hard-won by those who have gone before, though adaptable as circumstances might require to the vicissitudes of everyday political life.[54]

Feaver's appreciation of Oakeshott's thought about democracy is for the most part accurate, but he undervalues the contingency of democracy in Oakeshott. The fact that democracy is, for Oakeshott, more comprehensive than the role of government escapes his attention. He does not make reference to, and one can only suppose he did not have access to, the early texts from Oakeshott published in *What Is History? And Other Essays*. In the two essays I have cited above, especially "The Voice of Education in the Conversation of Mankind", Oakeshott not only emphasizes the contingent nature of democracy, but its discursive essence. Feaver's analysis would have benefitted from a reading of these texts. Nonetheless, Feaver ends his summary of Oakeshottian democracy with valuable insight:

> Oakeshott aims not to dismiss democracy but to find appropriate grounds for depicting it as a tangible feature of contemporary civilization in the changed historical circumstances of an ongoing human adventure ... . There can be no pristine "liberal democracy", no unipolar regime of liberty or equality. The adventure is, as always in the human estate, more a matter of Box and Cox, in which liberty requires authority. Notably, Michael Oakeshott closed the last book published in his life with a recreated essay on the theme of "The Tower of Babel" ... that is by turns funny and mordant, a barely concealed parody of those who yearn to dwell in Elysian fields of "democracy", led there by the politics of faith, or collectivism, or enterprise association.[55]

Suvi Soininen understands Oakeshott's earlier remarks about democracy to have close similarity to his characterization of a "proper" understanding of political activity altogether. Further, she correctly notes that whereas democracy in his earlier work is more of a tradition than a doctrine, it also "is used in many respects to describe the "universal" — and I take this to mean the Western — activity of politics".[56] Whereas this could seem contradictory, I think Soininen is right in seeing both tradition and contingency theorized on the one hand and a "universal"/ Western idiom of politics theorized by him on the other — both as essential aspects of democracy. This is no contradiction because politics itself is every bit as tradition-bound and contingent as is democracy, as I will demonstrate below.

---

54   *Ibid.*, 156.
55   *Ibid.*, 158–59.
56   Soininen, 138–39,

Political Philosophy, Political Activity, and Political Discourse

At this juncture, we cycle through the texts above, as relevant, and consider others, so as to determine what relationship exists between Oakeshott's theorization of political philosophy, political activity, and political discourse on one hand, and democracy or democratic theory on the other. I have, of course, covered the material in which he deals with democracy explicitly, so the rest of the chapter will consider texts which I will argue offer less explicit reasons to make conclusions about Oakeshott's conceptualization of democracy. Because my arguments below are of an inferential kind, an appropriate degree of tentativeness and humility is necessary. Nonetheless, to say that an argument is inferential does not mean it is weak, let alone, illegitimate. If what Oakeshott argues about political philosophy, activity, discourse, and other matters comports rationally with certain views of democracy and disallows other views, one cannot avoid some conclusions as to how his thought in one area or another implies certain conceptions of democracy he must (rationally) hold, or at minimum, that he can rationally hold.[57] In addition to taking his texts in roughly chronological order, I will also want to deal with political philosophy, political activity, and political discourse in just this order. Importantly, it must be added, however, that these matters obviously flow into one another and therefore no neat and clean distinction can always be made between his theorization of philosophy, activity, and discourse. This being the case, patience is asked of the reader when she encounters a mixture of these concerns, or one of them seemingly "out of place" in the treatment below. Further, I will shortly explore dimensions of Oakeshott's thought that I have separated from political philosophy, which, clearly in a broad sense, are all a part of political philosophy (this is easy to see in respect to "Rationalism and Ideology" and "Liberalism and Freedom" but is also true of the other section headings). This being said, the reader could take the remainder of this chapter to be about political philosophy altogether; but I have divided the chapter for reasons I think economy and manageability demand. Although it is the case that all of the matters below bear upon one another, and therefore there is an artificiality involved in my sectional distinctions, it simply seems that such organization is the better alternative over against other, or no divisions.

---

57 Of course it is possible that Oakeshott can be nonrational or irrational and not see the proper relationship between two or more conceptions. I mean only to argue here that, if there is no evidence to the contrary, one should take Oakeshott's conception in one respect to either allow or affirm a conception in another respect if rationality seems to require this relationship. I will argue that certain of his conceptions imply certain things as to what he would most likely take democracy to be. By "most likely", I mean that which rationality either allows or affirms, given the particularities of the text(s) and other relevant features of the argument.

Political Philosophy

Three facts confront us at this juncture: first, Oakeshott has written a considerable amount of political philosophy; second, a great deal has been written about his political philosophy; and third, nearly all of political philosophy can in one way or another be connected to democracy and democratic theory.[58] Therefore, the challenge before us here is to *limit* discussion both in scope and depth, so as to only concern the reader with the aspects of his political theory that most clearly and importantly bear on questions of his thought about democracy. This is no small challenge and what follows would profitably be read as an indication of paths to follow more than the final word on the relationship between philosophy and democracy in Oakeshott's earlier work.[59]

Not only must one rely upon essays in order to ascertain Oakeshott's political philosophy before *On Human Conduct*, one should note that he employs no consistent methodology, nor does he consistently work on a particular project.[60] He moves between disciplines, most notably (but not exclusively), history and philosophy, and operates at different levels of analysis: practical, ideological, and theoretical. He often bypasses description, often fixes upon explanation, and subtly, but occasionally, dips into prescription.[61] At times, only careful attention allows the reader to notice where he is in respect to these conceptual locations. At times, he occupies more than one location at once.

A number of themes emerge in the collection of essays that give one Oakeshott's political philosophy before *On Human Conduct*. Here I should like to identify and describe those that I think are most important. Among

---

58 Oakeshott offers insight into the problem of conceptualizing and *containing* political thought. That is, not only can very much in political theory be connected to democracy, he adds that very much beyond the political can be connected to political theory. In "Political Thought as a Subject of Historical Inquiry", in *What Is History? And Other Essays*, 403–21, especially, 415, 419. See also his comment in the "Introduction to *Leviathan*" that political philosophy concerns "the whole intellectual life of our civilization; it is the whole intellectual history organized and exhibited from a particular angle of vision. Probably there has been no theory of the nature of the world, no theology or cosmology, perhaps even no metaphysics, that has not sought a reflection of itself in the mirror of political philosophy..", *Rationalism in Politics*, 225. Note also his claim that political philosophy is "the consideration of the relation between civil association and eternity" in his "Introduction to *Leviathan*", *Rationalism in Politics*, 291.

59 The careful reader will note that I have used "philosophy" and "theory" inter-changeably. Below I will note Oakeshott's use of these terms, and the subtle move made from the former to the latter term. Nothing should be understood as to hang on the difference between the terms; that is, they should not be taken here to mean different things, but seen as synonyms.

60 It is my view that *On Human Conduct* is Oakeshott's *magnum opus*, in part, because the single clearest theme of his life's work can be collected under the rubric of human conduct, particularly in its social forms. He alludes to this possible understanding in the preface of *OHC*.

61 Cf. Soininen, 11, 18. Soininen thinks that Oakeshott "cannot always sustain his insistence on the separation of practice and theory". I will consider her argument below. Benjamin Barber, perhaps more than all others, sees a prescriptive intention in Oakeshott; but he does not offer a sustained argument for this view. See Barber, *The Conquest of Politics: Liberal Philosophy in Democratic Times* (Princeton: Princeton University Press, 1988), 175.

them would be his concern to disengage philosophy proper, or theorizing, as he later comes to call it, from practical concerns. This does not mean, of course, that Oakeshott does not do philosophical work that bears upon practical matters, let alone that he has no practical concerns. It means that he is at some distance from Marx and all others who think that philosophy is at its most authentic when directly engaged in shaping political institutions, regimes, and outcomes. For Oakeshott, theory is marred, truncated, and diminished when it is bent (or, mangled!) to provide specific, and especially narrow, political purposes. To use theory in this way is to de-theorize it, and any short-term gains made by such use are more than offset by the damage done to the philosophical enterprise itself. Treating philosophy in this manner not only violates its nature, but then, in some sense, doing so would also ruin philosophy in the long run.

Various interpreters have identified the unbridgeable or, at least, large gap between theory and practice in Oakeshott as a key component of his political philosophy. Notably, Paul Franco and Terry Nardin do so.[62] Candreva notes that "Oakeshott is well-known for his view that philosophy, or theory, one the one hand, and practice or politics, on the other, are separate realms of activity and that the former cannot and should not be understood as a guide to the latter". She adds, however, that "others ... detect a shift in Oakeshott's views, in which the later works are said to abandon the separation between theory and practice posited in his earliest writings".[63] Suvi Soininen makes the argument that this gap is bridged more often than most think. She writes:

> Oakeshott cannot always sustain his insistence on the separation of practice and theory, or philosophy, ideological thinking, and practical politics, and he oscillates between what he sees as "real", non-partisan, descriptive political philosophy and normative theory ... .
>
> Nor do I wish to belittle Oakeshott's attempt to avoid falling into the trap of a *theoretician*, who intends to replace the everyday experience and knowledge of the cave-dwellers with his own superior, theoretical understanding.[64]

It seems that Soininen identifies something important in respect to this aspect of Oakeshott's thought when she refers to his "insistence on the separation of practice and theory". She thinks the insistence breaks down (while recognizing it as *insistence*), whereas others focus more on Oakeshott's philosophical claims than on the coherence between his claims and his arguments. Martyn Thompson echoes Soininen, "despite

---

62   Franco, *The Political Philosophy of Michael Oakeshott*, 161; Nardin, 11–12, 225–26. Note Hanna Pitkin's strongly negative view in this regard as well, in her "Inhuman Conduct and Political Theory", *Political Theory* 4, no. 3 (August 1976), 301–20.

63   Candreva, 74–75. Despite her reference to "others", the only person she identifies as holding this view of "detecting a shift ... " is Gerencser. Candreva's own view is closest to Franco.

64   Soininen, 18. The second sentence refers to a claim Oakeshott makes in *OHC*, 30, which we will visit in the next chapter.

Oakeshott's repeated insistence that philosophy has no direct practical impact", he writes, " 'The Voice of Poetry' is explicitly concerned to show that it may have a significant indirect impact on human conduct".[65] Steven Gerencser argues that the "commonplace" view of this "strict separation" between philosophy and politics is incorrect, and he also challenges it.[66] To note this focus on his claims is not (at least necessarily) to find fault with those commentators who focus on them. To seek to understand philosophical claims is simply an enterprise different from taking measure of one's consistency in acting on those claims. In my view, even insofar as Soininen is correct, Oakeshott still stands at a very great distance from the Marxian and critical theory views that authenticate philosophy just to the degree that it produces practical guidelines, (immanent) critique, and action. More important, perhaps, because of his own liberal convictions, he stands a great distance from much, if not most, of modern and contemporary liberal theory, in its desire to shape outcomes, such as policies of distribution.[67]

A brief journey into some of his early writings about political philosophy will shed some light on this question of the relationship between theory and practice. I will identify and/or summarize this literature and then offer concluding remarks. In his 1924 essay in which he critiques the Cambridge School of Political Science, or more accurately, evaluates the curriculum then used at Cambridge, Oakeshott writes that "Political Science" is an inaccurate concept and should be replaced with "Political Philosophy". Why? Because "science" misunderstands the endeavor, insofar as the proper study to be undertaken involves phenomena much wider than anything "science" can properly name. He claims that "there can be no study so intimately connected with *our life* as this we call Political Philosophy".[68]

---

65   Martyn P. Thompson, "Intimations of Poetry in the Practical Life", Corey Abel and Timothy Fuller, eds., *The Intellectual Legacy of Michael Oakeshott* (Imprint Academic, 2005), 282. It seems clear that if Thompson holds this view in respect to the essay "The Voice of Poetry in the Conversation of Mankind", he would hold it more broadly, i.e., in respect to other of Oakeshott's writings.

66   "Voices in Conversation: Philosophy and Politics in the Work of Michael Oakeshott", *The Journal of Politics*, Vol. 75, No. 3 (August, 1995), 724–42; and *The Skeptic's Oakeshott*, esp., Chapter 2, 33–51.

67   Will Kymlicka notes that most of the political philosophy of the last 30 years has addressed the question of how, if we are to treat persons as equals, we should protect them in their possession of certain rights and certain liberties; and how we should determine which rights and liberties deserve protection. Since Oakeshott is far more concerned with liberty than with rights, he has very much bucked the trend, as most contemporary liberal theory has concerned itself with rights, such as those justice demands. Kymlicka, *Contemporary Political Philosophy: An Introduction*, 2nd ed. (New York: Oxford University Press, 2002), 53. In addition to Kymlicka's claim, it should not be forgotten that liberal theory in its origins was concerned about shaping practical matters, and this has always remained an important part of liberalism; even if some of those practical concerns were to reduce state power and religious coercion.

68   In *What Is History? And Other Essays*, 65; italics are mine. Oakeshott here means "our life" in a comprehensive manner, not just political life narrowly construed. Cf. Footnote 56 above.

This echoes his claim in response to Morgenthau that "a science of politics is self-contradictory".[69]

In his 1938 "The Concept of a Philosophical Jurisprudence", Oakeshott seeks to "consider the meaning and possibility of a philosophy of law and civil society", which is a task, of course, related to, or a part of, political philosophy.[70] He makes a claim here which will be repeated in later work, almost verbatim. It is about the meaning of philosophy.

> A philosophical enquiry, as I understand it, is not a kind of enquiry different from all others ... [it] is simply thought and knowledge without reservation or presupposition. The aim in philosophy is to arrive at concepts which, because they presuppose nothing, are complete in themselves; the aim is to define and establish concepts so fully and so completely that nothing remains to be added ... philosophy is merely what occurs when thought is allowed to follow its own bent with unqualified freedom ... the aim in philosophical thought is the achievement, by means of a continuous process of redefinition, of concrete concepts ... .
>
> Philosophy is the attempt to redefine concepts concretely, that is, in relation to a universal context, the context of the totality of experience.[71]

In his "The Concept of a Philosophy of Politics", Oakeshott makes several claims entirely congruent with what I have documented immediately above, and in some cases, using identical language.[72] He adds that it must be emphasized

> that in philosophy, and consequently in a philosophy of politics, the criterion is never conformity with our ordinary view ... philosophy will conflict at every point with what happens to be the commonsense view, because a commonsense view must be expected to be incomplete ...
>
> Now, if this be the character of a philosophy of politics, there are clearly many purposes which it will not, and cannot, serve ... . It will not give us a view of political life in terms of purpose and end at all ... political life as achievement of certain ends is superceded by a view of political life in relation to the totality of experience .... A philosophy of politics, then, is unable to give guidance for action ... .[73]

Oakeshott makes very much the same claim in his "Political Philosophy". Here he adds that philosophy is inherently "radically subversive" and that it is what happens when "anchorage" is rejected, and the thinker permits each scene to supercede the one that came before. The metaphor he employs here is of climbing the stairs of a tower, and taking in increasingly grand vistas in which more is seen than before. Philosophers keep

69   "Scientific Politic", 103.
70   In *Politica*, 3 (published in two parts, September and December 1938), 203.
71   *Ibid.*, 345, 348.
72   For example, pp. 126–29; *Religion, Politics and the Moral Life.*
73   *Ibid.*, 135–7. This essay is tentatively given the date of 1946 by Timothy Fuller.

climbing upward while others stop along the way, not that it is the height that matters but the disposition of the climber. It is not achievement at the end of the climb, but the predisposition of ascent, that makes the climb philosophical. Whereas political philosophy has its "starting place" in political experience, it too is an unhindered ascent and exploration. As to the comprehensive nature of its concern, the "dominion over all things of the earth first given to man is the root of all political activity".[74]

Oakeshott argues that the political philosopher may properly offer reflection "in the service of politics", but in this case it follows that there is an absence of the "radically subverse impulse". The political philosopher may also offer reflection not to "determine" political activity, but to explain it. This is an enterprise toward the construction of "a political doctrine". This too, obviously, "falls far short of being radically subversive".[75] He adds the provocative claim that political philosophy makes claims that, if true, "things will be as they are; not as they were when we first caught sight of them, but as they *permanently* are".[76] Lastly, and by now, this is a familiar claim, the enterprise in political philosophy is

> to spread one's sails to the reflective impulse ... from a mooring-place of political experience ... [it is] the genuine, unhindered impulse of reflection ... [and] we must expect from political philosophy no practical political conclusions whatever. Political philosophy can provide no principles to be "followed" ... . Wherever there is genuinely philosophical reflection something is being said, such that if it is true, things will be as they permanently are — that is, as they are *not* in the world of practical politics.[77]

It seems that at least four matters demand some attention in respect to the question of the relationship between theory and practice in Oakeshott's early work. First, he holds a comprehensive view as to what philosophy addresses. For him, philosophy is relentlessly expansive, open-ended, unqualified, adventurous, even playful, and perhaps joyous.[78] This comprehensiveness, which properly belongs to philosophy generally, belongs all the more to political philosophy specifically. Second, related to its inclusivity and comprehensive nature, philosophy is inherently subversive. This is so because any conception or conclusion will be open to challenge and revision if there is yet more to be known and accounted for than the given conception or conclusion allows at the

---

74   *Ibid.*, 145. This essay is dated 1946–50 by Fuller.
75   *Ibid.*, 146–48.
76   *Ibid.*, 151–52 (italics are mine).
77   *Ibid.*, 152–55.
78   In his essay, "Work and Play", Oakeshott describes "play" as activity the purpose of which is to "illuminate the world", and claims that philosophy (like science, history, and poetry) is in this way *playful* and distinct from the world of mundane work. In *First Things*, 54 (June/July 1995), 29–33; and *What Is History?*, 303–14. Cf. Worthington's discussion of this matter, p. 134. Luke O'Sullivan dates the writing of this essay as "c. 1960".

moment. No conception or conclusion is complete, at least none which is more than trite; therefore data and phenomena not yet taken into account present at least the potential of subversion. Oakeshott writes that the political philosopher may offer reflection "in the service of politics, but that in doing so, the "radically subversive impulse" dissipates.

At this point, I am thrust into a dialectic which contains a potential, but not a necessary, contradiction. The third matter at hand, then, is the problem as follows. If, on the one hand, philosophy is comprehensive and radically subversive; and, on the other hand, if it cannot, by definition, offer recommendation of change or guidance in practical affairs, then one is caught in a contradiction. This contradiction would exist because if philosophy is truly comprehensive in scope, it must bear in some respects, upon some practical concerns, to put the matter in a minimal fashion.[79] In short, it seems impossible for philosophy to be as comprehensive in its concerns as Oakeshott claims, while denying it any entry into the realm of the practical, the concrete, and the political. His claim of radical subversiveness carries this same kind of problem. Subversiveness is conceptually related to change. If my ideas are subverted, I will likely or necessarily be lead to change them. If my ideas bear any relationship at all to the practical and political, and they are subverted, the result may be some change in practical and political matters.

However, I do not think it is necessary to see a contradiction of this sort in Oakeshott. He allows for philosophy "in the service of politics" and that philosophy can recommend change and offer guidance. His qualification is that when it does so it is no longer radically subversive.[80] It is clear that Oakeshott privileges philosophy which is, on his terms, radically subversive, but he allows that philosophy can be diluted or compromised and not lose its status altogether as philosophy. This is why I describe Oakeshott's thought about theory and practice as a dialectic. Insofar as philosophy is truly comprehensive, it cannot be entirely innocent of anything; and insofar as it is subversive, it may sooner or later bear a relationship to the changing of practical and political matters. The dialectic consists of a pure, abstract philosophy on one end, and a sullied philosophy that concerns itself with politics, on the other. There is no doubt that Oakeshott valorizes one side of the dialectic and that he worries about the other. In his "Rationalism in Politics", Oakeshott writes that a proper role for philosophy is to "explore the relations between politics and eternity". This is a very wide dialectic, indeed, but it is clear that eternity does connect, through some

---

79 Of course, analytically, taking our language at face value, if philosophy is truly comprehensive it bears upon everything and therefore, upon *all* practical matters however small and policy-oriented. But Oakeshott is not doing analytical work here, but rather a different kind of philosophy. He is using rhetoric (in the best, nonpejorative sense) to make a point.

80 *Religion, Politics and the Moral Life*, 146, 154–55.

fettered path, after all, to politics.[81] Even in his thought, however, it seems that there can be no unbreachable wall between the camps. Whereas he fails to fully appreciate what comprehensivity and subversiveness must imply, he still allows that political philosophy can be political in practical ways. Inasmuch as he is anxious about political philosophy becoming diminished and distorted by its involvement in concrete affairs, I think the philosopher can only join Oakeshott in that worry.

The fourth issue which calls for the reader's attention is, I think, entirely related to my argument above. Oakeshott writes that philosophy makes claims that, "*if true*, things will be as they permanently are — that is, as they are *not* in the world of practical politics". I italicized the qualifier "if true" in the sentence just quoted, because while he offers this platonic notion, it does not follow that he thinks the philosopher is in the habit of uttering such truths. That is, it is consistent with his views in this early period, about the comprehensiveness of philosophy that Oakeshott thinks there can be — conceptually speaking — permanent "things". This consistency does not mean that he thinks philosophers grasp the comprehensiveness, subversiveness, or permanence of matters. He only thinks that philosophers are those who are inclined to keep ascending the tower stairway so as to gain broader vistas. His view is that philosophers think more relentlessly and rigorously than others, without qualification and with an adventuresome spirit (and as I suggested earlier, hopefully because they find a good measure of joy in such thinking).

All can agree that politics is a realm where things are not pure, abstract, permanent, and true in a platonic sense, but this does not mean that the political philosopher can only run in horror away from the muck and mire of politics. It is true that insofar as the philosopher concerns herself with practical politics, it is likely that she will be less than radically subversive; but (again) Oakeshott simply notes (and perhaps laments) the loss of this subversiveness, not the entire loss of the philosophical enterprise.

Oakeshott theorizes political philosophy as at some distance from political activity and he thinks the practical and concrete diminishes the philosophical project. I have also shown that he allows for philosophy to be in

---

81   In *Rationalism in Politics and Other Essays*, 34. Let me here add a brief comment about my use of the term dialectic in this context as a means to describe Oakeshott's thought. It seems to me to be an unnoticed, or at least underdetermined feature of his thought in at least one respect, that it is dialectical (I am uncertain how this dialectical pattern owes to Hegel, but clearly Hegel has no small influence on Oakeshott). Not only does Oakeshott valorize (pure) philosophy over against (sullied) politics; but we see a similar dialectical relationship in these pairs: self-enactment/self-disclosure, civil association/enterprise association, *universitas/societas*. In respect to each pair, Oakeshott deeply values the former conception while at the same time realizing some necessity and value in the second. The claim I am here making will be seen more fully as we deal with these dialectical pairs below.

For a view of self-enactment/self-disclosure which bears affinity to my own, see Glenn Worthington, *Religious and Poetic Experience in the Thought of Michael Oakeshott* (Imprint Academic, 2005), 64–81.

service of politics, and although he does not give political actors advice in a direct and sustained manner, he is concerned about practical matters. Recall, for example, that he offers a critique of the Cambridge School of Political Science. It turns out that in this critique, he is willing to suggest just what it is that should be done at Cambridge. He could allow that offering advice to Cambridge is much different from offering it to Members of Parliament; but, of course, Oakeshott would not have suggested such a preposterous idea because he would recognize that similarities far outweigh the differences. He knew that the curriculum at Cambridge was at least as much a result of politics as a result of pedagogy. He might allow that when offering suggestions to Cambridge, he was not doing philosophy at all. This is much more likely, but not entirely satisfying because his work in this essay is very much like most of his work. It is a work of serious thinking, analysis, and clarification; and when doing such work generally, he understands himself to be working and writing as a philosopher.

These comments must suffice as to the consideration of the relationship between theory and practice, philosophy and politics, but I have meant to lead us toward a transition. Oakeshott is not content to theorize about philosophy and political philosophy, but he also theorized political *activity*, to which I now turn.

Political Activity

In his essay "Freedom and Power", Oakeshott claims that "It may be the business of philosophy to explore a world in which the opposition between these extremes [the exercise of freedom and submission to power] is theoretically reconciled; but as practical people we are not concerned with abstract absolutes, but with concrete relativities".[82] It is clear that Oakeshott is far from entirely disinterested in practical matters such as politics. This essay is an occasion for reflection on the meaning of freedom, and he notes that freedom "leads to the *recognition of certain forms of behaviour as the embodiments of the idea of freedom* and as consequently desirable".[83] Here again, then, one sees a relationship between idea and embodiment, between theory and behavior. He connects freedom, in fact, to certain political structures, specifically, government in which power is "broken up", "separated", and constituted by "independent sources". He ends this essay with the claim that a society should "exploit its own manner of thinking and get as much out of it as it can".[84] Oakeshott seems to have a practical concern in mind here. He is not writing about "getting as much out of it as one can" in respect to philosophical matters. He is concerned about what works best for a society (in this case, to promote and

---

82　In *What Is History? And Other Essays*, 235. This essay was written in the 1950s.
83　*Ibid.*, 237–38.
84　*Ibid.*, 242.

protect freedom). Clearly, the institutions or "embodiments" of freedom he endorses are those which have an historic and necessary relationship to democracy. Because Oakeshott had a life-long concern about freedom and saw freedom as, in part, bearing an essential relationship to the diffusion of power, it follows that at least some aspects of democracy are important to him. That is, insofar as democracy is an institutionalization of the diffusion of power, Oakeshott would find it of crucial moral and political importance.[85]

A brief and second visit to Oakeshott's "Conduct and Ideology in Politics" reminds one that for him political activity shapes political thought, much more so than the obverse. This is because as with all things, "we do not begin with an abstract idea but with an activity … ".[86] It follows, for Oakeshott, that "Words like 'Democracy' … are abstract statements of characteristics observed in conduct … " and that " 'democracy' … means a set of principles which set out in short-hand certain complicated ways of behaving".[87] One here sees the important Oakeshottian theme of practice shaping thought and theory. In politics, it is no different. Political activity shapes political thought, much more so than the other way around. Oakeshott offers the same argument in his Harvard lecture "The History of Political Thought", in which he notes, for example, that democracy names a "complex and intricate manner of behaving reduced to a generality", and that "'the democratic style of politics' is the same sort of expression as 'the baroque style of architecture.' 'The baroque style of architecture' is the product of reflection upon buildings that have actually been constructed".[88] One is reminded of Oakeshott's review of Spearman's *Democracy in England*, where he writes approvingly of understanding democracy as a "by-product" of political activity and other contingent factors, rather than as a "design".[89]

Oakeshott argues along these same lines in "Political Education", where writes,

> Politics is the activity of attending to the general arrangements of a collection of people … . To suppose a collection of people without recognized traditions of behaviour, or one which enjoyed arrangements

---

85 Of course, democracy of even the most minimal kind involves, by definition, a diffusion of power; but differing democratic theories and institutions theorize and embody more or less diffusion.
    For an insightful argument that democracy is and ought to be about the diffusion and control of power, see Ian Shapiro, *The State of Democratic Theory* (Princeton: Princeton University Press, 2003). For a related argument, one that sees democracy as equality and as necessarily deliberative (and thus, a diffusion of power), see Kevin Olson, *Reflexive Democracy: Political Equality and the Welfare State* (Cambridge, MA: MIT Press, 2006).
86 In *What Is History? And Other Essays*, 250–51.
87 *Ibid.*, 252–53.
88 In *Morality and Politics in Modern Europe*, ed. by Shirley Robin Letwin (New Haven: Yale University Press, 1993), 14, 15.
89 In *What Is History? And Other Essays*, 281.

> which intimated no direction for change and needed no attention, is to suppose a people incapable of politics. This activity, then, springs neither from instant desires, nor from general principles, but from the existing traditions of behaviour themselves ... . The arrangements which constitute a society capable of political activity ... are at once coherent and incoherent; they compose a pattern and at the same time they intimate a sympathy for what does not fully appear. Political activity is the exploration of that sympathy ... .[90]

The kind of empirical priority that activity has to theory and ideology means that political activity has a certain importance unmatched by political philosophy. This is worth mentioning because it seems that various interpreters take Oakeshott's claim that political philosophy is diminished when it seeks to provide a political program or otherwise create change, as a carelessness about actual political activity. To read Oakeshott in this way, however, is to read into him a premise he does not himself admit. His claim that it is a political theorist's role to think rather than to act, is no denigration of political activity per se. If political activity shapes political theory, as he argues in several places, it cannot follow that political thought has a kind of value of which political activity is but a scant reflection or (worse yet) aberration.

A reflection of political activity as the "pursuit of intimations",[91] in what are surely the most quoted words of "Political Education", signifies the claim I am making here.

> In political activity, then, men sail a boundless and bottomless sea: there is neither harbour for shelter nor floor for anchorage, neither starting place nor appointed destination. The enterprise is to keep afloat on an even keel; the sea is both friend and enemy; and the seamanship consists in using the resources of a traditional manner of behaviour in order to make a friends of every hostile occasion ...
>
> A depressing doctrine it will be said ... But in the main the depression springs from the exclusion of hopes that were false and the discovery that guides, reputed to be of superhuman wisdom and skill, are, in fact, of a somewhat different character. If the doctrine deprives us of a model laid up in heaven ... at least it does not lead us into a morass where every choice is equally good or equally deplored. And if it suggests that politics are *nur für die Schwindelfreie*, that should depress only those who have lost their nerve.[92]

It is not only the contingency of political activity, and the role of tradition which is of interest here, but that political activity is properly engaged between false and heavenly hopes on one hand, and complete *aporia* or

---

90 In *Rationalism in Politics*, 56–57.

91 *Ibid.*, 66–69.

92 *Ibid.*, 60. Oakeshott's use of the German: "for those afraid of dizzying heights". This famous passage touches upon a number of Oakshottian themes, but it should be remembered when we discuss contingency below.

cynicism on the other.[93] Political activity is for the stout of heart, those not afraid of dizzying heights, for those who have not lost their nerve. If this is the case, it does not follow that political activity is of little importance, or only for the most craven or self-serving among us. There is a vast sea of contingency, invitation, and opportunity the navigation of which necessitates no metaphysical or empirical certainty. Yet, there is no call for political activity to be abandoned. Political activity requires both technical and practical knowledge, Oakeshott tells us, and again, he does so without dismissing the validity or importance of such activity. Both kinds of knowledge equip those with the nerve for such engagement, that is, the engagement of "attending to the general arrangements of a set of people ... ", the arrangements of a "society",[94] and pursuing intimations found in the traditions, behaviors, and practices of such a group of persons.

The last text that must receive attention as I consider Oakeshott's understanding of political activity is Suvi Soininen's. She offers a book-length treatment of Oakeshott's theorization of political activity and it merits consideration (although here, my consideration must remain brief). Central to her argument is the conclusion that Oakeshott's thought about political activity changed dramatically over the course of his career. She argues that he moved from a near contempt for politics, seeing it as a "necessary evil",[95] to a serious appreciation of politics as a reflective and deliberative activity. The argument is that Oakeshott's later work theorizes politics in an original way, as an "art of contingency". My own argument in this project parallels hers in various ways, but because I have organized my approach by dividing Oakeshott's work into two periods, I will not consider the entire scope of Soininen's argument in this chapter. This means that I will have occasion to return to her work. For now, I concentrate on her understanding of Oakeshott's earlier conception(s) of political activity.

She writes that her "main theme can perhaps be best expressed by presenting two quotations" from Oakeshott. First, from 1939, "Political action involves vulgarity, not merely because it entails the concurrence and support of those who are mentally vulgar, but because of the false simplification of human life implied in even the best of its purposes".[96] Second, in 1975 Oakeshott writes that politics calls for " ... so exact a focus of attention

---

93   Reflections on this passage in relationship to contingency can be found in J.G.A. Pocock, *The Machiavellian Moment* (Princeton: Princeton University Press, 1975), 8–9; and Kari Palonen, "Das 'Webersche Moment'", *Zur Kontingenz des Politischen* (Opladen/Weisbaden: Westdeutscher Verlag, 1998), 12. Cf. Soininen, 189.

94   *Rationalism in Politics*, 13, 44, 45.

95   The claim that Oakeshott in his earlier years saw politics as a "necessary evil" is an allusion, which Oakeshott himself uses toward the end of "Political Education" to F.H. Bradley's sentence, "The world is the best of all possible worlds, and *everything* in it is a necessary evil", in the Preface of F.H. Bradley, *Appearance and Reality*. See *Rationalism in Politics*, 66.

96   "The Claims of Politics", in *Religion, Politics and the Moral Life*, 93; Soininen, 1.

and so uncommon self-restraint that one is astonished to find this mode of human relationship to be as rare as it is excellent".[97] As I have intimated, I will deal with Oakeshott's more positive and robust embrace of political activity as seen in *On Human Conduct* in the next chapter. What is clear at this point is not only that Soininen sees these paradigmatic quotations as marking the boundaries of his movement from disdain to appreciation, but that her argument must be considered.

Soininen argues not only that Oakeshott's valuation of political activity changes so significantly, but that the "elements" or dynamics he increasingly understands to be a part of political activity implies a growing understanding of politics as a reflective and discursive activity, as opposed to activity which is merely the habitual continuation or preservation of political tradition.[98] Fittingly, she sees the conception of contingency, in both explicit and implicit ways, as permeating Oakeshott's political thought. In this respect, her work is particularly close to that of David Mapel, although she sees the theme of contingency running throughout much of his *oeuvre*. For Mapel, the importance of contingency does not come into focus until *On Human Conduct*.[99] Below I will have more to say about contingency in Oakeshott and its relationship to democratic theory. In addition to this permeating theme of contingency, Soininen investigates what she calls Oakeshott's "central conceptions" — power, authority, ideology, and tradition — in relation to his conceptions of political authority. This approach allows for the conclusion that his appreciation of political activity changes substantially over his career.[100]

Soininen notes that although in 1939 Oakeshott claims that political activity has nothing significant to contribute to a society's traditions (artists and poets offer more), and that political systems are relatively superficial, resting upon deeper traditions; in his immediate postwar thought, *political* tradition is seen as the pinnacle of politics properly understood. She thinks that his characterization of politics as conversation acquires an increasingly precise content (I think it acquires ever more *richness* in content, I doubt that precision is the best way to describe the development of Oakeshott's thought in this respect). So while in 1939 Oakeshott saw politics as at least potentially injurious, by the late 1940s he is concerned to

---

97   *OHC*, 180 (in the 1975 ed.); Soininen, 2.

98   Soininen, 2, 229.

99   On p. 12, Soininen notes that Oakeshott himself "emphasizes the contingency of human associations" in *On Human Conduct*. Further, she writes that "later", in *OHC*, he "speaks more emphatically about the specific contingency of 'theorizing' ", p. 189, footnote 437.

100   Soininen's approach is thematic rather than chronological; see pp. 83–84. Yet, her methodology must concern itself with chronology in a secondary, yet still important, manner. Her approach then, is the inverse of my own, as I am seeking to submit the thematic concerns to a larger chronology. Of course, neither Soininen nor I can succeed entirely in keeping themes and chronology from spilling into one another.

articulate the difference between political activity properly understood and carried out and politics badly conceived and executed. His most famous rubric for "bad" politics is "Rationalism", which I will investigate below. From 1958 onward, Soininen observes (as have others), Oakeshott substituted the concept of tradition with that of practices and uses "tradition" in quotation marks. He begins to emphasize politics as rhetorical and discursive activity, and "tradition" becomes understood as a conceptualization "used in political argumentation". By this point in his career, ideologies belong no longer to Rationalism, but rather, they are "understood as specific vocabularies of political discourse". In his later theorization, ideologies are seen as "tools of argumentation which can be used in contingent political situations".[101] Whereas Soininen notes that tradition and ideology became, for Oakeshott, conceptions used for political discourse and political activity, she fails to observe sufficiently that political discourse and activity generate and help shape tradition and ideology, both as an empirical matter and in the thought of Oakeshott.

Soininen argues, then, that Oakeshott "continually 'updated' and manipulated his own political thinking ... following the many 'intimations' of his own texts" over five decades. She refers to his "re-descriptions" and his "metaphors on politics as conceptual innovations or reformulations".[102] Again, she notes the pervasive theme of contingency, and that by "On Being Conservative" (1956), the "gloomy tone" of his commentary on politics has receded. I would add that being "at home" in the world — the essence of what he means by "conservatism" — is intimately linked with appreciating the ubiquitous nature of contingency. Lastly, she argues that in Oakehott, political theory and political activity have a "playful" relationship with one another, as theory is as contingent as is activity. She concludes by suggesting that Oakeshott's "late description of political activity as a *deliberative engagement* also implies his hope that political activity may to some extent utilize and learn from other activities as well as relate to them *conversationally*, without attempting to dominate them".[103]

I have offered an exceedingly brief summary of Soininen's argument. In my judgment she argues forcefully and convincingly that Oakeshott's theorization of political activity developed over the course of his career, and did so such that his near disdain for politics became, by the end of *On Human Conduct*, a rather explicit and robust appreciation of political activity properly understood.[104] Key to the development of his thought is the

---

101 *Ibid.*, 215–18.
102 *Ibid.*, 219–20.
103 *Ibid.*, 229–30; italics are mine.
104 Of course, I did not here analyze and evaluate Soininen's argument, but only summarized it. A close inspection and detailed account given on these pages would not assist this project and,

increasing attention paid to the contingent and *deliberative* dimensions and dynamics of political activity. This is to say that insofar as he recognizes and engages the contingent and deliberative aspects of power, authority, tradition, ideology, and so forth, his conception of politics, political theory, and political activity must follow in this direction. I will note Soininen's understanding of the relationship between contingency and discourse with a bit more detail when I turn my attention to Oakeshott's theorization of political discourse.

What I want to add now, before I move to consideration of discourse, is a brief reflection about the relationship between Oakeshott's understanding of political activity and democratic theory and democracy. I have drawn attention to Soininen because I think her argument helps in the development of the conclusions I make here.[105] I will limit my remarks to three. First, there is a logical and practical relationship between contingency and democracy that should be noticed. If political traditions and practices, the complex and organic fabric of civic association (to use the term Oakehsott employs later), are as thickly contingent, and distant from platonic ideals and rationalist engineering as he theorizes, it follows that persons as such, citizens as well as office-holders, constitute the living, breathing, developing set of phenomena Oakeshott recognized as democracy. I am here suggesting that contingency leads to democracy in at least some ways, and that a diffusion of power leads to contingency. If contingency, like political activity, is not to be feared — if it is for those not afraid of dizzying heights and those who would sail boundless and bottomless seas — it is for *all* those with such "nerve". Nowhere in Oakeshott is it suggested that only political officials have such nerve, indeed, quite the contrary. As I have shown, he explicitly argued that democracy is carried forward by citizens, not merely politicians and bureaucrats. In human conduct and civil association, *people* contingently constitute the countless going-ons of life and democracy; his thought about this materializes in his early career, even if it does not crescendo until *On Human Conduct*.

Second, and I can put this succinctly, insofar as Oakeshott values politics, he esteems (his account of) democracy. As was seen in the first part of this chapter, Oakeshott does indeed value democracy, but additionally, an inspection of his work overall shows that his appreciation for political activity also grows to the point where it too, one can fairly say, comes to be

---

indeed, would take it off course. In all particulars where I think Soininen can offer a better understanding or argument, the difference between our considerations does not add meaningfully to the argument I am making in this text.

105 Soininen's work helps in respect to drawing these conclusions, but her argument is not necessary to them.

valued by him.[106] One can be certain that Oakeshott values democracy (on his understanding of this concept, of course) and that he increasingly comes to value politics; my point here is that because his idea of politics properly understood and carried out are democratic in various basic respects, his growing appreciation of politics might also reflect a growing appreciation of democracy. Here I use the word "might" to intentionally *understate* my view, although by the end of this project, and after consideration of *On Human Conduct*, I hope to have shown that there is a parallel between his growing valuation of politics and a growing valuation of political association that must be, if it is to be coherent, seriously democratic. In sum, if Oakeshott's appreciation of political activity grows, then too, must his appreciation of democratic forms of political activity.

Third, and perhaps anticlimatically, I would add that once one can see that Oakeshott's thought about something as substantial as politics and political activity changes quite significantly, one must realize that his thought about other substantial matters may themselves have changed as well. My claim here is a support to the stronger claim made immediately above. If Soininen is correct — and her conclusions are in keeping with the conclusions of Oakeshott scholars in general in this respect — that Oakeshott continuously seeks to understand (having never seen himself to have come to a complete understanding of anything) and that he displays a facility and flexibility of mind, such that his thought is always in *process*, then it stands to reason that his views about democracy are in flux (as I have already shown); and more permutations of democratic thought are possible, and indeed, likely.

Political Discourse

Soininen has helped bring us to a consideration of Oakeshott's theory of political discourse because she sees the discursive and deliberative dimension of political activity as becoming (in intrinsic relationship to contingency) the key element of Oakeshott's mature thought about politics. In this section, I will consider three of Oakeshott's essays: "Political Discourse", "The Voice of Conversation in the Education of Mankind", and "The Voice of Poetry in the Conversation of Mankind". The reader will then be in a position to agree with Soininen about the growing importance of discourse and deliberation in Oakeshott, yet one will also discover that his valuation of discourse emerges relatively early in his career. I caution the reader once again, however, in offering the reminder that the fullest expression of these themes in Oakeshott's thought comes in *On Human Conduct*, and therefore my consideration of various of these themes are

---

106 Although Soininen offers the most rigorous, detailed, and sustained argument for the development of Oakeshott's appreciation for politics, her argument is not entirely *sui generis* insofar as others *notice* (rather than adventurously explore) changes in his theorization of politics.

truncated at this point, from the perspective of Oakeshott's complete work.

"Political Discourse" was first published in the 1991 edition of *Rationalism in Politics*, but it is entirely in keeping with his earlier "The Voice of Conversation in the Education of Mankind" (1948). It is the one text in this chapter first published after *On Human Conduct*. I do not know when it was written, but it fits the literary and conceptual context of *Rationalism in Politics* as well as fitting so consonantly with the 1948 essay. In this section I am addressing essays out of their chronological order because the latter two parallel each other so closely it makes sense to consider them next to one another. In "Political Discourse", Oakeshott immediately identifies the relationship between political discourse and contingency, noting not only that discourse is a response to contingent events but that it shapes events as well. He goes further than these two simple observations; however, he claims that "a political situation is one to which there is no *necessary* response".[107] The idea of radical contingency as intrinsic to discourse is of great importance to Oakeshott, and it emerges often. It follows, inasmuch as politics is discursive, that political decisions, actions, and practices are not bound, in their particulars, to necessity.

Oakeshott notes that political discourse can take various forms, for example, that of argument, "ideology", or "logical design". Ideologies are "special vocabularies" and "idioms of deliberation and discourse". And "logical design" names the kind of discursive practices most common in political discourse; it is " ... argument to persuade without being able to prove. And it gets this design from the logical status *given* to the *beliefs* which compose its vocabulary of discourse — the status of maxims or the components of maxims: beliefs generally held to be true, and values generally held to be important".[108] At the heart of his essay is his recognition of the concern to go beyond this kind of discourse, "Can we not do better", he asks, "than these surmises and conjectures, shots in the dark and actions recommended because they are marginally preferable to others?" He raises the specter of the "emancipation of political deliberation from conjecture and opinion about the probable consequences of actions .... we are asking for *apodeictic* political discourse".[109] What Oakeshott means by such discourse is "demonstrative political discourse ... a kind of argument

---

107 *Rationalism in Politics*, 73.

108 *Ibid.*, 80–81; emphasis is mine. Oakeshott anticipated "the linguistic turn" in a number of respects; among them, he rejected the notion of "fact" as existing apart from "non-fact." His claim that a "logical status is *given to beliefs*" ties to this aspect of his thought. I will have occasion to address this dimension of this thought in Chapter Three as I consider the work of Mapel, Mouffe, and Gerencser, who consider this matter. Cf. also Soininen, 125–26, 145, 157, 198–200, 203.

109 *Ibid.*, 81–82.

capable of proving or disproving the "correctness" of political proposals".[110] His reference is, of course, to reason-giving, justificatory discourse—which the reader will encounter in the deliberative democrats summarized in Chapter Four.

Oakeshott considers the relationship between demonstrative political discourse and ideology and reasoning. He argues that for all of Marx's effort and brilliance in laying out the possibility of solid and foundational demonstrative political discourse, based upon categorically informative, true anthropology, and historical interpretation, the project fails. The hope of liberating political deliberation from opinion and conjecture remains. He writes that

> the naive attribution of the status of axioms to what are nothing more than opinions is the vice of much contemporary political argument ... Further, a craving for demonstrative political argument may corrupt us by suggesting that we have not got to make choices ... . And, what is equally important, this craving for demonstrative political argument may make us discontented with ordinary political discourse which, because it is not demonstrative, we may be tempted to regard a species of unreason ... . In this matter Aristotle and Isocrates are better guides than Plato and Marx ... [demonstrative political argument] might discourage the only sort of intellectual effort capable of improving the quality of our political discourse. I mean the effort to understand our "principles" and our "admitted goods" in such a way as to recognize each as a choice we have made for ourselves on our own moral responsibility ... the effort to support our proposals with relevant arguments in which conjectures are not confused with certainties nor opinion with demonstrable truth.[111]

I end this description of "Political Discourse" with a lengthy quote because it represents a summarizing crescendo of the essay that warrants more than superficial consideration. In this essay, Oakeshott despairs of rational choice theory, utilitarianism, and the epistemological foundations upon which such social theories and other consequentialist moral theories rest.[112] He is critical here of what he elsewhere calls "Rationalism". Most to the present point, he finds political discourse which is a reflection of such propositional thinking to be corrosive and corrupting, a "disastrous error". It is the narrative and rhetorical form and the stress on *kairos*, the "fitness for the occasion" of Isocrates and Aristotle, which comports more coherently and valuably to our best political discourse, more than the rationalistic, propositional, calculating, and deterministic language of Plato and Marx. Analogical narrative surpasses analytic argumentation. Note that he values "ordinary political discourse", which is no less reasonable for being ordinary. Note that the valuation of "ordinary" political

---

110 *Ibid.*

111 *Ibid.*, 95.

112 Although he does not use these terms of rational choice theory, utilitarianism, rationalism, and so on, in this essay, they are clearly implied.

discourse has egalitarian and, therefore, democratic overtones and implications. When Oakeshott suggests that it is an understanding of our principles and goods which is the *"only sort* of intellectual effort capable of
improving the quality of our political discourse" he echoes not only Aristotle but many contemporary republicans and communitarians, including
MacIntyre, Taylor, Sandel, Benhabib, Walzer, and Beiner. This impulse is
also a democratic one, insofar as our principles and goods are constituted
through narrative and discourse, community, and tradition, and we do
not hold our principles and goods as "atomistic" (Taylor), "unencum-
bered" (Sandel), or "un-situated" (Benhabib) selves.[113] Note too, that
while Oakeshott embraces argument as having a legitimate place in political discourse, he does not equate argument with what he calls "demonstrative political discourse". The "effort to support our proposals with
relevant arguments" stands against what I might call a certainty of certainty and of demonstrable truth. In short, "Political Discourse" is an argument in which one is meant to see the inherent relationship between
authentic discourse and contingency. Choices have to be made, just as reasons are to be given and arguments offered, but truth and certainty offered
in propositional and analytical form often corrupt the best kind of political
discussion and have a harmful effect upon political discourse. After all,
statements of "truth" and certainty tend to stifle and truncate, and often
end, discussion. Our most valuable discourse does not operate at the level
of utilitarian calculus or rational choice theory; it is not deterministic.
Political discourse at its best is a contingent and inviting, non-hierarchical
conversation about our principles and goods, about the choices citizens
make and the moral reasons they make them. Several of the themes introduced here by way of, and within "Political Discourse" are elaborated in
"The Voice of Conversation in the Education of Mankind", to which I now
turn.

    Because I have touched upon this essay in the first part of this chapter, I
can truncate my examination of it here. As I wrote above, in this essay
Oakehsott robustly and enthusiastically articulates an intrinsic relationship between democracy and discourse, while rejecting thinner views of
democracy. He also writes various things about the meaning of discourse
and conversation that are quite relevant to this inquiry. He argues that
conversation is the most civilized and civilizing of all the arts. Conversation is nonpurposive; it is akin to the delight of juggling, with a "dialectic

---

113 See, e.g., Alasdair MacIntyre, *After Virtue: A Study in Moral Theory* (Notre Dame: The
     University of Notre Dame Press, 1981); Charles Taylor, "Atomism", in *Philosophy and the
     Human Sciences: Philosophical Papers Vol. 2* (New York: Cambridge University Press, 1985);
     Michael Sandel, *Liberalism and the Limits of Justice* (New York: Cambridge University Press,
     1982); Michael Walzer, "The Communitarian Critique of Liberalism", *Political Theory*, 18, no.1:
     6–23; Ronald Beiner, *What's the Matter with Liberalism?* (Berkeley: The University of California
     Press, 1992); and Seyla Benhabib, *Situating the Self: Gender, Community and Postmodernism in
     Contemporary Ethics* (New York: Routledge, 1992).

of its own; circular, without beginning or end. Up go the balls, the plates, the hats, the whole miscellany of the juggler's box; up and over, in and out, spinning and leaping ... . It is enough that they are moving before us in the air, graceful and enchanting. The art of conversation is not to let them fall".[114] He continues to note that although some people regard conversation "as a kind of intellectual bottle-party at which the most welcomed guests are those who come with some exotic contribution", such elitism ruins conversation, there is "a certain inertness about even the most brilliant epigram which makes it inappropriate in conversation: it detains the flow of talk without being able to set it off in a new direction".[115] Conversation, he adds,

> springs from the movement of present minds disposed to intellectual adventure. Its enemies are the tedious, pernicious talkers, resisting the flow ... . Conversation cannot easily survive those who talk to win ... those who won"t forget or who cannot remember, those who are too lazy to catch what comes their way or who ... are too unresponsive to do anything but let it stick ... the dialectic of conversation must be given its head; bit and bridle are out of place ... . The object is not to persuade or to convince, not to overpower an opponent by reasoning or by eloquence ... . Conversation wanders, responsive to every breeze. The lust of domination ... is absent ... . It is a mean between extremes and therefore appropriate to the civilized man, who is neither a genius nor a fool ... [it] requires more than the inspiration of the Graces; but it requires less than that of the Muses. Somewhere between these ideas lies its world; a world, both in its greatness and in its littleness, fit for mortals.[116]

I have constructed the paragraph above from a barrage of elegant lines on the art of conversation. Indeed, Oakeshott's prose is often so beautiful it is at once tempting, and hard to refrain from invoking. My purpose, however, is to give the reader a sense of the egalitarian and inclusive, nonelitist fabric of conversation, on his account. One need not be a genius; it is an art fit for the ordinary "civilized" person. In this essay, Oakeshott ties democracy strongly to just *this kind* of conversation. Again, the nonpurposive, contingent nature of conversation is presented. Conversation is an internal good; it is not simply for some end beyond itself; it is entirely, or in good measure, its own end. It is what civilized beings do, as a high-water mark of their civilization. Dominating, scoring points, having one's own way, these aims are *nonconversational*. Political discourse in democratic civilizations is meant to approximate this character of conversation. As to the democratic and egalitarian nature of such conversation, Kenneth Minogue

---

114 *What Is History? And Other Essays*, 187.
115 *Ibid.*, 188.
116 *Ibid.*, 189–91.

notes this about Oakeshott, "When he talks of conversation he is thinking of the local pub, not Oscar Wilde at the Café de Paris".[117]

It is important to caution the reader against the suspicion that Oakeshott may mean different things by "discourse", "deliberation", and "conversation". It is clear that he does not distinguish between these terms in any technical senses. Clearly, what he means by conversation applies to discourse beyond the political, but it includes political discourse and deliberation. Obviously Oakeshott knows that some conversations must be "fact"-finding, decision-oriented, and the like. He is not making the absurd claim that conversations can never include purposes of any kind. He is making the deeper, philosophical claim that human beings and human communication, given the kinds of creatures people are, ought to be aware of contingency, agency, freedom, equality, and *poiesis* (to which I will turn shortly). His reflections on discourse mirror the Aristotlean insight that our conversation ought to be as fully human as possible; that is, it ought to reflect the kind of creatures we are: contingent, free, equal, rational, and creative. There is no doubt that Oakeshott thinks political discourse no less than other conversation ought to approximate this conception as much as possible.

He writes that conversation is "a disposition of the human soul; it may often reveal itself in talk, but it is capable of civilizing *any* of the activities in which humans engage".[118] All the more,

> if there is one activity more than another which has benefitted from the civilizing touch of conversation, it is politics. That politics is a subject suitable for conversation, only a barbarian would deny. But the view that I want to suggest is that politics is good for *nothing else*. Moreover, this approximation of politics to conversation is, I think, the gist and meaning of democracy … politics, alone among the subjects of discourse, belongs solely to the realm of conversation … .[119]

The reader may recall this quotation from my use of it earlier in this chapter, but the claim made here bears repeating. Hardly as robust a statement is made by any contemporary deliberative theorist. It is also worth mentioning here that this passage, and this essay altogether, endorses my earlier claim that Oakeshott conflates the meaning of politics and democracy. This conflation is not careless or accidental, of course, rather, Oakeshott conceives of politics as democratic politics. Note, for example, his claim that at "its lowest democracy appeared as a device for talking out the dogmatic reformers; at its highest, it is the politics of conversation".[120]

This essay is also an early presentation of Oakeshott's thought about the relationship between contingency, conversation, and politics. It is the

---

117 In "Oakeshott's Rationalism Revisited", Abel and Fuller, eds., 192.
118 *Ibid.*, 193 (emphasis, mine).
119 *Ibid.*, 194–95, (emphasis, mine).
120 *Ibid.*, 195.

politics of conversation that can rescue us [from] ... the illusion of the evanescence of imperfection. All life is necessarily imperfect; it is full of possibilities, but sparing of certainties. The politics of conversation alone recognizes this necessary imperfection ... . It is the only style of politics that recognizes unequivocally that rulers and subjects alike are neither gods or heroes ... . And we ... must gather together all the powers of conversation in order ... to turn aside the still undefeated forces of barbaric dogmatism ... . This at least recognizes the two main ingredients of human life: chance and choice ... the values and the conduct appropriate to mortal human beings are those that belong to conversation ... . In conversation, as in life, chance and choice are unconfined, united only upon rare and notable occasions. In both, poise in imperfection is the only perfection, and achievement is not to be mistaken for a conclusion.[121]

In respect to contingency, discourse, and politics, Soininen nicely summarizes,

Oakeshott's understanding of political activity as responding to contingent situations which are the product of choices represents a direct opposition to deterministic or mechanistic models of politics ... . [Here] I think we come rather close to Oakeshott's notion of good political conduct on a practical level. At no point is there any *necessary* response to a given political situation. The openness to conversation refers to the contingency of politics ... .[122]

McIntyre also recognizes the importance of discourse in Oakeshott's political theory. He writes that Oakeshott "believes that the character of political discourse is implicit in his concept of practical activity".[123] In the context of McIntyre's discussion, his use of the word "implicit" means not "suggested" so much as it refers to an observation that "goes without saying", or is unquestioned.

I have noted that there are significant parallels between "The Voice of Conversation in the Education of Mankind" and "The Voice of Poetry in the Conversation of Mankind". Accordingly, I can now turn to this second, and better known essay. Here, Oakeshott is concerned to say something about poetry and the relationship between poetic discourse and other kinds of discourse, and it is his thought about both conversation and poetry that is of interest here. While he writes about "poetry", it is clear that Oakeshott means something broader than poetry in the technical and literate sense, as he says so explicitly. What he means by poetry is *poiesis*, the creative dimensions and actions of humankind.[124] Much of what he has to say about conversation is just what he wrote in "The Voice of Conversation in the Education of Mankind". For example,

---

121 *Ibid.*, 196–98.
122 Soininen, 102–03.
123 McIntyre, 170.
124 He writes that what he means by "poetry" is "the activity of making images of a certain kind and moving about among them in a manner appropriate to their character". But "images" is not to be taken (only) literally.

> In a conversation the participants are not engaged in an inquiry or debate; there is no "truth" to be discovered, no proposition to be proved, no conclusion sought … . Of course, a conversation may have passages of argument and a speaker is not forbidden to be demonstrative; but reasoning is neither sovereign nor alone, and the conversation itself does not compose an argument … . Thoughts of different species take wing and play round one another, responding to each other's movements and provoking one another to fresh exertions … voices which speak in conversation do not compose a hierarchy.[125]

There is no need to quote additional texts in this regard, this passage and those in the previous essay give the reader sufficient understanding of his theorization of conversation. Oakeshott writes that two voices have come to dominate our civilizational conversation: the voices of science and of practical activity. Politics, he sees as a species of practical activity.[126] Practical activity, he continues, is the most common manner of imagining; that is, we can hardly absolve ourselves from it. Further, he argues that practical activity has an intrinsic relationship to morality. Selves "in moral activity are equal members of a community of selves … . The moral skill in practical activity, the *ars bene beatique vivendi*, is knowing how to behave in relation to selves ingeniously recognized as such".[127] Practical language, political discourse, preeminently, is moral language; politics is practical and, therefore, saturated with moral consideration.[128]

Oakeshott connects *poiesis* to contemplation and, even, "delighting" (" 'delighting' is only another name for 'contemplating' "); and he writes that "those who would enjoy the difficult delights of contemplation must be ready to enter by whatever door chance or circumstance may throw open to them".[129] As his essay unfolds, he comes to the point where he can conclude that poetic imagining *is* contemplative activity, the voice of contemplation *is* the voice of poetry, and poetry is contemplating and delighting.[130] There is a contemplative and delightful, contingent freedom in *poiesis* and the poetic use of images can move into any number of discourses. For example,

> the word "democracy" for some people represents a quasi-scientific image, for many it signifies a practical image … for de Tocqueville it stood for an historical image, but for Walt Whitman it was a poetic image. In short, the character of an image is revealed in its behaviour,

---

125 *Rationalism in Politics*, 489–90.

126 He thinks that whereas politics has become a modulation of the practical voice in modern Europe, in ancient Greece, politics was understood to be a poetic activity. See ibid, 493.

127 *Rationalism in Politics*, 502.

128 *Ibid.*, 504. Oakeshott's intimations about morality in this essay are elaborated and theorized in *OHC*. I will pay attention to his moral theory in the next chapter.

129 *Ibid.*, 514, 516.

130 *Ibid.*, 516.

in the sort of statements which can relevantly be made about it and in the sort of questions which can relevantly be asked about it.[131]

I have now come to a place where it can be seen how Oakeshott's theorization of conversation and *poiesis* relates to political discourse, democracy, and politics. While politics, as practical activity, is not the voice of poetry, it does not remain out of conversation with poetry, it need not remain untouched by *poiesis*, and it can approximate the character of poetic imagining, contemplation, and delight. Each voice speaks in its own idiom, to be sure, but the voices are capable of hearing and responding to one another.[132] "We find in practical activity itself intimations of contemplative imagining capable of responding to the voice of poetry".[133] Oakeshott uses the example of how love and friendship, although poetic in nature, are also "ambiguously" practical activities which "intimate contemplation and may be said to constitute a connection between the voices of poetry and practice … . Further, there is, perhaps, in 'moral goodness' [a part of practical activity] … a release from the deadliness of doing and a possibility of perfection, which intimates poetry".[134] The voice of poetry, according to Oakehott, is at times itself ambiguous, and "pre-eminently conversable", so one should not be surprised that it can be found not only in conversation with politics, but that it can in some ways, now and again, charm politics into becoming a better and more humane conversational partner. Candreva puts it this way, alluding to his claim that poetry is "a dream within the dream of life", she writes that for Oakehsott, "there is no separation between dream and truth: the world of imagination *is* the world of reality".[135] What Oakeshott says about *poiesis* tracks closely to what he says about conversation, as he explicates conversation in both of these essays.[136] He argues in both essays that there are conversational,

---

131 *Ibid.*, 518.

132 Franco correctly notes that Oakeshott "develops an image of culture as a conversation between various modes of discourse that compose our civilization." In *Michael Oakeshott: An Introduction*, 116. The idea of culture as conversation and politics as conversation, as being not so much two different things as two ways of conceptualizing the same thing, seems right to me, as my exegesis in the next chapter will, in some measure, indicate.

133 *Ibid.*, 536.

134 *Ibid.*, 538.

135 Candreva, 90; see "The Voice of Poetry...", *Rationalism in Politics*, 541.

136 Bearing in mind that Franco sees conversation as an Oakeshottian metaphor for culture, and Soininen sees conversation as Oakeshott's "master metaphor" (p. 145), and the close relationship between conversation and *poiesis* that I am arguing; note that Coats understands Oakeshott's account as one of "the poetic structure of all mediated human experience." It is this poetic structure which, according to Coats, "provides the basis for Oakeshott's critique of rationalism in political and moral life." For Coats, Oakeshott theorizes a "poetic character of human activity", and I agree. See Wendell John Coats, Jr., "Michael Oakeshott and the Poetic Character of Human Activity", *Political Theory and Practice: Eight Essays on a Theme* (Selinsgrove: Susquehanna University Press, 2003), 109. Additionally, Timothy Fuller understands Oakeshott as offering a "poetics of the civil life", which is a conception similar to that of Soininen, Franco, Coats, and me. See his "The Poetics of the Civil Life" in Jesse Norman,

dialectical, deliberative, discursive, and (in the second essay) poetic characteristics that either belong to politics, or which politics is meant to approximate, or that can and should affect politics. Further, he understands democracy to be just that form of politics which is not only politics proper, but the dimension of politics which is straightforwardly most similar and connected to conversation, discourse, deliberation, *and* poetic and contemplative imagining. Conversation is such a deep and rich metaphor in Oakeshott's literary and intellectual arsenal that it cannot be dismissed in seeking to understand his theorization of politics, and especially of democracy.[137] The connections are by turns, several, sophisticated, intimated, explicit, suggestive, and theoretically powerful. One can confidently assert that for Oakeshott, politics is conversation (not merely conversational) in the deep and rich sense of his understanding of that concept. All the more then, democracy is conversation.[138] My claims here do not signify a leap or extrapolation from Oakeshott, for in *his* words, we need a "politics of conversation."

I have discussed Oakeshott's understanding of political philosophy, political activity, and political discourse so as to show that he is far from hostile to, or even dismissive of democracy, even democracy understood in the mode of discourse, but rather that his thought moves between implicit and explicit acceptance and endorsement of democratic conceptions in keeping with "the deliberative turn" in democratic theory. Yet there are still other conceptions to be explored in his early work, in respect to what relationship they may bear to democracy. And so, we now turn our attention to them.

The State, Authority, and Law

As with "political philosophy" and "political activity", the rubric of state, authority, and law could easily lead one into the whole of Oakeshott's political theory and leave hardly any dimension of it undisturbed. Here, as above, then, I must rein in my exploration and exegesis; and the reader is again invited to take what follows as suggestive, as it cannot be exhaustive.

In his 1929 essay, "The Authority of the State", Oakeshott does something he does often: he questions a set of assumptions people hold in

---

ed., *The Achievement of Michael Oakeshott* (London: Gerard Duckworth, 1993). Podoksik offers a significant reflection on Oakeshott's use of the metaphor of poetry in his *In Defence of Modernity*, 103–20. Lastly, for all the virtues of Worthington's *Religious and Poetic Experience in the Thought of Michael Oakeshott*, his failure to exegete the relationship between *poiesis* and conversation in Oakeshott's thought seems to me to be a serious shortcoming.

137 Soininen's reference to Oakeshott's "master metaphor" of conversation is accurate and what the metaphor signifies is important. Gerencser pays significant attention to Oakeshott's use of the metaphor of conversation, and it warrants our concern; but I will turn to Gerencser in this respect when we consider skepticism.

138 Oakeshott's discussion of deliberation in *On Human Conduct* will help validate this claim.

respect to meanings, in this case, of "authority" and "state". This is a frequent pattern in his work, to expose assumptions and conventions, to call them into question and show their weaknesses, and only then to offer his own thought. His own thought in respect to the meaning of authority is that it exists only in an individual person's acceptance of something as authoritative and as something that exists with a kind of inescapable authority that places it beyond preference. This means that authority cannot be coercive; it cannot rest upon on its own recommendation. Further, "what compels me to believe is never the mere cause which produces the belief, but always the whole ground which sustains it … . The 'authority' of what is external (the 'authority', for example, of the expert) is, then, derivative and dependent, it has no power of its own to compel obedience … ".[139] This is a constant theme throughout Oakeshott's career in respect to authority. What is authoritative is so only insofar as those who would subject themselves to that authority do so because they recognize what they invest with authority to be authoritative. Any given datum or person or institution cannot be authoritative in a vacuum, it cannot carry authority in itself, its authority derives from contingent events and circumstances. These two claims are intrinsically related and interdependent. There can be no authority which is external, coercive, and disassociated from the contingencies that create the relationship(s) between authority and those who recognize that authority. If this is what Oakeshott means by authority; what does he mean by "the state"?

I simply note, though I cannot explore this matter here, that he begins his reflection on the meaning of the state by lamenting that "the prospects of political thought today are darker even than those of theology. For the theory of politics has fallen on evil days … ".[140] In this context, Oakeshott's point is that there is far too little coherence and value in theorization about the state. Importantly, his own understanding avoids the too-easy and too-confining limitations of rival conceptions (this again, is typical Oakeshott). For him, the state is something more than government and law, or "any other subcategory of the totality of relationships among individuals". Rather, the state is "the totality of goings-on that is never fully revealed by any of the particulars … . No single purpose could ever define what 'state' is in Oakeshott's sense".[141] In short, Oakeshott describes the

---

139 *Religion, Politics and the Moral Life*, 77–78.

140 *Ibid.*, 80. His critique of the state of political theory in comparison to the state of theology is damning commentary indeed, given the pitiful theology of 1929. It seems two world wars, and especially the *Shoah*, were necessary to shake European and American theology out of its complacent slumber. The theology against which Oakeshott complains needed rescue by Karl Barth (although I am not suggesting, of course, that Oakeshott endorsed Barth's program).

141 *Ibid.*, 12. I am quoting from Fuller's Introduction. In my view, it is the inclusive, comprehensive nature of the state that we see in Oakeshott's theorization of "civil association" and *societas* in *On Human Conduct*, and it is this expansive nature which leads interpreters to inconsistent and

state as "the social whole", and he explicitly disallows a distinction to be made between state and society.[142]

In respect to what the authority of the state might mean, it follows that the state can have no authority in and of itself. The state, Oakeshott argues, has authority that is entirely derivative, and therefore talk of the state's authority is in one respect merely an abstraction and a "legal fiction ... not a fact". It cannot be "itself the real authority which actually compels any belief or action".[143] So far, his understanding seems uninteresting and common; but Oakeshott adds that he is not theorizing the authority of the state as deriving through consent, and in fact, he argues that consent "can never create or maintain authority; authority is never authoritative because it is consented to". He thinks that whatever is authoritative must be so because it is "absolute and independent of our acceptance or recognition: consent itself requires an authority upon which to rest".[144]

What he is getting at is this. The government or law cannot have authority in itself, nor can the people have authority in themselves. Neither the government as such nor the people as such can be authoritative. Rather, there is "a whole ground" upon which authority rests. Authority rests upon the state, and recall, the state is more than government or law or any other subcategory; the state is the "social whole". The authority of the state "resides solely in the completeness of the satisfaction which the state itself affords to the needs of concrete persons. Apart from its completeness, the state has no authority ... ".[145]

Oakeshott's theory of state authority would seem to invite attack from a number of angles, yet it may be superior to any of the most theorized historical options: to see authority as imposed on people by a state external to them, or to see the state as indistinguishable from the people, or to see authority as obtaining in people disconnected from institutions of authority. The first two options reified are totalitarianism and the third reified is anarchy. In any case, what is important for my concern here is two things. First, although I will have reason to consider Oakeshott's understanding of authority with greater scrutiny in the next chapter, his theorization of authority holds to this root understanding throughout his career. Second, his understanding of authority has important implications for democracy and relates in a congenial fashion to what the reader has already discovered about Oakeshott's democratic theory. I will explicate these

---

confusing statements about civil association, sometimes identified as civil society, sometimes identified as the state.

142 *Ibid.*, 84. It is this inseparability, the refusal of distinction between state and society, to which I refer in the preceding footnote; that is, what I think many commentators fail to see in civil association.

143 *Ibid.*, 86.

144 *Ibid.*

145 *Ibid.*, 87.

implications at the end of this section, when I have considered the state, authority, and law a bit more fully.

In an essay that may have been written in 1959, Oakeshott makes two claims worth noting here. First, he offers a conception of government as umpire, stabilizer, peacemaker, and reconciler. This is, of course, the classical liberal, *modus vivendi* view of government. Interestingly, however, and this is the second claim, he thinks that umpirage means "preventing any single substantive condition [from] imposing itself to the exclusion of all others".[146] I find the second claim interesting in light of the first because it assumes that in a liberal society, events will not occur naturally such that any single "condition" might not come to be hegemonic. He does not sufficiently explicate what he means by "condition" in this essay, so the reader is left at sea about this; but, in any case, it is his view that the government has a role to umpire and reconcile, while at the same time *prevent* any single substantive condition from "imposing" itself. Perhaps he is not so much assuming that hegemony cannot develop in a liberal society, as much as he is worried about *imposition*. That is, in imposing a single substantive condition there is a violation of liberal and moral civil association. I point this out here because just what is allowed substantively and purposively in civil association is a matter of debate, in respect to how this matter is theorized in *On Human Conduct*; and here it seems worthwhile to notice a connection between his early and later work, as I have been doing occasionally.

The other, and obvious, connection Oakeshott's liberal view of government has to democracy is that such a government will have little business interfering in democratic activity, and in such a liberal society a vast space is left open for the robust exercise of democracy. This is not to say, of course, that liberalism means or equates to democracy, as though all liberal societies are deeply democratic, but clearly, the historical and theoretical relationships between liberalism and democracy are not merely accidental. I will turn shortly to a few more words about Oakeshott's liberalism and its relationship to democracy and democratic theory.

In his 1958 Harvard Lectures, Oakeshott spoke of the activity of governing, the political theory of individualism, and the political theory of collectivism. Here I want to give brief attention to the latter two parts of *Morality and Politics in Modern Europe*, the last five lectures. I should add that the issues I now engage interpenetrate much of what is to follow throughout the rest of this chapter: matters of liberalism, freedom, individuality, skepticism, and rationalism. Therefore, as I indicated above, the reader should keep in mind that there is some degree of artificiality between these categories and that they bear interdependent relationships with one another. I am dealing with the political theories of individualism and collectivism

146 "Current Ideas about Government", *What Is History? And Other Essays*, 295, 298.

here only because of the necessary relationship to the state, authority, and law that are implied or explicated; but for Oakeshott, individualism is a matter of personhood and agency before it is a matter of politics.

In the first part of the book he argues that the rise of individualism, and especially the "morality of individuality", came to supercede the tradition and communal-bound middle ages, and especially the "morality of communal ties". This individualism is the most important development of modernity.[147] Although Oakeshott values individualism properly understood, he observes that even where present, it is not always an unqualified good. Where individuality had come to dominate life, it all too often destroyed the morality of communal ties without replacing it with the proper morality of individuality. This left a significant number of Europeans who were "unable or unwilling" to make choices for themselves, docile, and overcome with the morality of "anti-individualism" in which "security" is preferred to "liberty", "solidarity" to "enterprise", and "equality" to "self-determination". This is the morality of collectivism that lies at the heart of the political theory of collectivism.[148] This is the foundation upon which is built Parts II and III.

In Part II Oakeshott is concerned with the politics of individualism, in Part III, with the politics of collectivism. The political theory of individualism is organized around the use of Locke, Kant, Smith, Burke, Bentham, and Mill in sequential order, because these figures represent steps and directions in the development of individualism.[149] Oakeshott argues that all of these figures up to Mill theorized government as an umpire. Kant certainly reifies and valorizes the power of the individual, and Oakeshott claims that Adam Smith sees human beings and government in much the same way as Kant, only so much more "clumsily". Burke sees government as a restraint on human passions, so the idea of restraint is added to that of referee. Bentham's contribution is in respect to his understanding of government's role in institutionalizing tolerance. With all of these men, society is an aggregate of individuals, not a community. It is with Mill that the political theory of individualism begins to change, he is a transitional figure. Oakeshott finds him to offer three distinct theories of government, two of

---

147 Cf. Charles Taylor, *Sources of the Self: The Making of the Modern Identity* (Cambridge: Harvard University Press, 1989). Here Taylor agrees with Oakeshott's assessment that the discovery of the idea of individualism is the single most important development of modernity, and he reports this development with insight and acuity.

148 Michael Oakeshott, *Morality and Politics in Modern Europe*, ed. Shirley Robin Letwin, (New Haven: Yale University Press, 1993), 27; cf. Kenneth Minogue's Introduction, x–xi.

149 This does not mean that Oakeshott understands the development to be a simple linear movement such that what follows is better than what came before. He values Locke, for example, while he does not value Bentham. On p. 53 Oakeshott writes that the greatest thinkers who "saw to the bottom of the task" in respect to constructing a political theory of individualism are Spinoza, Hobbes, and Locke.

them are formal and "genuinely individualist, but the third is substantial, and, although its starting-place is individualist, it collapses into collectivism."[150]

The first theory of government is democratic because only democracy is appropriate to individuals who are self-directed, free, and spontaneous. The second theory of government comes into play because of Mill's distinction between "self-regarding" and "other-regarding" acts. Whereas in respect to self-regarding acts, government has no say, in respect to "other-regarding" acts, the government has a proper role to protect persons from harm. It is this function of government which leads to the third theory of government, which has to do with Mill's belief in the progress and "ultimate perfectability of mankind".[151] Oakeshott concludes that in the final analysis, Mill did not regard the individual as an end in himself, but as an instrument and servant of progress for society or humankind. It is clear enough as to how this conceptualization of government leads to collectivism.

By "the politics of collectivism" Oakeshott means an understanding of government in which its proper office is the "imposition upon its subjects of a single pattern of conduct, organizing all their activities in such a manner that they conform to this pattern. It understands governing as the activity of creating a "community" by determining a "common good" and enforcing conformity to it".[152] He sees collectivism as diminishing or obliterating the ability of persons to makes choices, which generates a morality of "solidarity". Such a government has the power not only to maintain "prescriptive" rights but to create new rights. Oakeshott writes that the growth of power in European governments over the past four centuries is due to meeting the needs of "those who have been unable ... to enjoy in any significant degree the experience of individuality".[153] Here and elsewhere, he seems to think that individual freedom is too much a burden for modern peoples. Nikolai Berdyaev has written about the "terrible freedom" people want but cannot handle, and so they diminish it for themselves. Oakeshott, it seems, shares this Berdyaevian idea; and sees collectivist governments as reflecting this fear of, or withering under, freedom.

There are idioms of "perfection" which reflect three different versions of collectivism. Oakeshott identifies a religious version, where "perfection" is understood as righteousness or moral virtue; a "productivist" version were "perfection" is understood as a condition of prosperity; and a "distributionist" version, where "perfection" is understood as security or

---

150 *Ibid.*, 79.
151 *Ibid.*, 81. It seems that Oakeshott may be overstating the case here. I am not sure Mill believed in the "ultimate perfectability of mankind".
152 *Ibid.*, 89.
153 *Ibid.*, 92.

welfare. Calvin's Geneva exemplifies the first, the Baconian worldview has generated the second, and the third version is connected to theories of redistribution and egalitarianism, "its central idea is an "equalitarian" society", and "welfare economics" is the means to realizing this vision.[154] It is not necessary for our purposes to evaluate the cogency or coherence of his views. What is of interest is the relationship between anthropological and psychological conclusions and the role of government. Free people who cherish their freedom will create governments that are limited and therefore do not violate people's freedom. Collectivism develops in relationship to an erosion of fidelity to freedom. When people no longer know how to make choices or give up on the challenge of doing so, they give that power to government or allow government to take it from them. This is the Oakeshottian narrative. It suffers from the weaknesses that have been exposed in various forms of libertarianism for quite some time. For example, Oakeshott is innocent of the interdependent relationship liberty and equality must have in order for either conception to be coherent and robust.[155]

One can see the connections and common ground of these three early texts. If the state is an Aristotlean or Hegelian "social whole"[156] and the authority of the state emanates from the historically contingent relationships between persons and offices, etc., which constitute the state, it follows that the anthropological and psychological embrace of freedom or "anti-freedom" (to which I will turn momentarily) would have an organic connection to government. As in "Current Ideas about Government", in his Harvard Lectures, he presents the basic liberal idea that a limited state is essentially and necessarily related to freedom. Although he does not make the argument in these texts, as I indicated above, Oakeshott did think that a limited state, which leaves maximum room for freedom is essentially and necessarily related to democracy. One recalls at this juncture what Oakeshott wrote about democracy in *The Social and Political Doctrines of Contemporary Europe*, where his thought about liberalism and democracy is tied together in just this way. There is obvious truth in this conclusion, and throughout Oakeshott's life, the relationship between the erosion of democracy and the centralizing power of government is also

---

154 *Ibid.*, 107, 109.

155 It must be noted that Oakeshott makes at least one claim that would take issue with my own. He writes, " ... I think in the end, it is impossible to keep the concepts of *liberty* and *equality* apart", *Religion, Politics and the Moral Life*, 131. My point is that, such claims aside, Oakeshott does not give anything close to a sufficient account of the relationship between freedom and equality.

156 Franco refers to Oakeshott's "full-blown Hegelian definition of the state" in which Oakeshott "goes on to reject the separation of the state from society". In *The Political Philosophy of Michael Oakeshott*, 77.

unquestionable when one considers the rise of totalitarian states.[157] What he fails to see, or grossly underdetermines, however, is that free and democratic peoples might freely and democratically choose to work through the agency of government, collectivizing their choices (say, in a Rousseauian manner) for some purposes beyond Hobbesian or libertarian purposes. This theme will be visited in the next chapter with more scrutiny than we need apply here.

One might simply take Oakeshott to be warning against a conflict between authority and individualism, whereby authority is by definition seen as a threat to individualism. This would be a libertarian reading of Oakeshott, but mistaken; Oakeshott's thought is more original, nuanced, and flexible than "isms" allow. We need only recall his claims in the Introduction to *Leviathan* where he writes

> ... it is Reason, not Authority, that is destructive of individuality ... .What, indeed, is excluded from Hobbes's *civitas* is not the freedom of the individual, but the independent rights of spurious "authorities" and of collections of individuals such as churches, which he saw as the source of the civil strife of his time.
>
> Hobbes is not an absolutist precisely because he is an authoritarian ... . Indeed, Hobbes, without being himself a liberal, had more in him of the philosophy of liberalism than most of its professed defenders.[158]

This passage indicates not only Oakeshott's skepticism about the power of reasoning, but complexifies and problematizes a simple authority-versus-individuality perspective. Authority, he claims, is not necessarily destructive of individuality, and authority properly conceived and executed can keep the state from "absolutism", or totalitarian tendencies. Authority properly understood, as I have indicated, is emergent from the state itself, which is the "social whole", not a government or set of laws set over against the people, nor merely at the disposal and whim of the people. Democracy is not anarchy. Oakeshott's liberal democratic civil association (a term he uses in his Introduction to *Leviathan*) strongly valorizes individuality, but by no means averts authority. It is the way that authority is constituted that matters, and if constituted along liberal and democratic lines (as he theorized them), such authority supports, protects, and promotes individual freedom.

It is not surprising that Oakeshott's theory of law reflects the understanding of the state and authority summarized above. Here I briefly summarize his early theorization of law (keeping with my simple organizational division in which everything before *On Human Conduct* is "early", and *On Human Conduct* and other writings after it are "late"). For

---

157 Soininen points out that Oakeshott's conception of power and the collectivization of power has an economic dimension; in Soininen, 91–98.

158 *Rationalism in Politics*, 282–83.

example, fitting with his theory of the state as all social relationships in their various networks and complexities, and that government cannot coerce or compel belief or acceptance of "its" authority, Oakeshott thinks citizens do not obey laws, but rather, they "subscribe" to them. This will be explicated in the second essay of *On Human Conduct*, but it is also his understanding presented in "The Authority of the State". That the law itself, as such, is authoritative is a "legal fiction", and law "always draws its power from a source outside itself".[159] This is the only understanding of law congruent with his theorization of the state and authority.

One can recall that "The Concept of a Philosophical Jurisprudence" undertakes a consideration "of the possibility of a philosophy of law and civil society".[160] Even putting his objective in this way intimates an intrinsic relationship between law and, not government, but civil society, which is bigger than government and carries the implications of his idea of the state, indicated above. Here Oakeshott is critical of thin and limited conceptions of the law, and concomitantly, their weak relationships to philosophy, in which philosophy "stands to the philosophy of law merely as a presupposition".[161] His theorization of law and civil society stresses the necessity of philosophical depth and of the relation of law to civil society, as an embodiment of the meaning of such a civil society.[162] He writes that "In a philosophical doctrine the *what* and the *why* are genuinely inseparable … ".[163] Congruent with what I have reported about his theorization of state and authority, law has an organic and intimate connection, holding no authority "on its own", deriving "its" authority from both its philosophical anchorage and meaning and, more importantly, from its part in and reflection of the "social whole" discussed above.

One recalls our observation above that one way to theorize democracy is as a diffusion of power, and further that this understanding of democracy is found in Oakeshott, here and again, mostly in implicit, but nonetheless, real ways. Consider then, what he writes about government by rule of law in "The Economy of Freedom":

> But government by rule of law … while losing nothing in strength, is itself an emblem of that diffusion of power which it exists to promote, and is therefore peculiarly appropriate to a free society. It is the method of government most economical in the use of power; it involves a partnership between past and present and between governors and governed which leaves no room for arbitrariness; it encourages a tradition of resistance to the growth of dangerous concentrations of power … . Particular laws, we know, may fail to protect the

---

159 *Religion, Politics and the Moral Life*, 85–86.
160 *Politica*, 3 (1938), 203.
161 Franco, *The Political Philosophy of Michael Oakeshott*, 73, 78.
162 What Oakeshott refers to as "civil society" in 1938, he will come to write of as "civil association" by 1946, in his Introduction to *Leviathan*.
163 *Politica*, 3 (1938), 358.

freedom enjoyed in our society, and may even be destructive of some
of our freedom; but we know also that the rule of law is the greatest
single condition of our freedom ...
The diffusion of power inherent in the rule of law leaves government with insufficient power to operate a collectivist society.[164]

By this point in this investigation, it is clear that for Oakeshott, the
meaning, substance, and function of law and the rule of law are democratic. Law is not authoritative *in se*, it is not external to citizens, it is not
imposed, it is not obeyed but rather "subscribed to", and it is a democratic
legal regime resistant to the danger of the concentration of power.
Oakeshott's conception of law is similar to the idea of law as "constitutive
rhetoric" put forward by James Boyd White. The law, White argues, is concerned with the question "What kind of community should we be? ...
What kind of language should the law constitute, should constitute the
law?" Law, he continues, is "a culture of argument, perpetually remade by
its participants".[165] White rejects utilitarian ways of theorizing or using the
law and also what Oakeshott called "Rationalism". He rejects the understanding of law that "results in a reduction of the human to the material
and the measurable, as though a good or just society were ... not a set of
shared relations, attitudes, and meanings".[166]

In keeping with a chronological approach, I end this section with consideration of a few references from the Harvard Lectures. First, he writes
that "Law and morals normally have the same centre but not the same cir-
cumference ... to have achieved a distinction between crime and sin in one
of the characterizations of modern European societies".[167] So, and again,
this will be explicated in Chapter Three. While the law is imbued with
moral character for Oakeshott, it does not follow that the law ought to simply prescribe sanctions against immorality or sin (let alone prescribe positive obligations to morality and righteousness).[168] Relatedly, when
Oakeshott considers the thought of Montesquieu, he takes him to be offering "an analysis of the dispositions of a current political character" and
"the aptitudes of the modern European political character". Among the
"dispositions" and "aptitudes" of democracy is the idea that law is meant

---

164 *Rationalism in Politics*, 390–91, 399–400. For an account of democracy which *is* "resistence to
dangerous concentrations of power", see Michael Hardt and Antonio Negri, *Multitude: War
and Democracy in the Age of Empire* (New York: The Penguin Press, 2004). Note that Oakeshott,
Hardt, and Negri all agree that *any* concentrations of power are dangerous.

165 James Boyd White, "Law as Rhetoric, Rhetoric as Law", Austin Sarat, ed., *The Social
Organization of Law* (Los Angeles: Roxburg, 2004), 64, 65.

166 *Ibid.*, 67.

167 *Morality and Politics in Modern Europe*, 16–17.

168 For further reflection on this problematic, see my "Authority and the Rule of Law as
Contingent Moral Practice in Michael Oakeshott's Civil Association", *Law, Justice, and Civic
Virtue*, ed. David Keller, (Orem, UT: Proceedings of the Sixth Annual Utah Valley State College
Conference by the Faculty, 2005), 79–88.

to "promote the common good".[169] Further, Oakeshott claims that the rule of law is meant to be "recognized as an emblem of the necessary conditions for the enjoyment of individuality."[170] Here, I have touched upon part of Oakeshott's reflection on the relationship between morality and law and, at this point, have seen how his theorization of law comports with his understanding of the state and authority. One should recognize, I think, the democratic contours, intimations, and *necessities* of this theorization, even in those places where it remains implicit. One would do well also to remember that often matters are left implicit because they are thought to be obvious. No small amount of Oakeshott's democratic thinking and democratic sensibilities "go without saying." This becomes an inescapable conclusion, when considering his work as I have.

Liberalism and Freedom

I have already considered some Oakshottian texts which indicate his classical liberalism. I need not belabor the point of his liberalism here, I only want to summarize it most concisely and to identify what I think is most at its heart. Two things can quickly be stated as a preface to my remarks. First, a number of commentators have seen in Oakehshott's liberalism something quite important. For example, John Gray has written that Oakeshott has "isolated and identified the very kernel of 'liberalism' "[171] and David Walsh writes that Oakeshott has given "the most profound expression" of "postmodern liberal philosophy" and "the theoretically most profound account of liberal political order currently available".[172] The second matter is simply that there is a literature which, in effect, gives shape to an argument as to whether Oakeshott is best considered a "conservative" or a "liberal". I find this literature surprising, uninteresting, and, in some respects, odd. Those who want to claim him for "conservatism" focus on a minority of his earlier work, his skepticism, and his separation of theory and practice. Those who see in him various philosophical conceptions, commitments, and values of liberalism, e.g., that of liberty and individuality, see him as a liberal. What is clear is that he is a Whig liberal, a conservative liberal. "Conservative" modifies "liberal" in respect to his thought. The growing body of literature sees this matter as I have just identified it, and the great balance of literature considers the nature of his

---

169 *Morality and Politics in Modern Europe*, 39–41.
170 *Ibid.*, 52.
171 John Gray, *Liberalism* (London: Routledge, 1989), 199. Gray is referring to *OHC* but his remarks are also relevant to Oakeshott's work before *OHC*.
172 David Walsh, *The Growth of the Liberal Soul* (Columbia: The University of Missouri Press, 1997), 56, 57.

liberalism, not the question of whether he is a liberal.[173] Some think there are two Oakeshotts, the "conservative" of *Rationalism in Politics* and the "liberal" of *On Human Conduct*.[174] Further, there are now coming into view interpretations of Oakeshott as a postmodernist.[175]

Oakeshott's liberalism is important for this project because of the deep and important conceptual and historic relationship liberalism and democracy share. Here I take liberalism only to mean what it means uncontroversially, that is, an historical movement in which the value of the individual came to have such importance that it was concomitantly seen that the state should have limited power, and be coercive only when necessary and that religion should be voluntary and never coerce. Persons are (meant to be) free to pursue life plans and identities, and institutions are (in the main) meant to enjoy such freedoms as well. It means government and law, which protects and promotes such freedoms, fundamentally by protecting "negative" freedoms but also, at times, by promoting

---

173 For interpretations of Oakeshott as a "conservative", see David Spitz, "A Rationalist *Malgré Lui*: The Perplexities of Being Michael Oakeshott", *Political Theory*, 4 (1976), 335–52; Perry Anderson, "The Intransigent Right at the End of the Century", *London Review of Books*, 14 (24 September, 1992), 7–11; Russell Kirk, *The Conservative Mind* (London: Faber and Faber, 1954), 413–14; Kirk F. Koerner, *Liberalism and Its Critics* (London: Croom Helm, 1985), 270–308; Hanna Pitkin, "The Roots of Conservatism: Michael Oakeshott and the Denial of Politics", *Dissent*, 20 (1973), 496–525; Jeremy Rayner, "The Legend of Oakeshott's Conservatism: Sceptical Philosophy and Limited Politics", *Canadian Journal of Political Science*, 18, no. 2 (June, 1985), 313–39; and Anthony Quinton, *The Politics of Imperfection: The Religious and Secular Traditions of Conservative Thought in England from Hooker to Oakeshott* (London: Faber and Faber, 1978), 90–96.

For interpretations of Oakeshott's liberalism, see Corey Abel, *Michael Oakeshott's Liberalism: The Epistemology of Experience and the Morality of Individualism* (PhD diss, University of Chicago, 1995); Wendell John Coats, "Michael Oakeshott as Liberal Theorist", *Canadian Journal of Political Science*, 18 (1985), 773–87; Lawrence E. Cahoone sees him as a conservative liberal in, *Civil Society: The Conservative Meaning of Liberal Politics* (New York: Blackwell, 2002); Paul Franco, "Michael Oakeshott as Liberal Theorist", *Political Theory*, 18 (1990), 411–36; John Gray, *Post-liberalism: Studies in Political Thought* (New York, Routledge, 1993), 40–46; Jacob Segal, "A Storm from Paradise: Liberalism and the problem of Time", *Critical Review*, 8. no. 1, 1994, 23–48; Michael Williams, "Liberalism and Two Conceptions of the State", D. MacLean and C. Mills, eds., *Liberalism Reconsidered* (Totowa, NJ: Rowman and Allanheld, 1983), 117–129. In respect to interpreters we have referred to so far in this study, those who take Oakeshott as a liberal include Franco in both of his books, Gerencser, Nardin, O'Sullivan, McIntyre, Podoksik, Soininen, and Worthington.

174 For example, Charles Covell, *The Redefinition of Conservatism: Politics and Doctrine* (London: Macmillan, 1986), 136; and Anthony Farr, *Sartre's Radicalism and Oakeshott's Conservatism: The Duplicity of Freedom* (London: Macmillan, 1998), 241–55.

175 For example, Richard Rorty, "Postmodernist Bourgeois Liberalism", *Objectivity, Relativism, and Truth: Philosophical Papers I* (New York: Cambridge University Press, 1991), 197–202; and Fred Dallmayr, *Polis and Praxis* (Cambridge, MA: MIT Press, 1984), 41–44, 60–66, 209–18. For a consideration of the relationship between conservatism and postmodernism that makes use of Oakeshott, see Bruce Pilbeam, "Conservatism and Postmodernism: Consanguineous Relations of "Different" Voices?" *Journal of Political Ideologies*, 6, no. 1 (2001), 33–54. For a consideration of Oakeshott and Rorty in relation to one another, see Soininen, 42–53; and my unpublished paper, "The Strong Poet or the Voice of Poetry in the Conversation of Humankind: *Poiesis* and Morality in Richard Rorty and Michael Oakeshott". Mouffe, and in some ways Mapel, may think of Oakeshott as a postmodernist as well. I will investigate their interpretations of Oakeshott in the next chapter.

"positive" freedoms. It also means a robustly or relatively free market, which follows from the freedoms mention above. Such dimensions of liberalism mean also, then (at least derivatively), a pluralism and diversity in such liberal societies (or at minimum, an openness and possibility of pluralism and diversity). In liberal societies, there are no controlling projects, agendas, ideas, or values. There are a plurality of goods and ends sought and enjoyed.[176] Efraim Podoksik offers this summary of Oakeshott's liberalism in what I am referring to as his "early" career: "in his writings on politics prior to *On Human Conduct* Oakeshott reveals a strong liberal sentiment, promoting the ideas of freedom, individuality, and the rule of law".[177] Podoksik gets it right in respect to the core values at the heart of Oakeshott's liberalism, though he would have been well served to include here Oakeshott's valuation of pluralism. He repairs this omission when he notes a few pages later that Oakeshott, "pushes his assertion of plurality as far as possible".[178] One recalls, for example, Oakeshott's words from *The Social and Political Doctrines of Contemporary Europe*, that "society must not be so unified as to abolish vital and valuable differences …. the imposition of a universal plan of life on a society is at once stupid and immoral … ".[179] Here one can also note that Kenneth Minogue sees the repellent Rationalism of Oakeshott's conceptualization as, above all else, "mono-modalism", a "relentless drive toward monism", its "reduction of the variety of the world to a single world of understanding", which emits in a "politics of uniformity".[180]

Even Oakeshott's essay "On Being Conservative" is, in good measure, a statement of liberalism. Its primary thrust is that the "*disposition*" of being conservative means the ability to enjoy whatever is available rather than to wish for something else, and that government ought not to be zealous to violate this sense of delighting in the present by pushing too hard for change.[181] No serious reading of Oakeshott can doubt his endorsing theorization of and deep commitment to individual agency, individuality, "the morality of individuality", freedom, limited government, a neutral state

---

176 I have touched upon an important debate within liberalism, one I cannot explore here, but it is about whether liberalism itself is a controlling good and end and about whether liberal government can be or ought to be the neutral umpire Oakeshott and others claim it is and must be. Do liberal values, commitments, and laws sometimes, in some respects, trump other values, commitments, and laws– even, at times, by force of coercion? While liberals argue as to the best answers to these questions, all liberals, by definition, theorize a relatively robust space for pluralism and diversity.

177 Podoksik, 179.

178 *Ibid.*, 204.

179 On page xix.

180 In Abel and Fuller, eds., 183, 188, 192, 193.

181 *Rationalism in Politics*, 407–37, see esp. pp. 407–08, 423, 432.

seen in the metaphor of an "umpire" or "referee", and the plurality of goods and ends in proper human life and conduct.[182]

It should readily be seen that the valuation of all the conceptions and commitments above lead to, are related to, and are often led to by democracy. Just to the extent that one valorizes the importance of individual worth, individual liberty, robust agency, limited government, and pluralism, one is going to endorse some serious form of democracy or fail to do so at the cost of incoherence.

Individuality and Anti-Individuality

Closely related to liberalism and democracy is, as I have just indicated, the idea of the importance of the individual *qua* individual. This is a significant theme in Oakeshott, as the reader will have already concluded. While the reader has discovered some of Oakeshott's thought in this respect, a few further remarks are in order. I will begin by simply noting that Horst Mewes, for example, argues that Oakeshott is "one of the great political theorists of modern European individualism";[183] and when Patrick Riley authored his memorial essay on Oakeshott, he chose as its title, "Michael Oakeshott: Philosopher of Individuality".[184] Words that Riley invoke are as useful as any as a window into Oakeshott's Kantian esteem of individuality.

> Morality consists in the recognition of individual personality whenever it appears. Moreover, personality is so far sacrosanct that no man has either a right or a duty to promote the moral perfection of another: we may promote the "happiness" of others, but we cannot promote their "good" without destroying their "freedom" which is the condition of moral goodness …
>
> But this pursuit of individuality, and of the conditions most favourable to its enjoyment, was reflected in an understanding of the proper office of government … . In what we have come to call "modern representative democracy".[185]

This brief passage says much as to Oakeshott's view of the connections between morality, freedom, liberalism, government, and democracy. Morality "consists in the recognition" of individuality. Soininen is correct, as I will discuss below, that "Oakeshott considers *morality* as the appropriate

---

182   On Oakeshott's understanding and valuation of agency, see Robert Orr, "A Double Agent in the Dream of Michael Oakeshott", *Political Science Reviewer*, 20 (Spring, 1992), 44–62; and Tregenza, *Michael Oakeshott on Hobbes*, 53–62. For his understanding and valuation of plurality, see "On Being Conservative", *RP*, 429; and Loren Lomasky, "Liberal Obituary?" in Tibor R. Machan and Douglass B. Rasmussen, eds., *Liberty for the Twenty-First Century: Contemporary Libertarian Thought* (Lanham, MD: Rowman & Littlefield, 1995), 246.

183   Horst Mewes, "Modern Individualism: Reflections on Oakeshott, Arendt, and Strauss", *The Political Science Reviewer*, 21 (Spring, 1992), 116.

184   *The Review of Politics*, 54, no. 4 (Fall 1992), 649–64.

185   "The Masses in Representative Democracy", *Rationalism in Politics*, 367–68.

context for understanding politics".[186] Individuality is "sacrosanct", writes Oakeshott. As discussed above, the anthropological conclusions about the fundamental importance of individuality are foundational to the *necessary* form of government that is coherent with our individuality: democracy. That is, Oakeshott's interest in individuality and freedom is not primarily psychological in nature, but rather, he is interested in the consonant forms of government, authority, and law, the kinds of human and civil association that reflect, protect, and promote individuality and freedom properly understood.

Mewes and Riley are by no means alone in seeing individuality and freedom as a crucial part of Oakeshott's thought. For example, Franco, Nardin, Podoksik, Tregenza, and Worthington all devote significant space in their books to the exploration of the meaning of individuality and, concomitantly, freedom, in Oakeshott. In *Rationalism in Politics and Other Essays*, the themes of individuality and freedom are widely present; "The Political Economy of Freedom" is only one essay taking up these matters. There it is clear that for Oakeshott, not only is freedom a moral concept but individuality is also. It is difficult to find him addressing the concept of individuality without theorizing it as a moral term or considering it in a moral context, for purposes of moral understanding.[187]

Oakeshott theorizes not only individuality and freedom in the senses he thinks proper and fitting but also the figure who stands in contrast to the free individual: the "individual *manqué*", the "anti-individual", and the "mass man". All of these figures, from the free individual to the anti-individual in rationalistic and cowardly bondage, are moral characters. In "The Masses in Representative Democracy", one is introduced to these characters, whom "the course of modern European history has thrown up" to us. Whereas the emergence of the "disposition to be an individual is the pre-eminent event in modern European history",[188] the development of the "mass man", the "individual *manqué*", and the "anti-individual" is entirely regrettable. In keeping with his profoundly contingent theorization, the individual is an historical event; he is not natural, metaphysical, or teleological.[189] The development of individuality grew out of the "morality of communal ties", as persons became ever more able and willing to make choices for themselves.[190]

The gradual disintegration of the morality of communal ties led to the development of the lesser character as well. "There were some people ... less ready to respond to this invitation: and for many the invitation to

186 Soininen, 84.
187 Cf., e.g., Tregenza, 53–79; Podoksik, 149–57; and Worthington, 44–51.
188 *Rationalism in Politics*, 370.
189 *Ibid.*
190 *Ibid.*, 365.

make choices came before the ability to make them and was consequently recognized as a burden".[191] Whereas the development of individuality grew concomitantly with a morality of the individual, so too, the development of the anti-individual brought a commensurate morality. Whereas individuality

> constituted a considerable moral revolution ... the weight of this moral victory bore heavily upon the "individual *manqué*" ... .
>
> In some, no doubt, this situation provoked resignation; but in others in bred envy, jealously, and resentment. And in these emotions a new disposition was generated: the impulse to escape from the predicament by imposing it upon all mankind. From the frustrated "individual *manqué*" there sprang the militant "anti-individual", disposed to assimilate the world to his own character by deposing the individual and destroying his moral prestige.[192]

As I wrote above, Oakeshott is not interested in individuality and anti-individuality for their own sakes (whatever this might mean), and he does not separate morality and politics. He is interested in the morality of individuality, or I might more accurately say that he is interested in morality (part of which implies or necessitates his conception of individuality) just insofar as morality and political activity are intrinsically related and are, in important ways, slightly different ways of conceptualizing the same phenomena. That is, the "social whole" of the Aristotlean state is deeply and inherently related to the morality consonant with individuality and the individuality coherent with morality. Franco correctly writes of Oakeshott's "obvious sympathy for the disposition of individuality and his tying of liberal democracy to it ... ".[193] Concomitantly, he is interested in the morality of the anti-individual in the same way, because of its relationship to human association and political activity, particularly the state as described above. Oakeshott's theorization of the state, authority, law, freedom, individuality, and morality are all of a whole; these concepts are so tightly interwoven that to pull one loose would unravel the fabric of the constellation.

This summarization is endorsed by the Harvard Lectures. When lecturing on the activity of governing, Oakeshott immediately wades into the relationship between morality and government in modern Europe. This leads him to explicate the historical rise of individuality and, once again, the "morality of the individual" and of the "anti-individual".[194] From this juncture, he discusses, as I have shown, "The Political Theory of Individualism"

---

191 *Ibid.*, 370–71.

192 *Ibid.*, 372.

193 *Michael Oakeshott: An Introduction*, 110.

194 The individual and anti-individual appear again in the third essay of *On Human Conduct*. It is worth mentioning here that Oakeshott's theorization of an historic "character" whom he calls an "individual" and of another "character" called the "anti-individual" have been contested as a less than adequate historical approach. It seems that these characters are, in considerable

and "The Political Theory of Collectivism." It is of no surprise that the "mass man", the "individual *manqué*", and the "anti-individual" lead to a kind of political association that can be defined as collectivism. Of course this is a kind of reading of history and theorizing of human experience and conduct, related to his understanding of the matters I have discussed above, which stays with Oakeshott and comes to light in new ways in *On Human Conduct*, where civil association and *societas* emerge as fresh and sophisticated elaborations of the politics and morality of individuality, and enterprise association and *universitas* appear as equally sophisticated and elaborate versions of the politics and morality of the anti-individual. Oakeshott both complexifies and clarifies his earlier conceptions by his elaboration in *On Human Conduct*, but my point here is only to note the continuity in respect to these important themes and theorizations.

Skepticism

Here I will proceed with, first, a summary of Oakeshott's argument in *The Politics of Faith and the Politics of Scepticism* and then other considerations of his skepticism from various other sources. I might have interrogated this book on several occasions above, in addition to its direct passages about democracy, because much of what Oakeshott has written here comports with themes I have explored. In the scheme of this chapter's organization, however, it seems most valuable as a statement of Oakeshott's skepticism and an important precursor to a review of rationalism, ideology, and con-tingency. As my comment above suggests, I have already encountered thought much like that presented in *The Politics of Faith and the Politics of Scepticism*, most particularly in "On Being Conservative", "The Masses in Representative Democracy", and *Morality and Politics in Modern Europe*. The primary change from his earlier work to these latter two is that the poles of modern European consciousness and politics are no longer described as "faith" and "scepticism", but as "individuality" and 'anti-individuality'".[195]

In "On Being Conservative" Oakeshott compares what Franco aptly summarizes as a "politics of passion" and a "politics of skepticism". As with other pairs in the dialectical pattern I described above, Oakeshott con-siders one to be strongly preferable, more helpful and valuable, without rejecting the other in its entirety. He considers "the politics of skepticism" to

measure, caricatures, and Oakeshott, in my view, may or may not know sufficiently that they are so. See David Boucher, "Politics in a Different Mode: An Appreciation of Michael Oakeshott 1901–1990", *History of Political Thought*, 12, no. 4 (Winter, 1991), 728. Boucher argues that Oakeshott's abuse of historical data violates his own "postulates of history." Oakeshott acknowledges that he may have stretched or simplified some figures and events so as to fashion these "characters" and make his argument in "On the Character of a Modern European State." See his "On Misunderstanding Human Conduct: A Reply to My Critics", *Political Theory*, 4, no. 3 (August, 1976), 359–60. Cf. Worthington, 42, n. 2.

195 Franco, *Michael Oakeshott: An Introduction*, 107–08.

have much the advantage over the "politics of passion".[196] It is the kind of skeptical conservatism, the "politics of skepticism", that Oakeshott presents in "On Being Conservative" that is present in *The Politics of Faith and the Politics of Scepticism*. It is an aversion to the allure of perfection and a disposition to handle the temptation of the not-yet-known with care.[197] It is a call to be wary of our passions, however well-intentioned,[198] and a humility born of the awareness of the human condition, of contingencies, and hubris. Radical ventures are welcome in many respects, but in regard to government, wide-eyed notions are all too often dangerous and destructive.[199]

The politics of faith and the politics of skepticism stand for two quite different ways of understanding the human person, political association, political activity, and the office of government. Just as Oakeshott sees Francis Bacon as the first important figure in the productivist version of collectivism, he sees Bacon as the first and "most adventurous of the perfectionist politics of faith".[200] Indeed, it is not accidental that the politics of faith and the political theory of collectivism mirror one another, just as the politics of scepticism and the political theory of individualism echo each other. In respect to his skeptical warning against perfectionism, it is worth noting a criticism he makes of Eric Voegelin at about the same time he writes *The Politics of Faith and the Politics of Scepticism*. He writes, "Perhaps the most serious defect of the whole account is the underestimate of the strength and vitality throughout modern European history of what may

---

196 However, note an important qualification to the conservative "disposition" Oakeshott promotes: that "it is not at all inconsistent to be conservative in respect of government and radical in respect of almost every other activity". It follows for him, then, that "there is more to be learnt about this disposition from Montaigne, Pascal, Hobbes, and Hume than from Burke or Bentham", *Rationalism in Politics*, 435.

197 On Oakeshott's "sceptical conservatism", see Robert Eccleshall, "Michael Oakeshott and Sceptical Conservatism", *Political Science Since 1945: Philosophy, Science, Ideology*; Leonard Tivey and Anthony Wrights, eds. (Brookfield, VT: Ashgate, 1992), 173–95.
    Whereas skepticism is a pillar of conservatism, conservatism does not reduce to skepticism. It is my suspicion that some interpreters who cast Oakeshott as a conservative come too close to conflating skepticism and conservatism.

198 However, Oakeshott does not, it is important to note, agree with the Platonic and Aristotlean notions of the near-absolute danger and certain inferiority of the passions.

199 Oakeshott's theorization of the "conservative disposition" has little in common with the conservatism that emerged in the United States from the 1950s onward. His is an honest skepticism about human knowledge and power and a deep appreciation for contingency, in addition to such an appreciation for life on its own, present terms. I find plenty to criticize in Oakeshott's "conservatism", but it has an historically and philosophically informed depth and coherence almost entirely missing in the glob of ideas and practices that somehow go by the name of "conservatism" in the United States. The latter "conservatism" is rarely skeptical of its own ideas or programs, for example, and is as much a form and proponent of what Oakeshott called "Rationalism" as is nearly all the political ideologies recent U.S. "conservatives" attack. Of course another way to cast this claim is that the neoconservatism of recent U.S. history bears little resemblance to historical and actual conservatism. Cf. Franco, *Michael Oakeshott: An Introduction*, 104.

200 Franco, *Michael Oakeshott: An Introduction*, 105.

be called neo-Augustinian politics as both the partner and opponent of Gnostic [perfectionist] politics".[201]

The two extreme "poles of governing" and "styles of politics", described as the politics of faith and skepticism, are not merely anarchy or collectivism, although they could be reified respectively into these ideologies. Both of these "poles of an activity and poles of an understanding" are extremes "which make intelligible the ambivalence of our conduct in governing and the ambiguity of our political vocabulary".[202] One might think that Oakeshott undertakes the task of eliminating such ambiguity, but rather, he claims,

> if there is any conclusion I wish particularly to avoid, it is the fruitless conclusion that virtuous politics would seek simplicity and "shun ambiguous alloy", that what we ought to aim at is a resolution of the ambivalence and ambiguity of our politics or at least a formula under which they can be vanquished.[203]

This embrace of ambiguity comports with his appreciation of contingency and also his theorization that the politics of faith and skepticism are interdependent. When, in fact, "either of these styles of politics claims for itself independence and completeness, it reveals a self-defeating character. Each is not less the partner … . each stands in need of the other to rescue it from self-destruction … ".[204]

To the end of describing how citizens ought to live in and use this ambiguity, both styles of politics, Oakeshott refers to Halifax's *Character of a Trimmer* (published in 1688) as the character most appropriate to our circumstances. The trimmer does not put all the weight of a ship on one side, or point all the sails in a single direction, but rather, he constantly makes adjustments in response to the needs and conditions of sailing and seas, all in order to keep the boat on an even keel.[205] Oakeshott's reference to Halifax's metaphor is used to explain that "the politics of faith alone regards ambiguity as worthless" and that "politics is a *conversation* between

---

201 Review of Voegelin's *The New Science of Politics* in the *Times Literary Supplement*, August 7, 1953, 504. In Franco, *An Introduction*, 106.

A brief note about Oakeshott on Augustine: Oakeshott considered Augustine one of the two most remarkable persons who ever lived (Montaigne being the other). This remark was made in a letter to Patrick Riley and recounted in Riley's "Michael Oakeshott: Philosopher of Individuality", 661. See Wendell John Coats, "Oakeshott and Augustine", in his *Oakeshott and His Contemporaries: Montaigne, St. Augustine, Hegel, et al.* (Selingsgrove, PA: Susquehanna University Press, 2000), 28–38.

202 Michael Oakeshott, *The Politics of Faith and the Politics of Scepticism*, 17.

203 *Ibid.*, 20.

204 *Ibid.*, 91–92. Cf. Franco, *Introduction*, 106–07.

205 *Ibid.*, 123–28. Cf. Franco, *ibid.*, 107. One cannot miss the relationship between the image Oakeshott borrows from Halifax and his own image of "sailing a boundless and bottomless sea … where the enterprise is to keep afloat on an even keel … ", *Rationalism in Politics*, 60.

diverse interests".[206] That is, politics *is* a conversation, a discourse by which the ship of state is kept on an even keel. Patrick Deneen uses *The Politics of Faith and the Politics of Scepticism* to argue that just as politics can be a version of Oakeshottian "faith", similar forms of "democratic faith" are also dangerous, or "out of keel", so to speak.[207]

The interdependence of the politics of faith and of skepticism, even if faith is much more dangerous, bears mentioning, for, among other reasons, some interpreters see Oakeshott's skepticism as so radical that they fail to appreciate the "trimming" necessary between the two "styles of politics". This seems particularly true of Neal Wood's "A Guide to the Classics: The Skepticism of Professor Oakeshott". Wood argues that Oakeshott's "conception of philosophy is fundamentally skeptical" and most "apparent when he discusses political activity".[208] In Wood's defense, he published this article in 1959 and, therefore, could not have access to *The Politics of Faith and the Politics of Scepticism* and other of Oakeshott's work. Nonetheless, a robust skepticism in Oakeshott continues to be advanced by, for example, Roy Tseng, who writes that "no *fundamental* change in spirit has ever occurred in Oakeshott's idea of philosophy in terms of a sceptical character".[209] In any case, a virtue of Tseng's book is in his treatment of skepticism as the proper Oakeshottian antidote to rationalism.

Just as Tseng takes Oakeshott's skepticism to be, along with his idealism, the most important constant of his philosophy altogether, and therefore one of the two necessary keys to understanding Oakeshott; similarly, Steven Gerencser sees skepticism at the heart of Oakeshott's political philosophy (along with a matter much related to skepticism: his affinity to Hobbes). Unlike Tseng, Gerencser argues that after *Experience and Its Modes*, Oakeshott moves away from idealism and replaces it, in effect, with a radical skepticism, at least in respect to the possibility of philosophical understanding.[210] Gerencser is interested in explicating the transformation in Oakshott's thought from the idealism of *Experience and Its Modes* to the skepticism that is signaled in "The Voice of Poetry in the Conversation of Mankind", and to a somewhat lesser extent "Political Philosophy".

---

206 *Ibid.*, 130 (emphasis, mine).

207 Patrick J. Deneen, *Democratic Faith* (Princeton: Princeton University Press, 2005), 49.

208 In *The Journal of Politics*, 21, no. 4 (November, 1959), 650, 651.

209 Roy Tseng, *The Sceptical Idealist: Michael Oakeshott as a Critic of the Enlightenment* (Imprint Academic, 2003), 5. Tseng, of course, deals with *The Politics of Faith and the Politics of Scepticism* and its use of Halifax's metaphor; but I am unable to conclude from his book a sufficient sense of accommodation to Oakeshott's accommodation of the politics of faith.

210 Steven Anthony Gerencser, *The Skeptic's Oakeshott*, 2–3, 34. Cf. McIntyre, *The Limits of Political Theory*, 34. Cf. Soininen's discussion of Gerencser's understanding of Oakeshott's skepticism in Soininen, 70–77, 104–06. Whereas McIntyre has important disagreements with Gerencser's interpretation of Oakeshott's skepticism, Soininen is in agreement with Gerencser on this matter.

For my purposes, however, what is interesting about Gerencser's under-standing of Oakeshott's skepticism lies in its relationship to conversation.

Just to the extent that gulfs of understanding between autonomous modes are replaced by voices in conversation, skepticism increases, at least on an account of skepticism correlative to a suspension of certainty. In "The Voice of Conversation", Gerencser argues that Oakeshott begins to direct his skepticism to the claims of philosophy itself. Further,

> by using the image of conversation, Oakeshott provides a manner of interaction that can be meaningful and yet with conditions to protect against irrelevant claims of supposed authority ... .
>
> When understood as voices in conversation ... there is nothing restrictive or necessary about this interaction, except the paradoxical recognition that there are no certainties within it ... . The skeptical ele-ment of his thought is evident in his rejection of the certainties of any voice in the manifold of human utterance.[211]

At this point one can see the connection between skepticism and conver-sation that touches upon our concerns. Indeed, recall Oakeshott's claim in "Scientific Politics", that the "root of so-called 'democratic' theory is not rationalist optimism about the perfectibility of human society, but scepti-cism about the possibility of such perfection".[212] Yet at least equal to the force of skepticism in Gerencser's exposition is the import of contingency. Just as politics as conversation is skeptical about certainty, it is skeptical about directions and outcomes. It is the matter of contingency in Gerencser's theorization that interests me more than his focus on skepti-cism, in the next chapter. At this moment, the mutually reinforcing rela-tionship between skepticism, contingency, and conversation should be kept in mind.

Rationalism and Ideology

Rationalism names a constellation of closely related ideas, and the reader has just caught a glimpse of it in the quote from "Scientific Politics", imme-diately above. Rationalism also names what is perhaps the single theme having received the most attention in Oakeshott's work before *On Human Conduct*. His theorization of rationalism is primarily clustered in a number of essays collected in *Rationalism in Politics and Other Essays*.[213] I have just noted that Tseng's understanding of Oakehshott's skepticism as having value is in good measure because it is a means of countering rationalism. I will briefly summarize what Oakeshott means by Rationalism and demon-strate what relationship it bears to ideology, in Oakeshott's account,

---

211 *Ibid.*, 39–40.
212 *Religion, Politics and the Moral Life*, 109.
213 "Rationalism in Politics", "Rational Conduct", "The New Bentham", and "The Tower of Babel", are, I think, the most helpful.

before investigating in what respects it might relate to democracy and democratic theory.

Minogue notes that Oakeshott's "Rationalism" is a "social critique" similar to concepts put forward by various others, including "scienticism", "technology", "ideology", and "the colonization of the *Lebenswelt*". Oakeshott's rationalism, as Minogue sees it, is "the deliberate attempt to catch happiness", and the Rationalist is "supremely the mono-modal bore targeted in *Experience and Its Modes* for whom everything is really practical … . Further, the infection is progressive … . Rationalism goes on entrenching the toxin".[214]

Rationalism is Oakeshott's term for a distortion of practical activity by the misguided effort of applying theory, or what looks to be "useful" theory. The Rationalist is guided by such concepts as efficiency, productivity, and use in ways that are irrelevant, inappropriate, or in violation of the enterprise in which they are sought to be "applied".[215] The rise of rationalism comports with the rise of modernity and the inclination to reduce practical reasoning to (moral and other) rules of conduct, technical knowledge, and technique.[216] Of course, rules of all kinds have their place, but the rationalist fails to see that rules are abridgements, abstractions, and distillations of practical activity. Rationalism is also the disposition to reject habit and convention, to jettison the acceptable for the better, and valorize "reason" over experience. The rationalist appears in "the New Bentham" as the *philosophe* who

> is an inventive, ingenious, mildly perplexed and easily satisfied mind; there is vitality but no discrimination. All knowledge appears equally significant [but] … there is neither time nor inclination to learn anything profoundly … . he is unconscious of his vulgarity … .
>
> He does not know what it is to be perplexed; he only knows what it is to be ignorant. And he is protected from the dilemmas of doubt by a tough hide of self-confidence … .
>
> He believes that what is made is better than what grows, that neatness is better than profusion and vitality. The genius of the *philosophe* is

---

214 In Abel and Fuller, eds., 183. Minogue's reference to "technology" alludes to critiques made by, perhaps, Christopher Lasch and Jacques Ellul; his reference to the "colonization of the *Lebenswelt*" refers, of course, to Habermas. His claim that rationalism is progressive reports Oakeshott's claim to this effect in "Rationalism in Politics".

215 This part of what Oakeshott means by Rationalism has significant similarities to MacIntyre's critique of "applied" ethics. They share the conviction that there are certain conceptions, practices, and conventions that cannot simply be "applied". For both MacIntyre and Oakeshott, morality is one such, nonapplicable, practice. I will say more about this in Chapter Three. See Alasdair MacIntyre, "Does Applied Ethics Rest on a Mistake?" *Monist*, 67 (1984), 498–513.

216 Oakeshott writes, "Rationalism is the assertion that what I have called practical knowledge is not knowledge at all, the assertion that, properly speaking, there is no knowledge which is not technical knowledge", *Rationalism in Politics*, 15.

> a genius for rationalization, for *making* life and the business of life
> rational rather than *seeing* the reason for it ... .[217]

Nardin correctly notes that a "chief mistake of Rationalism is to assume
that conduct is only rational when it is guided by "theory", that is, by general ideas that we can formulate as propositions or laws".[218] Yet theory and
knowledge are not the only matters distorted and misconceived by the
rationalist. Morality, too, is the recipient of such a fate.

> The morality of the Rationalist is the morality of the self-conscious
> pursuit of moral ideals, and the appropriate form of moral education is
> by precept, by the presentation and explanation of moral principles ...
> . it is morality reduced to technique, to be acquired by training in an
> ideology rather than an education in behaviour. In morality, as in
> everything else, the Rationalist aims to begin by getting rid of inher-
> ited neiscience and then to fill the blank nothingness of an open mind
> with the items of certain knowledge ... .
>   Like the politics of the Rationalist (from which, of course, it is insep-
> arable), the morality of the Rationalist is the morality of the self-made
> man and of the self-made society: it is what other peoples have recog-
> nized as "idolatry".[219]

Rationalism has had a deteriorating and devastating effect in modern
understandings of knowledge, politics, morality, and more. It has been
culturally cancerous and toxic.[220] Rationalism is the "politics of the felt
need"[221] and the "politics of perfection". It is politically manifest in the
activity of governments who pursue illusions and the consolidation of
power necessary to seek the achievement of those illusions. "The Political
Economy of Freedom" is a critique of the growing power of government
and other rationalistic dimensions of politics. I mentioned earlier that
Oakeshott's theorization of collectivism is, in effect, another permutation
of rationalism, but at bottom, rationalist politics are not all of the collectivist or "leftist" variety. One can recall his response to Hayek's *Road to Serf-
dom*: it too is "a doctrine", and "a plan to resist all planning may be better
than its opposite, but it belongs to the same style of politics. Only in a society already deeply infected with Rationalism will the conversion of the
traditional resources of resistance to the tyranny of Rationalism into a

---

217 *Rationalism in Politics*, 138–39.

218 Nardin, 92. The first two paragraphs of my summary of Oakeshott's "Rationalism" owes to
     Nardin, 90–93.

219 *Rationalism in Politics*, 40–41.

220 Oakeshott writes that rationalism is "the most remarkable intellectual fashion of post-
     renaissance Europe", *ibid.*, 5; that "the history of Europe is littered with the projects of the
     politics of Rationalism", *ibid.*, 10; and that it has exerted its influence over nearly every aspect
     of human experience, including art, literature, science, education, religion, and the "conduct of
     life itself", *ibid.*, 22. Cf. Candreva, 23–24.

221 *Rationalism in Politics*, 27.

self-conscious ideology be considered a strengthening of those resources".[222]

One can recall Oakeshott's claim in "Scientific Politics" that

> parliamentary government and rationalistic politics do not belong in the same tradition and do not, in fact go together ... [and] that the institutions of parliamentary government sprang from the least rationalistic period of our politics ... . The "root" of our so-called "democratic" theory is not rationalist optimism about the perfectibility of human society, but scepticism about the possibility of such perfection.[223]

In short, democracy and rationalism cannot have a happy relationship, for they are enemies.

I have now quoted Oakeshott twice in places where he used "Rationalism" and "ideology" as closely related concepts, and it remains to say a word about the relationship these conceptions have for him. Soininen writes,

> It is a well-know fact that the concept of ideology generally appears with negative connotations in Oakeshott's work and is closely connected to his ideal type of rationalist politics. Ideology is described as a comprehensive, self-legitimating, and often pseudo-scientific program of action; a plan which intrinsically belongs to the strain of politics referred to by Oakeshott as rationalism. It is purported to be a set of independently premeditated abstract principles which supply in advance a formulated end (or ends) for a society to pursue.[224]

I have suggested that there is a close relationship between rationalism and ideology for Oakeshott, but the real question is whether they are closely related or two ways of naming the same thing. To answer this question, I will utilize Paul Franco's and Suvi Soininen's discussion of ideology in Oakeshott. I will then be able to describe the Oakeshottian relationship between rationalism, ideology, and democracy. According to Franco, "Rationalist politics are, above all, ideological politics — the simplicity and (illusory) self-containedness of a set of abstract principles being preferred to the complexity and relative open-endedness of a tradition of behavior".[225] As this sentence suggests, Franco writes of rationalism and ideology together, and in roughly synonymous ways (he considers ideology in

222 *Ibid.*, 26–27. For more on Oakeshott's conception of Rationalism and the rationalist, see Franco, "Oakeshott's Critique of Rationalism Revisited", *Political Science Reviewer*, Vol. 21, No. 43 (1992), 15–43; *The Political Philosophy of Michael Oakeshott*, 107–56; *Michael Oakeshott: An Introduction*, 81–115; John Gray, "Michael Oakeshott and the Political Economy of Freedom", *The World and I*, Vol. 3 (September, 1988), 607–17; Robert Grant, *The Politics of Sex and Other Essays: On Conservatism, Culture, and Imagination* (New York: St. Martin's Press, 2000), 23–49; Tseng, 131–74; Candreva, 21–99; and Soininen, 89–98.

223 *Religion, Politics and the Moral Life*, 109.

224 Soininen, 124. Note that Soininen's limitation of rationalism to politics in this passage is unwarranted, as the summary above should make clear.

225 *Michael Oakeshott: An Introduction*, 83. Cf. his statement in *The Political Philosophy of Michael Oakeshott*, "by far the most significant characterization of rationalist politics for Oakeshott is that they are ideological politics, 'the politics of the book'" 112.

his chapter on Rationalism); and he does so, I should add, because Oakeshott does so.

Franco notes that Oakeshott's historical account of the emergence and appeal of rationalism is "curiously" uncomplicated and truncated, given the fact that he "argues so forcefully against abridged and ideological history."[226] Whereas Franco's observation is certainly correct, Oakeshott's inconsistency in following his own advice does not tell against his conception of Rationalism and ideology *for my purposes*. That is, I am interested in what Rationalism and ideology mean for him, and how this meaning is related to democracy. Only if, and to the degree that his simple and truncated account of Rationalism and ideology impact its relationship to democracy, does this matter become my concern.

Oakeshott writes,

> How deeply the rationalist disposition of mind has invaded our political thought and practice is illustrated by the extent to which traditions of behaviour have given place to ideologies, the extent to which the politics of destruction and creation have been substituted for the politics of repair .... This conversion of habits of behaviour, adaptable and never quite fixed or finished, [fit] into comparatively rigid systems of abstract ideas ... .[227]

Importantly, Franco notes that ideology is what it is just insofar as it is a departure from the politics of tradition. For the historical sea-change that took place between what can be summarized by "tradition", on one hand, and "Rationalism" and "ideology", on the other, is a key element of Oakeshott's conception. Franco, however, finds "Oakeshott's valorization of habit, custom, and the unself-consciousness of tradition" to be "profoundly anachronistic". He continues, "This may be the way politics were conducted in aristocratic societies, but it is irrelevant to modern democratic societies".[228] I think that Franco misses much of the weight of Oakeshott's argument, and he is not entirely accurate in his conclusion. That is, I think Oakeshott's valorization of tradition does have some value for "modern democratic societies". I want, however, to delay my argument against Franco, because only at the end of this project will my argument in opposition to his be finished. That is, this project as a whole is, in part, a response to Franco's claim.

Here I will only elaborate his claim, but minimally. Franco uses Hegel to make his point: "the fundamental principle of the modern age, deriving from the Reformation, is that everything must be justified at the bar of human reason, must be justified by thought. Modern politics are unavoid-

---

226 *An Introduction*, 86.
227 *Rationalism in Politics*, 26.
228 *An Introduction*, 96.

ably ideological, though not necessarily in the negative sense disparaged by Oakeshott".[229]

He sees development in Oakeshott's understanding of ideology, claiming that his later discussions of tradition and political discourse "pay far more serious attention to this ideological dimension of politics".

> In a reply to one of his critics in 1965, for example, he makes it plain that a tradition consists of general ideas, principles, and norms. His fundamental objection to rationalism now is that it fails to grasp the radical diversity of these ideological beliefs … .
>
> Given the radically diverse nature of a tradition — Oakeshott calls it a "multi-voiced creature" — political deliberation becomes a matter of striking a balance between competing goods. There is nothing that precludes ideological debate …
>
> The unavoidably ideological character of modern politics receives even more emphatic acknowledgment in … "Political Discourse".[230]

Franco, then sees rationalism and ideology in roughly synonymous ways, and he thinks that earlier in his career, Oakeshott's understanding of tradition — in opposition to ideology — was simplistic and anachronistic, but by 1965, and especially in "Political Discourse" (first published in 1992), he has developed a properly complexified understanding of tradition, so that it makes room for (a more developed understanding of) ideology. Although, as I have noted, the argument I make in this book will respond to Franco's understanding of Oakeshott's conception of tradition, his own recognition of the development of Oakeshott's thought in this regard goes some way toward anticipating part of my own argument.

Soininen gives considerable attention to ideology, and she thinks that it plays "a central role in his view of (rationalist) politics until the late 1950s".[231] She argues that Oakeshott replaces the concept of doctrine with that of ideology in order to more accurately describe what he means, that is, that ideology speaks to "a way of life", and as such it is not necessarily pejorative. "Ideology is a concept belonging to the sphere of political thought *per se*."[232] This does not mean that Oakeshott does not use the concept of ideology, most often, as he used "Rationalism", that is, in a derogatory way; but she is correct in noting that he does come to use the word in a more philosophical way, denoting a conception that is not negative or positive *per se*. One can see, then, that she has some disagreement and some agreement with Franco. Franco seems not to sufficiently appreciate the more philosophical use of ideology in Oakeshott; but he also seems to recognize, rather obliquely, an indirect development of the concept insofar as

229 *Ibid.* Franco is alluding to, nearly paraphrasing, a passage in G.W.F. Hegel, *Elements of the Philosophy of Right*, ed. Allen Wood; trans., H.B. Nisbet (Cambridge: Cambridge University Press, 1991), 22.

230 *Ibid.*, 96–97. Note that Franco again uses rationalism and ideology synonymously.

231 Soininen, 126.

232 *Ibid.*, 132. On page 206 she notes succinctly his modification of the concept of ideology.

it must play off of "tradition", and tradition becomes a more richly developed idea in Oakeshott's work, over time.

In his "Conduct and Ideology in Politics", probably written around 1955, Oakeshott clearly uses the word in such a way that in cuts in both directions. That is, it is at once a politics which is concerned with questions like What is liberty? What is justice? What is democracy? Yet when he writes "our politics have become what we call 'ideological' politics", it is not a complement.[233] A narrow fixation upon such "ideological" questions is far less than what politics should be, or be concerned about. Along these lines, he writes to Karl Popper in 1948 of the rationalism I have described above and adds "But political life only becomes this when it is governed by ideologies: *normally*, in the 19th century, it never was this".[234]

Soininen notes that although Oakeshott's conception of ideology "belongs to the 'scheme' of rationalist politics", in the late 1940s and early 1950s it is "a sort of caricature that emphasizes the contrast between Oakeshott's notion of 'proper' politics and rationalist politics". Indeed, for Oakeshott, "ideological politics" is not actually politics at all, but the "abolition of politics".[235] One finds then, in Oakeshott's account of ideology, both a pejorative use of the term in which it is essentially a synonym for rationalism *and* a development of the term which treats the concept more philosophically, with greater nuance and complexity, most importantly, recognizing it as not pejorative in principle. Soininen is clearer than is Franco in drawing these conclusions, but there is substantial agreement between them. I have meant to endorse their investigations and readings of Oakeshott in this regard.

The last thing to be said about Soininen's interpretation of Oakeshott on ideology is, in respect to our purposes, the most important. She undertakes her discussion of ideology in relation to Oakeshottian texts on democracy and rightly sees him as theorizing democracy as an antidote to rationalism and ideology. She observes, for example, that when writing of a tradition of ideas that live in contradistinction to rationalism and ideology, and in opposition to the "crude and negative individualism" that is consonant with rationalism and ideology, he refers to this "tradition of ideas" as "Representative Democracy".[236] She adds that it is "important to note that the doctrine of Representative Democracy as 'constructed' here

233 *What Is History? And Other Essays*, 245.

234 *A Letter to Karl Popper*, in Soininen, 134. The emphasis is Soininen's but I have maintained it as it does indicate the "sea-change" I indicated above, between tradition and rationalism and ideology — and that fact that he sees traditional politics as "normal".

235 Soininen, 137. Soininen is quoting Kenneth Minogue in respect to the negation and abolition of actual politics. Minogue's essay is "On Identifying Ideology", in M. Cranston and P. Mair, eds., *Ideology and Politics* (Firenze: Badia Fiesolana, 1980), 27–42.

236 *Ibid.*, 229. She is here referring most specifically to p. xvii of *The Social and Political Doctrines of Contemporary Europe*, but her conclusion of democracy as an antidote to rationalism and ideology reaches beyond this text alone.

by Oakeshott, clearly informs us of the 'positive side' of his dual conception of politics leading up to the final conception of politics in civil association or *societas*".[237] By the "dual conception" of politics, she means traditional, nonideological politics, on the one hand, and rationalistic and ideological politics, on the other. That is, she connects democracy to traditional, nonideological politics. One might also note that when she sees the development of Oakeshott's thought about democracy beginning in *The Social and Political Doctrines of Contemporary Europe* and culminating in his theorization of civil association and *societas,* she anticipates the argument of this book.

In related fashion, Soininen notes that the metaphor of conversation is a part of an appropriate understanding of political activity, or politics proper, which is also an antidote to rationalism and ideology.[238] This observation comports, of course, with Oakeshott's "conversational politics" and "politics of conversation", and indeed, his view of politics *as* conversation.

In this section, I have summarized and interrogated Oakeshott's conception of rationalism and ideology. I have shown that rationalism is an enemy of politics proper, of individuality and freedom, and of tradition. It is impossible not to surmise that it is also an enemy of democracy. I have demonstrated that in his earlier work and overwhelmingly in respect to what he wrote about ideology, it is virtually synonymous with rationalism, but I have also noticed that in the later 1950s Oakeshott begins to treat ideology in a more philosophically astute and complex manner. Ideology, while it most often retains its pejorative sense, now also becomes, especially in "Political Discourse", a conception which is not pejorative *per se;* thus, the close identification with rationalism is severed.

One sees, then, that Oakeshott's theorization of rationalism and ideology bears two different relationships to democracy. First, insofar as ideology is rationalism, it is nondemocratic or antidemocratic. Franco is right that Oakeshott's caricature of rationalism and ideology is less historically informed and complex than it should be, but in respect to the purposes of this investigation, it is clear that rationalism and rationalistic ideology stand for just about everything that democracy is not. Or put differently, rationalism and rationalistic ideology are constituted by ideas and practices in opposition to those which undergird and constitute democracy. The second bearing of ideology to democracy (now leaving rationalism aside, which is unqualifiedly negative) turns on the developed and richer account of ideology that Oakeshott comes to articulate. Just insofar as ideology becomes a neutral concept akin to a "way of life", it need not be opposed or dangerous to democracy. Just to the extent that Franco and

237 *Ibid.,* 131.
238 *Ibid.,* 135.

others are correct that all of modern politics is ideological, in this nonpejorative sense, it does not necessarily pose a threat to democracy. One can recall that as early as circa 1955, Oakeshott described modern politics as ideological and concerned with questions such as, What is democracy? Narrow fixation on such questions as the exclusion of other matters aside (which is what vexed Oakeshott), concerning ourselves with such questions is not less than democratic! In short, democracy comports with conceptions, values, and practices that run counter to rationalism and to rationalistic ideology; but ideology in the more richly developed sense may also be consonant with democracy.

In "Rationalism in Politics", Oakeshott writes, "To explore the relations between politics and eternity is one thing: it is something quite different, and less commendable, for a practical politician to find the intricacy of the world of time and contingency so unmanageable that he is bewitched by the offer of a quick escape into the bogus eternity of an ideology".[239] Here one finds a connection between three matters I have touched upon in this chapter and one yet to be explored further. Politics proper is described as the exploration of the relationship between politics and eternity; ideology is described as the result of bewitchment and escape into a bogus eternity, a failure of nerve to face the world as it is;[240] and that real world from which many seek ideological escape is demanding and threatening just because it is intricate and contingent. Victor Serge said, "The world is always new, if your nerves are strong enough". Oakeshott's concern is that just *because* the world is always new, our nerves need to be strong enough.

Contingency

Stephen Batchelor writes that "To be empty of a fixed identity allows one to enter fully into the shifting, poignant, beautiful and tragic contingencies of the world".[241] I have shown that Oakeshott valorizes tradition over rationalism and ideology, but one should not take his conception of tradition to reduce to rigidity, let alone permanence. He notes often in one way or another, that tradition is never "fixed or finished". He agrees entirely with Batchelor: the world as it is, full of shifting contingencies, is poignant, tragic, beautiful, and inviting. Podoksik ends his book with this sentence, "On the whole … the dominant sentiment in Oakeshott's writings is an appreciation of present enjoyment even when decay is inevitable, as it is

---

239 *Rationalism in Politics*, 34.

240 My use of "failure of nerve" is meant to echo Oakeshott's words in "Political Education", which I used earlier in this chapter. We recall that he claims politics is for the *nur für die Schwindelfreie*. It takes some courage to sail the boundless and bottomless sea of politics.

241 In *Verses from the Center* cited in Michael Schellenberger and Ted Nordhaus, *The Death of Environmentalism: Global Warming Politics in a Post-Environmental World*, 26.

for everything historically contingent."[242] The reader has come upon the theme of contingency in Oakeshott already, here and there; but as the final thematic reflection of this chapter, a summarizing account is needed, and of course, especially in respect to its bearing upon democracy and democratic theory. One reason I must explore contingency in Oakeshott's thought is that it is an important element both in respect to the arguments Mapel and Mouffe make about Oakeshott's democratic theory (to be analyzed below) and because *On Human Conduct* is permeated implicitly and explicitly by this concept. Additionally, however, contingency is an important theme in Oakeshott's earlier work as well (in this respect as in so many others, *On Human Conduct* shows itself to be a culmination and crescendo of Oakeshott's intellectual career).[243]

I end this chapter with consideration of contingency because it is related to everything to which I have given attention. Oakeshott's understanding of political activity and discourse, agency, individuality, freedom, liberalism, skepticism, rationalism, ideology, etc., is infused with a sense of, and no small degree of writing on, contingency. Without knowing the importance of contingency in his thought, understanding these others matters well is impossible. For Oakeshott, contingency is not accident nor is it limited in scope. Contingency names not merely accidental relationships between phenomena, but rather, it has an explanatory function (not that all things can be explained, of course). That is, it is an explanation of human conduct and history, of personal agency and of events. One's own choice in a moment, and a civilization's choices over time, are all products of contingency. Our choices can be intelligent and nonintelligent (in a technical sense); they are responses to antecedent phenomena. Contingency "makes an occurrence intelligible as a significant event in relation to other significant events", further, "actions that are contingently related ... throw light on one another and thereby render one another more intelligible".[244] Contingency is a consequential relationship between actions and/or events which is neither accidental *or necessary*. It is the inescapable condition of human conduct and the defining presupposition of human agency and historical explanation.[245] Events are joined, and the human experience is an assembly of differences.[246] Contingency brings ambiguity in its wake

---

242 Podoksik, 232.

243 Nardin notes, "Woven through Oakeshott's reflections on human experience are the ideas of modality, contingency, and civility", 230. He nicely unpacks this sentence in the conclusion to his book.

244 Nardin, 138, 139.

245 For Oakeshott's conception of contingency as historical understanding, see Nardin, 161–66; O'Sullivan, esp. 163–67; and Podoksik, 99–100.

246 *Ibid.*, 231. Cf. Tregenza, 72; and McIntyre, 69.

and is also a product of ambiguity.[247] According to Oakeshott, our world is "infected with contingency".[248]

David Walsh discusses Oakeshott's contingency in relationship to his nonfoundationalism. He writes, "Michael Oakeshott provides the clearest illustration of how a nonfoundational liberal order is still capable of identifying the dangers that tend to undermine it and finding the appropriate means to defend itself. It is not stuck irretrievably in the morass of historicist contingency".[249] For Walsh, the nonfoundational contingency of Oakeshott's theorization is rescued from being "stuck in a morass" because of the way he understands civil association in respect to its being *moral* association. I will elaborate upon Walsh's claims in the next chapter, but I mention it at this moment for two reasons. First, with Walsh, I think it is important to warn the reader against an assumption that contingency results in nothing more than conceptual, historical, and practical muddles. For Oakeshott, radical contingency does not imperil meaning or purpose in life; it does not lead to, for example, a moral relativism of the worst sort.[250] This leads to the second observation toward which Walsh moves the reader, for Oakeshott contingency and morality implicate one another profoundly. Morality is contingent and therefore contingency does not escape a moral dimension. I am not here claiming that various actions and events are moral, that claim is but a truism. I am claiming that contingency itself is intrinsically related to what it means to be a moral agent. Of course, as I have indicated, I will have to explain this below. Walsh thinks that liberalism contains, and Oakeshott specifies this kind of liberal theory, the resources for its own nonfoundational and contingent meaningfulness. Rorty endorses Oakeshott just to make claims of this sort in his account of "The Contingency of Community".[251]

One need only notice the title of Soininen's book to properly intuit the importance she sees in Oakeshott's understanding of contingency. The reader will recall that for her, Oakeshott's conception of political activity moves, over the range of his career, from a "necessary evil" to the "*art of contingency*". She notes that for Oakeshott, the contingent nature of our

---

247 Cf. Podoksik, 225.

248 *OHC* (1975), 73.

249 Walsh, 65.

250 Moral relativism, in contrast to popular views, names more than one theoretical account of morality. By relativism "of the worst sort", I mean the caricature of relativism in which it is said that there are no means possible to make any moral judgments whatsoever, and that, concomitantly, all moral views and actions are equally valid. It is not certain that anyone actually holds this view, or that it is a view which can be held.

251 Richard Rorty, *Contingency, Irony, and Solidarity* (New York: Cambridge University Press, 1993), 57–60. Cf. Rorty's similar use of Oakeshott in *Objectivity, Relativism, and Truth: Philosophical Papers*, vol. 1 (New York: Cambridge University Press, 1993), 25, 28, 195, 197. Along these lines, Soininen writes, "Both Rorty and Oakeshott have a certain level of trust in the prevailing liberal culture and its possibilities, although its only 'guarantee' is the existence of people who are willing to unflinchingly stick to their own convictions" 53.

world should sometimes lead the political actor to work against change. This idea is present, unsurprisingly, in "On Being Conservative", where the task is said to be "like the 'governor' which, by controlling the speed at which its parts move, keeps an engine from racketing itself to pieces".[252]

She also discusses contingency in relationship to Oakeshott's understanding of conversation and deliberation, noting, for example, that "politics, *as* a deliberative, reflective activity, *is* the ... 'recognized contingency' of the human choice and situation".[253] She also correctly sees that relationship in Oakeshott between contingency and law (which was intimated above). She writes, "Oakeshott's deep understanding of the contingency of current arrangements and *lex*, and the role of politics in changing them, thus also implies an understanding, or at least a possibility of the 'republican ideal' of citizenship".[254] I think that Soininen is correct in seeing republican intimations, sensibilities, and possibilities in Oakeshott (and this will become clearer by this book's end). At this moment, however, I need only to note the relationship between republicanism and democracy. Not only are the words related, but these conceptions share, of course, an interpenetrating history. Both ideologies share the root idea of persons (usually, "citizens") controlling their own fortunes through some means of collectivizing their wills. Clearly, as a liberal, Oakeshott does not endorse all manner of republican ideas, but he is not in all ways at a great distance from republicanism.[255]

Dick Howard writes that

> Living with indeterminancy is a source of anxiety; democracy is inherently unstable, indeterminable. Attempts will be made to re-create unity, to find a worthy (symbolic) representative of it ... to understand the meaning of a unity that is always on the horizon but can never quite be domesticated. This is the history of modernity — a modernity that is ... political and democratic ... .
>
> The politicization of society is in principle characteristic of democratic societies, not of their totalitarian enemy. In a democracy, it is in principle always possible for a domain of life that seemed immune to politics to lose its neutral status and become the object of political interrogation ... [for we are] faced with the indeterminacy of democracy.[256]

I bring Howard's reflections to this discussion because I see it as a sober acknowledgment of the necessity of democracy in contingent times. It is also a statement of the contingency of democracy. Neither I nor Oakeshott

---

252 *Rationalism in Politics*, 434. Soininen, 175.

253 Soininen, 184 (emphasis, mine).

254 *Ibid.*, 186.

255 See Wendell John Coats, "Some Correspondences Between Oakeshott's 'Civil Condition' and the Republican Tradition", *A Theory of Republican Character and Related Essays* (Cranbury, NJ: Associated University Presses, 1994), 63–77.

256 Dick Howard, *The Spectre of Democracy* (New York: Columbia University Press, 2002), 122, 132.

share the kind of resignation that seems present in Howard's reflections about these matters, but it is the connection between politics *as* democratic *as* contingent, and contingency *as* making *democratic* politics necessary that I think resonates strongly with Oakeshott. Whereas Howard thinks of democracy as inherently unstable, Oakeshott would reply in a Churchill-like manner, that however unstable, it is surely not only better than its alternatives, but that it is, in the long run, more stable than its alternatives as well. This is one of the aspects of Oakeshott's hopefulness (despite all of our rationalism and rationalist ideology) that Rorty and Walsh find appealing. One need only recall Oakeshott's review of Spearman's *Democracy in England* to see how charged it is with the contingency of democracy and the conviction that democracy is the best suitable political response to the fact of contingency in our lives. Here he argues that democracy is not the result of "design", nor should it be, that rightly comports to the "vicissitudes" of our collective experiences and choices.

I have offered a glimpse, I hope, of why it is that contingency leads to democracy and democracy is consonant with contingency. We are the makers of our world, in some meaningful measure, for Oakeshott; as a liberal who valorizes agency, freedom, and individuality, he thinks it best that we not turn our lives over to others, most of all, to government. Insofar as we are makers of our world, we have the moral grounding to act as citizens, to diffuse power, to shape our futures for ourselves. For some, such moral and political commitments necessitate anarchism; but for Oakeshott, they necessitate democracy. True, the contingency of this world means that we are not entirely makers of our world, but this fact does not lead Oakeshott to find any reason for the diminishment of democratic ideals. Soininen is correct to recognize the relationship between discourse and contingency, and law and contingency, in Oakeshott. I have interrogated his thought sufficiently as this juncture, to know that if discourse and law are contingently-infused, and proper responses to contingency, it follows that democracy is also infused with and responsive to the contingent nature of our human conduct, politics, and history. To be reminded of Oakeshott's notion of democratic politics as the "pursuit of intimations" and the navigation of boundless and bottomless seas is to be reminded of just why democracy is the best response to contingency.

Conclusion

In this chapter I have investigated a wide range of Oakeshott's thought, both in terms of its time span and in terms of its volume. There has been a substantial breadth and depth into which my interrogation has proceeded. I began by identifying and commenting upon virtually all of the occasions in Oakeshott's work before *On Human Conduct* in which he utilized the words "democracy" or "democratic". I then turned to an exploration of several themes in his "early" (before *On Human Conduct*) work which, I have argued, bear some relationship to democracy and democratic theory.

This investigation has been, as I warned, filled with some conceptual danger. For much more could have been said and other themes discussed.[257] I sought to be as concise as possible while at the same time, addressing everything necessary. The result has been a chapter which one must hope strikes an ephemeral balance between saying too much and saying too little. The reader can here recall Feaver's words that although Oakeshott "had a good deal to say about democracy", his "insights and asides about the character of democracy" were "uttered in an idiom that was exploratory, tentative, or ironic; rather than definitive in tone", and that his "lifelong interest in democracy ... usually appeared as the shadowy background of his wider philosophical essaying into the character of government and politics in modern Europe".[258] Feaver is correct in this conclusion. What we have done here is separate all that Oakeshott wrote about democracy explicitly, from all that is suggestive as to democracy. The shadowy explorations, tentative claims, and irony are present in some (differing) respects in the first, explicit literature, as well as the implicit texts.

Nonetheless, I have demonstrated that there is a body of work in Oakeshott's early career relating to democracy and democratic theory. In fact, the first part of this chapter, which addresses the explicit discussions of democracy in Oakeshott, is by itself, a significant contribution to the Oakeshott literature.[259] Yet it is in probing the other literature as I have, seeking to understand the possible and necessary relationships between other thematic concerns and democracy that deepens my analysis and creates a kind of *gestalt* by which to understand Oakeshott's underdeveloped democratic theory. Whatever faults may attend the second part of this chapter, however, they should not be allowed to diminish the clarity of his thought about democracy present in the first part.

One will recall that in *The Social and Political Doctrines of Contemporary Europe*, Oakeshott claims that democracy "is by no means either a complete or a satisfactory expression as it stands" and that it is in need of "a radical restatement".[260] Oakeshott has then, himself, provided the invitation for us to explore his own democratic thought and wonder as to what the content of such a restatement might be if he were to make it. I have argued that in exploring Oakeshott's thought about political philosophy proper, political activity, political discourse; the state, authority, and law;

---

257 Most notably, we might have pursued the theme of tradition in Oakeshott's thought.
258 Feaver, 133, 155.
259 I make this claim, in good measure, because I have considered a number of texts here which Feaver does not.
260 pp. xvi, xviii.

liberalism and freedom; individuality and anti-individuality; skepticism; rationalism and ideology; and finally, contingency, I am able to glean a sufficient amount of information to draw conclusions about the character and constitution of his democratic *gestalt*. In some respects, my findings must have a degree of tenuousness, as I wrote about what his thought permits and seems to imply; in almost all cases, however, these conclusions seem inescapable, and in these regards I wrote about conclusions his thought demands.

In short, taking his thought and theorization of these matters as a whole, and added to what he writes about democracy and democratic theory straightforwardly, one must conclude that not only does Oakeshott hold democracy (on his understanding) to have substantial value but that there are resources in his thought that constitute the possibility of extending it into democratic theory proper. The province of democracy touches upon much of his philosophy; and indeed, he sometimes seems to be treading into democratic territory, penetrating democratic theory, unaware. Of course, one must avoid making Oakeshott say anything he does not in fact say; but by gathering his relevant thought carefully, pulling it together in relationships that do not violate the meaning of the respective claims and texts, I ask what the implications of his thought are for democratic theory. That is, I am asking, if Oakeshott has a democratic theory, what does it look like? I am arguing that there is an answer to this question.

This chapter has gone some way in answering this question, but much work remains to be done. I must interrogate *On Human Conduct* and a few other later texts (Chapter Three); and must also consider what we mean by democratic theory and just what kind of democratic theory seems a most promising conversational partner with Oakeshott (Chapter Four). I will finally need to bring Oakeshott and contemporary deliberative democratic theory into dialogue and see what fruit that conversation bears (Chapter Five).

On Human Conduct

The reader should recall the claim made on several occasions in Chapter 2 to the effect of "but we will explore this matter more fully in the next chapter". I have made clear my conclusion that *On Human Conduct* contains not only Michael Oakeshott's most mature work, but that it is a culmination and crescendo of much of his life-long work. In this conclusion, I am iterating a claim widely agreed-upon by Oakeshott scholars. Oakeshott states in the Preface, "The themes explored here have been with me nearly as long as I can remember … ".[1] If this widely-held conclusion is correct, coupled with Oakeshott's proclamation that he is taking up themes that have long been with him, it should not surprise us that he will have any number of things to say in *On Human Conduct* relevant to the themes I have discussed, including, of course, democracy.

In addition to his *magnum opus*, there are a few other texts I will consider in this chapter, but nearly all of the focus will be on *On Human Conduct*. The texts interrogated have been published no earlier than 1975. I will, of course, at times reach back and revisit earlier texts, but I will keep this backwards glance to a minimum, just as I sought to minimize reaching forward in the previous chapter.

I will proceed as follows. First, I will quite briefly summarize the project of *On Human Conduct* and, most importantly, the second essay, "On the Civil Condition". Second, I will describe and explain what Oakeshott means when he writes of "civil association *as* moral association", that is, I will explain his moral theory and, in particular, its relationship to civil association and *societas*. Third, I will interrogate Oakeshott's theorization of human conduct, the civil condition, and the character of the modern European state in respect to contingency and deliberation. Fourth, I will analyze and evaluate the arguments made by Mapel, Mouffe, and Gerencser in respect to their understandings of the relationship between civil association and *societas*, and democracy.

---

1   *OHC*, vii.

On Human Conduct and the Civil Condition

On Human Conduct is composed of three connected essays: "On the Theoretical Understanding of Human Conduct", "On the Civil Condition", and "On the Character of a Modern European State". Each essay builds from theory presented before it. Franco notes that it is a "résumé and restatement" of several themes in his earlier career; among them,

> the rule of law versus central planning; British democracy versus socialism; the politics of the diffusion of power versus collectivism; the politics of skepticism versus the politics of passion; the morality of individuality versus the morality of the common good; representative democracy or parliamentary government versus popular government.[2]

Franco immediately and importantly adds this caution against an overly simplistic account of Oakeshott: he "is always fighting a two-front battle. It is not only socialism or collectivism that comes in for criticism; what conservatives and libertarians generally oppose to these ideologies — whether it be the free market, natural rights, fundamental values, or religion — is also criticized".[3] As I have suggested, I agree with Franco (and others) that a continuity is found in Oakeshott's earlier work and his later work, including *On Human Conduct*, and that this continuity is primarily of a thematic nature (although Oakeshott employs a variety of new terms in *OHC*). At the moment, one can simply observe that as Franco summarizes the fundamental themes in Oakeshott's work, "British democracy", "the diffusion of power", and "representative democracy or parliamentary government" are listed as three of the six things he prefers over their antithetical partners.[4] Of course, I have meant to show that the other three themes Franco lists are also related to democracy. In a word, what is of note here is that in various ways, these themes are taken up again in *On Human Conduct* and a considerable part of his later work.

McIntyre rightly claims that any adequate judgment of Oakeshott's contribution to the understanding of political activity depends upon an examination of his understanding of the world of practical activity, or as he phrases it in his most considered essay on the subject, the world of human

---

2 *The Political Philosophy of Michael Oakeshott*, 157.

3 *Ibid.*

4 I do not think Franco is sufficiently clear about how "diffusion of power" and "popular government" find themselves in opposition in Oakeshott's thought. Indeed, I think putting "popular government" forward as a regrettable phenomenon to be opposed is a misleading way to put the matter, and not something Oakeshott actually wrote against, as such. What Oakeshott opposed was mere majoritarianism, mere aggregate forms of (minimal) "democracy", and appealing to the "lowest common denominator" in citizens' manipulation of citizens, the use of suspect information and arguments, etc.; what Nietzsche called *grosse Politik* and he called "Rationalism in politics" and rationalistic ideology. But nearly all contemporary democratic theorists oppose these phenomena, and most certainly they are opposed by all deliberative theorists. Indeed, what Oakeshott did oppose is, for the most part, itself opposed to the "diffusion of power".

conduct.[5] I have noted that the essays in *On Human Conduct* depend upon one another in a sequential logic; McIntyre is making essentially the same point. Oakeshott's understanding of the character of human conduct is intrinsically related to his understanding of the character of civil association. Wolin concludes that in this book:

> Oakeshott's theorizing is remarkable not only for its sensibility toward the nuances of human conduct, the ambiguities of human situations, and the elusiveness of human meanings, but also for its conviction that the observance of formalities is a deeply moral undertaking and that theorizing about propriety is equally so.[6]

This tightly packed description of *On Human Conduct* begins with an identification of the nuances of human conduct from which the other matters follow. One should also note that Wolin's references to ambiguity and elusiveness can be read as approximations of or allusions to contingency.

I will, then, briefly summarize the most important parts of "On the Theoretical Understanding of Human Conduct". This essay is comprised of three areas of analysis. First, an account of understanding itself, where he offers a nonfoundationalist conception in which he moves from the language of modes of understanding he theorized rigorously early in his career,[7] to what he now calls "platforms of theorizing". Here, he makes a transition from the use of the term "philosophy" and utilizes "theory" it its place.[8] Nonetheless, he warns against the "theoretician", who is one who "deserts his own [proper] character as a theorist". This claim is an update from his earlier dismissal of the *philosophe*, who is also an "imposter" in place of the philosopher. The theoretican replaces the *philosophe* as one engaged in rationalism (to use an earlier idiom, not repeated in *On Human Conduct*), and again, both are imposters of worthwhile callings.[9] Second, Oakeshott's analysis concerns the moral dimension of human conduct; and third, he theorizes the contingency of human conduct.

Theory, for Oakeshott, has the same character as did philosophy earlier. It is a skeptical enterprise. Nardin correctly notes that it is

> not a special method of thinking, much less a particular kind of knowledge. It is simply thinking made as critical as possible ... . The more skeptical and subversive the criticism, the more likely we are to call it 'philosophy'. Philosophy is simply the effort to understand, theorizing

---

5   McIntyre, 41.

6   Sheldon S. Wolin, "The Politics of Self-Disclosure", *Political Theory*, 4, no. 3 (August 1976), 326. Cf. the fine summary of *OHC* by Bhikhu Parekh, "Michael Oakeshott" *Contemporary Political Thinkers* (Oxford: Martin Robertson & Co., 1982), 100–23.

7   Michael Oakeshott, *Experience and Its Modes* (Cambridge: Cambridge University Press, 1994). First published 1933.

8   Parekh notes that Oakeshott's "increasing dissatisfaction over the years with the term 'philosophy' comes to a head", 100.

9   *OHC*, 26–31.

pushed to the limits. It is thinking that emerges from and is continuous with the thinking about which it thinks.[10]

Although Nardin employs "philosophy" here, as well as "theorizing", he recognizes that the latter term overtakes the former in *On Human Conduct*. Theorizing is "the unconditional engagement of understanding", it seeks to "abate mystery rather than achieve definitive understanding", and although the "notion of an unconditional or definitive understanding may hover in the background … it has no part in the adventure".[11] "The irony of all theorizing is its propensity to generate, not an understanding, but a not-yet-understood."[12]

Like so many of his concepts, Oakeshott's "human conduct" is itself an "ideal character".[13] That is, conduct itself is not performed but, rather, it names a way of understanding and theorizing the postulates and conditions of human actions and utterances.[14] Human conduct is always "*inter homines*", performances understood as transactions between agents. Agents are persons who are able to make free choices and respond "intelligently"[15] to contingency; and such agents employ deliberation as an important means to respond to their contingent situations. Just as "theory" replaces "philosophy", so too, the contingent and conditional context of human conduct, or actions, which in *Rationalism in Politics* Oakeshott called "tradition", he now calls "practice". In a reply to various of his critics, he writes that his idea of a practice should be read not only as a replacement, but as a corrective to what he had written earlier about tradition.[16] A practice consists of the exchanges and encounters of reciprocity in which agents converse, deliberate, and respond to one another. A practice is a

---

10   Nardin, 53.
11   *OHC*, 1, 3.
12   *Ibid.*, 9.
13   Oakeshott's "ideal character" is not unlike Weber's "ideal type", and *OHC* makes uses of several such "ideal characters" which include law (*lex*), membership (*civis*), association (*civitas*), civil practices or rules of conduct (*respublica*), and most importantly, the "master" ideal character of "civil association", which "hovers over and nourishes these lesser embodiments". In Wolin, 323. See *OHC*, 109. Of course, it follows that "enterprise association" is also an ideal character. I should also mention that *societas* is the approximation of civil association which has appeared in history, and *universitas* is the historical approximation of enterprise association.
14   *Ibid.*, 31; cf. Tseng, 187.
15   Oakeshott's connection of agency and "intelligence" has nothing to do with *how* intelligent agents are or act, in quantifiable or (especially) qualifiable terms. This term refers to decisions agents make with any degree of reflection, such that the resulting actions are not merely unconscious. Scratching one's nose automatically because it itches is not, for example, an instance of agency. Scratching one's nose to send a signal would be an instance of agency.
16   "On Misunderstanding Human Conduct: A Reply to My Critics", *Political Theory*, 4 (1976), 364. For an explanation as to why Oakeshott saw his earlier discussions of tradition as inadequate, see Tregenza, 70–71. We have no need to explore this matter here, but only to see that his conceptualization of "theory" is now seen as a clarification of, and perhaps some improvement upon what he earlier meant by tradition.

"language" of "self-disclosure" spoken only by agents. Human conduct is, again, "*inter homines*", agents

> disclosing themselves in responding to their contingent situations by choosing what they do in relation to imagined or wished-for outcomes ... what is learned in this transaction is languages of self-disclosure and self-enactment; not what to do or say, but the arts of agency.
>
> In respect to their generality and pervasiveness, the two most important practices in terms of which agents are durably related to one another in conduct are a common tongue and a language of moral converse.[17]

For Oakeshott, agency is not only contingent and "intelligent" but also formal. It is formal in that human beings are free, that is, agents, by definition. Agency is a universal, but it can only have particular expression. Agents will act contingently in such ways as to create practices. In addition to the obvious claim that creating and using common languages are an important human practice, he adds that the other is "the language of moral converse". That is, morality is both a practice and a kind of "language". A practice is a "prudential or a moral adverbial qualification of choices and performances, more or less complicated, in which conduct is understood in terms of procedure". The stoic *apatheia* and the "chivalry" of the Middle Ages are two such practices, according to Oakeshott. Practices, of course, may be institutionalized, be elastic, compose hierarchies, and overlap one another.[18] Parekh describes Oakeshott's concept of practice as "the basis of his discussion of civil society" (by which he means civil association).[19]

For Oakeshott, the postulates of human conduct include intelligence, agency, individuality, and freedom.[20] Indeed, to be without the freedom of agency is to be less than human.[21] So fundamental is Oakeshott's conception of human conduct that it stands in place of a conception of human

---

17 *OHC*, 59.

18 *Ibid.*, 55–56. For a concept of practices similar to Oakeshott's, see MacIntyre, *After Virtue*, op. cit., especially, 190–210. MacIntyre nicely discusses relationships between practice and tradition which not only enrich his own work, but is not inconsonant with Oakeshott's theory. Franco discusses Oakeshott's shift from tradition to practice in *The Political Philosophy of Michael Oakeshott*, 171–72. John Casey and David Walsh rightly connect Oakeshott's theory of practical knowledge and practice with tradition, and also to Aristotle's understanding of *phronesis*. See Casey, "Philosopher of Practice", ed. Jesse Norman; *The Achievement of Michael Oakeshott*, 59–60; and Walsh, 56–61.
   To *apatheia* and chivalry, one can add the Christian practice of forgiveness, for this reason: doing so indicates how practices and traditions are not entirely coherent, which is to say, not understood or practiced thoroughly; and so again, we encounter the importance of the concept of an ideal character in the enterprise of theorizing.

19 In "The Philosophy of Michael Oakeshott", *British Journal of Political Science*, 9, no. 3 (July, 1979), 491.

20 As noted above, for Oakeshott an agent is free by definition, so "free agent/agency" is redundant, although the term "free will" strikes him as even more redundant. See Oakeshott, *The Voice of Liberal Learning* (Indianapolis: Liberty Fund, 2001), 2–3.

21 *Ibid.*, 5–6. John Liddington notes that for Oakeshott, our "free" agency is our "definitive condition", In "Oakeshott: Freedom in a Modern European State", eds. Zbigniew Pelczynski

nature. That is, for him, conduct is the irreducible feature of human *being*.[22] Human conduct, in all its wild, contingent, free, and moral irreducibility, emits to practices. I will revisit several of these conceptions when I consider Oakeshott's moral theory and other matters pertaining to the civil condition.

The second essay of *On Human Conduct*, "On the Civil Condition", constitutes the heart of the book. The first sentence of this essay identifies the *condition* being addressed with a *relationship*: "In this essay I shall attempt to identify and go some distance in theorizing what I shall call the civil condition or civil relationship. This is an ideal character ... it is a certain mode of association ... I shall call it the relationship of civility."[23] Further, he even refers to the civil condition *as* human conduct.[24] In fact, he presents us with a conception and theorization of conduct/condition/relationship/association; that is, these terms are essentially treated as synonymous in this essay. There is a kind of logic involved in this theorization, although Oakeshott does not explicate, but mostly seems to assume it. It is this: human conduct is basic to our humanity; it is irreducible (replacing "nature" in terms of conceptualizing our essential human feature).[25] Our conduct not only creates the conditions, relationships, and associations of civility but are also constituted by such conditions, relationships, and associations. That is, there is an intrinsic, inseparable, and reciprocal relationship between conduct and the media of conduct. The phenomena are mutually constitutive of one another. It follows that "a civil condition", a "relationship of civility", and "civil association" could only be, at least roughly, synonymous. In a rather accidental way, the secondary literature endorses the claim made here insofar as various authors use these terms in interchangeable ways. That human conduct itself is also theorized in synonymous ways with these other conceptions strikes one as a somewhat more challenging, but not unacceptable, conception. The fundamental thing to be seen here is Oakeshott's interchangeable and intrinsic connection between conduct, condition, and association. I will argue below that this theorization bears upon democratic theory, but one can already note that the conceptions of agency, individuality, freedom, and contingency which I argued were so pervasive in Oakeshott's earlier work and are important in the first essay of *On Human Conduct*, are also intrinsic and

---

and John Gray; *Conceptions of Liberty in Political Philosophy* (New York: St. Martin's Press, 1984), 298.

22   Cf. Robert Orr's reflection on this matter, op. cit.

23   *OHC*, 108.

24   *Ibid.*, 112.

25   It is clear, however, that Oakeshott does not consider human conduct in ontological terms, but this is in contrast to human nature, which is, of course, conventionally theorized in ontological terms.

fundamental to civil association.[26] The relationship of civility (constituted by the fundamental criteria of agency, individuality, freedom, and contingency) is the very kind of association which authentically manifests the human condition, which is, conduct.[27]

Describing civil association, Terry Nardin writes:

> The rule of law may be premised on individual freedom, but it is nevertheless a mode of association that is realized through obligatory and enforceable laws … . The result is an unavoidable tension between citizenship and freedom … we may say that civility and individuality are conceptually related. Civil association presupposes citizens who regard themselves as separate persons, each pursuing his or her own self-chosen purposes.[28]

He is not only articulating my claim above that Oakeshott's theorization of the person and his theorization of society and state must be entirely congruent, but he also notes the tension that is created by robustly free individuals living together. This problem is, of course, at the heart of democratic theory. Democracy names (whatever else it names) a way to negotiate this tension. Nardin begins his reflection on the civil condition by noting that many Oakeshottian themes "are brought together" here; and he describes the civil condition as Oakeshott's effort to "answer one of the fundamental questions of political theorizing: How can human beings be related within an order that constrains their conduct while respecting their individuality?"[29] There is nothing surprising about the way Nardin casts Oakeshott's project, and he is certainly correct in both of these claims. I quote it here because one can immediately see how civil association *must*, at least indirectly, have some relationship to democracy or democratic theory. Indeed, one can think of many (democratic theorists, at least) who would answer Nardin's question with just the word "democracy". This way of casting Oakeshott's theorization of the civil condition also helps one see how unsurprising it is that a significant literature has been produced in interpreting it.[30]

Just as does democracy, civil association also presupposes citizens who are, and understand themselves to be, separate persons who are individuals

---

26 Note, however, that Oakeshott does not follow Hegel in seeing the state as the culmination of human association; rather, he sees civil association as the ideal character which best incarnates authentic civil relationship, the civil condition.

27 In addition to the criteria I have listed, Oakeshott understands the "postulates" of the civil condition to include *civitas*, *cives*, *respublica*, *lex*, civil law, adjudication, authority and obligation, legislation, justice, policy, and politics; ix, 108–09. Agency, individuality, freedom, and contingency stand in a metatheoretical position in relationship to these more specific and narrowly circumscribed "postulates."

28 Nardin, 211.

29 *Ibid.*, 183.

30 Various treatments of civil association are valuable, but I will here note the one book- length project given to its explanation, Kenneth McIntyre, *The Limits of Political Theory: Oakeshott's Philosophy of Civil Association*.

pursuing their self-chosen purposes, who embody the freedom inherent in agency, in self-disclosure, and particularly, in self-enactment. Such freedom and individuality does not disallow one from participation in community or association; indeed some forms of community or association encourage the extensive agency, individuality, and freedom that Oakeshott values. Association is not coercive by definition, and purposive enterprises can be freely chosen. The state is a compulsory association, so no state can simply reduce to, or be identified as a civil association, but states can approximate Oakeshott's civil association to greater and lesser degrees. The very thesis and purpose of *On Human Conduct*, according to Anthony Farr,

> seeks to quell the ambitions of the theorist, to limit the scope and intrusiveness of the political engagement of its citizens. It thereby offers ordinary people the space to find their own way … As an assault upon the morbidity of conformity *On Human Conduct* belongs to the tradition of *The Sickness Unto Death* and *Being and Nothingness*. But it lacks the otherworldliness of both; either the neurotic strenuousness of Kierkegaard or the intellectualism of Sartre. This is a very down to earth earnestness … .
>
> It advises how to think about human life … . Freedom, intelligence, deliberation, and choice have no meaning apart from the concrete identity of "human conduct".[31]

I have used Farr to once again underwrite the connection between the importance of agency, individuality, and freedom to human conduct properly understood and then also to civil association. He sees deliberation as having a close, if not intrinsic, relationship to such agency, individuality, and freedom; and I will show such a theorization in Oakeshott below. The "space" Oakeshott "offers" to "ordinary people" to "find their own way", on Farr's account, cannot be conceived apart from democracy because a lack of democratic culture and structures would severely limit that space. Further, one can only imagine an "assault upon conformity" occurring, at least above ground, and without fear of punishment, in a democratic society.[32]

---

31 Anthony Farr, *Sartre's Radicalism and Oakeshott's Conservatism: The Duplicity of Freedom* (New York: St. Martin's Press, 1998), 224. Farr's comment that Oakeshott's theory is to "limit the scope and intrusiveness of the political engagement of its citizens" is not quite accurate. As I will show shortly, civil association does not *necessarily* limit political engagement; what it does is eliminate instrumental and purposive political engagement understood in a particular way. Oakeshott clearly wants the power of the state to be limited, but this is something different from a limit on political engagement. If Farr were correct, this would tell against democracy in Oakeshott's theory. (I might add that Farr seems to misconceive Kierkegaard, but I obviously must resist the temptation to defend Kierkegaard here.)

32 Of course I am aware of pervasive and deadening forms of conformity that also occur in democratic societies, especially, perhaps, those most engulfed by capitalism. Various observers have explored this problematic, notably, Christopher Lasch.

Franco claims that Oakeshott takes freedom "as the starting point for his political philosophy".[33] Mapel considers civil association as "the *only kind* of polity to *necessarily* respect individual freedom" and that "*The defining aim* of civil association is to express and protect the realization *by* 'agents' that they *are* 'agents.'"[34] Coats thinks that "the search for a basis for freedom in contingent acts of choice within a framework of general laws" and "that the freedom of *cives* arises not in *silence*, but in the generality of the laws, or terms of association 'is a move' unique to political theory based upon ... individualist assumptions".[35] Coats also finds within civil association "an ethos to cultivate the freedom (to choose) inherent in moral agency".[36] Tregenza recognizes that Oakeshott sees the rules of conduct in civil association as creating authority that protects, rather than diminishes, free agency.[37]

Oakeshott writes that "Freedom, like a recipe for game pie, is not a bright idea ... to be deduced from some speculative concept of human nature. The freedom which we enjoy is nothing more than arrangements, procedures of a certain kind ... ".[38] Civil association is his theorization of those arrangements and procedures which constitute and protect freedom. In other words, freedom names certain practices, not abstract notions. Practices, in keeping with the "adverbial", contingent nature of agency, freedom, rules, law, and morality, "prescribes conditions for, but does not determine, substantive choices and performances of agents. In short, what joins agents in conduct is to be recognized as 'practice'; that is, a procedure proper ... only in the *subscriptions* of agents".[39] Since practices are subscribed to, Oakeshott's theory of practice presupposes agency, individuality, and freedom; indeed the reciprocity between agency and practice is clear — those who learn to participate in practices, learn not what to do or say, but the "arts of agency".[40] Walsh thinks that just because civil association is a practice, it is "remarkably stable", because, as a practice, it has "the living variability and durability of custom that is capable of changing and remaining the same at the same time".[41] Oakeshott employs the analogy of language, and makes Walsh's point. The rules of language,

---

33   Franco, *The Political Philosophy of Michael Oakeshott*, 167.
34   Mapel, "Civil Association and the Idea of Contingency", 392–93 (emphasis mine, except for "by" and "are").
35   Coats, "Some Correspondences Between Oakeshott's 'Civil Condition' and the Republican Tradition", 67.
36   *Ibid.*, 70.
37   Tregenza, 107.
38   *Rationalism in Politics*, 54.
39   *OHC*, 55.
40   *Ibid.*, 59.
41   Walsh, 58–59. Recall that Parekh thinks that Oakeshott's concept of practice "is the basis of his discussion of civil society" (again, by which he means civil association). In "The Political Philosophy of Michael Oakeshott", 491.

which cannot be fully specified, tell us how to speak, not what to speak. Language provides order to an endless diversity of communications. Language is a practice of order and authority, and *therefore*, freedom and communication.

So far I have sought to show that the deep importance of agency, individuality, and freedom that is important in Okaehsott's early work and inherent in human conduct properly conceived, is equally manifest in the ideal character of civil association. I have also begun to intimate that the radical agency, individuality, and freedom intrinsic to proper conduct and association are intimately and essentially connected to practice, contingency, deliberation, structures of authority (recall the "postulates" identified in footnote 27), noninstrumentality and nonpurposiveness, morality and, of course, democracy. Of course, more remains to be said about these additional aspects of civil association.

Oakeshott understands human conduct as intercourse between free individuals that can be analytically distinguished into two kinds or aspects; each kind is present in any actual performance. One aspect is substantive, in which action/conduct/performance is understood as a specific and intelligent choice to do *this* rather than *that* in order to achieve a particular outcome or satisfaction. The other is the formal aspect, in which action/conduct/performance is understood as being made under the conditions of practice or practices. What this means is that conduct is always performance oriented in some way or degree toward achieving substantive outcomes, but under general conditions which do not specify the character of the action or the outcomes desired.[42]

Concomitantly, associations are to be understood as belonging to one of two "modes of association". One mode of association is in respect to the substantive element of human conduct, and the pursuit of specific outcomes and satisfactions. This he calls "enterprise association". The second mode of association is in respect to the formal character of human conduct, in terms of practices which govern these actions and performances. This is, of course, civil association. Both are, it needs to be emphasized, ideal characters; and each kind of association is found in mixture with the other in all modern European societies.[43] In enterprise association, members are joined by the primary purpose of pursuit of a goal or achievement. In civil association, the formal rules, the conditions of the association itself, constitute the

---

42 Podoksik, 182.
43 McIntyre writes that according to Oakeshott, "human beings are associated in terms of purposes and in terms of non-instrumental rules. These two types of association are exclusive of one another, but do not deny the existence of each other", 158. But they are exclusive of one another only analytically, in the sense of ideal characters; not in fact.

Although Oakeshott doesn't theorize sub-societal and sub-state groups as such in *OHC*, it is likely that some measure of the character of both enterprise association and civil association must also be found in all such groups; for example in religious, civic, or recreational organizations.

association's meaning; and there is no overriding, comprehensive purpose or achievement sought; that is, unless one takes the purpose of civil association to be something like the expression and protection of the "realization *by* 'agents' that they *are* 'agents.'"[44] In Oakeshott's language, it is nonpurposive and noninstrumental (just as enterprise association is purposive and instrumental). Civil association utilizes, and is in part constituted by, general rules to which citizens (*cives*) subscribe, whereas enterprise association requires specific commands which persons follow or obey. As Barber puts it, "In the language of the first essay, the civil condition would appear to be a condition of self-enactment rather than self-disclosure, defined by common rules, not common ends".[45] Clearly, matters of authority, legitimacy, and law are conceived in a distinctive way as they are a part of civil association, and I will consider this matter below, but it is now certain that Oakeshott's valuation of agency, individuality, freedom, and contingency comport with civil association.

The third essay of *On Human Conduct* can be quite briefly summarized, given my discussion of the first two essays. "On the Character of the Modern European State" involves Oakeshott in some historical description and analysis whereby he seeks to understand the emergence of the modern European state from the circumstances of medieval life and thought. Modernity is not pristine and parsimonious but is full of "confidence-trick[s]", "ambiguity", and "confused and sordid expedients for accommodating the modern disposition to judge everything from the point of view of the desirability of its outcomes in policies and performances and to discount legitimacy".[46] He thinks that enterprise association has gotten the better of civil association and overwhelmed it.

> The notion of the state as an all-embracing, compulsory corporate association and of its government as the manager of an enterprise is, then, to be recognized as one of the most obtrusive of the strands which constitute the texture of modern European political reflection....
>
> It is an understanding of the character of a state which has bitten deep into the civil institutions of modern Europe; it has compromised

---

44 Mapel argues that this is the purpose of civil association "in at least a definitional sense", "Civil Association and the Idea of Contingency", 393. It is not clear that civil association can have even this purpose, even in a "definitional sense", and it is not clear what such a "definitional sense" might mean. McIntyre denies that it can have such a purpose, McIntyre, 183. My own view is that little rides on the claim as to whether or not this is the purpose of civil association. But notice how this question mirrors the debate in liberal theory as to whether liberal political associations can properly promote liberal values, or whether liberalism is by definition neutral in respect to all values.

45 Barber, 163. I would suggest an insertion of the qualifier "mere" before "self- disclosure". That is, persons disclose themselves to others in civil association as well as practice self-enactment, but there is little room for self-enactment in enterprise association. I will say more about the relationship of and difference between self-disclosure and self-enactment when I consider moral practice below.

46 *OHC*, 93.

its civil law and corrupted the vocabulary of civil discourse … . [this is] the withering away of civil association.[47]

These are horrified words, coming from Oakeshott, but they describe an understanding that has become dominant. Nevertheless, it still remains, as indicated earlier, that although there is a regrettable and gross asymmetry and imbalance between civil association and enterprise association, some mixture of the two ideal characters still show themselves concretely in modernity.

The third essay undertakes to interrogate in actual historical form, the ideal characters theorized in the second essay. Oakeshott chooses to employ two late medieval words to reflect what he called civil association and enterprise association on previous pages. Civil association is now *societas*, and enterprise association becomes *universitas*; and as mentioned, the latter has come to overtake, but not eliminate, the former.

McIntyre offers a summary of the flow of *On Human Conduct* moving from the third essay to the first. Reading the organization of the essays in this backwards way helps one see the nature and purpose of the third essay, but also the logic of the book as a whole. Oakeshott, he writes,

> constructs from his understanding of modern European political experience. Oakeshott's political philosophy is best understood as a further articulation of the character of the modern state conceived on the analogy of a *societas* … . Oakeshott's elaboration of the theory of civil association is an attempt to restate and clarify Hegel's account of the state by eliminating the non-essential references to actual historical states which vitiate the philosophical character of civil association in Hegel's account … . Further, the appropriate theoretical context of Oakeshott's political philosophy is his understanding of human conduct. He situates his essays on the character of civil association and the rule of law within a larger consideration of the character of practices and conduct, and his conception of the state as a rule-articulated association can be understood only within the context of his general theory of human conduct.[48]

I have demonstrated that civil association/*societas* is intrinsically related to agency, individuality, and freedom; but it is also certain that his theorization of civil association is intimately and inherently related to morality and moral practice, and this important matter must now demand our attention.

Civil Association *as* Moral Association

It is my view that Oakeshott's moral theory appropriately invites a book-length treatment, and the fact that Oakeshott's civil association is a moral association in the most essential and irreducible way is a matter I

47   *Ibid.*, 311–12.
48   McIntyre, 159.

think to be underdetermined in the literature. Of course, the attention given here must also be limited, but because moral theory is a crucial aspect of civil association—and of democracy—I must give it sufficient consideration. While I intimated a small part of Oakeshott's conception of morality in the previous chapter, particularly when considering individuality, the anti-individual, and rationalism; I postponed a discussion of morality in his earlier work so as to consider it here. While this decision backtracks a little, I will give most attention to *On Human Conduct* and the larger themes that concern his thought on morality, taking his work altogether. First, then, I offer a summary "standard account" of morality against which to understand Oakeshott's account. Second, I summarize his earlier reflection on morality. Third, I describe his thought in *On Human Conduct*.

Below I will make reference to Oakeshott's "moral theory". I employ the word "theory" as does Oakeshott, to signify comparatively rigorous thinking, not thinking of a particular, technical kind.[49] Oakeshott is not a moral theorist in the sense that it is a specialty, or he writes texts dedicated to exegeting moral theory, or that he constructs a moral system of his own. By theory, I do not mean system. He is a moral theorist in the same sense he is a democratic theorist—he writes about each, and much of what he writes indirectly or implicitly relates by way of necessity to morality and/or democracy. When I write of his moral theory, I mean only to reference his thought about morality and nothing more technical than this. In one sense he is not a moral theorist, and that is the sense of the "antitheory" articulated by a number of contemporary, and other, writers.[50] I will say a bit more about this below.

A "Standard Account" of Morality

I offer such an account of morality to lay bare the rather hegemonic view of morality against which Oakeshott's account is an alternative. I borrow the rubric of a "standard account" from Stanley Hauerwas and David Burrell, but there is nothing novel in their view, or in mine, and there is no doubt

---

49   Here I am also taking what he writes about philosophy to be applicable to what I mean by theory.

50   Some of the important contemporary "antitheory" texts are, Annette Baier, *Postures of the Mind* (Minneapolis: University of Minnesota Press, 1985); Garrett Barden, *After Principles* (Notre Dame: University of Notre Dame Press, 1990); Albert R. Jonsen and Stephen Toulmin, *The Abuse of Casuistry: A History of Moral Reasoning* (Berkeley: University of California Press, 1988); Julius Kovesi, *Moral Notions* (London: Routledge and Kegan Paul, 1967); Alasdair MacIntyre, *After Virtue* (Notre Dame: University of Notre Dame Press, 1984); Martha Nussbaum, *The Fragility of Goodness* (New York: Cambridge University Press, 1985); John McDowell, "Virtue and Reason", *Monist*, vol. 62 (1979), 331–50; Edmund L. Pincoffs, *Quandaries and Virtues: Against Reductivism in Ethics* (Lawrence: University of Kansas Press, 1986); Richard Rorty, *Mind in Action: Essays in the Philosophy of Mind* (Boston: Beacon Press, 1988); and Bernard Williams, *Ethics and the Limits of Philosophy* (Cambridge: Harvard University Press, 1985). Aristotle is considered an antitheorist by some, and Nietzsche is widely considered as such.

that there is something like a "standard account" which is, at least, roughly as I shall describe it. The standard account is an amalgam of deontological, utilitarian and other consequentialist theories, intuitionism, and liberal convictions (for example, the priority of the right over the good). This matrix of moral beliefs is nearly unquestioned at the level of concrete practice and only becoming more than rarely questioned at the level of theoretical reflection (as the recent publication of the texts indicated in footnote 50 imply).

So what are the basic features of this account? Hauerwas and Burrell write that

> the hallmark of contemporary moral theory, whether in a Kantian or utilitarian mode, has been to free moral behavior from the arbitrary and contingent nature of the agent's beliefs, dispositions and character. Just as science strives to free the experiment from the experimenter, so ethically, if we are to avoid unchecked subjectivism or relativism, it is thought that the moral life must be freed from the particularities of agents, caught in the limits of their particular histories. Ethical rationality assumes it must take the form of science if it is to have any claim to being objective.[51]

Reference to the idioms of the categorical imperative, the ideal observer, universalizability, "the original position", and nearly all features of consequentialism illustrates Hauerwas's and Burrell's point. Such concepts promote the idea that moral judgments must be made from anyone's point of view (or, in another sense, from no one's point of view).[52]

MacIntyre's work is a sustained attack upon the standard account, and his (like Hauerwas's) has been an important voice in identifying and constructing an alternative account.[53] In his 1989 lecture "The Privatization of the Good", MacIntyre regrets what thin and scattered shared moral values we have, that we have them so incoherently, and that they reflect no shared conception(s) of the good. In fact, he doubts that modern and contemporary Western culture agrees that there is any such thing as the human good.[54] He gestures toward a body of literature which argues that liberal morality must remain neutral in respect to contending versions of the good. Of course, the argument that liberal morality necessitates neutrality has many liberal opponents, who see (non-neutral) liberal moral

---

51   Stanley Hauerwas and David B. Burrell, "From System to Story: An Alternative Pattern for Rationality in Ethics" in *Truthfulness and Tragedy: Further Investigations into Christian Ethics* (Notre Dame: University of Notre Dame Press, 1977), 16.

52   *Ibid.*, 17.

53   MacIntyre, *After Virtue*; "The Privatization of the Good", *The Review of Politics*, 52, no. 3 (Summer, 1990), 344–61; *Whose Justice? Which Rationality?* (Notre Dame: University of Notre Dame Press, 1988); *Three Rival Versions of Moral Inquiry: Encyclopedia, Genealogy and Tradition* (Notre Dame: University of Notre Dame Press, 1990); *Dependent Rational Animals: Why Human Beings Need the Virtues* (Chicago: Open Court, 1999).

54   Although I am referencing "The Privatization of the Good", this theme is present in much of his work, and in various ways, in all the texts cited in the footnote immediately above.

principles and values as meriting protection and promotion. In this debate, the latter camp has, I think, won the day. They have shown that absolute neutrality is incoherent and that liberal values need protection and promotion even for many illiberal values to be protected. Yet this counter-argument against complete neutrality does not damage MacIntyre's claim because the kind of indeterminacy and neutrality he critiques in the first camp remains in the second group of liberal theorists as well. Their arguments typically allow for, and even promote, wide disagreement about the human good and a fear of coming to consensus about such a good.

Yet MacIntyre also argues that the good has been *privatized*, and he notes the "remarkable degree of concurrence" among liberal theorists in this respect. He cites as examples Virginia Held, Ronald Dworkin, and John Rawls.[55] He observes that these views all share the conclusion that no conception of the good has established a claim to rational superiority and, yet, that rationality is exactly what should win our consent to visions of the good (and moral arguments more generally). He adds that it is not that we do not have enough recommended methods for arriving at rational conclusions about the right and the good; rather

> we have all too many methods, each of them incompatible in important ways with the others … we have a range of types of Kantianism, a similar range of types of utilitarianism, and of intuitionism, contractarianism, and various blends of these … [yet] [r]adical and *de facto* ineliminable disagreement confronts us.[56]

Further, he argues that such fragmentation takes place not only at the level of theory but also among ordinary nonphilosophical persons in respect to currency of everyday practical discourse. He thinks that our moral platitudes merely float on the rhetorical surface of our culture.[57] With those others I have suggested "won the day", MacIntyre argues that liberalism offers its own vision of the good, and that "genuine debate between rival conceptions only occurs when the actualities of one mode of social life … are matched against the actualities of its rivals".[58]

I have used Hauerwas, Burrell, and MacIntyre to assist in sketching out the basic features of a "standard account" of morality. This account takes morality to be based upon or intrinsically related to rationality and, particularly, rationality patterned on scientific accounts of rationality. It is an amalgam of theories, all with important irreconcilable differences. The

---

55 For example, Held, *Rights and Goals* (Chicago: University of Chicago Press, 1984), 19; Dworkin, "Liberalism", in *Public and Private Morality*, Stuart Hampshire, ed., (Cambridge: Cambridge University Press, 1978), 127; Rawls, *A Theory of Justice* (Cambridge: Harvard University Press, 1971), 447–48.

56 MacIntyre, "The Privatization of the Good", 348.

57 *Ibid.*, 448–49.

58 *Ibid.*, 355.

amalgam takes morality to be, in important senses, objective and universalizable. Morality is taken to offer theoretical conceptions which can then be "applied" to problems and quandaries of various kinds.[59] This holds true for morality conceived in both Kantian and consequentialist (and other, e.g., intuitionist and contractarian) terms.[60] A paradox exists in which moral theory, "applied" to moral problems, is understood to render answers and solutions, while at the same time, a deep indeterminancy exists.

Such titles as *Moral Reasoning: A Philosophic Approach to Applied Ethics*[61] and a wide range of modifiers to "Ethics" signify the standard account. Such modifiers include not only "Applied", but "Professional", "Business", "Environmental", "Bio", "Medical", "Sexual", and the like, let alone the incoherent "Personal", "Social", and "Virtue". The ubiquitous talk of "values" marks a dimension of this muddle in our culture; it is a vacuous term in popular discourse, admitting, however unintentionally (and ironically), the indeterminancy of our moral language.[62] It is as if the modifiers strive for precision while our adherence to "values" identifies our confusion. Joel Kupperman notes that the stilted moral theories that comprise this "standard account" have "tended to be framed so that character, habits, and past decisions (unless they generated specific obligations) of the moral agent dropped out of the picture". The effect of this omission is "like that of the cardboard cutouts in which tourists can insert their faces and be photographed as the cowboy and the saloon lady. Moral choice is presented as totally impersonal, apart from specific obligations that may have been incurred".[63]

I have tried to show various features of a "standard account" of morality in order to supply a backdrop against which to consider Oakeshott's account. The value of this modest tactic will be seen only when I interrogate his moral theory. One might suspect or know that Hauerwas and Burrell are

---

59   See MacIntyre, "Does Applied Ethics Rest on a Mistake?" *Monist*, 67 (1984), 498–513; and Edmund Pincoffs, "Quandary Ethics", *Mind*, 80 (1971), 552–71; reprinted in Hauerwas and MacIntyre, eds., *Revisions: Changing Perspectives in Moral Philosophy* (Notre Dame: University of Notre Dame Press, 1983), 92–112.

60   Of course, Kant and later deontologists emphasize this feature of morality with a greater sense of importance, sophistication, and conviction than do utilitarians, and other consequentialists, who are more likely to also be relativists of some kind. MacIntyre is probably right that "For perhaps the majority of later philosophical writers, including many who are self-consciously anti-Kantian, ethics is defined as a subject in Kantian terms. For many who have never heard of philosophy, let alone Kant, morality is roughly what Kant said it was". In his *A Short History of Ethics* (New York: Macmillan, 1966), 190.

61   Richard M. Fox and Joseph P. DeMarco, *Moral Reasoning: A Philosophic Approach to Applied Ethics*, 2d ed. (New York: Harcourt, 2001). Such titles are numerous. Here I mean to draw attention to the ways "reasoning" and "applied" function in the title and the conception of the book.

62   On the matter of the confusion of our moral language, see MacIntyre, *After Virtue*, Chapters 1 and 2; and Jeffery Stout, *Ethics After Babel* (Boston: Beacon Press, 1988).

63   Joel J. Kupperman, *Character* (New York: Oxford University Press, 1991), 151.

influenced by Aristotle, Aquinas, and MacIntyre; and that the moral theories of Hauerwas, Burrell, and MacIntyre are shaped by attention to virtue, vice, the role of habituation, and so forth. Although this is true, it does not follow that to reject the standard account one must give oneself over completely to Aristotelianism or any other *aretaic* theory, as the antitheorists demonstrate. I have used their accounts not to bend our discussion toward *aretaic* theory, but only to help sketch a background for our understanding of Oakeshott.

Earlier Moral Theory

Here we quite briefly return to Oakeshott's writing before 1975 to orient us to his more focused and mature reflection on morality in *On Human Conduct*. For Oakeshott, moral conduct cannot be separated or differentiated from any other kind of (agent-oriented and free) conduct. Moral behavior does not describe behavior of a certain kind, but all human behavior which is "intelligent" (as described above) and chosen by agents who are free (need it be said that this understanding does not mean that all human behavior is right or good?). This means, of course, that he supposes no human *telos*. Moral conduct is characterized by

> human affection and behaviour determined, not by nature, but by art. It is conduct to which there is an alternative. This alternative need not be consciously before the mind; moral conduct does not necessarily involve the reflective choice of a particular action ... a man's affections and conduct may be seen to spring from his character without thereby ceasing to be moral. The freedom without which moral conduct is impossible is freedom from a natural necessity which binds *all* men to act alike ... . It identifies moral behaviour as the exercise of an acquired skill (though the skill need not have been selfconsciously acquired) ... .[64]

The substantive freedom inherent in morality does not mean that moral conduct reduces to a world of arbitrary choices, let alone such choices as mere responses to appetite. Morality consists of valuations (as well as appetites, of course) and is "composed not merely of ... desire and aversion but also of ... approval and disapproval".[65] Although Oakeshott deeply values individuality, morality is constituted in virtue of its being *shared*. Morality is also an historical achievement:

> Selves in moral activity are equal members of a community of selves: and approval and disapproval are activities which belong to them as

---

64 Michael Oakeshott, "The Tower of Babel", *Rationalism in Politics*, 466. Oakeshott's two essays given this title are important reflections on morality, especially the first, which is quoted here. It was first published in the *Cambridge Journal* in 1948. The second is published in *On History and Other Essays* (Indianapolis: Liberty Fund, 1999), and was first read at Trinity College, Oxford in 1979.

65 "The Voice of Poetry in the Conversation of Mankind", ibid., 501. Cf. Candreva, 103. My summary of Oakeshott's moral theory before *OHC* owes to Candreva's Chapter 5, "Philosophy and the Moral Life".

members of this community. The moral skill in practical activity, the *ars bene beatique vivendi*, is knowing how to behave in relation to selves ingeniously recognized as such.

In general, then, moral activity may be said to be the observation of a balance of accommodation between the demands of desiring selves each recognized by the others to be an end and not a mere slave of somebody else's desires ... and one "morality" differs from another in respect to the level at which this balance is struck ... .[66]

Oakeshott identifies three forms of moral life in Europe's history. The first and most ancient of these he calls the morality of communal ties. As Candreva points out, his description of this morality is much like Constant's "liberty of the ancients". The second is the morality of individuality. The third is the morality of the common good.[67] As the political and social structures of the Greco-Roman world disintegrated, a new moral sensibility began to emerge. Oakeshott describes this as "the disposition to cultivate the 'freedom' inherent in agency, to enjoy individuality, and ... to concede virtue to this exercise of personal autonomy acquired in self-understanding".[68] Even though "the liberty of the moderns", to use Constant's idiom, overtakes that of the ancients, Oakeshott also thinks that Aristotle understood some of the key features of the civil condition and that individuality properly conceived has roots in at least this one ancient source.[69]

Of course, the dissolution of the morality of communal ties is very much, on balance, all to the good for Oakeshott, as it opens up opportunities for freedom and what he will identify in *On Human Conduct* as self-enactment. Yet the same conditions that bring opportunity for freedom, bring the possibility and sad actuality of the anti-individual and the individual *manqué*, as described in the previous chapter. Candreva points out that Oakeshott's description of this unfortunate character reminds one of Nietzsche's "last man", who, born of resentment, despises what is unequal, superior, or distinct. The "last man" refuses the risks of self-definition and creativity. Oakeshott cites Nietzsche along these lines as he writes of the "image of a new barbarism" found in the anti-individual.[70]

In 1948's "The Tower of Babel", Oakeshott identifies two "forms" of the moral life: the "morality of habit" (a "habit of affection and behaviour") and the "morality of reflection". All forms of the moral life are combinations of these two elements; it is impossible for a morality to consist of only

---

66 *Ibid.*, 502; cf. "The Moral Life in the Writings of Thomas Hobbes", *RP*, 296.
67 "The Moral Life in the Writings of Thomas Hobbes", *RP*, 296.
68 *OHC* 239; cf. Candreva, 104–05.
69 *OHC*, 108–11, 245–46; cf. Candreva, 105.
70 "The Masses in Representative Democracy", *RP*, 376; Candreva, 107. Cf. Oakeshott's comments in *OHC*, "The individual *manqué* had suffered not only substantive loss but also moral defeat... he is an historic and derivative character, the victim not only of the dissolution of familiar beliefs and relationships but also of another's more lively response to this dissolution. And hidden in his character was a seed of resentment", 277.

one. He thinks, however, that the best form of morality is one in which, although both are present, habit is dominant. This will strike some as at odds with his radical valuation of agency, individuality, and freedom, the "liberty of the moderns". Yet for Oakeshott, to act in accordance, or even "out of" custom and habit is not to act (necessarily, of course) arbitrarily, irrationally, or blindly. In fact, the difference between the two forms of the moral life mirrors the difference between practical (much like Aristotelean *phronesis*) and technical knowledge. Both have their place, but technical knowledge is more restricted in its usefulness, and finds its proper place in the milieu of practical knowledge. As with all practical knowledge, moral habits and customs draw on flexible, fluid, organic forms of understanding; but in so doing, they do not necessarily restrict agency, individuality, and freedom. Indeed, as was discovered above, certain customs, traditions, and habits may very well protect and promote such individuality and freedom, as Oakeshott argues.

Of course, many republican and communitarian theorists—ancient, modern, and contemporary—have argued for the virtue of custom and habit over against individualism. Yet most of these arguments have rested in foundationalist assumptions or explanations (e.g., Burke). Oakeshott's theory is nonfoundationalist, however; and for this reason Rorty adopts him as a model in this respect. He sees himself following Oakeshott when he writes that moral principles "only have a point insofar as they incorporate tacit reference to a whole range of institutions, practices, and vocabularies of moral and political deliberation. They are reminders of, abbreviations for, such practices … ".[71] Another way Oakeshott is distinguished from many other theorists who valorize "the morality of habit" is in his conception of the fragility, flexibility, and malleability of such morality. For most theorists of this kind, habit is strong and stable, and the stability (the relative nonmalleability) of tradition is what makes it strong (again, Burke stands as a good example).[72] He compares the morality of habit to language, and like language, habits withstand a number of uses, abuses, distortions, changes, and partial breakdowns without having their essential character destroyed or even significantly altered.[73]

Again, Oakeshott thinks that neither the morality of habit or of reflection "taken alone" is less than properly moral, and alone these are "ideal

---

71 Richard Rorty, *Contingency, Irony, and Solidarity* (New York: Cambridge University Press, 1997), 59. Rorty correctly notes that "this point is common to Hegel … Annette Baier, Stanley Fish, Jeffrey Stout, Charles Taylor, and Bernard Williams". I agree that these "antitheorists" understand morality in ways that comport significantly with Oakeshott's understanding.

72 Here, Oakeshott writes quite similarly to MacIntyre, who stresses the changeableness of tradition, in *After Virtue*.

73 "The Tower of Babel", *RP*, 468. Cf. *OHC*, 63–67, for a description of the analogy between morality and language. Cf. Candreva, 110.

extremes", but the morality of reflection, he thinks, tends to undermine the morality of habit in a way that does not work in the opposite direction.

> And together with the certainty about how to *think* about moral ideals, must be expected to go a proportionate uncertainty about how to *act*. The constant analysis of behaviour tends to undermine, not only prejudice in moral habit, but moral habit itself, and moral reflection may come to inhibit moral sensibility.[74]

Indeed, as one might expect, his criticism of the morality of reflection echoes his criticism of rationalism, and he explicitly associates the two in "Rationalism in Politics". Both overemphasize (a scientific account of) rationality and certainty; both equate thought and activity with the technical application of rules and procedures, and the purposive achievement of ends; both understand education as mere training, risk replacing judgment with information; and both prosper the notion that activity springs from thought and that conduct derives from reflection, that practice follows theory.[75]

The morality of reflection can appear either as the pursuit of ideals or as the reflective application of rules. The distinction between these forms is, of course, often blurry, and they are not mutually exclusive. This analytical distinction, however, allows Oakeshott to write of a morality of rules and of a morality of ideals. This comports with his aversion to perfectionism in all its guises. For him, the pursuit of perfection is dangerous and often leads to horrendous results. The "pursuit of perfection as the crow flies is an activity both impious and unavoidable in human life" ... "every moral ideal is potentially an obsession; the pursuit of moral ideals is an idolatry. ... this is a form of moral life which is dangerous in an individual and disastrous in a society".[76]

I identified three kinds of morality theorized by Oakeshott, the ancient morality of communal ties, the modern morality of individuality, and the contemporary morality of the common good; but I have not yet commented upon the third version. It unsurprisingly bears affinity to "the politics of faith" I discussed in the previous chapter and the collectivism associated with such political and moral faith. In his second (1979) "The Tower of Babel" essay, he sees in the Genesis story a tale of the morality of the common good and how even noble purposes can so easily and often go bad. Here, a single condition is imposed on all kinds of activity and on all people, and the character of the anti-individual is predominant. It expresses the consequences of rationalism and clearly shares similarities and sensibilities with what he will call "enterprise association" and "*universistas*". Candreva nicely sees a similarity between Oakeshott's

74   "The Tower of Babel", *RP*, 475.
75   *Rationalism in Politics*, 37–42; cf. 100–02, 110, 115–17, 474, 480. Cf. Candreva, 111.
76   "The Tower of Babel", *RP*, 466, 476.

thought about what rationalism and the morality of the common good do to people, e.g., decreasing people's wonderment for God — and Nietzsche's proclamation of the "death of God".[77]

Although Oakeshott clearly, on balance, prefers the "liberty of the moderns" over the ancients, he also thinks much has been lost in the transition from antiquity to modernity.[78] He writes:

> The real life of a society is expressed most clearly in terms of love/friendship, of the principle of the good, and to venture upon the discovery of the true nature of these is at once the final and the most difficult chapter in our own account of the self and its life. To pause for a moment and see how far we now are from the speculations on governmental form and organization which occupy the major part of our political "philosophers" today, is to see how far modern political philosophy has strayed from a true view of its proper subject matter.
>
> It was a wise dictum of Aristotle that the perfect law-giver has more regard for friendship than for justice, for the latter cannot exist except in a society founded upon and moved by the former.[79]

Candreva makes a statement that may be provocative to some who endorse Oakeshott's liberalism: "it appears that Oakeshott may have a clearer idea about the good life than he is willing to admit".[80] I will hold this claim in abeyance for the time being. After I consider his moral theory and civil association more fully, taking into account *On Human Conduct*, one may come to agree with Candreva and conclude that his moral vision is robust in certain respects and comports with democratic society in such a way that it intimates an understanding of the good life. Charles Beitz writes that "Political theories can be 'democratic' in two different, although related, senses. Democratic theories in the narrower (and more traditional) sense speak to the question, what is the best form of government? Those in the broader sense ask, what is the best society?"[81] My argument is that Oakeshott theorizes answers in both senses.

---

77   Oakeshott: "among its other connections, it is certainly closely allied with a decline in the belief in Providence: a beneficient and infallible technique replaced a beneficient and infallible God … ", in "Rationalism in Politics", *RP*, 23. In respect to Nietzsche's claim, see *The Gay Science*, ed. Bernard Williams (New York: Cambridge University Press, 2001), 119–20 (3.125). Candreva, 119.

78   An appealing study would compare Oakeshott and MacIntyre, as they theorize this movement. MacIntyre thinks much more has been lost than does Oakeshott, but the dialectic between them might be instructive.

79   "The Nature and Meaning of Sociality", *Religion, Politics and the Moral Life*, 59. Cf. Candreva, 123. Note the similarity to Marx, who thought that in the fullness of communism such friendship, kindness, and love would exist that justice would become unnecessary.

80   Candreva, 102.

81   Charles R. Beitz, *Political Equality: An Essay in Democratic Theory* (Princeton: Princeton University Press, 1989), ix.

On Human Conduct

Paul Franco correctly notes:

> The key to Oakeshott's understanding of civil association is the idea of a moral practice developed in the first essay of *On Human Conduct*. Civil association is, most fundamentally, association or relationship in terms of a moral (i.e., noninstrumental) practice. By defining civil association in this way, Oakeshott is able to overcome the atomism that has dogged liberal theory from Locke to Mill. A moral practice — and hence, civil association — does not compromise the freedom inherent in human agency because it does not determine the substantive choices of agents but only prescribes procedural or adverbial conditions to be taken into account when choosing and acting. Far from being an external limit on agency, a moral practice is indispensable to it. There is no agency that is not an acknowledgement of a moral practice, just as there is no utterance that is not any language in particular. Freedom and morality mutually imply one another.[82]

I quote Franco at some length because he has packed a number of themes tightly into one paragraph and has shown their relationship not only succinctly but also somewhat artfully. I have considered some of the themes he raises and will need to discuss some others. I begin where his paragraph leaves off, in considering the relationship between morality and freedom, and the other necessary aspects of morality theorized in the first essay of *On Human Conduct*. When the first essay's claims are understood, one can then see how it is that civil association *is* "most fundamentally", moral association.

One may recall how important agency, individuality, and freedom have been to Oakeshott in his earlier writing. The first essay of *On Human Conduct* continues to present this importance. Both Franco and Nardin, for instance, see individuality and freedom[83] as the central and defining core of his moral theory. Franco writes, for example, that in the first essay Oakeshott "elaborates a teaching about human freedom that serves as the basis of his liberal theory of civil association. Though it cannot be doubted that individual freedom was always at the heart of Oakeshott's political vision, it is only in *On Human Conduct* that he finally provided a philosophical account of it".[84]

Freedom, for Oakeshott, does not mean "the quality of being substantially 'self-directed' which an agent may or may not achieve"; this is, in fact, more "properly called 'self-determination' or 'autonomy.'"[85] As indicated earlier, human conduct and the freedom inherent in it are not to be

---

82   Franco, *Michael Oakeshott: An Introduction*, 154.

83   I have written of "individuality and freedom" several times above, but this pairing carries the danger of allowing the reader to misjudge how closely related these concepts are for Oakeshott. While distinct, they are nearly synonymous, and it is close to redundant, on his terms, to write of "individuality and freedom".

84   Franco, 146.

85   *OHC*, 36–37.

distinguished from habitual, spontaneous, or irrational conduct but from biological and genetic impulses. Human conduct is a matter of agency, freedom, beliefs, understandings, and meanings. Freedom, for Oakeshott, is "inherent in agency". It is not, however, only a formal condition, for it could remain formal and have little purchase in real lives and real politics. As important as the formal and definitional character of freedom is, Oakeshott also theorizes a civil and political order which, predicated on the formal condition of freedom, he sees as robustly protecting and promoting it as well.

One may recall that what Oakeshott theorized under the rubric of "tradition" he now theorizes, in *On Human Conduct*, as "practice". "Tradition" communicates to some, although Oakeshott never intends this meaning, a fixed, unchanging phenomenon. "Practice" carries, connotatively, it seems, a sense of the "adverbial" character of human conduct he wishes to emphasize. The analogy of practice with language which he begins to employ in earlier writing becomes more pronounced in *On Human Conduct*.

> Thus, a practice may properly be recognized as a language … . It does not impose upon an agent demands that he shall think certain thoughts, entertain certain sentiments, or make certain substantive utterances. It comes to him as various invitations to understand, to choose, and to respond. It is composed of conventions and rules … and is continuously invented by those who speak it and using it is adding to its resources. It is an instrument to be played upon, not a tune to be played. Learning to speak it is learning to enjoy and to explore a certain relationship with other agents.[86]

Oakeshott distinguishes and describes two kinds of relationship: "transactional" relationships in which agents pursue substantive ends and "practical" relationships which are "adverbial" in nature. Such "practical" relationships can be understood as comprised of two different kinds of practices. There are practices which "are designed to promote the success of the transactions … they govern". On the other hand, there are practices that are not instrumental to any purpose. Such practices are "noninstrumental" and "nonpurposive"; these are, Oakeshott writes, moral practices.[87]

> A morality is the *ars artuim* of conduct; the practice of practices; the practice of agency without further specification … a moral practice is not a prudential art concerned with the success of the enterprises of agents; it is not instrumental to the achievement of any substantive purpose or to the satisfaction of any substantive want … Nor is morality a court of arbitration in which different and often conflicting purposes of agents and their chosen acts are reconciled to one another and

---

86   *OHC*, 58; Franco, 150.
87   *OHC*, 59–62.

mean satisfactions authorized ... .

> In short, a morality may be identified as a practice without any
> extrinsic purpose; it is concerned with good and bad conduct, and not
> with performances in respect of their outcomes. And a moral relation-
> ship is not association for the achievement of a common purpose.[88]

Further, and as intimated above, there

> is no agency which is not the acknowledgment of a moral practice, and
> no moral conduct which is not the exercise of agency ... . The condi-
> tions which compose a moral practice are not theorems or precepts ...
> [but] a vernacular language of colloquial intercourse ... .
>
> Every such vernacular of moral converse is a historic achievement of
> human beings ... . It is never fixed or finished ... . It *is* its vicissi-
> tudes ... .
>
> Moral conduct is not solving problems; it is agents continuously and
> colloquially related to one another in the idiom of a familiar language
> of moral converse.[89]

It is clear that Oakeshott is at some distance from the "standard
account" of morality I summarized above. In contemporary terms, he is
undoubtedly an "anti-theorist". In fact, his "antitheory" theory reminds
one not only of certain contemporaries such a MacIntyre, Baier, and Williams (recall footnote 50) but also of Thomas Aquinas, who taught that
moral practice is roughly what Oakeshott says it is.[90] Morality for him is
also in some important ways Aristotelian (as he himself points out),[91] for
example, in respect to the nonreductionistic approach shared by both, and
the method of further elaboration of "vernacular" understandings, customs, and intuitions commonly held. It is Kantian at least insofar as the
important distinction between prudential and moral conduct. It is
Hegelian in respect to the analogy of morality and language.[92]

For Oakeshott, moral rules are "abridgements"

> which concentrate into specific precepts considerations of adverbial
> desirability which lie dispersed in a moral language ... . Moral rules
> specify performances in terms of obligations to subscribe to injunc-
> tions. What a moral practice intimates as, in general, proper to be said
> or done, a moral rule makes more explicit in declaring it is *right* to do

---

88   *Ibid.*, 60–62.

89   *Ibid.*, 63–64.

90   I refer, of course, to Thomas's *Summa Theologica*. Two texts which elaborate and explain the
claim I make here are Jean Porter, *Moral Action and Christian Ethics* (New York: Cambridge
University Press, 1999) and Charles R. Pinches, *Theology and Action: After Theory in Christian
Ethics* Grand Rapids, MI: Eerdmans, 2002). Both authors take many clues from, and frame their
arguments on Thomas's "Oakeshottian" account of morality. Of course, all three are doing
theology and therefore make various important claims Oakeshott does not make.

91   "On Misunderstanding Human Conduct", 363. Note that it is not surprising that Oakeshott's
moral theory would be, in some measure, both Aristotelian and Thomastic insofar as the
importance of Aristotle for Thomas.

92   Franco, *Michael Oakeshott: An Introduction*, 151.

      ... . Rules, duties, and their like (moral principles and dogmas) are,
      then, passages of stringency in a moral practice.[93]

Morality, for Oakeshott, is adverbial, and therefore it is always a moral distortion to mistake rules, duties, principles, theorems, *theoria*, ideals, or dogma for morality.[94] Abridgments abridge something more substantial than themselves. He writes that no moral practice can be reduced to the rules of duties, or the 'ideals' it obtrudes, and *rightness* is never more than an aspect of moral response, for they are used in conduct, not applied to conduct; and the moral reflection in which they may be brought to bear upon choosing is *deliberative*, not demonstrative.[95] He adds that moral rules are not criteria of good conduct and, therefore, not primarily instruments of judgment, but that they are "prevailing winds which agents should take account of in sailing their several courses".[96] It is by now clear that Oakeshott's valuation for agency, individuality, and freedom continues to be conative in his theory of moral practice; indeed, freedom and morality come to look much the same in his thought.[97]

What I have been describing is the kind of moral practice Oakeshott calls "self-disclosure". This is conduct relating to the intercourse of agents, each concerned with procuring satisfactions and seeking them, at least in some measure, in the responses of others. Such conduct is composed of performances in response to contingencies and for the achievement of outcomes.[98] There is another kind of moral practice he theorizes; he calls it "self-enactment". In self-enactment, "the consideration in doing is not what is intended to be achieved but the sentiment in which it is done ... what the agent chooses to think is related to his understanding and respect for himself, to the integrity of his character, and not at all to his understanding of ... [how] he must respond by choosing an action".[99] In self-enactment, "doing is delivered, at least in part, from the deadliness of doing, a deliverance gracefully enjoyed [for example] in the quiet of

---

93   *OHC*, 66–67.

94   The adverbial nature of moral practice is famously illustrated in Oakeshott's claim that as an example, criminal law "does not forbid killing or lighting a fire, it forbids killing 'murderously' or lighting a fire 'arsonically,'" *OHC*, 58.

95   *Ibid.*, 68. The emphasis is mine. As the reader may well guess, I emphasize "deliberative" because of the larger concerns of this project. I will argue below that there is a meaningful relationship between Oakeshott's moral theory, deliberation, and the democratic features and implications of civil association.

96   *Ibid.*, 70.

97   For an insightful and challenging text which explores the intimate relationship between morality and freedom, see Jacques Ellul, *The Ethics of Freedom*, trans. and ed., Geoffrey W. Bromiley (Grand Rapids: William B. Eerdmans, 1976).

98   *Ibid.*

99   *Ibid.*, 73.

religious faith".[100] It is knowing how to be "loyal" to oneself and is reflective of what, in part, virtue theorists mean when they consider the virtue of
an agent. The compunctions of self-enactment are demands that an agent
places upon himself, "a *délicatesse* of conduct which cannot be required of
him by another... ".[101]

Self-enactment is quite similar to Charles Taylor's idea of a notion that
came into existence only in late modernity, that

> there is a certain way of being human that is *my* way. I am called upon
> to live my life in this way, that is *my* way, and not in imitation of any-
> one else's life. But this notion gives a new importance to being true to
> myself. If I am not, I miss the point of my life; I miss what being human
> is for *me*.
>
> This is the powerful moral idea that has come down to us. It accords
> moral importance to a kind of contact with myself, with my own inner
> nature, which it sees as in danger of being lost, partly through the pres-
> sures of outward conformity, but also because in taking an instrumen-
> tal stance toward myself, I may have lost the capacity to listen to this
> inner voice ... .
>
> Being true to myself means being true to my own originality, which
> is something only I can articulate and discover.[102]

It is important to note that Taylor also argues that modern identity is
intrinsically political because it ultimately demands *recognition*. One's self
is not constituted only by inner discovery and reflection; it must also be
intersubjectively recognized by other such selves if it is to have coherence
and be ascribed proper identity and value.[103] The idea that modern politics
is based on the principle of universal recognition comes from Hegel; but
increasingly that universal recognition based on a shared humanity is
insufficient — particularly among groups who have experienced profound
discrimination and disenfranchisement — and, hence, modern politics
turns, with contemporary politics, into demands for recognition of group

---

100 *Ibid.*, 74. Oakeshott does not mean here that self-enactment is manifest only in, or even
(necessarily) primarily in, religious faith. He does think, however, that it is perhaps most often
enjoyed in religious faith; thus my insertion of [for example]. Oakeshott adds some reflection
about religious belief to his consideration of morality in *OHC*, 81–86. For a discussion of the
relationship between religion and self- disclosure and self-enactment, see Worthington, 64–73.

101 *Ibid.*, 75, 77. "Character" and "integrity" are words that are also used by some to signify, at least
in part, what Oakeshott calls self-enactment. E.g, cf. Joel Kupperman, *Character* (New York:
Oxford University Press, 1991); and Christine McKinnon, *Character, Virtue Theories, and the
Vices* (Orchard Park, NY: Broadview Press, 1999).

102 Charles Taylor, *Multiculturalism and the Politics of Recognition* (Princeton: Princeton University
Press, 1992), 30–31. Taylor's interrogation of the meaning of self-enactment (to use
Oakeshottian language), or authenticity and self-fulfillment, is extended beyond essay length
in his insightful book, *The Ethics of Authenticity* (Cambridge: Harvard University Press, 1991).
Originally *The Malaise of Modernity*, the book's first title, intimates a relationship between the
(proper) need for self-enactment and a crisis of modernity, wonderfully developed in the text.

103 On the relationship of the self to liberal political theory (and rival ideologies), see Peter
Digeser, *Our Politics, Our Selves?: Liberalism, Identity, and Harm* (Princeton: Princeton
University Press, 1995).

identities.[104] This matter of recognition of selves, and groups, of mulit-culturalism and identity politics is of acute importance in all liberal democracies. Indeed, it is recognized that the very meaning of democracy itself is tied to this problematic.

Hegel's importance to Oakeshott has been noted, and I am suggesting here that Taylor's insight about modern self-discovery and self-truth is deeply consonant with Oakeshott's conception of self-enactment, both in respect to the inner turn but also in respect to the realization that inner selves have no coherence or meaning apart from engagement with other self-enacted selves. This is to say that self-enactment needs self-disclosure, and, in turn, then, self-disclosure needs self-enactment. The centrifugal and centripetal tendencies and needs of persons are mutually necessary. For Oakeshott, civil association and the civil condition, morality and human conduct, bear such intimate and intrinsic relationships as a necessity, in part, to bear the relationship between self-disclosure and self-enactment or, in Taylor's terms, authenticity and recognition. Walsh touches lightly upon this relationship in his remark that because the moral life, for Oakeshott, is based on "a living practice", a "habit of affections and behavior become established when certain ways of living become connected with our amour propre, our *sense of ourselves*".[105]

Since morality is a practice on the understanding I have summarized, it does not "prescribe choices to be made or satisfactions to be sought; instead, it *intimates considerations* to be *subscribed to* in making choices, in performing actions, and in pursuing purposes". It postulates free agents, but it does not mean a kind of moral autonomy which requires moral choice to be a gratuitous, criterionless exercise of the "will".[106] In sum, human conduct

> is agents disclosing and enacting themselves in responding to their understood contingent situations by choosing to do or say *this* rather than *that* in relation to imagined and wished-for outcomes … *presided over* by a practice of moral conduct … a moral practice, as the *ars artium* of agency, is agents related to one another in terms of conditional properties which are expressly or tacitly recognized in the conditions of all other special prudential relationships and manners of being associated in conduct.[107]

Oakeshott's Moral Theory in Civil Association

Here I summarize Oakeshott's moral theory and, in so doing, must attend to its inherent relationship to the civil condition or civil association. I have

---

104 Francis Fukuyama, "Identity, Immigration, and Liberal Democracy", *Journal of Democracy*, 17, no. 2 (April, 2006), 9.

105 Walsh, 57 (emphasis, mine). Walsh means "ourselves" to be understood both in terms of individual selves, as well as collectively; in terms of both self-enactment and self-disclosure.

106 *OHC*, 79 (emphasis, mine).

107 *Ibid.*, 86, 88 (emphasis, mine).

started this brief work already in my use of Taylor, and the paragraph immediately above, but there are several strands above that need to be pulled together. In the quote from Franco I used to begin this section, he claims that "Oakeshott is able to overcome the atomism that has dogged liberal theory" because the freedom it postulates and promotes does not determine substantive choices but is adverbial, noninstrumental, and nonpurposive. It turns out, then, that morality is "indispensable" to freedom rather than a limit upon it. "Freedom and morality mutually imply one another." It is also Walsh's insight to see how Oakeshott's theory of freedom and morality are the basis for a new vision of liberal association. Civil association names a liberal order, yet it is imbued with Aristotelianism; and because of this unique Oakeshottian synthesis of Aristotelian, liberal, Hegelian, and other insights, the moral practice which is civil association, is "remarkably stable". Morality, standing without foundational presuppositions, is stable in good measure because it is not reducible to any further reality; it is already concrete as a practice which synthesizes self-disclosure and self-enactment. Thus, the absence of criteria (rules, theorems, dogma, ideals, etc.) used as a moral yardstick does not lead to the inevitability of interminable and incommensurable moral disputes. The fact that moral formation and judgment are personal does not entail that it is merely subjective. The "living practice" that names both morality and civil association need not have, and cannot have, substantive purposes; yet this aspect of its coherence also leads to stability. This nonintrumental and nonpurposive practice is freedom, and the robust enjoyment of freedom so conceived assists such stability as liberal orders seek. It follows that "this noninstrumental understanding of morality is the key to Oakeshott's conception of civil association".[108]

Oakeshott understands morality as a practice; as described above, it is noninstumental and nonpurposive, and moral relationships do not exist for the achievement of any common purpose (Mapel notwithstanding). Morality does not "*prescribe* choices or satisfactions to be sought", but it does "*intimate considerations* to be *subscribed* to" when making choices, performing actions, or pursuing purposes. Morality is "adverbial", and it "*is*", Oakeshott tells us, "its vicissitudes". It is intrinsically related to freedom (Franco is right that freedom and morality mutually imply one another); and is the "*ars artium* of agency" the practice of practices, constituted by self-disclosure and self-enactment which exist in mutually supporting and necessary ways, it is inviting, open, nonjudgmental in the senses of Kantianism or consequentialism, yet not undemanding of moral seriousness. Because it is all these things, born of an intellectual synthesis of various traditions (from Aristotle, Hobbes, Kant, Hegel, and more), it is a liberal order which is comparatively stable. Its stability does not exist

---

108 Walsh, 62 and 57–62.

despite its nonfoundationalism and contingency, but, in part, because of these factors.[109]

If one were to pull from the paragraph immediately above all features of civil association, little would be left. In *On Human Conduct*, civil association names the moral association I just described. I began the paragraph, "Oakeshott's moral theory ... ". but everything written above is relational and associational. Oakeshott theorizes a civil association of a certain kind: what kind? a moral association on the terms of a moral practice as summarized above. Civil association would be, at most, a tattered ghost of an idea if somehow the substance of its morality could be taken from it. It may be even more precise to say that as he theorizes human conduct and is led inevitably to conceptualization of the civil condition; his thinking on these matters leads him inevitably to theorize practice generally and moral practice specifically as he does, and thinking about the relationship between human conduct, the civil condition, practice and morality, leads him inevitably to theorize civil association (and concomitantly, *societas*, enterprise association, and *universitas*). In short, civil association is just the kind of noninstrumental, nonpurposive, adverbial *association* which is its constituting and conative moral practice.

Contingency and Deliberation

Two important features of the moral association Oakeshott identifies as civil association are also important in the democratic theory that will also be discussed in the next chapter: contingency and deliberation.

Contingency

I have, of course, already considered contingency in some measure, in respect to Oakeshott's work before *On Human Conduct*, and I mentioned that much is made of this aspect of Oakeshott's theory of civil association by Mapel. I will interrogate Mapel quite shortly, so engagement with his thought can be postponed. Here, I will only summarize what he has to say about contingency and the civil condition in *On Human Conduct*. Contingency and deliberation have an intimate relationship in Oakeshott's thought; but I have chosen to treat each separately for analytical purposes.

Oakeshott theorizes contingency in the first essay. As mentioned in the last chapter, contingency does not name merely accidental events. He

---

109 Although I have mentioned strands of Aristotelianism, Kantianism, etc., that influence or resonate with Oakeshott's theory, recall our earlier claim that he stands closest to the "antitheorists" and is considerably distant from the "standard account" of morality I have given. Perhaps the short summary of Oakeshott's moral theory presented here gestures toward the claim made above, that his account of morality deserves book-length treatment. Much work could be fruitfully done to show how his moral theory agrees with and differs from a large number of sources; of course his own theory can be explicated in far more detail than what I can offer here.

notes that an understanding of contingency, that is, the relationship of dependence or inter-dependence among phenomena, enhances our intelligibility of goings-on. Second, contingency names an inter-/dependent relationship different from teleological, evolutionary, mechanistic, and organic kinds which exist "in virtue of the regularities which constitute the process or the structure ... [or the] system ... [or] relations of necessity".[110] Contingency names a relationship between "goings-on" that exhibit human agency and inter-/dependence. "Incidental" signifies such a relationship. Of course there are often sequential relationships of such events, where occurrences are recognized as conditional upon previous occurrences.[111] Such convergences constitute "an *eventum*; not a merely recorded occurrence, not itself an assignable action or an assignable response to an action, but the contingent outcome of the choices and encounters of assignable agents and understood as this outcome".[112] Of course, reaching such an understanding is often difficult, if not evanescent; what is and is not an "outcome" in any given set of phenomena is a matter rarely, if ever, concluded, with absolute certainty. "Like all adventures in theorizing", Oakeshott writes, the engagement to understand a substantive performance in terms of its contingent conditions "is an engagement to abate mystery rather than to achieve a suppositious definitive understanding".[113]

If this is the description of the formal character of contingency, more remains to be said. Why does Oakeshott consider contingency in *On Human Conduct*? Why does he undertake a seven-page theorization of it? As has been understood by Mapel, Walsh, Soininen, and several interpreters, contingency plays an important role in his theory of human conduct/civil condition/civil association. Here I offer a short description of this importance.

"All religions, nearly all philosophies, and even part of science itself testify to the unwearying, heroic effort of mankind desperately denying its contingency", writes Jacques Monod.[114] Human history is filled with concerted efforts to refuse, contradict, or at least diminish contingency. Against this historical grain, however, and in ways that are crucial to his theory, Oakeshott writes of conduct, morality, and moral association as noninstrumental, nonpurposive, and contingent. The "ideal character of 'human conduct' [is] the relationship concerned [with] contingency".[115] Of course, Oakeshott does not deny that people often engage in conduct

110 *OHC*, 101.
111 *Ibid.*, 103–04.
112 *Ibid.*, 107.
113 *Ibid.*, 106.
114 Cited in John Gray, *Straw Dogs: Thoughts on Humans and Other Animals* (London: Granta Books, 2002), 1.
115 *OHC*, 101.

which is instrumental, purposive, and meant to abate contingency, but two things: first, he is remarkably comfortable with contingency and consistently communicates a laxness about the need to diminish it; second, he recognizes that human conduct need not be instrumental and purposive and that it is essentially, at root, not so. His nonfoundational theory is tied to his embrace of contingency. If one eschews metaphysical foundations and teleology, contingency will not be kept at bay nor will one see the reason to be anxious about this, one only need recall the nonnecessariness of contingency. Oakeshott is quite at peace in a world and a politics in which so very much is not necessary.[116]

Although noninstrumentality and nonpurposiveness are not identical conceptions and both are different from contingency, Oakeshott uses these terms in roughly synonymous ways.[117] He does so not because he is confused but because the meaning he legitimately makes of them coherently allows them to be used in this way. Clearly, noninstrumentality, nonpurposiveness, and nonnecessariness are closely related. The world is thoroughly contingent, so human conduct and association are as well (whether or not this is recognized by any given agent at any given time). He writes that the agent is "what he understands himself to be" and "his contingent situations are what he understands them to be … . He has a 'history', but no 'nature'; he is what in conduct he becomes … what he enacts for himself in a diurnal engagement, the unceasing articulation of understood responses to endlessly emergent understood situations … ".[118]

Similarly, he writes that practices "are not stable compositions of easily recognized characteristics … . they are footprints left behind by agents responding to emergent situations, footprints which are only somewhat less evanescent than the transactions in which they emerged … ".[119] Human conduct and practices are radically contingent, so it follows that the moral practice of civil association is so as well. Tregenza notes that Oakeshott's civil association privileges "a contingent, historic disposition to cultivate individuality".[120] McIntyre also notes the intimate relationship between contingency and individuality.[121] Podoksik describes Oakeshott's conception of freedom (and therefore of individuality, moral practice and

---

116 His thought in "On Being Conservative", and about *poeisis*, especially in "The Voice of Poetry in the Conversation of Mankind" comes immediately to mind.

Oakeshott's skepticism, can be argued, I think, to bear some relationship to his understanding of contingency, especially in respect to its nonnecessariness. Strains of this skeptical tradition follows from Pyrrho, Sextus Empiricus, and stoicism generally.

117 To deny purpose is one thing; to deny instrumentality, or the means to purpose, is another. It is worth noting that Mapel and others use these terms in the "roughly synonymous" ways I suggest follows from Oakeshott's own usage.

118 *OHC*, 66.

119 *Ibid.*, 100.

120 Tregenza, 125.

121 McIntyre, 69.

civil association) as "recognized contingency".[122] Soininen argues that "politics in civil association is presented as a *deliberative*, reflective activity ... a heightened recognized contingency".[123]

Indeed, one will remember that Soininen's study of the development of Oakeshott's theorization of political activity is described as moving "from a 'necessary evil' to the *art of contingency*". On the face of it, one is struck by the odd notion of art and contingency related in the manner she suggests. Her use of the term "art", however, signifies Oakeshott's embrace of, and work with, contingency. The meaning of contingency is not that humans are helpless or ought to be passive. Persons do indeed give shape to their conduct, practices, relationships, associations, and events. Morality, in part, is meant to "endow human conduct with a formality in which its contingency is somewhat abated".[124] This abatement of contingency will be discussed in the next section, but at this point one need only see that there is a kind of work and play, a kind of *poeisis* in respect to one's contingent circumstances that Oakeshott theorizes and Soininen seeks to capture in her notion of the "art of contingency".[125]

Like Tregenza and McIntyre, she notes the inherent relationship of contingency and individuality within civil association; that is, these are mutually supportive, and even mutually defining, phenomena.[126] It is, however, the relationship between contingency and politics, which is to say, the relationship between contingency and civil association, which concerns her most. Politics just *is*, on Soininen's account, response to contingency. Of course, in one respect, this claim is simply a truism, but she means that for Oakeshott nothing guides politics. "At no point is there any *necessary* response to a given political situation". She immediately continues, "The openness of conversation refers to the contingency of politics; the idiom of political discourse is persuasive, not demonstrative".[127] At the moment, it is the first sentence quoted that captures our attention, but I extend the quote to the next sentence because her view that conversation and discourse have an intrinsic relationship to the role of politics and civil association, all saturated in contingency, is an insight I will pursue immediately below. In noting the nonnecessariness of political action in civil association, she is echoing Mapel's argument about the fundamental and important role contingency plays in civil association. This is a matter that leads to questions about the role of democracy in such association.

---

122 Podoksik, 57.
123 Soininen, 217 (emphasis, mine).
124 *OHC*, 74.
125 Cf. Oakeshott's early essay "Work and Play", op. cit., which echoes the sense of contingency and our relationship to it that Soininen and I both seek to express.
126 Soininen, 78.
127 *Ibid.*, 102, 103.

One can recall Oakeshott's complaint against rationalism and note that much of that criticism is about the rationalistic attempt to escape the "intricacy of the world of time and contingency".[128] It follows that political actors should keep from confusing politics with eternity and "acquire an understanding of contingency".[129] Soininen prospers a consideration of contingency in Oakeshott's theorization of political activity in a thirteen-page section of her book. Here I briefly summarize that reflection. This section is also much concerned with deliberation, and she begins by once again drawing the two matters together, noting their intrinsic relationship.[130]

She claims that "Oakeshott's deep understanding of the contingency of current arrangements and *lex*, and the role of politics in changing them, thus also implies an understanding, or at least a possibility of the 'republican ideal' of citizenship".[131] I have briefly noted my supposition that there are various republican features of civil association and referenced Coats in that respect. Here I would note not Soininen's agreement, but that just insofar as an understanding of contingency leads to appreciation for republicanism, then it also leads in some respects to democracy. This claim embodies the notion, of course, that republicanism and democracy bear important and essential relationships to one another (in the thought of various theorists, they are synonymous), and I have also touched upon this in the previous chapter. I am also at the moment simply accepting Soininen's claim that an appreciation of contingency leads to an appreciation of republicanism.

Not only are republicanism and democracy underwritten by contingency, but so too is the legitimation of politics.[132] In this, her claim mirrors that of Walsh, who sees stability in Oakeshott's moral practice of civil association. She writes that small innovations along the way — trimming,

---

128 *Rationalism in Politics*, 34; cited in Soininen, 154.

129 Soininen, 163.

130 *Ibid.*, 184, cf. 190.

131 *Ibid.*, 184, 186. Although Oakeshott is radically liberal in important ways, I think, as I have indicated above, that his theorization of the civil condition is full of Aristotelian, republican, Hegelian, and communitarian sensibilities and dimensions. This claim is mundane in respect to his Hegelianism, as, for example, seen in Franco's work which elucidates much of Oakeshott's connections to Hegel.

132 Habermas, of course, theorizes a consistent "legitimation crisis" insofar as any state (particularly in respect to its government) is never entirely "legitimate" for all relevant persons, most specifically, its citizens. The failure of complete legitimacy has both normative and various descriptive, democratic, and deliberative dimensions; and all such dimensions are interrelated to the others. For example, certain theoretical claims can be made against a state action, although a large majority of people may endorse that action; conversely, a large majority may reject a possible state action which is determined to be normatively praiseworthy by philosophers, social scientists, and theologians. He sees capitalism as undermining and crisis-creating, especially vis-à-vis states overdetermined by it. Discursive democracy is work toward reducing illegitimacy. See Jürgen Habermas, *Legitmation Crisis*, trans. Thomas McCarthy (Boston: Beacon Press, 1975); and (on the matter of discursive democracy), *Between Facts and Norms: Contributions to a Discourse Theory of Law and Democracy*, trans.William Rehg (Cambridge: MIT Press, 1988).

as Halifax put it, and Oakeshott echoing him, agreed — serve as preserva-tive measures in political activity, especially in civil association. And these small adjustments stem from "the acknowledged contingency of a com-munity".[133] So it is, she concludes, that political activity does not always "work against change, because contingency and change are built-in aspects of the understanding of 'civil freedom' in a civil association ... . If politics were understood in any other manner than as a (deliberate and reflected) channel of change in *lex*, it would not respond to agents' contin-uous modification of the vernacular language of morals in their perfor-mances and (desired) self-understanding as contingent agents".[134]

I have sought to demonstrate that contingency is an important matter in Oakeshott's theory of civil association for a number of reasons. He is radi-cally comfortable with the fact of contingency, without being stoic, deter-ministic, fatalistic, or utterly passive about it. Moral practice and political activity are about being at work and play in relationship to our contingent circumstances. As individual agents are as bound by contingency as are associations, their activities can serve to "abate contingency". The perfor-mances and relationships of agents can, then, in the contingency of free-dom, serve to constitute republican or democratic spaces, energies, politics, associations, and their deliberations.[135]

Deliberation

I will here, as earlier, make nothing of the difference among the terms con-versation, discourse, and deliberation, and their cognates, unless a partic-ular contextual reason demands I do so. As with contingency, I will summarize Oakeshott's conceptualization of deliberation in *On Human Conduct*, before I move on to consider the most helpful claims made in the secondary literature. An obvious and direct connection with deliberative democracy is now at hand. Clearly, not everything Oakeshott has to say about conversation, discourse, or deliberation will have import in respect to democratic theory; but no small amount of his thought about these mat-ters will have some such importance. To conclude that Oakeshott values the idiom, and even the practice of conversation generally, and deliberation

---

133 Soininen, 191.
134 *Ibid.*, 197. Soininen actually writes that political activity "does not work against change". I added the qualifier "always" into the claim to make it coherent. She certainly must recognize, on reflection, that sometimes political activity does seek to diminish or stop change of some kind. Her comment can be sensical only if she means something like the Heraclitusian claim that change is constant/all things are always in some stage of change. If that is her point, her claim is uninteresting. Recall that Oakeshott writes that morality is, in part, about the abatement of contingency.

I also disagree with her in respect to her view that for Oakeshott, politics is only understood as deliberate, reflective change in *lex*; but I will consider this matter in the next section.
135 I have limited our discussion of the secondary literature, but substantive and helpful considerations of contingency are to be found in Nardin, O'Sullivan, Podoksik, Tregenza, and Tseng.

among, say, members of parliament does not mean that he endorses, let alone theorizes, a robust or sophisticated deliberative democratic theory, *as such*. Nonetheless, I will find his reflection on conversation and deliberation — coupled with many other features of civil association — to lead us some way down the road to deliberative democratic theory. Certainly everything written here should be understood in relationship to the consideration of conversation and discourse in his earlier work, offered in the previous chapter.[136] As with other themes (e.g., agency, moral practice, contingency), *On Human Conduct* is an elaboration and sophistication of matters addressed earlier; and there is a continuity of thought, far more than a discontinuity, between the earlier and the later work. Tseng's discussion of "Oakeshott's concept of 'substantial conversation'" underwrites this claim.[137] While he explicates Oakeshott's consideration of conversation in his earlier texts, it is striking how this "substantial conversation" prefigures what he writes about deliberation and intercourse in *On Human Conduct*.

Oakeshott's theorization of deliberation immediately ties it to matters of contingency: first, in that although there are limiting conditions that ought to be taken into account when choices are made, nevertheless, "the eligible alternatives in conduct are virtually unlimited"; and second, that deliberation is done (if done wisely) in recognition of the "likelihood of uncertainties".[138] Importantly, he then stipulates that the conditions of deliberation are the postulates of conduct; and, as such, deliberation

> is the only kind of argument in which an agent can recommend an action to himself, and its reasons are the only kind of reasons which may legitimately be adduced for having made *this* rather than *that* choice … .
>
> Doing as an engagement of reflective consciousness, then, postulates a deliberation … But deliberating as a specific activity … may be recognized as a counterpoise to the inherent uncertainty of doing.[139]

That is, deliberation is a necessary or essential aspect of what a person chooses, if that choice is a reflection of intelligence (on Oakeshott's terms, as discussed above), and one might also clearly conclude if such choice is to be rational. This is a mode of thought which is personal before it becomes interpersonal. Further, deliberation is a means to "abate contingency". Unsurprisingly, having discussed deliberation as I have just summarized, he turns to the matter of persuasion and persuasive speech. Because deliberation is "the characteristic idiom of reflection in conduct,

---

136 McIntyre in particular emphasizes the continuity between Oakeshott's discussion of persuasive speech in *On Human Conduct* and "Political Discourse", 70, 169.

137 Tseng, 174–79.

138 *OHC*, 44. In respect to Oakeshott's discussion of deliberation in the summary that follows, he is using the term, quite clearly, as will be seen, to signify a particular kind of conversation or discourse.

139 *Ibid.*, 45.

persuasion may be said to be the characteristic idiom of speech". His point seems to be that persuasion is the "distinctive character" in "argumentative discourse, in negotiation, or in debate" where such utterance is "unequivocally" about "persuasive argument" designed to recommend and to prompt choice about what shall be done.[140] Although he offers an argument for the claim that persuasion is the characteristic idiom of speech, it is, I think, unpersuasive. His argument aside (it is a small matter for the concerns here, so I need not examine it), it is hard to conclude that persuasion is what is characteristic about speech. I have quoted this claim, however, because it does intimate the importance for Oakeshott of not only deliberation but also of persuasion.

After explaining deliberation in the first essay, he turns to its application and meaning in the second, in respect to the civil condition. What distinguishes political thought and utterance, he argues, "is its character as deliberation about *respublica* in terms of the *bonum civile*; that is, about the conditions *cives* should be authoritatively required to subscribe to and be constrained to observe".[141] This engagement is deliberative and argumentative and intends to be persuasive. Such political deliberation is "conditional upon the postulates of human conduct, and of moral and civil association … ".[142] Importantly, he folds the meaning of deliberation, argumentation, and the intent to persuade into the parameters set by the proper postulates of human conduct and civil association, which he notes is moral association. Indeed, he writes, "Civil association is a moral condition" as he begins his discussion of what deliberation entails.[143] Deliberation and argument, then, among other things, will properly respect the agency, individuality, freedom, contingency, and moral character of others.

It follows that, because civil association is a moral condition,

> it is not concerned with the satisfaction of wants and substantive outcomes but with the terms upon which the satisfaction of wants may be sought. And politics is concerned with determining the desirable norms of civil conduct and with the approval or disapproval of civil rules which, because they qualify the pursuit of purposes, cannot be inferred from the purposes pursued … .
>
> Civility, then, notes an order of moral (not instrumental) consider-

---

140 *Ibid.*, 46, 47–48.

141 For Oakeshott, *respublica* names "the comprehensive conditions of [civil] association, *OHC*, 108.

142 *Ibid.*, 173. One notices that Oakeshott claims there are conditions to which citizens should be "authoritatively required" to "subscribe". For those unfamiliar with Oakeshott, this can only sound nonsensical. How does one subscribe as a requirement? Isn't subscription different than obeying? Subscription is a highly abstract theorization in Oakeshott, and the meaning he parses is not easily agreed to by all. But we will discuss this matter in the next section.

143 *Ibid.*, 174.

ations ... [prompting] recognition of civil association as itself a moral and not a prudential condition.[144]

Oakeshott's description of civil association as a moral condition and, as such, association which seeks not substantive outcomes in terms of the satisfaction of wants, but rather seeks to establish the terms upon which satisfactions may be pursued, goes to the heart of the next section. While this matter will be discussed momentarily, my purpose in quoting this text here is to show what he conceives deliberation to be most fundamentally about. It is employed in politics to determine the very norms and conditions, the political and constitutional infrastructure, of such political association (which is at once both intrinsically moral and civil). Importantly, he does not disallow the possibility that in deliberating about the "civil desirabilities" of civil association, *cives* may take into consideration "intimate moral relationships", and he means "only that what is civilly desirable cannot be [directly] inferred or otherwise derived from general moral desirabilities". For example, "no civil rule can be *deduced* from the Golden Rule or from the Kantian categorical imperative".[145]

Unsurprisingly, given his long-standing admonishment against rationalism and the politics of faith, what he is warning against here is an understanding in which civil association would be, or provide a condition of, deliberation in which a "Civil Reason" or "Civil Imagination" with the character of a "*cosmopolis*" would be *imposed* upon *cives*; after all, "no moral conclusions can be drawn from such imaginary models". He argues that "Norms of civil conduct ... are contingent choices which may have reasons but not causes ... . In short, political proposals are conclusions, and whether or not they have been significantly deliberated, they are deliberative conclusions ... ".[146] For Oakeshott, deliberation is, then, intrinsic to the politics of the moral condition which is civil association. Such deliberation is an exchange with contingency, not deduced from platonic abstractions, such as the imaginary model of Civic Reason, or other such ideas that have been foisted upon various peoples from time to time.[147] Further, even when conclusions, which are the fabric of politics, are not "significantly" deliberated, they are still *deliberative*; that is, deliberation names something intrinsic to the conduct and discourse that constitutes political activity in civil association. Deliberation signifies a character of conduct and discourse that is larger than particular forms of argumentation. To put it otherwise, deliberation is not a form of discourse on one side of a line defined by criteria; but rather, discourse can be more or less deliberative,

---

144 *Ibid.*, 174, 175.

145 *Ibid.*, 175, 174.

146 *Ibid.*, 176–77.

147 As earlier, I do not mean to use the conception of platonic abstractions as those owing only to Plato, but rather as a *kind* of abstraction.

and the criteria defining it has some purchase (little to much) all along the continuum or range of kinds of discourse.

As a part of theorizing deliberation, Oakeshott notes that

> *respublica* is the work of local human intelligences and ... it cannot be expected to display any notable elegance or economy of design; nor can it escape being ragged at the edges, intimating situations to which it has no precise response. And it is recognized to be undergoing continuous modification ... in contingent circumstances.[148]

But despite the ragged, *ad hoc*, and contingent nature of deliberation, he also states that "civil intercourse" can also be understood "in terms of general theorems, of varying degrees of abstraction ... and even more general moral ideas (such as fairness and humanity) ... ".[149] Of course, one can pose two questions to Oakeshott: how a "general" moral idea is to be differentiated from an idea insufficiently general, e.g., the Golden Rule and the categorical imperative, and why such a distinction should be made. It seems that too-specific moral ideas may, in his view, lead to, or be intractable from, substantive outcomes and the satisfactions of wants, but he is not clear about this. In any case, deliberation and "intercourse" extend along a range of discourse that includes the conditions of civil association, general moral ideas, and general theorems displaying varying degrees of abstraction (which can, presumably, include rather nonabstract, but concrete, theorems or ideas).

Oakeshott summarizes his theorization of deliberation and intercourse as follows:

> political deliberation, a practice of civil discourse ... is neither quiescent nor agitated; it is a situation of continuous responses to circumstances in terms of rules. And it is this situation which provides not only the subject of political deliberation but also the intellectual equipment available to be employed when critical attention fastens upon some small or large part of it and deliberate innovation is canvassed ... criteria of approval or disapproval untouched by contingency are necessarily absent ... . The anchorage of this deliberation and argument is a sea-anchor. Demonstrative conclusions are necessarily impossible; final solutions and alternative ideal systems of *lex* are persuasive subterfuges or corrupting delusions.
>
> The considerabilities of political deliberation are, then, aids to reflection rather than indisputable criteria of choice. None can escape the characteristic conditionality of such deliberation, but that some are more solid than others can hardly be doubted.[150]

He explicates three conditions he argues are important for such deliberation, but they are offered as illustrations of what he has in mind, not definitive or exhaustive criteria: first, that a civil prescription is undesir-

---

148 *Ibid.*, 177.
149 *Ibid.*
150 *Ibid.*, 178.

able if it cannot be enforced; second, that consideration of what harm to others may result from decisions should be employed; and third, that any innovation prospered should have its feasibility considered, "such that the *respublica* concerned can accommodate it".[151]

One should notice that in all of the summary offered here, no mention is made of hierarchical or official systems or contexts for such deliberation and intercourse. Indeed, the substance of the discussion is applicable to all persons (although, obviously, some are better equipped to deliberate and argue, and more interested in doing so than others). Political actors, such as members of parliament and administration officials, are, I would add, perhaps those most likely to come up with "final solutions and alternative ideal systems of *lex*" which are "subterfuges or corrupting delusions".[152] Everything in his discussion of deliberation allows for egalitarian and democratic possibilities; there is no comment which closes the way off to such possibility. Certainly, Oakeshott does not in a thoroughgoing manner explicate and elaborate egalitarian and nonhierarchical features of his theory, but it is clear he, at the least, allows for it. He concludes, "In short, the consideration here is that what is being attended to and deliberately reformed in politics is a *vernacular language* of civil intercourse." When he has perhaps the most opportune place to put this responsibility in the hands of the few, the experts, or the assembly, he does not: "it calls for so exact a focus of attention and so common a self-restraint that one is not astonished to find this mode of human relationship to be as rare as it is excellent".[153] It is just here that he might add that only those with special training or inclinations or electoral credentials are up to the task. Similarly, he writes that engagement in politics, and therefore, deliberation, requires a "disciplined imagination", but he does not add that only experts have such imaginations. The egalitarian and democratic possibilities remain wide open.

Soininen's conclusion about the role and importance of deliberation and conversation in Oakeshott's thought is worth summarizing. The word "deliberation" does not appear in the index of her book, although the word is used in various places; "conversation", by contrast, earns several page citations. Her discussion endorses my claim that, in most cases, Oakeshottian references to "deliberation", "discourse", and "conversation" can be understood in interchangeable ways. She writes of a "Rortyan-Oakeshottian" version of liberalism which is a "politics of

---

151 *Ibid.*

152 I add this comment, but one can easily imagine Oakeshott agreeing, given the low esteem in which he generally held public officials. He considered the Tories, for example, to do "less damage" than the Labour Party (which was typically in power during his career).

153 *Ibid.*, 180.

change and conversation".[154] She notes that he was a defender of parliamentary government and of "a *conversational* culture".[155] Soininen agrees with my claim above that Oakeshott is interested in answering the question, What is the best society? His answer is the moral association, which is civil association, and such association is conversational, deliberative, and prospers freedom in contingency. In civil association, the "openness to conversation refers to the contingency of politics".[156] She also writes of the "conversation of politics in a society", the "politics of conversation", and, as mentioned earlier, conversation as Oakeshott's "master metaphor".[157]

She writes that the Oakeshottian politics of conversation is not only about present political activity but also signifies conversations and political activity between past, present, and future. Further, it "*includes* the concrete model of parliamentary conversation". She immediately cites his claim that conversation is the "gist and meaning of democracy" from *The Voice of Conversation in the Education of Mankind*.[158] If conversational politics "includes" parliamentary deliberation, it is more than such deliberation. Her immediate invocation of Oakeshott's broad claim about democracy suggests that she sees in his reflection a kind of conversational democracy that goes beyond the legislative body and is, in some significant sense, cultural and societal, as she has already claimed. She communicates less directly what Wallach correctly states succinctly, when he writes of Oakeshott's theorization of conversation, "the free-flowing, open-ended, tolerant exchange of views — as the proper form for a community's moral and political deliberations".[159]

In the Epilogue to his *Introduction* to Oakeshott's thought, Franco summarizes civil association as follows:

> Oakeshott's ideas of civil association and the conversation of mankind are ... linked in several ways. First, both ideas reflect Oakeshott's consistent opposition to the reductive and Gnostic tendencies of our age and his profound appreciation of the variety, contingency, diversity, and complexity of human life. Second, the theory of culture embodied in the conversation of mankind in many ways provides the ultimate justification for Oakeshott's ideal of civil association. The gift of civil association ... is a negative gift, making possible the more substantial

---

154   Soininen, 52. This version is opposed, by Soininen, to the "politics of consensus" and the "politics of conflicts" theorized by Raz and Berlin. See Joseph Raz, *The Morality of Freedom* (Oxford: Clarendon Press, 1986); and Isaiah Berlin, "Two Concepts of Liberty", in Berlin, *The Proper Study of Mankind: An Anthology of Essays*, H. Hardy and R. Hausheer, eds. (London: Pimlico, 1988).

John Wallach refers to the nonteleological communitarianism of Rorty, "and his guide, Michael Oakeshott", in "Liberals, Communitarians, and the Tasks of Political Theory", op. cit., 591, cf., 598.

155   *Ibid.*, 102

156   *Ibid.* Cf. Franco, "'Conversation,' like 'intimation,' evokes open-endedness and flexibility ... ", *Michael Oakeshott: In Introduction*, 93.

157   *Ibid.*, 103, 107, 112, 135, 145, and 155.

158   *Ibid.*, 156. "The Voice of Conversation", *What Is History?* 195 (emphasis, mine).

159   Wallach, 599.

fulfillment of human beings in the realm of culture understood as a conversation.[160]

Franco is correct in seeing the intimate connection between conversation and civil association, and one is assisted in this realization just insofar as deliberation is seen as a type of conversation, but yet entirely in keeping with everything Oakeshott says about conversation more broadly. Franco obviously sees no disjunction between Oakeshott's conceptualizing of conversation and civil association, and this can only mean that there is no second-class status, in his view, given to conversation, as opposed to deliberation. Franco is also correct in his agreement with Soininen, that the metaphor of conversation does not only apply to the style of politics he theorizes but that it is even larger; it signifies the kind of culture he conceptualizes. Civil association is widely described as Oakeshott's theory of civil society, and undoubtedly, connection between a culture of a certain kind and civil association is entirely warranted.[161] Franco also rightly notes the liberal character of civil association in that it allows for a wide variety of ways agents can pursue and find "substantial fulfillment" within such moral (free and noninstrumental) association.

It is hoped that my summary and consideration of contingency, and conversation, have prepared the ground for further reflection on civil association in respect to additional matters that relate to the question of democracy.

"A Democratic Oakeshott?"

As I mentioned in the first chapter, Mapel, Mouffe, and Gerencser deal with the question of in what respects Oakeshott is a democrat in explicit, albeit quite brief, ways. In this section I summarize their arguments and then respond to them. Here, then, I offer some part of my overall argument in respect to how I shall answer Gerencser's question, "A Democratic Oakeshott?" My interrogation of their arguments, coupled with my responses, goes some way toward my explication of a democratic Oakeshott. In short, I can forecast my answer: I think Mapel and Mouffe offer, overall, strong reasons to understand Oakeshott's theory as entirely compatible with participatory and deliberative democracy. I think Gerencser offers a flawed argument in which he sees Oakeshott's demo-

---

160 Franco, *Michael Oakeshott: An Introduction*, 184. Cf. Oakehshott, *Hobbes on Civil Association* (Indianapolis: Liberty Fund, 2000), 79. Franco continues, "By viewing Oakeshott's idea of civil association in relation to his conception of mankind, one sees that he offers us a political philosophy that is more comprehensive and inspiring than, say, the political liberalism of Rawls, and possibly any other liberalism since Mill's". In this conclusion, Franco agrees with Walsh; but it is outside our purview to consider Oakeshott's liberalism as such.

161 A valuable, perhaps book-length, contribution to Oakeshott studies would include a significant treatment of civil association in relationship to civil society theory, and in this context, the consideration of Oakeshott's reflections about culture. It is in such consideration that Franco cites *Hobbes on Civil Association*, 79.

cratic commitments as truncated at the level of constitutional authority. I believe I defeat his argument and show that Oakeshott's theory is at least as democratic as Mapel and Moufee argue.

David Mapel claims that "Oakeshott's view of authority is compatible with a wide variety of political arrangements, including ... . participatory democracy ... it is a mistake to think of civil association as a competitor with participatory democracy ... ".[162] What one should want to know is how Mapel comes to this conclusion. I will need to interrogate not only "Civil Association and the Idea of Contingency", but (to a lesser degree) an essay published two years later, "Purpose and Politics: Can there be a Non-Instrumental Civil Association?" which I will consider first. My investigation of Mapel, Mouffe, and Gerencser will serve as a vehicle to, among others things, help us exegete Oakeshott's conception of law and authority in civil association.

No small number of interpreters have been vexed by Oakeshott's claim that civil association is noninstrumental and nonpurposive. It is so because morality is noninstrumental and nonpurposive, and civil association is moral association; but then, many are confused by such an account of morality as well (the "standard account" has a strong hold in modern and contemporary culture). Mapel undertakes to show in what respect Oakeshott's theorization is coherent. His consideration of this question brings him to correctly state that civil association has authority "because it is acknowledged to have authority; there is no other basis on which it could have authority ... [and if]

> we distinguish the question of *how* a civil association *could* possess authority from the question of *why* it *should* have authority, this view is not as surprising as might first appear. It is roughly similar, for example, to the "positivist" view of legal theorists such as H.L.A. Hart, who base the existence of a legal system on ... "rules of recognition".[163]

I used the legal theorist James Boyd White in the previous chapter to make a similar point, but Hart is often cited for just the purpose displayed by Mapel—to help explain Oakeshott's theory of law and authority. Nevertheless, Oakeshott also writes that there are some requirements of justice in civil association that are "inherent, not in the notion of a just law, but of law itself ... . It is only in respect of these considerations that it may perhaps be said that *lex injusta non est lex*".[164] Mapel notes that this "appears to complicate matters greatly, since the claim that 'an unjust law is not law' is of course associated with the natural law position, not with ... legal posi-

162 Mapel, "Civil Association and the Idea of Contingency", 405. He refers to John Wallach, 599.
163 Mapel, "Purpose and Politics: Can there be a Non-Instrumental Civil Association?" 67. He cites Hart, *The Concept of Law* (Oxford: Clarendon Press, 1961).
164 Oakeshott, "The Rule of Law", *On History and Other Essays*, 152–53. Although the quote here is not from *On Human Conduct*, his theorization of law in both places is mutually supportive and similar.

tivism... ". The claim that an inner morality exists in legitimate law echoes the principal critic of Hart, Lon Fuller. Fuller argued that law must be understood as intrinsically "purposive". So here Oakeshott makes claims that align with both Hart and the positivists, on one hand, and Fuller and the natural law tradition, on the other. How is this (at least apparent) contradiction to be reconciled?[165]

Mapel correctly notes that Oakeshott's use of the conception of an "ideal character" and other features of his theorization of law and civil association places him in territory at some distance from both Hart and Fuller. He is not *defining* law at all but, rather, *describing* an ideal character called "civil association or 'the rule of law.'" In "The Rule of Law" Oakeshott

> summarizes the idea of civil association both in terms of the positivist idea of a procedure that allows us to identify law independently of morality and in terms of the inner morality of law. And he adds a third important feature ... [he] says that civil association is concerned with a justice of its own that is "neither arbitrary, nor unchanging, nor uncontentious, and that [is] the product of a moral experience which is never without tensions and internal discrepancies.[166]

Oakeshott adds that what

> this mode of association requires for determining the *jus* of law is not a set of abstract criteria but an appropriately argumentative form of discourse in which to deliberate the matter; that is, a form of moral discourse ... focused narrowly upon the kind of conditional obligations a law may impose, undistracted by prudential and consequential considerations ... ".[167]

So far, then, I have shown that Oakeshott, in describing (not defining) the relationship between morality and law, as a means to discovering law's authority, has noticed three historical dimensions or features of law: its proceduralism, its "inner morality", and what I shall call a "structural" morality. That is, law is authoritative insofar as it is consonant with morality and insofar as its own structure is of a moral kind. Such a structure demands that law cannot be arbitrary, unchanging, uncontentious, without tensions and discrepancies. Additionally, civil association is concomitantly and relevantly discursive, argumentative, and deliberative about the moral reasons that justify, endorse, or demand particular laws.

Mapel is troubled by Oakeshott's moral theory insofar as a moral practice, on his account, cannot be completely noninstrumental. I have just quoted and summarized Oakeshott's claim that moral discourse and deliberation in relation to the validity of specific laws is entirely true to civil association. Mapel would, it seems, see this as an instrumental feature of morality, but it is not, if what Oakeshott means by

---

165 Mapel, 68. Lon Fuller, *The Morality of Law* (New Haven: Yale Press, 1963).
166 Mapel, 70; "The Rule of Law", 155–56.
167 "The Rule of Law", 156.

noninstrumentality is properly (on Oakeshott's account) understood. Moral consideration of law is necessary to civil association when such consideration is not bent to predetermined outcomes, satisfaction of wants, or enterprises. Further, the imposition of moral theorems, rules, principles, systems, and the like, upon civil association violates the integrity of civil association. But the merit of laws or potential laws in relation to moral considerations does not necessarily impose such motivation or conduct as specified above on an association.

Yet Mapel goes some way in comprehending Oakeshott on his own terms when he argues that he must have "something like" the specification of moral and legal rules in mind when writing about "adjudication" and "legislation" in respect to civil association. Mapel borrows from Henry Richardson to explain that specifying a moral (or legal) rule is different from "applying" it deductively or "balancing" it intuitively; nor is it a combination of these methods. Specifying is an *ad hoc* procedure which is discursive in nature, and it both allows one to see the original point of a norm while at the same time, it extends the meaning of that norm. This means the norm cannot itself be absolute and must be revisable.[168] I see consonance between Richardson's theory and Oakeshott but am free of the anxiety which motivates Mapel to spell out this connection. Richardson is interested in determining a way to solve moral problems, but this agenda is, for Oakeshott, already mistaken. The respect in which Mapel understands Oakeshott on Oakeshottian terms is accurate insofar as Richardson's theory helps him to see that Oakeshott is not interested in moral deduction or balancing, but more interested in "amplifying" the "meaning" of *lex* by analogical- not analytical-reasoning.[169]

Mapel concludes that "we may discover that we need (and can provide) more 'normative' or 'substantive' moral and political theory than Oakeshott thinks possible". He continues,

> In short, I do not think that we are in a position to assess whether civil association is logically (let alone, practically) possible, if what we mean by a "civil" association is a completely "non-instrumental" form of association that adjudicates and legislates without ever 'balancing' various substantive interests ... . If we find that we cannot completely escape the need to consider external consequences in morality, law, and politics, then civil association will prove neither a defensible idea nor practical ideal.[170]

---

168 Mapel, 76; Henry S. Richardson, "Specifying Norms as a Way to Resolve Concrete Ethical Problems", *Philosophy and Public Affairs*, 19. no. 4 (Fall 1990), 279–310.

169 Mapel, 77. For an insightful comparison of analogical versus analytical moral reasoning and argument, see Kovesi, Porter, and Pinches, op. cit., but all three find the origins of this distinction in Thomas Aquinas. A critique of the "standard account" or morality summarized above would penetrate the analytical aspect of modern moral theories.

170 *Ibid.*, 78.

Mapel sees that civil laws do not involve particular purposes, but he also thinks that civil laws can and do forbid "action-types", and so in this respect civil association must involve some restriction of freedom. "Indeed", he writes,

> all laws have purposes. Therefore, a civil association must have as many purposes as it has laws. Yet … there is *no* set of purposes that it *must* have; in this sense, Oakeshott has articulated an interesting idea of a minimal state, one that is united by nothing other than an acknowledgement of its authority".[171]

Lastly, Mapel concludes that if the meaning of "nonpurposive" is "noninstrumental", then one cannot determine whether a completely noninstrumental association is possible. The assessment of this question hangs on to what degree laws can be "specified" rather than deduced, weighed, or balanced.

One need only address a few remarks to Mapel at this juncture, before we consider "Civil Association and the Idea of Contingency". It seems that Oakeshott has answered Mapel's question as to whether substantive interests and external consequences can be debated in civil association. He is clear that moral consideration of particular laws is appropriate, on the terms I have summarized above. There is nothing contentious in Mapel's conclusion that in civil association "action-types" can be forbidden and that certain kinds of freedom are curtailed. Oakeshott could not possibly disagree. Mapel is also clearly right in the conclusion that civil association disallows a set of *necessary* purposes and that it consists in respect to a particular understanding of agreed-upon authority.

Where he goes wrong, I think, is in the notion that Oakeshott's theory mandates a "minimal state". To be clear, Oakeshott certainly endorsed a "minimal" state vis-à-vis what he saw as many overreaching embodiments of Rationalism and the politics of faith alive and well in his day, but this fact is not related by logic or necessity to his theorization of civil association as such. Nothing in his conceptualization of civil association necessitates a "minimal" state, and indeed, the question of what a "minimal" state might even mean is not discussed by Oakeshott in those terms. The infrastructure of civil association allows for *cives* in all their diverse interests and robust freedom to give to the state whatever responsibilities they so choose, as long as powers given to the state do not, of course, obliterate the infrastructure of civil association. It is an interesting question if there are powers citizens might give the state such that the erosion of civil association is launched, if and when those citizens act consonantly to civil association in making their decisions. Mapel, however, has not engaged this complicated question; he only assumes a "limited" state as a necessary outcome of Oakeshott's theorization of civil association.

---

171 *Ibid.*

A civil association can contain any number of instrumental and purposive decisions *within* it, and, in fact, no alternative is possible. What a civil association cannot be, on Oakeshott's terms, is *itself* purposive and instrumental. If the claim, "Civil association is *for* ... " has an answer, is completed, Oakeshott's terms have been violated. It seems, however, that this claim can go uncompleted, and insofar as it need not be completed, civil association is possible. My point here does not seek to obviate the fact that civil association names an ideal character, and that no actual or pure civil association has existed. The point is only that Oakeshottian civil association, as I understand it, is not incoherent or logically impossible.

With Mapel's understanding of civil association as I have summarized it, in mind, and as background, I turn to a further consideration of his thought, this time, in respect to his reflection on the relationship of civil association and democracy. As above, I offer both a brief summary and a brief evaluation. Mapel argues that civil association is "unified by the 'hidden thought' of contingency" and (as one has already seen), that civil association does have one purpose in a "definitional sense", to

> express and protect the realization *by* "agents" that they *are* "agents".
> Put another way, civil association has the fundamental purpose of
> privileging the view that all human self-understandings are ultimately
> 'contingent' or foundationless ... this interpretation does make a kind
> of sense of Oakeshott's description of civil association as "purpose-
> less" and does establish a conceptual connection between civil associa-
> tion and political freedom. This interpretation of [*On Human Conduct*]
> also reveals a conception of authority that even Oakeshott's harshest
> democratic critics should be prepared to accept.[172]

Unsurprisingly, Mapel focuses on the dimension of meaning in contingency which consists in the ability of agents to choose particular, contingent, responses and actions. What makes enterprise association a "self-contradiction", as opposed to civil association, is that agents who are, by definition, free cannot be so in an association, which by its definition, diminishes freedom. "Only an association with no 'policies' whatsoever, that is, civil association, is fully compatible with respect for agency or freedom."[173] Of course, Oakeshott is not opposed to enterprises and so cannot be opposed to persons and groups pursuing them; what he is opposed to is any given enterprise giving ultimate and comprehensive guidance to a society. Mapel writes that what is opposed is an enterprise "state", and this is certainly correct.[174] Enterprise association consists in compulsory purposes and compulsory policies which turn laws into com-

---

172 David Mapel, "Civil Association and the Idea of Contingency", 392, 393.

173 *Ibid.*, 396. The reference to enterprise association as a "self-contradiction" is from *OHC*, 119.

174 *Ibid.* On my interpretation, if an enterprise association has sufficient influence over a society and yet somehow this influence is not institutionalized in the state, it could still violate the meaning of a civil association and that society would be an enterprise association (if I can employ these terms in a clumsy either/or way, for the moment). Mapel's reduction of the

mands, laws that are not subscribed to but rather obeyed, and laws that are commands are incompatible with freedom. Mapel writes that "individuals are certainly unfree whenever they perform an action solely because someone in authority demands that they perform it", and he sees this lack of freedom in civil, as well as enterprise association.[175]

However, Mapel does not fully appreciate Oakeshott's theorization of the ideal character of subscription. A citizen can freely perform an action because it has been demanded just insofar as the structure of demand, the system of authority, has been subscribed to, rather than coercively imposed. Again, my claim does not mean to obviate the fact that in real societies and states, citizens frequently do obey commands solely because they are commanded, but they also know of subscription. Most of us have membership in associations which are structured with such freedom, giving space for such freedom, that we do think we are subscribing to demands, endorsing them in one respect, even when we disagree with the particular substance of any given demand. Churches, for example, function this way. Persons subscribe to "demands" even when they disagree with all or part of the particularities of the demands, just because the infrastructure of subscription is seen to be more important than the particularities of the demands. Of course, such subscription tests one's ability to persist in subscribing, one does not continue in doing things unhappily if it can be avoided. In a system of subscription, the character and substance of demands are subject to change, so that one may come to "happily" subscribe to this or that demand. As an ideal character, and a theoretical construct, civil association is not incoherent if one sees Oakeshott's understanding of subscription in this way. Inasmuch as my understanding of subscription is correct, one can immediately see that it is a democratic conception. Indeed it is not far in its basic character from the contract theorists' conception that it is the will of the people that legitimizes and governs the state. Subscription means that authority derives from subscribers.

Oakeshott theorizes the difference between subscription to rules and obedience to commands in a way that comports with the description I have just suggested. However, Mapel does not accept this explanation. He writes,

> "Ask yourself", the Oakeshottian might say, "where does respect for agency come from? Does it come from the idea of the state as compulsory undertaking aimed at some (supposedly) common good? Or does

---

concept to the state seems to me to be too narrow an interpretation. On my account, agents could have their freedoms curtailed by enterprises not chosen by themselves in ways that can stand outside of the state. My claim is theoretical insofar as it is clear that in nearly all cases of enterprise association, the state is involved in the regimes and apparatuses that influence and enforce enterprises of the sort we are discussing. I am making a Foucaultian claim here, although space does not allow an elaboration of the argument.

175 *Ibid.*, 397.

it more likely come from the idea of civil association, which is essentially a translation of the idea of individual agency into operational
terms?"[176]

His reply to this way of putting the matter is that it reifies the ideas of
civil and enterprise association, that people and institutions exhibit tendencies while logical constructs or ideal types cannot. Also, he claims that
enterprise association can contain both rules and commands (whereas
civil association contains only rules), and so Oakeshott's either/or dichot-
omy breaks down. Mapel sees Oakeshott as relying, then, on false distinctions. Where enterprise association has policies and civil association has
rulings, what's at stake? "All rules can be redescribed in terms of their purposes and vice versa … . All rules are 'purposive' and constraining and
therefore 'substantive'; but all rules are necessarily general in character
and therefore 'formal' as well."[177]

I am not certain that I entirely understand Mapel's claim of reification.
After all, the "logical" constructs and ideal types he claims cannot exhibit
tendencies are constructs and ideal types ("characters") *of* and *about* people and institutions. When he sees policies and rules as interchangeable
and allows that rules can be described as to their purposes, this simply
seems to betray a misunderstanding of the distinction Oakeshott theorizes, rather than Oakeshott proffering a distinction which is false. All
rules are purposive and substantive only on the most minimal, and even
trite, meaning of "purpose" and "substance". Oakeshott has in mind the
kinds of substantive purposes that people invoke to justify, explain, and
guide their cultures, societies, and states. When the French go to war to
save culture, the Germans go to war to save the Fatherland, and Ameri-
cans go to war to make the world safe for democracy, we see enterprise
association and its concomitant commands rather clearly.[178] I am not suggesting that only purposes of this scope and power are substantive or purposive, but the meaning Oakeshott theorizes runs in this direction, toward
controlling ideas and identities. It seems to trivialize his theorization in
reducing it to *all* rules regardless of how small and narrow they are. Does
the rule to stop at a red light constitute an enterprise association? Is there a
threshold of a certain number of such rules that once crossed constitutes
enterprise association?

Mapel is more helpful when he addresses the relationship between civil
association and contingency directly. He notes that agency means the ability to question practices and, surely one should add, any and all aspects of
human conduct. It follows that

---

176   *Ibid*. Mapel notes "I owe this objection to Timothy Fuller".
177   *Ibid.*, 398.
178   Oakeshott notes that war "in a modern European state is the enemy of civil association", and
that a state turned to war has "indisputably turned in the direction of association in terms of
substantive purposes", *OHC*, 272–73.

any association that insists that certain purposes or conditions must be *necessarily* approved as rational, beneficial, or morally desirable cannot, therefore, be based on this understanding of the self as agent ... . this self-understanding rules out all compulsory enterprises that seek to ground their authority in terms of the rational necessity of some collective aim.[179]

Mapel rightly argues that one way civil association seeks to reflect this understanding of agency and contingency is to divorce approval and authority. This is true in the sense I sought to describe above when I discussed subscription; but there is also a dimension of authority coming from subscription, and therefore coming from approval. The question is, Approval of what? I wrote of the approval of a system of subscription, but this is, of course, civil association. That is, what citizens approve is their association and its structure of rules (*lex*), not the specifics of all specific rules or the specific outcomes of all ruling. Mapel puts it wonderfully,

We approve of civil association as a whole precisely because it does not require us to approve of *any* of its particular laws, purposes, or policies. And we approve of *not* having to approve of any particular laws or policies because we understand that as contingent beings we can *always* come to disapprove what we previously found desirable. In a civil association ...

Citizens understand that the purpose of divorcing approval and authority is not to insulate authority from criticism but to reflect their understanding that criticism is *always* possible. Political freedom is not merely compatible with this rationale for authority but intrinsic to it.[180]

I am at a point in consideration of Mapel's interpretation of Oakeshott where I can begin to turn to the implications of civil association for democratic theory. Mapel correctly notes that the separation of authority from approval, echoing in some ways, my description of subscription, does not lead to the conclusion that Oakeshott endorses authority such that he simply justifies the status quo. He quotes Oakeshott's observation that "the claims of governments to authority have been supported, for the *most* part, by the most implausible and gimcrack beliefs which few can find convincing for five minutes together and which bear little resemblance to the governments concerned".[181]

Once civil association is understood as entailing the conception of radical agency I have been arguing, agency that is capable of questioning and revising itself and all institutions, and once one sees that civil association is just the collective dimension, or civil condition of this agency, one can begin to see the openness, flexibility, and liveliness of civil association. Mapel rightly concludes that there are affinities between Oakeshott' conception of the modern state and that of Foucault. "For example, Oakeshott

---

179 *Ibid.*, 401.
180 *Ibid.*
181 *OHC*, 191 (emphasis, mine); Mapel, 403.

continually stresses that the development of the modern state has been accompanied by the growth of an enormous apparatus of control and surveillance and by a steady effort to impose a substantive conception of virtue on recalcitrant subjects."[182] If *On Human Conduct* and civil association cannot be a justification of any existing power, and if this theorization of civil association has the purpose of rethinking the relationship between power and authority, and redrawing the distinction between them along nonfoundationalist lines,[183] then democratic space is opened and is, it seems, intrinsic to civil association. This is the exegesis of *On Human Conduct* which allows Mapel to conclude that Oakeshott's view of authority is compatible with a wide variety of political arrangements, including participatory democracy. The structure of agency and authority described above "opens up the maximum amount of space for criticism. Participatory democrats should therefore recognize this view of authority as their own ... ".[184]

Certainly participatory democrats can conceptualize authority in ways at *some* distance from Oakeshott, and so if Mapel's claim is taken in a strict and most literal manner, it is an overstatement. But there is no doubt that Oakeshott's theorization of authority in civil association is a robustly democratic conception; it simply cannot be otherwise. I think it also true that no participatory democrat could conceptualize authority in ways far different than Oakeshott (which is perhaps the meaning of Mapel's claim). Mapel seizes upon the "maximum amount of space for criticism" in civil association as the leading indicator of participatory democracy. Oakeshott's theorization of agency, freedom, and civil association certainly does entail just this open space for criticism, the theorization of the relationship between authority and subscription should not be overlooked as yet another source for participatory democracy. This is to say that although subscription to rules is not inconsonant with critique, it is also necessarily related to mechanisms for agreement. The possibility of disagreement is crucial to democratic theory, but, of course, the possibility of agreement is as well. Authority by subscription names a system of agreement that also holds the possibility for criticism. This is an essential component of all democratic regimes of authority, and of liberal and democratic politics more generally.

Chantal Mouffe uses Oakeshott to conceptualize the nature of political community "under modern democratic conditions", and she argues that one needs to "go beyond the conceptions of citizenship of both the liberal

---

182 Mapel, 404. He cites *OHC*, 310. Cf. Mapel's comment that "If anything, in *HC*, Oakeshott is more contemptuous of the idiocies of the right than of the left", ibid, 403. Cf. my claim in footnote 174 that limiting enterprise association (and Rationalism and the politics of faith) to the state is too narrow and particular, and in this view I am agreeing with Foucault.

183 As Mapel correctly argues in *ibid.*, 405.

184 *Ibid.*

and the civic republican tradition while building on their respective strengths". She writes that Oakeshott's "idea of the civil association as *societas* is adequate to define political association under modern democratic conditions" in just the way that it transcends the limits of liberal and civic republican theories, and that it "can be very illuminating for such a purpose".[185] She reports on and endorses the conclusion that there is no basic and necessary incompatibility between republican citizenship and modern democracy,[186] thus opening the way for her use of Oakeshott.

She is concerned to formulate the moral character of modern citizenship as a way to escape the relevant limits of liberalism and republicanism. One on hand, an improved theory of citizenship would keep the liberal commitments to ethical pluralism, to the priority of the right over the good, and to freedom and equality for all. She sees these principles as constituting what can be called, in Wittgensteinian fashion, a "grammar" of political conduct. To be a citizen in such a conception is to recognize the authority of these principles and the rules in which they are embodied. This is a liberal democratic understanding of citizenship. On the other hand, she seeks a conception of citizenship that, while not postulating the existence of a common good, nevertheless, "implies the idea of commonality, of an ethico-political bond that creates a linkage among the participants in the association". This theorization would accommodate the distinctions between public and private, and morality and politics, which have been "the great contribution of liberalism to modern democracy, without renouncing the ethical nature of political association".[187] It is by now clear why she is inclined to turn to Oakeshott for help in building this conception. Mapel sees the heart of civil association as opening a wide space for criticism, and thus as profoundly democratic. Mouffe sees the core of his theory as maintaining the moral constitution of a political association without giving up important liberal and democratic commitments.

She reports some features of civil association with which we are now familiar, and particularly the absence of a single substantive idea of the common good and the valorization of individual liberty. Such an association, she writes, is contingent, "without definite shape or a definite iden-

---

185 Chantal Mouffe, "Democratic Citizenship and the Political Community", in *Dimensions of Radical Democracy: Pluralism, Citizenship, and Democracy*, Chantal Mouffe, ed. (London: Verso, 1992), 225, 232. Much of this chapter is also published in Chantal Mouffe, *The Return of the Political* (London: Verso, 1993), 16, 66–73.

186 *Ibid.*, 228. She cites Quentin Skinner, "The Idea of Negative Liberty: Philosophical and Historical Perspective", in R. Rorty, J. B. Schneewind, and Q. Skinner, eds., *Philosophy in History* (New York: Cambridge University Press, 1984); but others, of course, make this basic argument, e.g., Richard Dagger, *Civic Virtues: Rights, Citizenship, and Republican Liberalism* (New York: Oxford University Press, 1997). Note that Dagger's text postdates Mouffe's writing.

187 *Ibid.*, 231.

tity and in continuous re-enactment".[188] She notes that Oakeshott criticizes the liberal view of the state as conciliator of interests, and considers this kind of liberalism as remote from civil association as the idea of a state as a promoter of an interest. She invokes his claim that "it has been thought that the 'Rule of Law' is enough to identify civil association whereas what is significant is the kind of law: 'moral' or 'instrumental'"; and what she finds useful in his conception of civil association is that "while allowing for the recognition of pluralism and individual liberty, the notion of *societas* does not relinquish all normative aspects to the sphere of private morality".[189]

Of course Mouffe is aware of the "conservative use" Oakeshott makes of the distinction between *societas* and *universitas*, but, she writes, "I believe that it is not the only and necessary one".[190] She thinks that the "conservative content" he pours into *respublica*, which can be replaced with "radical principles", is the result of a "flawed idea of politics". This flaw runs counter to Mapel's conclusions in one respect. She thinks that his conception of politics as a shared language of civility is only adequate for one aspect of politics, the "we" side, the "friend's side". "What is missing in Oakeshott is division and antagonism, that is, the aspect of the 'enemy.' It is an absence that must be remedied if we want to appropriate his notion of *societas*."[191] The remedy is not difficult, however, because *societas* can accommodate and include the introduction of "more radical principles"; it can also receive the broadening and conflict-aware features she sees missing. Whereas Mapel appreciates the open space for criticism in civil association, Mouffe sees it as too one-sided, too innocent of antagonism and conflict. Of course, Mapel and Mouffe are not completely at odds here;

---

188 *Ibid.*, 233. Mouffe employs the word "community" (which I have changed to "association"), and seems not to notice Oakeshott's caution about this word in *OHC*. He is careful to note that a civil association, because of its liberal features, is not a community. My comment here should not be taken, however, to indicate that I think Mouffe misunderstands civil association in an important way.

189 *OHC*, 318, in Mouffe, 233, 234. It need not detain us here, but insofar as Mouffe thinks that liberalism advances the instrumental and purposive end of the promotion of self-interest, Oakeshott's civil association is not a liberal conception.

190 *Ibid.*, 234. She notes that, for example, although Oakeshott "targets the idea of redistributive justice", such opposition is not a necessary feature of civil association. "One can perfectly justify state intervention on the basis of a certain interpretation of *respublica*", 239.

  I think Mouffe is correct, as I alluded earlier in my criticism of Mapel's conclusion that civil association endorses a "limited" state. But I am troubled by her langauge: "of a certain interpretation of *respublica*". What we should want to know is what is the *best* interpretation of *respublica* (civil association) and *why* is it best? I think, as I'm sure does Mouffe, that the best interpretation of *respublica* disallows out of hand the exclusion of the possibility of any state intervention and, under the conditions I sketched above, allows robust state intervention. The key to the matter is what *cives* decide for themselves under conditions of contingency and profound agency and freedom. This is the interpretation most coherent and consonant with the whole of *On Human Conduct*.

191 *Ibid.*, 234. On the matter of the importance of conflict in politics, see Bonnie Honig, *Political Theory and the Displacement of Politics* (Ithaca: Cornell University Press, 1993).

their evaluations do not run head-long into one another because they are not dealing with the exact same questions. She is seeking to account for Oakeshott's "conservative content", Mapel is explaining the structure of civil association. Mapel's project need not include this part of Mouffe's, but in the end, they agree. Both see that civil association need not be confined to the interests to which Oakeshott is committed. They see that civil association is not confined to that which, in a sense, Oakeshott has confined it. Put otherwise, civil association accommodates far more than Oakeshott identifies, and Oakeshott obviously did not intend to identify every possible thing as it might be accommodated in civil association.[192]

Mouffe sees civil association as citizens bound together by "their common recognition of a set of ethico-political values. In this case, citizenship is not just one identity among others — as in liberalism — or the dominant identity that overrides all others — as in civic republicanism".[193] The private/public relationship is reformulated to transcend the limits of liberalism and republicanism. In civil association,

> every situation is an encounter between 'private' and 'public,' between an action or an utterance to procure an imagined and wished-for substantive satisfaction and the conditions of civility to be subscribed to in performing it; and no situation is the one to the exclusion of the other.[194]

The distinction of "private (individual liberty)/public (*respublica*) is maintained as well as the distinction individual/citizen, but they do not correspond to discrete separate spheres". These two identities exist in permanent tension that cannot be reconciled. "But this is precisely the tension between liberty and equality that characterizes modern democracy."[195] All situations are private while never immune from the public conditions specified in *respublica*. Wants, choices, and decisions are private because they are the responsibilities and responses to contingency made by agents, but the performances are public and are to subscribe to the conditions of civic association.

> Since the rules of *respublica* do not enjoin, prohibit or warrant substantive actions or utterances, and do not tell agents what to do, this mode of association respects individual liberty. But the individual's belonging to the political community and identification with its ethic-political principles are manifested by her acceptance of the common

---

192 Two small points in this context: First, I think it unhelpful to use the word "conservative" in conjunction with Oakeshott unless the meaning of the word is described just as Oakeshott uses it. As Mouffe employs the term, a reader insufficiently aware of Oakeshott could easily come to have misunderstandings about him. Second, I think "civil association" a better term over against *societas* because the latter term names the historical approximation to the ideal character which is civil association, and I am here doing the work of theory rather than the work of history.

193 *Ibid.*, 235.

194 *OHC*, 183.

195 Mouffe, 238.

concern expressed in the *respublica*. It provides the "grammar" of the citizen's conduct.[196]

Mouffe has meant to theorize a conception of citizenship that contributes to the extension of liberty and equality, which combines the ideals of rights and pluralism with those of "public spiritedness and ethico-political concern". She sees this conceptualization as combining the strengths of liberalism and civic republicanism, while transcending their weaknesses. She refers to this theorization as a "new modern democratic conception of citizenship" which could "restore dignity to the political and provide the vehicle for the construction of a radical democratic hegemony".[197] Indeed, she uses Oakeshott's theory of civil association as *the* essential ingredient of her construction.

My response to Mouffe is threefold. First, and to go beyond my previous comment, in the conflict between Mapel and Mouffe in respect to the question if civil association gives open space to criticism or forecloses it by focusing on the conditions of agreement, Mapel's argument is strongest. Another way to put this question is: How open to difference is Oakeshott's civil association?[198] Mapel sees this conception as profoundly liberal, and institutionalizing agency and freedom in robust ways, and therefore wide open to difference. Mouffe, while seeing Oakeshott's commitment to freedom and equality for all, somehow also sees his notion of "politics as a shared language" as limiting the space for antagonism and conflict. I am not sure why she apprehends this limitation in Oakeshott's theory. He makes it clear in a number of places that language is contentious, never fixed or finished, and that discourse, deliberation, and argument are about choices between *this* or *that*. Further, his theorization of contingency also opens wide space for difference and conflict.

I suspect that she allows what she sees as his "conservatism" to color her analysis. That is, perhaps she reads Oakeshott's conservative "disposition" simply as an endorsement of the status quo. Admittedly, if one were to read "On Being Conservative" apart from most of his work, such a conclusion would have some validity. Given his thought as a whole, it is clear, and especially so in *On Human Conduct*, that (as Mapel argues) Oakeshott has no interest whatsoever in simply abiding things as they are. Further, as both Mapel and Mouffe agree, even if it were the case that Oakeshott used his theoretical work to justify or warrant conventional, and therefore, nonconfrontational conclusions, decisions, or actions, it does not follow that this theory is meant to work exclusively in this way, or in this direc-

---

196   *Ibid.*

197   *Ibid.*

198   On the problem of negotiating difference in democratic politics, see William E. Connolly, *Identity/Difference: Democratic Negotiations of Political Paradox* (Ithaca: Cornell University Press, 1991).

tion. Mouffe thinks some degree of repair or "remedy" must be given to Oakeshott's civil association, where Mapel sees no such repair as being necessary. Even on Mouffe's own terms, however, that remedy is not difficult, one need only "introduce conflict and antagonism into Oakeshott's model".[199]

Second, Mouffe's recognition of the moral character of civil association is important. Her reference to Wittgensteinian moral "grammar" points to something quite similar to Oakeshott's theorization of moral practice.[200] Her rubric of an "ethico-political" community communicates the sense of the indivisibility of morality and politics. In *On Human Conduct*, Oakeshott rejects her language of "community" and rejects her appeal to moral principles. The moral rules he acknowledges are "abridgments" and abstractions, and although at times, perhaps necessary for moral discourse, they do not have the meaning and power that the conventional language of principles, which she uses, contains. Nonetheless, she is right that only civil association *as* a "moral relationship", a "moral condition", a "moral practice", and a "moral association" (all terms employed by Oakeshott) can do the work of transcending the weaknesses of liberalism and civic republicanism as she conceives it. Walsh provides a valuable asset for this part of Mouffe's work; he helps one see how civil association as a moral practice remains deeply liberal while absorbing Aristotelian insights and overcoming some liberal problems, particularly liberal struggles with foundations.

Third, Mouffe agrees with Mapel about the single most important aspect of civil association in respect to its democratic constitution and potential. Both argue that civil association *cannot* be understood as confined to conventional, modest, limited, unadventurous, and conservative dimensions. It seems that one can be satisfied with the status quo and have no interest in change as a member of civil association and do so without violating the terms of civil association; but one cannot coherently understand civil association to underwrite, yet mandate, such conventionalism.

Agents who are robustly free in radically contingent circumstances, who acknowledge the authority of rules that such agents would have created, are *cives* who will not endorse less than democratic association. Morality, on Oakeshottian terms, necessitates democratic relationships in political association. The moral agents who are free in contingency are just

---

199 *Ibid.*, 234.
200 Richard E. Flathman extends beyond Wittgenstein: "Oakeshott's idealized conception of rule of law association and of rule-governed practice more generally carries further the Montaignian-Hobbesian-Bakhtinian, the Wittgensteinian-Derridian exposure of the practices and institutions, and more particularly the beliefs and ideologies that most commonly inform and pervade them, that bear the names of ruling, rules, and rule following". In Flathman, *Reflections of a Would-Be Anarchist: Ideals and Institutions of Liberalism* (Minneapolis: University of Minnesota Press, 1998), 76.

those who "postulate a state in terms of *societas*". There can be no doubt that such a state is understood by Oakeshott as democratic; the interesting question is, Democratic in what respects? This is, of course, the question to which this book is bent, and it cannot be sufficiently answered at this point.

Steven Gerencser draws on the work of Mapel and Mouffe in order to make his own argument about Oakeshott's relationship to democratic theory. He seeks to answer the question posed by the title of his article, "A Democratic Oakeshott?"[201] We are best served, I think, to simply record Gerencser's own forecast and summation of his argument before I begin to examine and evaluate it. He writes,

> I will argue below that Oakeshott's account does offer the view of authority that Mapel identifies in it, and Oakeshott's conception of civil association does possess the opportunities that Mouffe claims for it. I do, though, suggest that there are some significant limits to Oakeshott's thought for those interested in democracy, and Oakeshott is not only aware of these limits, he explicitly advocates for them.[202]

I find his argument suspect, but only a careful interrogation will allow one to see why. Gerencser agrees that Oakeshott understands himself to have allowed for ample antagonism and conflict in politics and in the "principles" by which civil association is "structured", but Gerencser disagrees with Mapel and Mouffe in that he thinks Oakeshott disallows antagonism and conflict "concerning the recognition of the authority of the conditions specifying their common or public concern". That is, he understands Oakeshott to exclude from politics "all questions about authority of the institutions and conditions of political association".[203] Gerencser rehearses Oakeshott's understanding of the adverbial character of rules, that the recognition of rules as such constitute authority, and that this undergirds the conception of political association as not abusive of freedom because it only asks that its rules be recognized as having authority based on the understanding that they do, as such, not based upon their approval. He rightly notes that this form of recognition "opens up the maximum amount of space for criticism", agreeing with Mapel.

Then he makes an interesting move. Gerencser writes, "However, as much as Oakeshott wants to have done away with the need for consensus, clearly, it is still present: it exists in the unquestioned acceptance of a 'common language' of civility, in the consensus required for the recognition of

---

201   In addition to "A Democratic Oakeshott?", Gerencser treats the question of deliberation and authority in Oakeshott in the last two chapters of his *The Skeptic's Oakeshott*. The argumentation found in the book, however, is found more concisely in the article.

202   Steven Anthony Gerencser, "A Democratic Oakeshott?" *Political Research Quarterly*, 52, no. 4 (December 1999), 846.

203   *Ibid.*, 847.

associates of the authority of the state."[204] In this sentence Gerencser makes two mistakes, and they are the mistakes upon which his argument rests. First, he seems to assume that when Oakeshott calls for the recognition of authority of the rules, as such, of civil association (rather than a correlative relationship of authority linked to approval of the particulars of the rules), that he wants to do away with a need for consensus which is actually still present. His second mistake is the claim that there is a "need for consensus" built into a 'common language' of civility.

I can briefly respond to his connection of "consensus" and civil discourse, or a "common language of civility". Oakeshott understands conversation generally and conversation employed in political discourse to be a practice of freedom. Just because it is a practice of order and authority (rules of grammar, etc.), it makes possible communication, self-disclosure, and self-enactment. It enables freedom and is enriched by freedom. Oakeshott's analogy between morality and language is polyvalent; but one aspect of the analogy is just that because language can withstand abuses, distortions, changes, and even partial breakdowns without having its essential character destroyed, it tells something about moral practice. If both language and the civil condition as a moral practice enjoy such freedom, flexibility, diversity, and even abuse, how can a "common language of civility" demand "consensus"?[205]

Gerencser is eight pages into his argument when he writes this sentence, which is the turning point of his argument, but he has not yet written anything up to this point providing the reasons why he would make these two claims. At this point, this sentence appears as an assumption. Perhaps what he writes after this sentence informs the reader satisfactorily about its claims. He undertakes to understand how it is that *cives* come to recognize a rule, and *respublica*, as authoritative. Before I continue my analysis, it seems helpful to be reminded of what Oakeshott means by *respublica*. It is "a practice of civility specifying, not performances, but conditions to be subscribed to in choosing performances, and therefore the common or 'public' concern, not the common purpose, of *cives*".[206] It is here, in *respublica*, that Gerencser understands Oakeshott to disallow disagreement, but how is this claim made? He rightly acknowledges that *respublica*

> may have power, but that's not what maintains *respublica*, a common good may result from the civil condition, but this is not what it pursues ... .
>
> Civil association, by not founding authority upon the desirability or "approval of conditions the conditions it prescribes" or dependence on "approved moral ideals, with a common or general interest",

---

204 *Ibid.*, 853.
205 Again, see "The Tower of Babel", *RP*, 468; and *OHC*, 63–67 for a description of the analogy between morality and language. Cf. Candreva, 110; and Walsh, 56–62.
206 *OHC*, 183.

> allows for a wide range of what Oakeshott understands to be
> freedom ... .

Then, however, he continues,

> A difficulty remains, however, because civil association does still
> require a consensus about what ought to be acknowledged as authori-
> tative. Oakeshott has merely moved the place of required consensus
> from that regarding a substantive purpose, good or end, to that
> regarding authority.[207]

Gerencser repeats the same move. He assumes that because the authority of the civil condition does not rest upon approval of the specificities of
its rules, that the only understanding available is that somehow a "consensus" has come to exist that must be given undeliberated acquiescence.
Grerencser does not suggest either how Oakeshott accounts for the existence of this "consensus", let alone what he means by "consensus". He
uses "consensus" quite loosely, somewhat like "agreement". In that case,
he is saying that Oakeshott thinks that there needs to be agreement about
respublica, the authoritative adverbial rules specifying the conditions of
the common good. However, he thinks such agreement to have come
about in Oakeshott's theory, without discourse, deliberation, or argument
and, therefore, derivatively, without tradition, practices, or politics. If
Gerencser employs "consensus" in its accurate sense and means to indicate that Oakeshott theorizes *respublica* as necessarily constituted by absolute agreement, agreement without dissent, then the same problem holds,
and holds more strongly.

Of course the greater problem in Gerencser's account is the assumption
that authority of *respublica* exists without having come to exist. He thinks
that Oakeshott fails to give an account of civil association that explains its
authority because he understands Oakeshott to have, in telling us that the
rules of civil association have their authority simply because they are the
rules, made an impossible demand. Certainly Oakeshott is making an
impossible demand if he has written what Gerencser has taken him to
have written. Gerencser is certainly right that an agreement (but not consensus) is necessary "about what ought to be acknowledged as authoritative", but he still has not shown the reader where or how "Oakeshott has
merely moved the place of required consensus from that regarding a substantive purpose ... to that regarding authority". It is still impossible to see
where Oakeshott actually disagrees with Gerencser. In fact.

> Oakeshott never denies that there are disagreements about the desir-
> ability of the conditions of *respublica*; to the contrary, it retains a place
> for such disagreement. Politics is what Oakeshott understands to be
> the forum for deliberation and disagreement concerning the desirabil-
> ity of differing ideals to be incorporated in *respublica* ... . Politics is an

---

207 Gerencser, 854.

activity of deliberation about the particular conditions that constitute *respublica*.[208]

Gerencser rightly notes that it is here that the "conflict and antagonism" that Mouffe thinks needs to be introduced already exists. Yet what troubles Gerencser is that politics concerns the deliberation of conditions, "but not their authority".[209] He claims that Oakeshott "completely excludes from politics any discussion concerning whether those rules, or the institutions and procedures through which they are created and interpreted, are authoritative".[210] It is, however, still not clear where or how Oakeshott is guilty of this charge. Gerencser references page 128 of *On Human Conduct* in support of this claim, but I cannot see such support in this text. Gerencser writes that Oakeshott has "presumed consensus ... in the recognition of its authority", in reference to Oakeshott's statement that politics requires assent to authority (see footnote below), but there is no warrant for this conclusion. Oakeshott's claim is conventional and well understood: politics can only take place within a structure of authority. It does not follow that authority must exist apart from deliberation or disagreement. Indeed, in the text quoted, Gerencser seems to miss the import of Oakeshott's claim that engagement, exploration, and deliberation of the conditions of desirability in *respublica* requires a relationship to *respublica* — what can this mean if not a relationship to the *authority* of *resupublica*? — which is not only acquiescent, but also "*critical*".

Gerencser acknowledges that Oakeshott has made explicit arguments contrary to what he takes him to be claiming in *On Human Conduct*. He notes that in "Political Education" Oakeshott writes, "Politics is the activity of attending to the general arrangements of a collection of people ... . To suppose a collection of people ... which enjoyed arrangements which intimated no direction for change and needed no attention is to suppose a people incapable of politics."[211] He notes that in the Harvard Lectures, Oakeshott writes,

> Politics is an activity, not of governing, but of determining the manner and matter of government, and where those are predetermined and are regarded as immune from choice or change, there is no place for 'politics.' Thus political activity, the activity in which the composition and conduct *of authority* is considered, discussed, determined, criticized, and modified, may be said to be an invention of Western Europe ... . [Among those matters deliberated are] Thoughts and expectations

---

208 *Ibid.*

209 Oakeshott writes of the "engagement to deliberate the conditions prescribed in *respublica* in terms, not of their authority but of their desirability", and of political engagement as "an exploration of *respublica* in terms of the desirability of the conditions it prescribes, and this entails a relationship to *respublica* which is at once acquiescent and critical. The ingredient of acquiescence is assent to authority. Without this there can be no politics ... ", *OHC*, 163–64.

210 Gerencser, 855.

211 *Rationalism in Politics*, 56.

about the constitution, composition and authorization of the governing authority.[212]

In "The Rule of Law", written after *On Human Conduct*, Oakeshott considers again the relationship of politics and authority. Here he introduces discussion about justice and broadens the discussion about what is "civilly desirable". He writes that politics necessitates arguing that what the rule of law "requires for determining the *jus* of a law is not a set of abstract criteria but an appropriately argumentative form of discourse in which to deliberate the matter".[213] Gerencser concludes that in "The Rule of Law", Oakeshott "wants to emphasize that one can judge a law to be *injus*, or unjust, and still recognize it as a law with authority".[214] That is, in this essay written after *On Human Conduct*, Oakeshott argues that deliberation about matters at the heart of authority can be conducted without destroying authority. Oakeshott argued this before and after *On Human Conduct*, but Gerencser does not see it in *On Human Conduct*.

Gerencser thinks that in *On Human Conduct* Oakeshott has made a radical change in respect to the possibility and necessity of political deliberation and disagreement reaching to the constitution of authority in civil association. Such an interpretation, however, depends on reading texts in the latter book in unnecessary, if not entirely idiosyncratic, ways; and it asks the reader to conclude that Oakeshott is either unknowingly inconsistent, or that he changed his theory in such a substantial manner without explaining the change from views held earlier. Gerencser's interpretation also counts on *On Human Conduct* differing from an essay written after it, which reads more closely to the texts before *On Human Conduct*. His interpretation rests on implausible grounds. In ruminating on Oakeshott's claim that "every adjustment of a *respublica* is a disturbance of the tensions which hold it together and is liable to bring thitherto concealed discrepancies to the surface", Gerencser writes that Oakeshott is "perilously close" to admitting deliberation and disagreement about the authority of *respublica*.[215] Perhaps he is so "close" as to actually allow deliberation and disagreement where Gerencser does not see it.

Gerencser brings democratic theory into the discussion explicitly when he ties his argument to Oakeshott's claim in "The Rule of Law", that

> to favour a so-called democratically-elected legislature is to express a belief that its authority to enact laws will be more confidently acknowledgeable than that of a legislature assembled and constituted

---

212 *Morality and Politics in Modern Europe*, 8, 9 (emphasis, mine).
213 *On History and Other Essays*, 156.
214 Gerencser, 859.
215 *OHC*, 180; Gerencser, 858.

in any other manner; it forecasts nothing whatsoever about the *jus* or *injus* of its enactments.[216]

He sees in this passage the same problem he has identified earlier: the conclusion that Oakeshott has placed deliberation about authority out of reach. There is, however, no such meaning in this passage. He writes, "while he seems to mask it in places, civil association … demands consensus in the matter of belief about authority".[217] Indeed, it is abundantly clear that Oakeshott *does* demand a particular kind of agreement ("consensus", if you will) about authority: that the rules that constitute authority be recognized as such. This is simply a matter of definition for Oakeshott. This demand is, however, not the demand Gerencser sees. He continues to assume that the demand must somehow mean that authority is beyond deliberation. This claim cannot be coherent, once contingency, agency, and history are taken into account; yet Gerencser ascribes it to Oakeshott.

Of course the straightforward reading of this passage in "The Rule of Law" is only the conventional one that (democratically concerned) *cives* are more likely to acknowledge as authoritative laws enacted by democratically-elected legislatures than those constituted in less democratic ways. This is, anyway, the democratic "belief". Oakeshott's claim that such a legislature's constitution forecasts nothing about the justice or injustice of its enactments is also uncontroversial. In *On Human Conduct*, Oakeshott writes that "the word 'democracy,' which properly speaking signifies a manner of constituting a government and of authorizing it to rule, is also used to characterize particular acts or policies … ". He adds,

> This is often a piece of political subterfuge: confident of the approval evoked when 'democracy' is used in its proper constitutional meaning, the word is made to qualify a performance or a policy evoking the same approval. But this confidence trick is an emblem of ambiguity which has infected the vocabulary of all political discourse … ".[218]

Gerencser's conclusion from this passage is, "Now again, Oakeshott wants to preclude from politics any discussions concerning authority."[219] Again, how is this reading of Gerencser's present in the passage? Radical democrats of every and any variety can quite easily agree with Oakeshott here. The text says nothing nor implies anything about the disallowance of politics in discussions concerning authority. Oakeshott is here complaining about the misuse of the word and concept "democracy" when it is used to legitimize, authorize, and suspend critical inquiry about any given act or policy. To abuse a word or concept is to diminish and distort that word or

---

216 *On History and Other Essays*, 152; Gerencser, 859.
217 *Ibid.*, 860.
218 *OHC*, 192–93; Gerencser, 860.
219 *Ibid.*

concept. Radical democrats are no less offended by the misuse of "democracy" than any others.[220]

In sum, Gerencser sees a problem in Oakeshott that does not exist. Only implausible, if not a tortured, reading of selected passages allows him to construct his interpretation, an interpretation out of congruity and consonance with Oakeshott's political theory overall. Gerencser admits that Oakeshott comes "perilously close" to his own view and that Oakeshott "himself acknowledged the contingent and volatile relationship between beliefs about authority and the constitutions and legislative offices and procedures that claim to embody them". Yet he somehow sees Oakeshott as disavowing such deliberation as a part of politics.[221] Gerencser fails to see the depth and extension of Mapel's summary claim that in civil association citizens "understand that the purpose of divorcing approval and authority is not to insulate authority from criticism but to reflect their understanding that criticism is *always* possible. Political freedom is not merely compatible with this rationale for authority but intrinsic to it".[222]

As I briefly explained when discussing subscription, acquiescence does not foreclose difference or deliberation, but Gerencser takes the concept to mean such foreclosure by definition. The acquiescence to authority which Oakeshott—uninterestingly and unsurprisingly—requires is acquiescence to the authority of a civil association as such. If the rules that would constitute authority have no authority, no civil association can exist.[223] Certainly this is what is conventionally meant when one speaks of the necessity of the rule of law. It is *the rule* of law that is necessary, not agreement about any given number of laws. Acquiescence to the institution of *lex* and the constitution of *respublica* does not mean, for Oakeshott, that such institution and constitution are beyond deliberation and disagreement. It means that at the end of the day, one decides to remain a *cives* and

---

220 In "Talking Politics", Oakeshott also complains that the word "democracy" is often abused. For example, in being used as a "utilitarian device", as a "piece of machinery designed, not to express certain beliefs about authority but to fabricate rules and arrangements that promote certain interests". *RP*, 444.

He also refers to "democratic" as a "vague" word (458), and to "democracy" as an "irrelevant expression" (458). This last claim is certainly exaggerated, but his concern altogether in this essay is the "artless muddle" that political discourse has become. He by no means singles out democracy as the only abused, "vague", "confused", and "indeterminate" term in our political vocabulary, there are several such terms. "Talking Politics" was originally an address given in 1975.

221 *Ibid.*, 862.

222 Mapel, "Civil Association and the Idea of Contingency", 401.

223 I am not suggesting that Oakeshott holds a view of authority similar to that too often understood to be Hobbes's view (on what are in my view, poor readings of Hobbes): that any authority that exists is its own justification such that no dissent can be legitimate. To the contrary, Oakehott thinks that if the authority of the civil association cannot be subscribed to, secession and war are options.

Nor am I suggesting that Oakeshott sufficiently theorizes dissent, revolution, secession, or war as appropriate responses to unsubscribable (nonauthoritative) authority.

hope one's deliberation and disagreement directs matters, even matters of authority, in the right direction. It means that liberal and democratic civil associations are based in the authority of provisionally permanent conclusions, decisions, and rules. Traditions and practices are such, for Oakeshott, that they accommodate change while remaining stable. Indeed, it is their nonfoundational, contingent flexibility and adaptability which create stability. This contingent phenomenon, intrinsically connected to our agency and freedom, does not diminish authority; it is the only proper and most satisfactory basis of authority.[224] It "remains the most civilized and least burdensome conception of a state yet to be devised".[225] Flathman helps one see this when he writes that the

> distinguishing features of this vision [of the rule of law in civil association] ... are not its institutions or practices in what we might call their material, rule-governed form, but rather the understandings its *personae* have of themselves, of the relationships with one another, and of the arrangements to which they mutually subscribe ... subscribers to such associations would adopt an affirmative stance toward its rules and the requirements those rules place on them.[226]

It has been important to investigate Gerencser's argument with considerable detail and length. He acknowledges that theorists such as Mapel, Mouffe, Rorty, and Flathman see in Oakeshott a democratic ally.[227] Although he thinks Oakeshott's democracy goes some distance in the right direction, he concludes that as to the basic structure of authority in civil association, Oakeshott's theory comes up short. I have meant to show that the arguments of Mapel and Mouffe stand up against a failed interpretation offered by Gerencser. They think that there are robust democratic possibilities in Oakeshott's theory of civil association, such that Mapel invokes "participatory" democracy and Mouffe, "radical" democracy in connection to Oakeshott's theory. I have not here examined Rorty or Flathman but they, too, see Oakeshott as a robust democratic source. Even Gerencser, the least convinced of the group, sees Oakeshott's democratic *bona fides* as significant, if not sufficiently extensive. In answer to his question, "A Democratic Oakeshott?", Gerencser's reply is "Yes, but not enough". Mapel and Mouffe respond, "Absolutely!"

---

224 Again, Walsh's explanation of the relationship among contingency, tradition, and the authority of moral practice is helpful. Walsh, 56–69.

225 "The Rule of Law", 178.

226 Flathman, 72.

227 Gerencser was evidently unaware of Feaver's essay. In addition to Mapel, Mouffe, et al., he mentions a review of *Rationalism in Politics* in which Colin Flack writes, "Oakeshott is very close here to the foundation of any serious socialist thinking. Emphasizing the concrete and the historical, he is opposed to the politics of slogan and the empty framework of liberal (or any other) values; and his claim that we can only know where to go next on the basis of a thorough understanding of where we have come from is a profoundly Marxist idea". Flack, "Romanticism in Politics", *New Left Review*, 18 (January-February 1963), 68; Gerencser, *The Skeptic's Oakeshott*, 158.

A Democratic Oakeshott

George Feaver thinks that Oakeshott has had quite a lot to say about democracy, and Noël O'Sullivan thinks that Oakeshott offers "a much more precise concept of democracy than that which is found in discourse theorists".[228] O'Sullivan's claim is startling insofar as some discourse theorists have offered fairly developed conceptions of democracy. I do not agree with O'Sullivan in one respect, yet I do in another. In disagreement, there is little which is "precise" in Oakeshott's theorization of democracy inasmuch as he does not give a detailed account of democracy in any one place, following a formula of defining and explicating democracy *by name*. But more importantly, I agree with O'Sullivan insofar as Oakeshott gives detail and precision to his theorization of certain concepts and phenomena which bear some relationship to democracy, and/or it turns out to be democracy that he theorizes. For example, he theorizes agency, freedom, morality, and authority in civil association in precise and detailed ways, and there is no doubt that these conceptions are democratic in the sense that they either necessarily presuppose democracy and/or necessarily are conducive to democracy. To restate succinctly: O'Sullivan is correct insofar as Oakeshott's theory of civil association *is* a theory of democracy. In this section I have removed the question mark from Gerencser's essay title because I conclude with Feaver, Franco, Mapel, Mouffe, and O'Sullivan that Oakeshott was a democrat and has offered, *at the very least*, an incipient democratic theory.

So far, I have undertaken to demonstrate that in all that he writes about democracy explicitly, Oakeshott is an advocate of democracy. Further, he is clear that more extensive, or "radical", theorizations of democracy beyond "representative" and parliamentary versions are welcome and necessary. In those places where he is critical of the use of the concept, it is because "democracy" is being undervalued, diminished, or abused, as, for example, when it is taken to mean merely majority opinion and goverment reflective of majority opinion.[229] If majoritarianism and mere aggregation are criticized by Oakeshott, it is not a signal of antidemocratic impulses but of something closer to the embrace of radical, participatory, and deliberative democracy.

Further, I have meant to show that in all he writes in respect to various features of his political theory, the implications are profoundly democratic. I have chosen to separate his work into the pre-*On Human Conduct* corpus, which I have identified as his "early" or "earlier" work and then to consider, principally, but not exclusively, *On Human Conduct*. At this juncture, I can conclude that Oakeshott's life-long work penetrated democratic

---

228 Personal email correspondence of 3 July 2006.
229 For example, *OHC*, 192–93, 231.

theory here and there, even though he never wrote a sustained piece of democratic theory *as such — unless one takes* On Human Conduct *to be precisely such a theorization.*[230] While I think an argument can be made that this is an entirely coherent way to understand *On Human Conduct*, such an argument, as ironic as it might seem, is surprisingly beside the point. It is irrelevant insofar as one need not label *On Human Conduct* or any of Oakeshott's writings as a piece of democratic theory in order to see democratic theory within it.

I have been considering the relationship between Oakeshott's political theory, understood broadly, and democracy; but I have not yet undertaken a consideration of what is meant by "democracy", at least for the purposes of this project. Before I can advance the final phase and culmination of this argument, I must address the matter of what is meant by democracy and what conceptualizations of democracy are most compelling in respect to Oakeshott's theory. It is uninteresting to conclude that Oakeshott is a democrat if all that is meant is that he is a democrat in a vague or mundane sense. That is, if his theory has nothing to suggest beyond traditional "parliamentary" or "representative" democracy, I have not advanced an interesting thesis. What I shall want to show is that his political theory makes possible interesting and valuable insights into deliberative democratic theory, and that certain features of such deliberative theory cast light on my understanding of Oakeshott. In order to proceed, then, I must now turn to a consideration of the "deliberative turn" in democratic theory.

---

230 This is Franco's and O'Sullivan's understanding.

Chapter Four

Deliberative Democratic Theory

It is hoped that a foundation as been laid. I have meant to describe, specify, and examine features of Oakeshott's political theory sufficiently so as to place the reader in the position of juxtaposing it to democratic theory. I have, of course, identified, described, and interrogated various relationships between certain aspects of his theory and democracy. To the groundwork of the first three chapters, then, I will add a summary of the democratic theory of interest in this project and then, in our last chapter, construct the culmination of the argument. As Oakeshott himself notes, "democracy" has been and is used to mean a great many things. There is no need to rehearse even a small number of these meanings, for, as I have indicated, I am concerned to investigate what relationship might exist between Oakeshott and the "deliberative turn" mentioned in the Introduction. Of course, it must quickly be added that this literature is also far too extensive to receive, as a whole, any significant treatment in one chapter. The last two decades have given birth to a fecundity of thought about richer, more radical, participatory forms of democracy that have in common the essential concept of discourse and deliberation.[1] It should already be clear in some suggestive ways that the Oakeshottian importance of contingency, conversation, deliberation, as well as agency, individuality, and freedom, in conjunction with liberal commitments and his suspicion of Rationalism, the politics of faith, and the controlling power of the state, in addition to his theorization of civil association—all bend his theory toward deliberative democracy. This project is one of both discovery and construction: I will seek to identify with greater clarity (than heretofore possible) what ways his theory is "already bent", in this direction; and I will construct an argument as to how to bend it further (without "breaking", which is to say violating, it). Just as there are always theoretical extensions and elaborations which go beyond not only their immediate

---

1   The implicit comparison in this sentence is to forms of democracy that are (only) representative, majoritarian, aggregative, and constitutional (formal).

contexts, but their immediate understandings and "applications", I will seek to discover and construct the extension and elaboration of Oakeshott's underdeveloped democratic theory in its penetration of deliberative theory.[2]

I will begin by sketching out the meaning of deliberative democracy in its most general conception; that is, I will here offer a brief description and summary of deliberative theory altogether. Then I will offer a brief description and summary of four sources of such theory, those offered by Rawls, Habermas, Dryzek, and lastly, Gutmann and Thompson. The reasons for choosing these four figures (taking Gutmann and Thompson as one "figure") will be identified. It will not be my task to interrogate, examine, and evaluate their theories; but rather, to describe and summarize them.

Deliberative Democracy

The implosion of Soviet totalitarianism seems to have been the catalyst for the explosion of theory in respect to civil society and democracy.[3] Whatever the causes, the early 1990s saw democratic theory take a "deliberative turn". Indeed, the

> essence of democracy itself is now widely taken to be deliberation … .
> The deliberative turn represents a renewed concern with the authenticity of democracy: the degree to which democratic control is substantive rather than symbolic, and engaged by competent citizens.[4]

Deliberative democracy, at this juncture, should not be understood apart from discursive democracy; and for the purposes of this book they can be understood synonymously unless I point to a distinction between them. The idea of deliberation here does not simply refer to the deliberation of political professionals, such as those in the assembly. Rather, the idea is that discourse and deliberation held among a wide array of citizenry, in various ways and contexts, provide democratic legitimacy.

---

2   Note that I refer to Oakeshott's "underdeveloped" democratic theory, as opposed to a notion such as a "precise concept of democracy" Noël O'Sullivan sees in Oakeshott. But to be clear, certainly O'Sullivan is correct in at least one sense: Oakeshott is precise in respect to his theorization of many features of political and (especially) civil association, and such association is democratic, on Oakeshott's own terms. I only depart from Franco and O'Sullivan insofar as Oakeshott does not refer to what he is doing as constructing a theory of democracy.

3   Such an analysis is beyond the scope of this project, but it would be worthwhile, I think, to explore the overlap between civil society theory and democratic theory that seems to have been launched by the fall of the Berlin Wall. I would suggest that the overlap is not insignificant insofar as new democratic, and more democratic forms of citizenship have been theorized as alternatives to the state-centric models or aggregation of interests; and no small part of that democratic space is seen to be in civil society.

    I do not mean to suggest that no such work has been done, only that more needs to be done. See, e.g., Dryzek's fourth chapter in *Deliberative Democracy and Beyond: Liberals, Critics, and Contestations* (New York: Oxford University Press, 2002), "Insurgent Democracy: Civil Society and State", 81–114.

4   John Dryzek, *Deliberative Democracy and Beyond*, 1.

There are concomitant commitments that have an essential relationship to the importance of such deliberation. They include the view of citizens as free and equal, and the related commitments of respect, impartiality, and inclusivity that such free and equal status requires. It follows that citizens must not be coerced or restrained in respect to their access to and participation in democratic processes. Gutmann and Thompson build *Democracy and Disagreement* on the foundation of the principles of reciprocity, publicity, and accountability.[5] These principles also follow from the idea of citizens as free and equal and are, in various ways, a part of all discursive theory. They include the idea that citizens would be sufficiently informed (and educated) so as to carry forward meaningful discourse. Some notion of reasonableness and/or rationality is a part of all deliberative theory. Citizens need to be given reasons for the processes and outcomes that affect their lives, and this reason-giving criterion must be accessible to all (minimally educated adult) citizens.

They include that citizens would have deliberative opportunities in respect, perhaps most particularly, to those matters which affect their lives directly (and about which there are strong arguments for conflicting views) that citizens would have confidence in a relationship between deliberative forums and political action inside the assembly, such that decisions made deliberatively do not run aground in ignorance nor are sunk by hostility. As Dryzek succinctly puts it, "Authentic *democracy* can then be said to exist to the degree that reflective preferences influence collective outcomes".[6]

They include some degree of constitutional protection that is present in all discursive theorists (although how much and what kind of protection is a much-debated matter). That is, there must be legal institutionalization of democratic principles and constitutional and legal protection of the will formation which takes place through discourse. No deliberative theorist thinks that everything should be up for grabs at all times. Some political matters must be settled, if not once and for all, then with highly difficult obstacles to their overturn. The democratic process is seen to be open and dynamic, but eventually, many decisions must be (at least provisionally) binding. Deliberative procedures are seen to be continuous in respect to one matter or another (we never arrive at a perfect political order) and independent of external political validation, that is, they are autonomous.[7]

---

5   Gutmann and Thompson write, in a way all deliberative theorists would endorse: "Deliberative democracy asks citizens and officials to justify public policy by giving reasons that can be accepted by those who are bound by it. This disposition to seek mutually justifiable reasons expresses the core of the process of deliberation. More specifically, the disposition implies three principles- reciprocity, publicity, and accountability ... ", 52.

6   Dryzek, *Deliberative Democracy and Beyond*, 2.

7   Cf. Joshua Cohen, "Deliberation and Democratic Legitimacy," in *Deliberative Democracy: Essays on Reason and Politics*, James Bohman and William Rehg, eds. (Cambridge: MIT Press, 1997), 72.

All theorists committed to discursive democracy engage liberal theory. The continuum of appreciation for liberal constitutionalism and liberal forms of democracy run the gamut from full-blown liberal theories to those highly critical of liberalism. In any case, each deliberative theory must engage liberal democratic theory as it works out its own vision. It can be added that all discursive theory admits of some, liberal and/or republican, notion of popular sovereignty. Similarly, all deliberative theory engages the dialectic of proceduralism and metaphysics. That is, whereas many theorists argue that the ground of political legitimacy resides in the procedures of and in deliberation itself, others allow that metaphysical convictions can and do, for many, ground their political and moral views. The question is to what degree and in what respects can such metaphysical views be allowed in public political deliberation and to what degree must the deliberative process itself be seen as the sole legitimizing ground. As with the relationship to liberal theory, the answers among discourse theorists range widely.

Lastly, deliberative theory is advanced as having value in two general respects. Some theorists emphasize its intrinsic value, that the moral reasons behind deliberation are most important and that it is the best political means of recognizing and realizing the free and equal status of citizens. Other theorists emphasize the instrumental value of discursive democracy. In modern and contemporary liberal and pluralistic societies, it is seen to work better than the alternatives. Here too, I have identified a continuum: while any deliberative theorist may focus attention on either the intrinsic or instrumental value of such democracy, the other value is never absent. The fact of both kinds of value residing within discourse theory leads one to note a final component: its attention to moral values, concerns, and principles.

Indeed, deliberative theory is driven by a certain moral conviction — that other forms of democracy are insufficiently attuned to both our status as moral beings and to addressing moral problems. Put differently, deliberative theorists think that other democratic (let alone nondemocratic) conceptions fail to see how morality demands participatory, discursive democracy; such democracy is a political manifestation of broadly shared moral commitments. The intrinsic value of deliberative democracy is a reflection of conviction about moral norms; and the instrumental value of such democracy is a reflection of the conviction about moral actions and outcomes. The intrinsic value has deontological overtones; the instrumental value holds consequentialist permutations. In short, deliberative theorists are such for moral reasons and think that deliberative theory best responds to the moral challenges and opportunities embedded in politics.

It remains to be added that deliberative democracy will, from time to time, have a comfortable or uncomfortable fit (as any given case may be) with representation, aggregation, bargaining, electoral politics and voting, and power politics more generally; but it is not *necessarily* in conflict with these components of the political process. In fact, deliberative democracy may work best when employed in connection with and checked by other such institutions.[8]

Certainly the summary of criteria and commitments of deliberative democratic theory offered here can be judged to be too expansive or too limited. Nonetheless, I think its value resides in not saying too much or too little about what is meant by deliberative democracy; and while any given theorist might take issue with it in some comparatively small respect, it can confidently be taken to stand as a sufficient approximation of the most important components of such theory, taken altogether. With this summary as background then, I will pursue description and summary of four particular theories.

Rawls and Habermas are of unquestionable importance to deliberative theory: Rawls, because of the power and influence of his theory of justice, and the elaboration of it worked out in *Political Liberalism*; Habermas, because of his rigorous, intricate, and sustained attention to the problem of political and democratic legitimacy.[9] Both have been profoundly influential to a generation of political and democratic theorists. John Dryzek has developed a post-Rawlsian and post-Habermasian discourse theory which builds on their respective strengths but pushes the theory forward. Owing more to the critical theory of Habermas than to the liberal theory of Rawls, he engages other theoretical paradigms (e.g., rational choice, liberal, civil society, and "green" political theory) as a means to explicate and test his own argument. Gutmann and Thompson not only argue for their own version of deliberative theory but have written a widely engaged text on the relationship between such theory and the problem of moral disagreement. Their argument has been influential and contested. The theories utilized below, then, offer an important body of work, essential to the deliberative democracy literature. No candidates for inclusion here, as important as they might be, can be said to be more important.

Rawls

The discussion of Rawls which follows owes to Joshua Cohen, "For a Democratic Society", and Amy Gutmann, "Rawls on the Relationship between

---

8   Ethan Leib writes, "populist deliberative procedures, when checked by other institutions, are decent approximations of legitimacy, which is reason enough to give them a try", in Ethan J. Leib, *Deliberative Democracy in America: A Proposal for a Popular Branch of Government* (University Park: The Pennsylvania State University Press, 2004), 41.

9   Habermas is often thought of as the "father" of discursive democratic theory. Gutmann and Thompson write that "More than any other theorist", he is "responsible for reviving the idea of deliberation in our time, and giving it a more thoroughly democratic foundation". In *Why Deliberative Democracy?* (Princeton: Princeton University Press, 2004), 9.

Liberalism and Democracy"; both essays are contributions to *The Cambridge Companion to Rawls*. Between them, Cohen and Gutmann more than adequately describe, explore, and evaluate Rawls's theory in *A Theory of Justice* and *Political Liberalism* as it relates to democracy. What they do not do is consider his democratic thought in *Justice as Fairness*.[10] Whereas my discussion of Rawls on democracy in respect to the first two texts does not differ significantly from Cohen and Gutmann, I will add a consideration of *Justice as Fairness*. Both Gutmann and Cohen set out to answer the question of to what extent and in what ways Rawls's theory is democratic; and they both reach similar conclusions: it is quite significantly democratic, but it is not as radically democratic as they would like.

As Cohen points out, neither the word "democracy" nor any of its cognates has an entry in the index to *A Theory of Justice*. He adds that the only traditional problem of democracy that receives much sustained attention there is the basis of majority rule, "which is itself addressed principally in the context of a normative model of legislative decisions with an uncertain relation to actual legislative processes".[11] Cohen refers to Rawls's treatment in *Theory* as a "relative inattention to democracy" and as "something of a surprise" when Rawls writes that his conception of justice as fairness in *Theory* "constitutes the most appropriate basis *for a democratic society*".[12] Cohen, in my judgment, does not sufficiently appreciate the way in which Rawls's *Theory* is about democracy. I see *Theory* as concerned with democracy the way that Franco, O'Sullivan and I see Oakeshott's political theory, and *On Human Conduct* in particular, as being about democracy. Rawls and Oakeshott are simply assuming that their discussions are understood as belonging in the context of democratic societies and states. Further, and more to the point, each sees his theory as being so unambiguously democratic that it does not consistently dawn on either of them to explain their theories' democratic features—*as such*. Of course, because Rawls and Oakeshott see their own work in this way does not mean others see it as they do. Regardless of how well it is understood that they assume democratic structures and institutions, whether they sufficiently explicate those structures and institutions is another matter.

Cohen goes on to note that Rawls's work demonstrates a more "intimate democratic connection" from the 1980 Dewey Lectures forward and that the revised version of *Theory* more explicitly elucidates this connection. Rawls now writes that the ideas and aims of justice as fairness are "those of a philosophical conception *for a constitutional democracy*", which he hopes

---

10   We might reasonably suspect that the contributors to this book had to have their essays to the publisher before consideration of *Justice as Fairness* was possible.

11   Cohen, in Samuel Freeman, ed., *The Cambridge Companion to Rawls* (New York: Cambridge University Press, 2003), 86.

12   *Ibid.*

will "seem reasonable and useful ... and express an essential part of the common core of democratic tradition". Cohen simply concludes that although *Theory* is not a theory of democracy, it is a contribution to democratic thought; and in this respect he is exactly right, and commentators widely agree.[13]

Gutmann notes that in both *A Theory of Justice* and *Political Liberalism*, Rawls "does not speak directly about the design of democratic institutions", because the theory is "primarily normative rather than empirical"; nonetheless, he does have "a lot to say about the ideal of free and equal citizenship" and it "is this ideal and its principled implications ... that reveal most about Rawls on the relationship between liberalism and democracy".[14] As does Gutmann, Cohen considers *Theory* and *Political Liberalism* (hereafter, *Liberalism*) together, seeing no radical difference between the two texts in respect to Rawls's treatment of democracy.

Cohen sees three features of Rawls's theory which bear important connections to democracy, or, put differently, three concepts important to democracy that resonate with Rawls's theory. They are the idea of a democratic political regime, the idea of a democratic society, "which means a society whose members are understood in the political culture as free and equal persons", and deliberative democracy, "which means a political society in which fundamental political argument appeals to reasons suited to cooperation among free and equal persons, and the authorization to exercise collective power traces to such argument".[15] The fact that Rawls uses the term "democratic" to refer to both the form of a political regime and to the form of a society identifies an important conviction, that democracy is the political manifestation of the view that members of society are equal. This equality emits to democratic society, which emits to democratic politics.[16] Justice as fairness is democratic at its most basic level because it assigns to individuals the equal right to participate in politics (this right being based upon a more fundamental moral equality among persons, which is conceived in a liberal idiom). Democracy is, on Rawlsian terms, a matter of basic justice. It is addressed to a society of equals, and the content of its rules and agreements ("principles" and "norms" as Cohen puts it) are shaped by a public understanding of the above.

---

13   Cohen, 86–87; Rawls, *A Theory of Justice* (1999), xi (the emphasis is Cohen's). Further references to *Theory* in Cohen refer to the revised (1999) version.

14   Gutmann (in Freeman), 168–69. It seems that Gutmann misconceives the relationship between theory and a problematic such as the design of democratic institutions. While Rawls's work is theoretical, this alone does not keep him from considering such design; and there is no reason why it must. Of course, it is not important to my project here to interrogate or explain what I see as misconception on Gutmann's part. I only register my disagreement so as not to be understood as endorsing this claim as to why Rawls does not "speak directly" about the design of democratic institutions.

15   Cohn, 87, 91–92.

16   Cf. Cohen, 96–97.

For Rawls, the standards of justice are recognized through deliberative and legislative processes but are independent of such processes. The processes are not guaranteed to meet the standards, and, in fact, societies can only have imperfect procedural justice. In respect to a constitution, "The best attainable scheme is one of imperfect procedural justice".[17] When creating a constitution, and therefore the basic principles of a just society, democracy will be engaged in two ways: first, in respect to the necessity of the participation of free and equal citizens and, second, in respect to the outcomes that issue from the process conducted by such persons. Justice requires that democracy requires the opportunity of equal participation by equals and outcomes which do not violate the basic principles of free and equal citizens, of justice, nor of democracy. Rawls writes that "none should benefit from certain undeserved contingencies with deep and long-lasting effects ... except in ways that help others" as a "democratic conception". He adds that this conception is "implicit in the basic structure" of a society that satisfies the first principle of justice as fairness (that all people are to have maximum freedom, but no more freedom than others) and that it satisfies the requirement of fair equality of opportunity.[18]

"Lying behind" the practical role of justice as fairness is "a deliberative conception of democratic politics", writes Cohen. He adds that in *Theory*, Rawls "seems to endorse some variant of a deliberative conception".[19] Two things must be said here briefly, although I will elaborate upon them later. First, it is odd that Cohen can only muster this mild conclusion, given, at a minimum, Rawls's theorization of the "Original Position", "Reflective Equilibrium", and "The Idea of Public Reason". Second, read through the lens of *Liberalism* and other extensions and elaborations of *Theory*, there is no doubt whatsoever that deliberation is of crucial importance to his theory and that *Theory* itself discloses some part of this importance.

Yet, in spite of the understated view of Rawls in respect to deliberation given at the outset of his discussion of just this matter, Cohen continues,

> In presenting justice as fairness ... Rawls *supposes* that he is addressing himself to citizens who ... have the deliberative responsibility of presenting public arguments at least about fundamental laws and policies ... .
>
> Rawls *assumes* this view of democratic politics as an arena of argument rather than a tamed competition for power, fair aggregation of interests, or expression of shared cultural commitments. And he *supposes* that his task is to articulate the most reasonable view of justice for citizens and officials to use in their political deliberations—a con-

---

17   Rawls, *A Theory of Justice*, rev. ed. (Cambridge: Harvard University Press, 1999), 173; in Cohn, 93. Cf. Rawls, 74–75; and Cohen, 91.

18   Rawls, "Reply to Alexander and Musgrave" in his *Collected Papers*, Samuel Freeman, ed. (Cambridge: Harvard University Press, 1996), 246; in Cohen, 97.

19   Cohen, 100–01; Rawls, 199–200, 313–18.

cept of justice that is for a democracy in that it is intended to guide the judgments of citizens in exercising their deliberative responsibility.[20]

Rawls imagines that democratic deliberation can be fruitful because he theorizes such deliberation among a people who have shared moral intuitions or, in Cohen's words, a "consensus on principles of political morality". Rawls understands that liberal societies have the capacity for many conceptions of the good, but adoption of the two fundamental principles of justice as fairness means that "Political argument appeals to this moral consensus".[21] Of course, Rawls allows that there will always be some disagreement in democratic societies, and his theory of a well-ordered society accommodates this fact. Deliberation, for Rawls, does not drive difference and disagreement away; it orders and manages it within parameters defined by the two principles. This is possible where "politics is, in the first instance, a matter of deliberation".[22]

I noted above that Rawls's conception of persons as free and equal in a political sense is built upon a liberal notion of free and equal status in a moral sense. Cohen rightly notes that there is a concomitant connection in Rawls between the development of the moral powers of understanding and choosing both justice and conceptions of the good, and democracy: "the development of these powers is connected to the good of persons as free and equal members of a democratic society … . The underlying idea, modeled in the original position, is that we are to reason about justice by reference to the good … ".[23] Cohen correctly observes that this idea is insufficiently clear in the first edition of *Theory*, but the revised version adds clarifying commentary, for example, that "Primary goods are now characterized as what persons need in their statuses as free and equal citizens … ".[24] In short, democracy is both the form of political association that best embodies our moral status and moral powers as free and equal persons, and it also helps form and promote our moral status and moral powers. The moral infrastructure of a well-ordered, just society is necessarily democratic.

Cohen concludes that justice as fairness "requires a democratic form of government in which the authorization to exercise political power comes from fair processes of collective choice. This conception expresses a democratic idea of society (a society of equals), and it is meant to guide the judgment and public argument of members of a democratic polity … ". Although "democracy figures in Rawls's view in these … fundamental

---

20   *Ibid.*, 102. I have emphasized "supposes" and "assumes" to underwrite, in some modest measure, my claim above that Rawls assumes the democratic nature of his theory more often than he explicates it.

21   Rawls, 232; Cohen, 103.

22   Cohen, 103.

23   *Ibid.*, 107–08.

24   Rawls, xiii, cf. xvi and *Political Liberalism*, 302; cited in Cohen, 108.

ways, it might nevertheless be argued that the idea of democracy does not figure with sufficient prominence in justice as fairness and that Rawls assigns an unacceptable priority of justice to democracy".[25] Cohen responds to such claims (as does Gutmann) in the remaining, and roughly the second half, of his essay. The concern about the subordination of democracy is that

> justice as fairness understands actual democratic politics, and the debate surrounding it, to be guided and restricted by substantive principles that we arrive at through reasoning that can be conducted independently of open public argument between and among citizens ... .
> Even in the ideal constitutional and legislative stages ... principles of justice are set out in advance, and the problem of political life might be seen as the application of those prior principles, whose content is fixed prior to argument between and among citizens.[26]

Cohen cites Habermas's evaluation of Rawls, where it is claimed that citizens

> cannot reignite the radical democratic embers of the original position in the civic life of their society, for from their perspective all of the *essential* discourses of legitimation have already taken place within the theory; and they find the results of the theory already sedimented in their constitution. Because the citizens cannot conceive of the constitution as a *project*, the public use of reason does not actually have the significance of a present exercise of political autonomy but merely promotes the nonviolent *preservation of political stability*.[27]

Cohen notes that this critique can be understood in three ways: first, that Rawls's conception of justice offers an independent, philosophically derived standard of the desired outcome; second, that settling fundamental questions in advance denigrates the importance of democratic argument; third, that Rawlsian justice, insofar as it denigrates democratic exchange, is founded on a mistrust of citizens, who need to have their judgments confined by strictures set out in advance. It should be added that these three perspectives are not mutually exclusive and that if the first two concerns are addressed, the third melts away.

Cohen argues that these problems that may be seen in Rawls's theory are not supportable; that is, that they insufficiently understand his theory. For example, Cohen sees nowhere in Rawls where judicial review improperly eclipses political deliberation. In respect to the second claim that Rawls, in effect, subordinates citizens to philosophers insofar as claims of justice denigrate the importance of political participation, Cohen, again, disagrees. This worry is generated by such claims as, or at least the claim that, "The idea of right and just constitutions and basic laws is always

25   *Ibid.*, 111.
26   *Ibid.*, 112.
27   Jürgen Habermas, "Reconciliation Through the Public Use of Reason: Remarks on John Rawls's Political Liberalism", *Journal of Philosophy* 92 (March 1995), 128; in Cohen, 113.

ascertained by the most reasonable political conception of justice and not by the result of an actual political process."[28] In my view, this claim made by Rawls in isolation would by worrisome to the democratic theorist, but in conjunction with the rest of *Political Liberalism*, and indeed, his other (relevant) work, it seems at worse, an injudicious statement.

Rawls does not, it turns out, actually think that the content of justice is "fixed in advance". Rather, he offers an account of moral learning, and concomitant acquisition of understanding of the content of justice — and he writes that we come to understand justice more adequately just as we participate as free and equal citizens in political argument and deliberation.[29] In reference to the criticism that in the original position, the principles of justice are determined once and for all, Cohen correctly responds,

> How could the possibility of presenting the argument as a matter of what people who are free and equal would choose under hypothetical conditions suggest limits on political autonomy once we see the hypothetical choice argument simply as a way to express conditions on arguments addressed to persons thus understood? It is not as though actual persons are being constrained by hypothetical decisions ... .[30]

The meaning of the original position, one must remember, is what Rawls thinks persons such as "us" (western, liberal, democratic people) would decide under conditions that allow our decisions to be best considered. His supposition about what persons like "us" would consider just and fair is about who we are over time, not in some hypothetical moment.[31] Thus, the principles of justice are in Rawlsian terms, meant to guide citizen deliberation; they are not simply locked into place. Justice as fairness does not foreclose argument, but proposes terms on which it is to be carried forward. Cohen rightly notes that in this respect Rawls's theory is like every other plausible theory of justice and that the availability of principles of judgment does not necessarily eliminate the disagreements that result when citizens exercise their judgment, even while agreeing on fundamental principles. Reasonable disagreement does not "show any failure of principles or reveal their vacuousness. Instead it shows how political principles always operate: they provide a shared, public terrain of reasoning that enables mutually respecting parties to explore their disagreements".[32]

---

28 *Liberalism*, 233.
29 Cohen, 124; Rawls, *Theory*, 414.
30 Cohen, 126.
31 Of course that his theory of justice is "political, not metaphysical" was not clear in *Theory*, and only later in "Justice as Fairness: Political Not Metaphysical", *Philosophy and Public Affairs* 14 (Summer 1985), 223–52; and *Political Liberalism* (New York: Columbia University Press, 1993) did Rawls make this for "us"-ness clear. I am simply and appropriately understanding his claims about justice as fairness through the lens of his later explanations.
32 Cohen, 127–28.

Although Cohen defends Rawls against criticisms to the effect that his theory undervalues democracy, there is one respect in which Cohen thinks Rawls fails. He thinks that Rawls provides an inadequate account of democracy not because it endorses a substantive conception of justice but because it lacks a plausible account of political disagreement.[33] This seems odd inasmuch as Cohen argues, as my summary has shown, that Rawls allows for more argument and deliberation than some critics allow. In short, however, Cohen thinks Rawls does not allow enough. He sees in Rawls's conception of justice, a built-in assumption about homogeneity. That is, in the idea that political argument appeals to moral consensus, political disagreement is vanquished. In fact, he sees Rawlsian moral consensus as analogous to Rousseau's determinate general will, the content of which is given by the principles of justice. Cohen's critique is difficult to endorse insofar as it is hard to see the kind of thick, lock-step republican agreement Rousseau theorizes any place in Rawls; and further, even Cohen admits that in the revised edition of *Political Liberalism*, Rawls "emphasizes that democracies include a plurality of reasonable liberal political conceptions of justice, as well as a plurality of comprehensive doctrines and that social unity cannot be achieved, as a practical matter, through agreement on any specific conception of justice".[34]

This brings me to a simple observation of Cohen's argument: it is focused on *Theory* and gives insufficient attention to *Liberalism* (let alone the absence of attention to *Justice as Fairness* noted above). Yet surely a proper evaluation of Rawls's theory as it relates to democracy should not only take into account all of his relevant work but note that his theory develops in a self-conscious and intentional matter, just in order to shore up weaknesses and give greater clarity to earlier texts. Rawls was, one should not forget, quite clear about this process as it related to the scope of his project.

Here is, however, the key component of Cohen's critique of Rawls's shortcoming: "Because a well-ordered society is homogeneous in its understanding of justice, democratic politics excludes argument over fundamentals — excludes not by banning such argument ... but by *idealizing it away*".[35] Rawls considers whether he is making an unwarranted "assumption of unanimity", and he concludes that "the idea of unanimity among rational persons is implicit throughout the tradition of moral philosophy".[36] This is, of course, true. That is, theorists who do normative work trade in thought about what it is on which peoples ought to agree. Such work typically oscillates between the explicit and implicit. Rawls under-

33   *Ibid.*, 115.
34   *Ibid.*, 129; Rawls, *Liberalism*, xlviii–1.
35   Cohen, 130 (emphasis, mine).
36   *Theory*, 233; Cohen, 130.

stands himself to be doing nothing other than what political and moral theorists do typically, if not by definition. Yet Cohen pries apart a distinction in an unusual way. In response to Rawls's understanding that as a theory of justice, political and moral theory are intrinsically related, and as such, they cannot be entirely separated (which is, after all, a commonplace of political theory), Cohen writes,

> But politics and morality are different: moral thought is concerned in part with what *I* should do ... but democratic politics is concerned with what *we* should do .... As Rawls has argued in *Political Liberalism*, we cannot reasonably demand or even expect a single moral philosophy or doctrine to be embraced by citizens of a democratic society ... .[37]

Cohen misconceives morality and, in so doing, makes a false distinction between morality and democratic politics. There are distinctions to be made, of course, but an emphasis on *me* as the core of morality, in contrast to *we* as the core of politics, is not one which is proper in respect to long-standing and conventional understandings of morality.[38] Further, Cohen immediately follows his complaint against Rawls with an admission that Rawls and he are in agreement as far as *Political Liberalism* is concerned. It seems, then, that Cohen's criticism is against *Theory*, but if this is the case, why target the earlier text alone when Rawls wrote *Political Liberalism* as an effort to improve upon various parts of *A Theory of Justice*? Insofar as his complaint is in the end against *Theory*, this should be made clear.

Cohen concludes that "once we give up on the expectation of moral unanimity in a democracy, we should also give up on the expectation of political unanimity. It is unreasonable to expect all members to accept the same conception of justice and arguably [it is] a virtue of democratic politics that they disagree". He continues, "Justice as fairness may be the most reasonable conception of justice for a democratic society. We cannot, however, expect the most reasonable democratic society to be founded on an agreement about justice".[39] Cohen is correct in these judgments, but they are too thin to critically penetrate Rawls's theory. That is, of course a lack of moral unanimity pushes toward a lack of political unanimity, and certainly not all members of a democracy will hold precisely the same moral and political understandings and commitments. But to say this is to iterate a truism. What one would want to know is what, exactly, are the postulates and claims made by Rawls that are in violation of this truism? In what specific respects does Rawls make it clear that a kind of unanimity is necessary for the coherence of his theory, in such a case where such unanimity is not

---

37 Cohen, 130–31.
38 Cf. Habermas, *Justification and Application: Remarks on Discourse Ethics*, trans. Ciaran P. Cronin (Cambridge: MIT Press, 2001), 48–49; and many explications of discourse ethics altogether to see how different Habermas's understanding of morality is to Cohen's in this regard. For Habermas, moral questions are always to be put in the first person *plural*.
39 Cohen, 131.

possible or likely? Similarly, it is not clear that he has defeated the notion that the most reasonable democracy cannot be founded on an agreement about justice. Such a conclusion would have to entail a project he has not undertaken—to show what foundation is better. "So how might the most reasonable conception of justice be achieved in the most reasonable form of democracy?" he asks. Cohen's answer: "That question remains open".[40] One can agree that it remains open, but if it does, one does not yet know that Rawls's theory fails in just the way Cohen claims it does.

Nearly all of what Cohen has to say about Rawls's conception of democracy as it seeps from *A Theory of Justice* and (although insufficient attention is paid to it) comes from *Political Liberalism* amounts to an acute interrogation with accurate conclusions. It would be helpful, from the perspective of the democratic theorist, if Rawls would have been clearer and offered more detail and straightforward consideration of democracy in his work. It seems to me that he is not sufficiently careful about articulating the need for a more radical democracy than reading his work can imply is necessary. That is, it is not clear to just what extent Rawls sees *these* democratic features as necessary in his theory as opposed to *those* features, and why. Theorists such as Cohen and I would want him to be more clearly "with us". We must, however, keep in mind that Rawls is not constructing a democratic theory *as such*. I am not as certain as is Cohen that Rawls has "idealized away" sufficient democratic deliberation because I think we have inadequate theorization from Rawls so as to demonstrate that claim. Rawls would disappoint quite clearly if he were to make no more vigorous an argument for democratic deliberation than he has, *if* he did so in a text which meant to offer a democratic theory. Rawls offers, I think, some sure steps in the right direction, and his importance to deliberative theory is due to his thoroughly liberal theory and the influence of his work. An investigation of Rawls's democratic theory, however, offers only a mere beginning. Of course, we still want to know of Gutmann's evaluation of Rawls, and further examination is needed, particularly in respect to *Justice as Fairness*.

As stated above, Amy Gutmann also undertakes to evaluate to what extent Rawls's theory is democratic. I need not use her analysis of Rawls as extensively as I have used Cohen, for there is significant overlap between their treatments. Like Cohen, she responds to those who criticize Rawls in respect to being insufficiently democratic. Like Cohen, and except for Habermas, she fails to mention these critics and engage their work directly. In any case, because she sees the critics' evaluations cluster around these claims, her investigation of Rawls's theory considers the following questions. Does it devalue the equal political liberty of adults? Does it devalue the political process of majority rule? Does it devalue the

40   *Ibid.*

kind of civic discourse that relies on more comprehensive philosophies — both religious and secular — rather than on the free-standing political philosophy that Rawls's theory explicitly defends?[41] Gutmann
acknowledges that Rawls's texts "do not say explicitly much about democracy", so she can only offer "interpretation rather than demonstration".
She notes that because Rawls's theory "incorporates both democratic and
liberal values at its core and identifies those values with the same
source" — the political idea of the person as a free and equal citizen — "it is
more difficult than it otherwise would be to distinguish the liberal and
democratic elements of this theory".[42]

Gutmann thinks that Rawls's difference principle is democratic insofar
as it maximizes the capacity of the least advantaged members of society to
realize their aims and is consistent with protecting everyone's equal liberty. She also thinks that his understanding of citizens as free and equal
implies the need for a fair distribution of political power and that in
Rawls's theorization, personal and political liberties are, to borrow a
phrase used by Habermas, co-original.[43] However, Habermas sees the
co-originality of personal and political liberties as existing in Rawls only in
the original position and at the "first level of theory formation". He then
objects that personal liberty gains priority thereafter, "under the institu-
tional conditions of an already constituted just society". Rawls's response
to this understanding is that citizens are equally free at all levels and
stages of discourse: in the original position, in the formation of the constitution, and thereafter.[44] In *Liberalism*, Rawls defends the idea that there is a
family of ways demonstrating the free and equal status of citizens. The
original position is just one part of this family, and no family member is
privileged. In Gutmann's words, echoing Rawls's own invocation of Constant, she writes, "Rawls, like Constant, does not advocate the personal
liberty of the moderns to the exclusion of the political liberty of the
ancients … . Rawls absolutely rejects trading off political liberty for something other than another equal liberty … ".[45] Indeed, even if "co-original",
the political liberties are instrumental in preserving the other liberties. Yet,
political liberties are not merely instrumental; *expressing* our status as free

---

41 Gutmann, 168.

42 *Ibid.*, 168, 174.

43 *Ibid.*, 171, 173–76. Jürgen Habermas, "On the Internal Relation between Law and Democracy",
The Inclusion of the Other (Cambridge, MA: MIT Press, 1998), 259.

44 Habermas, ibid., 69; Rawls, *Liberalism* (rev. ed.), 381–96; Cohen, 177. The revised edition of
Political Liberalism includes the exchange between Habermas and Rawls published in *The
Journal of Philosophy*. Habermas's essay, "Reconciliation Through the Use of Reason: Remarks
on John Rawls's Political Liberalism" has been cited. Rawls's response is, "Political Liberalism:
Reply to Habermas", *Journal of Philosophy*, 92 (March 1995), 132–80.

45 Gutmann, 177–78; Rawls, *Liberalism*, 26–28; *Justice*, 221; Constant, "The Liberty of the Ancients
Compared with that of the Moderns" [1819], in Benjamin Constant, *Political Writings*
(Cambridge: Cambridge University Press, 1988), 309–28.

and equal citizens in political life is important to democracy.[46] Gutmann adds,

> The exercise of citizens' sense of justice is both instrumentally and intimately connected with the exercise of citizens' sense of their own good. This is an important insight of Rawls's theory and the most neglected relationship between liberal and democratic values ... .
>
> It would weaken the liberal and the democratic nature of political liberalism—which we now have reason to label a liberal democratic theory—to give priority to all personal over all political liberties, or vice versa".[47]

The second half of Gutmann's essay bears more directly on the question of the deliberative capacities of Rawls's theory (but one should notice that her emphasis on the importance of political liberty in his theory lays the groundwork for her second-half analysis). Unsurprisingly, her examination lays open the deliberative possibilities in conjunction with a focus on *Political Liberalism*, much more so than on *Theory*. Gutmann emphasizes the balance between Rawls's valuation of personal and political liberties to show that his theory is as democratic (political liberties) as it is liberal (personal liberties); but she then knows she must consider the question of how Rawls's theory handles the inevitable conflicts that arise between basic liberties.

First, she notes that his theory is simply open to such conflict and, therefore, argument and deliberation. Yet she also notes that his theory allows for limits on political participation, as such limitation is needed to protect basic liberties. Rawls writes that "a bill of rights *may* remove certain liberties from majority regulation ... ".[48] Of course, his "may" is only an allowance, and there is nothing in his theory to think that the majority in a Rawlsian society would often, if ever, threaten the basic rights of the minority. As to conflict and possible conflict in a well-ordered society, for Rawls, there must even be the right to advocate revolutionary and seditious doctrines (his argument in this respect, Gutmann thinks, is among the best ever offered in respect to the importance of protecting political speech).[49] When any two liberties conflict the means of determining which should give way to the other depends on an assessment of the relative importance of each in respect to the overall scheme of equal liberties (not an assessment of the overall importance of political versus personal liberties). Free and equal persons justify their balance of liberties in respect to

---

46   Rawls, *Liberalism*, 299; Gutmann, 179.
47   Gutmann, 180.
48   Rawls, *Theory*, 228 (201, revised); Gutmann, 182: (emphasis, mine).
49   Rawls, *Liberalism*, 340–56; Gutmann, 182.

what brings the greatest scheme of freedoms for all.[50] This means of deter-
mination is at least as democratic as it is liberal.

Gutmann is correct when she writes:

> Although Rawls does not develop this part of political liberalism, his
> theory has the resources to offer both instrumental and intrinsic rea-
> sons for citizens to treat their fellow citizens with mutual respect- or
> what Rawls calls 'civic friendship' ... when they reasonably disagree
> ... . Mutual respect entails that they offer reasons, as Rawls puts it ...
> [that] we might reasonably expect that they as free and equal might
> reasonably also accept.[51]

While Rawls might have offered a more robust theorization of "civic
friendship", as Gutmann suggests, there is no doubt his theory entails a
correlative relationship between mutual respect and reasonableness in
discourse and deliberation. I imagine Rawls would not object to his idea of
civic discourse being articulated much like Oakeshott's understanding of
the politics of conversation. Such reasonable disagreement in both theories understands persons in dialogue as acting with respect, reciprocity,
and reasonableness.[52]

> The ideas of civic integrity, magnanimity, and the economy of moral
> disagreement help demonstrate how political liberalism can be devel-
> oped ... When developed in this deliberative direction, political liber-
> alism explicitly recognizes that many reasonable disagreements about
> matters of justice depend for their fair resolution on reciprocity ...
> among citizens who enjoy equal political liberty.[53]

Thus Gutmann summarizes accurately and sees that while deliberative
democracy is not developed as such in Rawls's theory, the postulates of his
theory do push inevitably in this direction. Again, "in this direction" does
not amount to a theory of deliberative democracy; but deliberative theorists engage Rawls's theory with justification because his theory *necessitates* political deliberation and sketches features for its actualization.

Although Gutmann recognizes the "democratic strength" of Rawls's
political liberalism, she still asks if it is "sufficiently democratic once it is
developed in these directions?" (the directions I have summarized above).
One source of doubt is the familiar one of its strong constitutionalism, seen
by some to overwhelm the majoritarian decision making the theory also
contains. It is also clear that in *Theory* Rawls does subordinate the procedures of majority rule to the "political ends the constitution is meant to
achieve"; he adds, "There is nothing to the view ... that what the majority
wills is right".[54] So, the question is, Does valuing majority rule as a means

---

50 Rawls, *Theory*, 229–30 (revised, 201–02); Gutmann, 183.
51 Rawls, *Liberalism*, li; Gutmann, 185.
52 Rawls, *Liberalism*, xlvi.
53 Gutmann, 187.
54 Rawls, *Theory*, 356; Gutmann, 187–89.

to realize just outcomes make Rawls's theory less democratic? If the instrumental value of democracy overshadows its intrinsic value, is it less democratic? Rawls, like most democratic theorists, rejects the definition of democracy as being majority rule. There remains no compelling argument as to why mere majoritarianism should trump the protection of basic liberal, human, and political rights. Rawls is no different from the consensus of democratic theorists — majority opinion is not more important than the value (and protection) of basic equality and freedoms held by, and the realization of just legislation in accordance with the free and equal status of, citizens.[55] Of course, in this understanding, Rawls's theory comports with Oakeshott's. Although both are deeply liberal theories, they do not reduce to the individualistic atomism that would emit into mere majoritarianism. Indeed, we can quickly recall that where we find Oakeshott criticizing "democracy" he is criticizing just this thin facade of democracy — the rule of the majority and the rule of individual *manqué*, collectivized into "mass man". Gutmann nicely summarizes the relationship between majority rule and equal political liberties in a way that both Rawls and Oakeshott would endorse:

> Majority rule may be the most common and straight-forward way of expressing the equal status of citizens who actually have equal political liberties. But it is the expression of equal political liberties that does the *moral* work in affirming the value of majority rule, not the intrinsic value of majority rule itself.[56]

One can recall that for both Rawls and Oakeshott, the foundation or essence of liberal and democratic political association is constituted by moral intuitions and commitments.

In conclusion, Gutmann writes that the right, and I would add, the sufficient equal possibility, of citizens to deliberate is an important part of the equal political liberty that is basic to liberal democracy, although it does not follow that deliberation about politics has priority over all other parts of basic liberty and political association. Whereas *Theory* insufficiently addresses this matter, Rawls's idea of public reason and other features of *Political Liberalism* pushes much farther in respect to theorizing these mat-

---

55 Gutmann, 189.

56 *Ibid.*, 190. Gutmann offers an articulate and compelling argument about the relationship of majority rule and political equality, drawing on Brian Barry (pp. 190–92); but it is beyond the scope of our inquiry to consider her thought disassociated from her interpretation of Rawls. See Brian Barry, "Is Democracy Special?" in *Democracy and Power, Essays in Political Theory I* (Oxford: Clarendon Press, 1991). Gutmann and Thompson extend Barry's argument in *Democracy and Disagreement*, 27–33.

ters. *Liberalism* thus successfully manages to affirm a democratic conception of justice and deliberative democracy in ways beyond *Theory*.[57]

Cohen and Gutmann give careful attention to the relationship and possibilities in and of Rawls's work in respect to (especially deliberative) democracy. They draw similar conclusions. They recognize in Rawls's theory important and necessary democratic structures that are mostly implicit in *Theory* and become more explicit in *Liberalism*. Not only does this development from implicit to explicit grow between texts, but between revised editions of the two texts. There is a trajectory in Rawls's thought that both Cohen and Gutmann recognize; it is, one might say, what appears to be a developing understanding in Rawls's own reflection, of the essential nature of democratic theory to his theory of justice as fairness and of political liberalism. Cohen and Gutmann treat Rawls a bit differently of course, but again, one is compelled to notice the similarity of their readings and interpretations. My analysis of Rawls does not simply reduce to that of theirs, of course, but their understanding of Rawls should not be ignored. I endorse their understandings, with the only significant departure on my part being with Cohen in respect to his conclusion, as I indicated above. Yet, they have not reported everything to be said about Rawls's democratic theory. Below I will offer a short summary that will in some minor respects reiterate Cohen and Gutmann, but there is additional interpretation offered as well. Even aside from *Justice as Fairness*, more needs to be said than said by Cohen and Gutmann; but certainly the absence of consideration of this latter text on their part necessitates some commentary on my own.

First, I briefly consider *Justice as Fairness* and then, second and last, I conclude this section with an interpretation of Rawls on democracy that in ways go beyond Cohen and Gutmann. Unlike *Theory* and *Liberalism*, *Fairness* makes many references to democracy and contains a variety of types of references to democracy in the Index. Even a cursory look at this last text underscores my earlier claim of a growing awareness in Rawls, that he needed to give further explicit attention to democratic theory. One only need to read the first eight pages to see this.

Rawls now writes of "property-owning democracy" as a way to name his theory of a well-ordered society. He notes that "overlapping consensus" is crucial because "reasonable pluralism is a permanent condition of a democratic society" and that this pluralism is the first of five basic facts which are "especially important in justice as fairness." The fourth fact is that "the political culture of a democratic society that has worked reasonably well over a considerable period of time normally contains, at least

---

57   Gutmann, 196–97. Note that Rawls's Introduction to the revised edition of *Liberalism* refers to democracy at least eighteen times, and to deliberation and public reason nearly as often, whereas democracy as *explicitly* addressed in *Theory* is quite minimal.

implicitly, certain fundamental ideas from which it is possible to work up a political conception of justice suitable for a constitutional regime."[58] Cohen concludes that one cannot expect the most reasonable democratic society to be founded on an agreement about justice, and as I responded, this gets Rawls's notion wrong. Here, Rawls makes it clear that ideas of justice flow from democratic culture, clearly and succinctly reversing the order Cohen supposed.

Fundamental to Rawls's argument is the conviction that it is the "power of the public", the "power of free and equal citizens" who all have "an equal share in political power ... so far as possible", which constitutes democracy, just as they offer reasons which "all citizens can publically endorse in the light of their own reason. This is the principle of political legitimacy that justice as fairness is to satisfy".[59] To Gutmann's point about the balance in Rawls between political and personal liberties, he writes that in a democratic society "nonpublic authority, as seen, for example, in the authority of churches over their members, is freely accepted". Yet although such personal liberty has its place in democracy, in a democratic society, "we may over the course of a life come freely to accept, as the outcome of reflective thought and reasoned judgment, the ideals, principles, and standards that specify our basic rights and liberties and effectively guide and moderate the political power to which we are subject".[60] This is "public reason".

Rawls considers a society embedding justice as fairness, made manifest in "property-owning democracy", to realize the main political values expressed by his two principles of justice and thinks that the capitalist welfare state fails to do so. He notes that the distinction between these two kinds of societies, or "social systems", is not sufficiently made in *Theory*.[61] Rawls sees the capitalist welfare state as violating justice as fairness and democracy because it fails to control the accumulation of wealth and capital in the possession of the minority. He notes that those with disproportionate wealth would control the economy and thus "political life as well". Property-owning democracy avoids this problem by "ensuring the widespread ownership of productive assets and human capital". It turns out, then, that in this social system, the least advantaged are not "the unfortunate and unlucky objects of our charity and compassion, much less our

---

58   Rawls, *Justice as Fairness*, 33–35; cf. 40.
59   *Ibid.*, 90–91.
60   *Ibid.*, 94.
61   *Ibid.*, 135–36. Rawls's two principles of justice are (1) "each person has the same indefeasible claim to a fully adequate scheme of equal basic liberties, which scheme is compatible with the same scheme of liberties for all"; and (2) "social and economic inequalities are to satisfy two conditions: first they are to be attached to offices and positions open to all under conditions of fair equality of opportunity; and second, they are to be to the greatest benefit of the least-advantaged members of society (the difference principle)," *Fairness*, 42–43. These two principles are reworked here from their first articulation in *Theory*, 60–61.

pity — but those to whom reciprocity is owed as a matter of political justice among those who are free and equal citizens along with everyone else".[62] Rawls is now explicit that democracy *means*, in part, economic justice (as to what extent or in what ways his theory is, in fact, just, is another question, and one I cannot explore). He now argues, more clearly than before, that democracy means the elimination of an underclass.[63]

In his explanation of property-owning democracy as constitutional democracy, Rawls invokes the necessity of "deliberative political discussion" and he ties deliberative theory to "civic republicanism". The principles of justice present in a well-ordered society are realized, he writes, by a constitutional regime consisting in the exercise of "the ideals of free public reason and deliberative democracy".[64] He also writes that in such a political association, the "conditions of deliberative democracy" and "the exercise of public reason" are to be "furthered"; and he again notes that this is "an aim justice as fairness ... shares with civic republicanism".[65]

Rawls summarizes some of the main institutions of a property-owning democracy, which include the following:

> Provisions for securing the fair value of the political liberties ... So far as practicable, provisions for realizing fair equality of opportunity in education and training of various kinds. A basic level of health-care provided for all ... . Note also that Mill's idea of worker-managed cooperative firms is fully compatible with property-owning democracy ... .[66]

Lastly, Rawls writes that the possibility of a stable pluralist and democratic society "may follow from the success of liberal institutions". On this account, he continues, "an overlapping consensus is not a happy coincidence ... Rather, it is the work of society's public tradition of political thought in developing a practicable political conception of justice".[67] In *Fairness*, Rawls's theory remains deeply liberal even as he admits of features his theory shares with civic republicanism. One of the consistent liberal components of his theory is its rejection of political *community* and its necessary embrace of "reasonable pluralism" as intrinsic to the democracy he theorizes.[68]

I have summarized Rawls's explicit considerations of democracy in *Justice as Fairness*. It is clear that he is not only much more explicit in explicating the intrinsic relationship between justice as fairness and democracy than in *Theory* and *Liberalism*; but he is also significantly clear as to what

---

62 *Ibid.*, 139.
63 *Ibid.*, 140.
64 *Ibid.*, 146, 148.
65 *Ibid.*, 150.
66 *Ibid.*, 176.
67 *Ibid.*, 197, 198.
68 *Ibid.*, 198–99.

the content of democracy is. Of course, he is not offering a work in democratic theory *per se*. Everything one might want to know about Rawls's
views on democracy is not to be found in *Fairness*, but what he writes here
has the value of clarifying much of what could only be inferred from his
earlier work. It is clear that his theorization of democracy pushes significantly beyond mere representation, aggregation, and interest-group
contestation. Many have seen a democratic socialism in Rawls, which is a
categorization he accepted, although he did not use that language as a
self-description. Whereas he does not theorize deliberation, he argues that
substantive deliberation is a necessary part of pluralistic and reasonable
public political discussion. One might argue that the discussion of democracy in *Fairness* is defeated by less than democratic structures in *Theory* or
insufficient democratic structures in *Liberalism*, but I am unaware of such
an argument and not sure how it could be made. It seems clear that *Fairness*
completes a trajectory of his work in which Rawls continuously
(stage-by-stage, we might say) explicated his theories of justice, liberalism,
and a well-ordered society. As this trajectory develops, he clarifies and
enriches his previous thought. This is never so clear as it is in respect to his
treatment of democracy.

I here conclude my consideration of Rawls and deliberative democracy
by reminding the reader of themes that are incoherent apart from deliberative democracy. I want to quite briefly reiterate the meaning of citizens as
free and equal, the original position, the two principles of justice, and a
conglomeration of themes closely related, that of public justification,
reflective equilibrium, overlapping consensus, and public reason. It is critical that one understand Rawls not to be offering merely formal ideals and
structures in relation to these conceptions. He is aware that if the ideals
and structures of a social system are not realizable, they are of little value.
He offers a normative theory, but he intends it to be "realistically utopian",
that is, he understands himself to be "probing the limits of practicable
political possibility".[69] This claim needs to be noted because if one were to
ask, "How would this *work*?" when considering his theory, one will be
unable to answer that question, as Rawls makes clear, without the answer
containing robust and deliberative democratic institutions and practices.

In respect to the status of citizens as free and equal, this means then, that
such freedom and equality cannot be only formal. Constitutional "guaran-
tees" of this status are insufficient for Rawls. What is necessary are the
political institutions and practices that make the free exercise of our rights
and liberties under actual conditions of equality (fair opportunity to various offices and practices, for example). Only democracy that consists in
deliberative opportunities, structures, and institutions meet these criteria
for the actual embodiment of free and equal citizenry. Rawls invokes the

---

69   *Fairness*, 4.

idea of "democratic political society" as linked to the idea of persons as having the moral powers which are "the basis of political equality". He also notes that citizens are free in that "they regard themselves as self-authenticating sources of valid claims".[70] This understanding of persons leads directly to the democratic construction of society he theorizes and provides the deepest foundation for the value of deliberation, for if persons are free, equal, and self-authenticating sources of valid claims, deliberation logically follows.

In respect to the original position, I have indicated what I take to be its proper understanding above, so will not need to add much more here. It needs only to be reiterated that the overwhelming power that some of Rawls's interpreters give the original position is unwarranted. That it, as stated above, Rawls does not mean for the original position to uniquely *contain* deliberative and constitutional political decisions so as to limit them. It is a device used to help us imagine *why* we would come to the kinds of rules, especially the two principles of justice, that would exist at the foundation of a sufficiently democratic society. As some commentators have rightly suggested, the original position is, in fact, of questionable value to Rawls's theory. That is, his work built from moral intuitionism and Kantian constructivism seems to do all the work necessary to construct his theory. In any case, the overdetermination of the original position made by some critics is a violation of Rawls's theory more than it is an accurate evaluation of it.

One notices that in his explanation of the original position, Rawls refers to it as a hypothetical abstraction from contingencies, the particular features and circumstances of persons, in order to think through how the conditions of fair agreement between free and equal persons would bring about the first principles of justice. He simply seeks to construct a heuristic concept in order to help readers think past historical advantages and disadvantages, accidental and arbitrary influences as a necessary means to conceptualize why persons would recognize and construct justice as he supposes they would.[71] Of course this imaginative exercise consists entirely in deliberation of the most uninhibited kind.[72] The idea is not to postulate deliberation as a once-and-for-all event, but rather as a way to

---

70   *Ibid.*, 21, 23.

71   *Ibid.*, 14–18.

72   Of course Rawls theorizes the deliberation that takes place in the original position takes place behind a "veil of ignorance" so persons are unaware of the advantages and disadvantages, strengths and liabilities, of their respective positions and statuses. One might argue that this mechanism truncates deliberation significantly (and so it has been argued by, for example, some feminist theorists). I think Rawls understands this imaginary mechanism to foster deliberation about the political matters that matter most, and to force the discussion in this helpful way. There is a literature on the original position, and this question has been debated. I only seek here to register observation of the notion that the original position can be seen as a means to limit deliberation, as well as to foster it.

think about how deliberation can be conducted so as to be clear about what is decided and why.

As to the two principles of justice, one recalls that these are absolutely basic. They form the grounding of all constitutional and postconstitutional rules, or laws. Along with the claim of persons as free and equal, they are the most dense claims as to the moral foundation of a well-ordered society, a political society of justice as fairness. I emphasize this fact because it helps one to more readily see that the equal indefeasible claim to a fully adequate scheme of basic liberties must include the full array of political rights and liberties that invite robust democratic deliberation. That is, moral foundations this basic would not fail to extend to the political infrastructure of a just liberal and democratic society. The second principle, whereby social and economic inequalities must be attached to offices and positions open to all under conditions of equal opportunity, and that they must be to the greatest benefit of the least advantaged, does not lead to deliberation directly. However, one cannot image a Rawlsian society being able to determine the matters that obtain in respect to this principle without deliberation. That is, surely how this principle would be applied in actual political life would require a great deal of deliberation. Certainly, because inequalities such as those specified here must be to the benefit of the least advantaged, the least advantaged would be incentivized, as free and equal citizens, to participate in the deliberation determining what actual directions need to be taken. Of course, the most advantaged are those typically engaged in political deliberation, whereas marginalized and disenfranchised citizens have little voice. Rawls's theory disrupts and addresses this immoral and unjust asymmetry and imbalance.

In respect to public justification, this, in conjunction with the related ideas I identified immediately below, is the last of Rawls's "fundamental ideas" set out at the beginning of *Fairness*. Rawls is direct: the aim of the idea of public justification (using this term to cover all the related ideas) is to specify the idea of discursive justification in and for a democracy characterized by pluralism. He writes that it is "worked out" for "the basic structure of a democratic society". The principles contained in these ideas "provide a mutually acceptable point of view from which citizens' claims on the main institutions of the basic structure can be adjudicated ... a shared basis for citizens to justify to one another their political judgments ...".[73]

In respect to the idea of reflective equilibrium, this is a personal as well as an interpersonal dynamic, but only the latter is of concern. In this regard, it concerns how citizens make their best considered judgments with others "without imposing on ourselves an external [coercive] authority". Citizens, when they achieve a wide (but not "full") reflective equilib-

---

73   *Ibid.*, 26–27.

rium, identify a mutually identified, public point of view from which all citizens can adjudicate their claims. This equilibrium, paired with the conception of justification, is what "best fits all of our considered convictions on reflection and organizes them into a coherent view". Rawls adds, "At any given time, we cannot do better than that".[74]

In respect to the idea of an overlapping consensus, it is introduced to make the idea of a well-ordered democratic society more realistic, as it accounts for historical and social conditions, the pluralism of democracies. Even when citizens affirm the same political conception of justice, they do not all do so for the same reasons, not all the way down. People have different "comprehensive doctrines", the beliefs, convictions, and worldviews (often religious in nature) that are often incommensurable. Nonetheless, persons of varying comprehensive doctrines can embrace the same political conception of political justice, if even for different reasons. This, Rawls thinks, is "the most reasonable basis of political and social unity available to citizens of a democratic society".[75]

Justice as fairness has three features that should help the development and actualization of overlapping consensus. Its requirements are limited to society's basic structure, its acceptance requires no particular comprehensive view, and its fundamental ideas and sensibilities are drawn from the familiarities of public political culture. Overlapping consensus is necessary because of the pluralism which Rawls sees as permanent in democratic societies. If a pluralistic society is to have stability, endurance, and security, an overlapping consensus will have to be achieved, because such a political society will need to be supported by a substantial majority of its citizens. Indeed, even highly conscientious and reasonable persons, after free and open discussion, are not likely to come to the same conclusions in all important respects.[76]

Two final remarks are in order. First, there is no guarantee that justice as fairness, "or any reasonable conception of a democratic regime, can gain the support of an overlapping consensus … . Many doctrines are plainly incompatible with the values of democracy". Second, "we start from the conviction that a constitutional democratic regime is reasonably just and workable, and worth defending. But given the fact of reasonable pluralism, we try to design our defense of it so as to gain allegiance of reasonable people and to win wide support".[77] Rawls is here getting at two notions:

---

74 *Ibid.*, 30–31. For a helpful discussion of reflective equilibrium, see Simone Chambers, *Reasonable Democracy* (Ithaca: Cornell University Press, 1996), 35–36, 61–62, 64–65, 169.

75 *Ibid.*, 32–33.

76 *Ibid.*, 34–36. Rawls notes a similar point made by Isaiah Berlin, namely, "that any system of social institutions is limited in the range of values it can accommodate … ". See Berlin, "On the Pursuit of the Ideal", in *The Crooked Timber of Humanity*, Henry Hardy, ed., (New York: Knopf, 1991).

77 *Ibid.*, 37.

that the means of pluralistic and just democratic society cannot violate its ends; therefore, no kind of bigotry (intellectual, moral, or otherwise) should be allowed to preempt the work toward overlapping consensus. As with reflective equilibrium, Rawls might have well pronounced, "We cannot do better than that".

Lastly, in respect to the idea of public reason, Rawls writes that this is "the form of reasoning appropriate to equal citizens who as a corporate body impose rules on one another backed by sanctions of state power". We may, he adds, and as I have quoted above, "over the course of life come freely to accept, as the outcome of reflective thought and reasoned judgment, the ideals, principles, and standards that specify our basic rights and liberties and effectively guide and moderate the political power to which we are subject".[78]

I am now in a position to show how these ideas or themes, considered together, relate to deliberative democracy. Indeed, it is not even necessary to explicate the relationship at length insofar as its contours are easy to see. Everything written on the previous five pages, from the idea of citizens as free and equal forward, interpenetrate at least some minimal idea of deliberative democracy and do so in order to be coherent. If we try to imagine a society which would incarnate Rawls's theory, thinking of the institutions, organizational structures and mechanisms, rules and laws, the means and the ends, as they would comport with everything we know about Rawls's conception of a well-ordered social system, I suggest such a society cannot be imagined without significant deliberative democracy. From the fundamental moral premises to the outcomes he theorizes, deliberation is required. Whereas he was unclear about this in *Theory* and insufficiently clear about it in *Liberalism*, he is quite clear about it in *Fairness*. Of course, he does not theorize what the character, procedures, boundaries, stipulations, etc., of deliberation would be. Again, his work is not in democratic theory as *such*, let alone deliberative theory. Rawls's work simply pushes the democratic theorist in the direction of deliberation; for more substantive reflection on what democratic deliberation might entail, the theorist must look beyond Rawls.

Before moving on, then, a word about method. One might interrogate each figure considered in this chapter from an Oakeshottian perspective and/or examine Oakeshott from the perspective of each, and otherwise compare each with Oakeshott. Doing so in respect to Rawls, would, for example, include a comparison of their respective liberalisms. I am, however, employing a different strategy, and only in the last chapter will we engage in a modest measure of comparison.

---

78   *Ibid.*, 92, 94. For a helpful discussion of Rawls's idea of public reason, see Chambers, 61–62, 71–77.

Habermas

Jürgen Habermas is in agreement, in the most basic ways, with Rawls. He thinks that persons are free and equal; and both are members of the "public reasons" approach which worries about matters of reasons and rationality as related to deliberation and democratic procedures and thinks that sufficient reasons permeating discourse is necessary to authentic democracy. As with Rawls, there have been significant changes in his theory, as he has developed it over time.[79] There is, however, no need to attend to these changes as such. With Rawls, it is necessary to describe and explain the changes because of a greater need to demonstrate a relationship between his theory and deliberative democracy and because the blossoming of this relationship does not occur until his last book. In regard to Habermas, however, I need only summarize *Between Facts and Norms*, and put it in the context of his larger moral and political project.[80] In *Between Facts and Norms* he gives full attention to deliberative democracy. Whereas it takes some effort to demonstrate Rawls's affinity with (let alone, theorization of) deliberative democracy, Habermas (as well as Dryzek, Gutmann and Thompson) is straightforwardly and robustly a deliberative democrat. This means that my treatment of Habermas, Dryzek, and Gutmann and Thompson will not necessitate the same kind of scrutiny given to Rawls.

Between Facts and Norms is an impressive assembly of thought drawn from various disciplines and discourses, constructed to utilize the merits of liberal theory and republicanism (or, alternatively, communitiarianism) while seeking to overcome the deficits of each. It is a discourse theory of democracy that pays great attention to the meaning and role of law in the proceduralism which provides democratic and political legitimacy. He aims to show that "the rule of law [*Rechtsstaat*] cannot be had or maintained without radical democracy".[81] His theory is procedural, rather than substantive; that is, democratic deliberation in conjunction with certain structures of democratic legitimacy bring about the outcomes that are fit-

---

79   Cf. Douglas Kellner, "Habermas, the Public Sphere, and Democracy: A Critical Intervention", in Lewis Edwin, Hahn, ed., *Perspectives on Habermas* (Chicago: Open Court, 2000), 266, 271, 273.

80   Two of Habermas's books are framed by consideration of democratic theory: *The Structural Transformation of the Public Sphere*, trans., Thomas Burger (Cambridge: MIT Press, 1989); first published in 1961 as *Strukturwandel der Öffentlicheit*. And *Between Facts and Norms: Contributions to a Discourse Theory of Law and Democracy*, trans. William Rehg (Cambridge: MIT Press, 1996); first published in 1992 as *Fakizität und Geltung. Beiträge zur Diskurstheorie des Rechts und des demokratischen Rechtsstaats*. Note that the accurate translation of the title's first words is "Facticity and Validity", and the argument of this book is meant to address the relationship of coherence between facticity and validity, the conditions by which such moments of coherence occur, or under which conditions there is a proper relationship between our facts and norms. Cf. Kenneth Baynes, "Deliberative Democracy and the Limits of Liberalism" in René von Schomberg and Kenneth Baynes, eds., *Discourse and Democracy: Essays on Habermas's* Between Facts and Norms (Albany: State University Press of New York, 2002), 15.

81   *BFN*, xlii.

ting to any given democratic society, given the conditions specified by the structures and procedures. One respect in which it is not substantive is that there are no *a priori* outcomes that democratic procedures must determine (except that outcomes, again, cannot violate the structures and procedures of the society and its state and laws). Habermas's theory is also procedural and deliberativist in that he holds to deontological notions of reasonableness that ought to guide deliberative procedures and procedural deliberation.

Schomberg and Baynes use Charles Beitz's conception of "complex proceduralism" to describe the proceduralism of Habermas; this is a worthwhile tactic insofar as Beitz offers a succinct description that Habermas fails to give. Beitz writes:

> Like other forms of proceduralism, [complex proceduralism] holds that democratic procedures should treat *persons* as equals; but it will not follow that the appropriate criterion for assessing procedures is the simple principle of equal power over outcomes. Instead, complex proceduralism holds that the terms of democratic participation are fair when they are reasonably acceptable from each citizen's point of view, or more precisely, when no citizen has good reason to refuse to accept them.[82]

Habermas theorizes ideal procedures that attempt to capture the idea of persons as free and equal, which is the basis of practical and public reason. Such reasonableness in practice makes manifest the idea of persons as free and equal. The processes which function in this way produce democratic and, therefore, political rightness or legitimacy. Legitimacy is, then, process and discourse-dependent. This is so in two respects: first, that the procedures come closest, given all alternatives, to the realization of persons as free and equal and more so than more determinate, substantive, or *a priori* values would; second, that the specification of these procedures remain sufficiently abstract, and the rights they express remain "unsaturated". The idea of saturation, for Habermas, is one of concreteness. He argues that rights can acquire their respective concrete and determinate character only through the exercise of citizens' collective autonomy. Citizens can only determine their rights through the deliberative and proceduralist processes of democracy.[83]

Habermas writes,

> Discourse theory invests the democratic process with normative connotations stronger than those found in the liberal model but weaker than those found in the republican model. Once again, it takes elements from both sides and puts them together in a new way. In agreement with republicanism, it gives center stage to the process of political opinion—and will-formation, but without understanding the constitution as something secondary … . According to discourse the-

82   Charles Beitz, op. cit., 23; in Schomberg and Baynes, 5.
83   *Ibid.*, 6.

ory, the success of deliberative politics depends not on a collectively acting citizenry but on the institutionalization of the corresponding procedures and conditions of communication, as well as on the interplay of institutionalized deliberative processes with informally developed public opinions. Proceduralized popular sovereignty and a political system tied into the peripheral networks of the political public sphere go together with the image of a decentered society. At any rate, this concept of democracy no longer has to operate with the notion of a social whole centered in the state and imagined as a goal-oriented subject writ large. Nor does it represent the whole in a system of constitutional norms mechanically regulating the balance of power and interests in accordance with a market model ... .

Discourse theory reckons with the *higher-level intersubjectivity* of processes of reaching understanding that take place through democratic procedures or in the communicative network of public spheres. Both inside and outside the parliamentary complex ... .[84]

A few pages later he writes,

In short, the ideal procedure of deliberation and decision making presupposes as its bearer an association that agrees to regulate the conditions of its common life *impartially*. What brings legal consociates together is, *in the final analysis*, the linguistic bond that holds together each communication community.[85]

I have presented this long quote, as well as the second, shorter one, not only because they summarize part of what I have discussed above but also because they introduce some concepts, the explanation of which will help the reader understand important features in and contextual elements of Habermas's theory. First, his reference to "communicative forms", "communicative network", and "communication community" brings us to a description of communicative reason and communicative action and then lets us move to discourse theory and discourse ethics, as this cluster of conceptions is at the foundation and in the background of his version of deliberative democracy.

It is easy enough to see that Habermas's work is a part of the linguistic turn that has permeated much of late twentieth-century philosophy and has invaded democratic theory. Habermas comes to makes this turn through his disenchantment with Enlightenment conceptions of rationality. This view is, of course, at the heart of the Frankfurt School's project and Habermas was most influenced in this direction by Horkeimer and Adorno's *Dialectic of Enlightenment*.[86] An important, and perhaps the central, problem for Habermas is to show how positivism, Weberian rationalization, Oakeshottian "Rationalism" (although he does not mention Oakeshott), all forms of "functionalist reason", and instrumental and stra-

---

84   *BFN*, 298, 299.
85   *Ibid.*, 306.
86   See, e.g., C. Fred Alford, *Science and the Revenge of Nature: Marcuse and Habermas* (Gainesville: University of Florida Press, 1985), 9–10.

tegic rationality are inadequate and how they threaten the humanity and full potential of human beings, especially how they bear on our social and political institutions and lives.[87] At the same time, as I have demonstrated, he is deeply committed to reason and rationality; but democratically and communicatively conceived.

Habermas conceptualizes communicative rationality and communicative action as a means to theorize how language can coordinate decisions and actions in mutually respectful, reciprocal, and consensual ways. He desires a means of communication and will-formation which is noncoercive and nonmanipulative. Although he is interested in how persons can come to agreement about all manner of things, it is the question of how they can come to rational and respectful agreement in regard to social and political matters that guide their common lives that interests him most. Mere compliance is not enough. The question is, How can decisions be both rational and consensual in the optimal or maximal ways? An intrinsically related question follows: What is the relationship between rationality and communal, democratic, mutual-respecting, discourse?

Whereas his monumental book, *The Theory of Communicative Action* is best known for the argument it makes as to how we should understand and critique modernity and discern what is of value in modernity, such that we would have grounds for "self-assurance", I am here more narrowly interested in the meaning of communicative action in respect to its bearing on his democratic theory.[88] Habermas claims that his theory of communicative action is a confrontation with the question of the normative foundations of critical theory, and by extension, of society. He wants to show that the "concepts of truth, freedom and justice are constitutively involved in the structures of linguistic communication as quasi-transcen-

87   Stephen K White, *The Recent Work of Jürgen Habermas: Reason, Justice, and Modernity* (New York: Cambridge University Press, 1988), 25. See Max. Horkheimer and Theodor Adorno, *Dialectic of Enlightenment* (New York: Seabury Press, 1972). Cf. Thomas McCarthy, *The Critical Theory of Jürgen Habermas* (Cambridge: MIT Press, 1994), 40–52; Stephen K. White, "Reason, Modernity, and Democracy", in White, ed., *The Cambridge Companion to Habermas* (New York: Cambridge University Press, 1999), 5; Georgia Warnke, "Communicative Rationality and Cultural Values", in White, 120–42; and David M. Rasmussen, *Reading Habermas* (Cambridge, MA: Basil Blackwell, 1990), 23–29, 35–36.

      Note that the positivism and Weberian rationalization that Habermas rejects is very much in keeping with everything Oakeshott means by the "Rationalism" he rejects.

88   White, *Cambridge Companion*, 8. Habermas, *The Theory of Communicative Action, Vol. 2, Lifeworld and System: A Critique of Functionalist Reason*, trans. Thomas McCarthy (Boston: Beacon Press, 1989), chapter 8; and Habermas, *The Philosophical Discourse of Modernity*, trans., Frederick G. Lawrence (Cambridge: MIT Press, 1987), chapter 1.

      The first of this two-volume work is *The Theory of Communicative Action, Volume1: Reason and the Rationalization of Society*, Thomas McCarthy, (Boston: Beacon Press, 1984).

dental fundamental norms that are closely tied to one another".[89] That is, normative foundations are to be found in language.

Communicative forms are primary for Habermas and his philosophy of language, and very much of all his theory rests on and emanates from this foundation. Rasmussen writes that this is "certainly the most fundamental claim of the entire corpus that constitutes the work of the later Habermas. The assumption behind it is that communicative claims are somehow emancipatory". And, this "primacy of the communicative mode constitutes the major theoretical insight sustaining the entire edifice Habermas has built ... . The theory of modernity ... . the discourse ethics ... the concept of politics and law — all can be systematically derived from this fundamental thesis".[90] Communicative action is opposed to strategic action, this latter kind of action being purposive. Communicative action is both rational and aimed at reaching understanding. Communicative action is noninstrumental, and cannot be "imposed". Communicative action carries an implicit validity claim because it is always, in principle, criticizable. One way communicative actions are foundational is in that they cannot be reduced to instrumental, purposive, or teleological actions.[91] It is worth noting that the language of purposiveness and instrumentality here is that of Habermas. One might think that I have slyly introduced Oakeshottian conceptions into Habermas's theory, but I am only reporting them. Communicative action, then, is similar in important ways to Oakeshott's understanding of civil association and the politics of conversation, whereas strategic action bears relevant similarities to Oakeshott's conceptions of rationalism and enterprise association. One should observe then, that the foundational importance of communicative action and, therefore, its importance to his deliberative democratic theory are not unlike the importance of Oakeshott's theorization of civil association as contingent, nonpurposive, and noninstrumental in respect to his political theory.

For Habermas communicative action is the original kind of communication, the originary form of discourse. It bears emphasizing that he sees it as emancipatory, as necessary for humane and just society and for democracy. It is the foundation of his discursive theory. He sees at least the possibility, if not the predictability, of communicative action as triumphing over strategic action as foundational to, and embedded in, radical democracy. Rasmussen thinks that Habermas's theory is an expression of politics much more than the science Habermas thinks lies at the root of his communicative theory, and he understands Habermas's political vision to be

---

89 Habermas, *Die neue Unübersichtlichkeit* (Frankfurt am Main: Suhrkamp, 1985), 215; and Albert Wellmer, *Praktische Philosophie und Theorie der Gesellschaft: Zum Problem der normativen Grundlagen einer kritischen Sozialwissenschaft* (Konstanz: Universitätsverlag, 1979), 10. In Detlef Horster, *Habermas*, trans. Heidi Thompson (Philadelphia: Pennbridge, 1992), 10.

90 Rasmussen, 26, 28.

91 *Ibid.*, 27. Habermas, *The Theory of Communicative Action*, 1, 339–402.

somewhat utopian.[92] Of course, Habermas sees himself as engaged in a program not unlike the view Rawls takes of his own, one of "feasible utopianism". Interestingly, Habermas distances himself from Rawls in this respect, as he sees the latter's theory as "purely normative". His own work, in contrast, is one of "*reconstructive* analysis", meant to "prove what we always tacitly assume, if we participate in the democratic and constitutional practices that have fortunately taken hold in our countries". He adds,

> I try to show that this normative self-understanding of our practices is not from the start illusory ... . Only a democracy that is understood in terms of communications theory is feasible under the conditions of complex societies ... in my model the forms of communication in a civil society, which grow out of an intact private sphere, along with the communicative stream of a vital public sphere embedded in liberal political culture, are what chiefly bear the burden of normative expectations. That is why ... nothing will change without the intervening, effective, innovative energy of social movements, and without the utopian images and energies that motivate such movements.[93]

In the interview quoted here, Habermas goes on to say that

> Communicative power can be formed only in public spheres that produce intersubjective relationships on the basis of reciprocal recognition and make it possible to use communicative freedoms ... Once a *public* starts moving, it does not march in unison, but rather offers the spectacle of anarchically unshackled communicative freedoms.[94]

He also admits that in his earlier work he had held to an "hermeneutic idealism", that he has recanted, as well as criticizing his own theorization of the "ideal speech situation", as a fallacy of misplaced concreteness.[95] This is to say that in his later work he moves some distance from the utopianism of which Rasmussen accuses him. Nonetheless, as I have noted, he sees a certain kind or level of utopianism as valuable.[96]

Communicative action, theory, reason, and community, then form the foundation of Habermas's theorization of democracy. *Between Facts and Norms* is peppered effusively with references to concepts all modified by the term "communicative": reason, rationality, action, power, freedom, and sociation. This study cannot explore or explicate this constellation of

---

92   *Ibid.*, 36.

93   Habermas, *A Berlin Republic: Writings on Germany*, trans. Steven Rendall (Lincoln: University of Nebraska Press, 1977); in Schomberg and Baynes, 242–43.

94   *Ibid.*, 249.

95   *Ibid.*, 251.

96   Habermas's view, in respect to the question of its utopianism, is, as I have indicated above, much like that of Rawls; and I am at a loss to understand how he sees Rawls's theory as utopian because "purely normative", when (a) it is not "*purely*" normative; and (b) Rawls sees his theory as holding concrete possibilities that seem not incredibly distant from Habermas's view of his own concreteness. Note that Rawls, like Habermas, builds his theory from the foundation of the shared moral intuitions of societies like ours, and writes that we do not start from scratch when discussing what kinds of rules and politics we would adopt and construct.

concepts beyond the necessary connections made here, but their importance is foundational to his larger program and the project of this book. Yet
additional contextual concepts must also be described, albeit more briefly,
before I return to his democratic theory. Communicative action leads to
discourse theory and discourse ethics, also foundational and contextual
concepts for understanding Habermas's theory of democracy.

Habermas tends to use "discourse theory" and "discourse ethics" in
synonymous ways, and the latter term is much more often referenced. His
use of "discourse" orbits loosely around a technical sense which refers to
the systematic examination of problematic validity claims.[97] Habermas
makes prodigious use of his concept of discourse in *Between Facts and
Norms* and unsurprisingly so in a book subtitled *Contributions to a Discourse Theory of Law and Democracy*. In this book, he references his earlier
development of the concept in *Moral Consciousness and Communicative
Action* and *Justification and Application: Remarks on Discourse Ethics*.[98]

I have noted Habermas's rejection of instrumentalist/functionalist
rationality, yet his hope in rationality otherwise conceived. Discourse,
along with the closely related conceptions of communicative action and
rationality, provides the means to theorize a program of justification, particularly, of moral claims. Discourse ethics picks up where the theory of
communicative action leaves off. What Habermas is looking for here is
some special kind of validity claim that pertains to commands and norms
and that can be identified within the context in which moral problems
emerge, i.e., the 'lifeworld'.[99] Discourse ethics, then, is situated in the
larger framework of communicative action and rationality, through which
Habermas argues that all communication requires consensual
intersubjective recognition of validity claims.

Habermas is particularly concerned about normative claims. He argues
that such claims have validity when they "*mediate a mutual dependence* of
language".[100] Further, and importantly, the validity of a norm rests on its
endorsement by all of those affected by it; "valid norms must *deserve* recognition by *all* concerned".

> True impartiality pertains only to that standpoint from which one can
> generalize precisely those norms that can count on universal assent
> because they perceptibly embody an interest common to all affected. It

97 Cf. William Outhwaite, ed., *The Habermas Reader* (Cambridge, UK: Polity Press, 1996), 368. And
    see William Rehg, *Insight and Solidarity: A Study in the Discourse Ethics of Jürgen Habermas*
    (Berkeley: University of California Press, 1994); and Rasmussen, 56–74.

98 *BFN*, xl. *Moral Consciousness and Communicative Action*, trans. Christian Lenhardt and Sherry
    Weber Nicholson (Cambridge: MIT Press, 1990); *Justification and Application*, trans. Ciaran P.
    Cronin (Cambridge: MIT Press, 1993).

99 Leslie Howe, *On Habermas* (Belmont, CA: Wadsworth, 2000), 30.

100 "Discourse Ethics: Notes on a Program of Philosophical Justification", in *Moral Consciousness
    and Communicative Action*, 61.

is these norms that deserve intersubjective recognition. Thus the impartiality of judgment is expressed in a principle that constrains *all* affected to adopt the perspectives of *all others* in in the balancing of interests ... . Thus the validity norm has to fulfill the following condition:

All affected can accept the consequence and the side effects its *general* observance can be anticipated to have for the satisfaction of *everyone's* interests (and these consequences are preferred to those of known alternative possibilities for regulation.[101]

Habermas rejects the liberal notion of a "neutral observer", whether of deontological or utilitarian varieties; and one can see republican strains in the quote above. Yet he uses Kantian conceptualizations in the construction of his theory, especially the principle of universalization (the first formulation of the Categorical Imperative).[102] Concretely, discourse ethics means the following:

1.   Everyone with the competence to speak and act must be allowed to take part in the relevant discourse.
2.   Everyone can question any assertion whatsoever.
3.   Everyone is allowed to introduce any assertion whatsoever.[103]
4.   Everyone is allowed to assert his attitudes, desires, and needs.
5.   No one may be coerced in any way from exercising their rights (1-4 above).[104]

In sum, Habermas's discourse theory demands that these terms are met, that "all affected can *freely* accept the consequences ... that the *general* observance of a controversial norm can be expected to have for the satisfaction of *each individual*". This summarization is then put in the form of a principle, (D): "Only those norms can claim to be valid that meet (or could meet) with the approval of all affected in their capacity as participants in a practical discourse."[105] It is important to be clear about what this normative theory is for Habermas: an idealization which we can approximate significantly. That is, Habermas thinks that his theorization of communicative action, discourse, and democracy is, although, normative, also partially descriptive and reasonably achievable. Complex philosophical details aside, it is straightforward as to how his discourse theory relates to

---

101   *Ibid.*, 65.

102   One can note his differences with Rawls as a signifier of his departures with aspects of liberal theory (the 1995 articles exchanged in *The Journal of Philosophy* are the best, but not only, documents which explicate this difference); but he is also in disagreement with communitarians in various respects as well. See Rasumussen, 62–73.

103   Note the important difference here between Habermas and Rawls. Rawls offers a strategy of avoidance, of taking some matters off the table in the public sphere, matters that are "comprehensive doctrines" or motivated by comprehensive doctrines, which he thinks are beyond the possibility of agreement because not subject to rational discourse by all participants involved.

104   "Discourse Ethics", 89.

105   *Ibid.*, 93. Cf. Howe, 36.

communicative action and communicative rationality, *and* how it relates to his democratic theory. Again one is reminded of the procedural basis and character of his program in general, and his democratic theory specifically.

Howe nicely summarizes as follows:

> In the end, Habermas wants to maintain that all forms of sociocultural life are geared to the support of communicative action through argumentation, no matter how poorly developed the latter might be ... . This means that trying to argue that there is no answer to moral questions is a pointless ... effort, but also that any attempt to devise a morality that excludes those who are affected by it is just as self-defeating. If Habermas is right, morality simply must be both inclusive and public ... .[106]

At bottom, we have to "find a way of regulating our communal life that is equally good for all".[107] Habermas's discourse ethics — combined with his democratic theory — is his means of doing just this. He converts his discourse ethics into a democratic theory:

> The discourse principle is intended to assume the shape of a principle of democracy ... by way of legal institutionalization. The principle of democracy is what then confers legitmating force on the legislative process. The key idea is that the principle of democracy derives from the interpenetration of the discourse principle and the legal form ... . One begins by applying the discourse principle to the general right to liberties ... and ends by legally institutionalizing the conditions for a discursive exercise of political autonomy.[108]

A few pages later he writes that

> Equal opportunities for the political use of communicative freedoms require a legally structured deliberative praxis in which the discourse principle is applied ... the *public use* of communicative freedom — call for the legal institutionalization of various forms of communication and the implementation of democratic procedures ... . Rights of equal participation for each person thus result from a symmetrical juridification of the communicative freedom of all citizens. And this freedom in turn *requires* forms of discursive opinion — and will — formation that enable the exercise of political autonomy in accordance with political rights.[109]

And finally, "Law is not a narcissistically self-enclosed system, but is nourished by the "democratic *Sittlichkeit*" of enfranchised citizens and a liberal political culture that meet it halfway".[110]

I have offered these quotes from *Between Facts and Norms* as a simple indication of the pervasive message that Habermas sends about the crucial

---

106 Howe, 37.
107 "Remarks on Discourse Ethics", in *Justification and Application*, 59.
108 *BFN*, 121.
109 *Ibid.*, 128.
110 *Ibid.*, 461.

and multifaceted relationship among discourse ethics, law, and democracy.[111] He transforms his discourse theory into political theory which is through-and-through, democratic theory. He writes also of a "democratic principle" by which legitimacy obtains only in the assent of all citizens in a discursive process. This process then results, where appropriate, in legislation.[112] But law and politics narrowly conceived are not the only proper forums of legitimate discourse and decision. There is a "lifeworld" and a "public sphere" outside of the legislative process that requires brief attention, for these concepts also have everything to do with Habermasian democracy.

Here I will be quite brief. Habermas borrows the term "lifeworld" (*Lebenswelt*) from Husserl, who used it to refer to the world as it is given to us through our experience, prior to the operation of science or of phenomenology in the philosophical sense. Habermas extends the concept further, using it to refer to informal aspects and ways of life, in contradistinction to market and administrative systems. The lifeworld is also, for him, a "horizon of meaning", that is, a way of ordering values and perspectives that are also alternative to market and administrative ways of conceiving "meaning".[113] The lifeworld "consists of individual skills, the intuitive knowledge of *how* one deals with a situation; and from socially acquired practices, the intuitive knowledge of what one can rely on in a situation, not less than, in a trivial sense [one's] underlying convictions".[114]

The lifeworld is the *context or setting* in which comunicative action and discourse takes place, not only in respect to a locus, but also in respect to a medium of understanding. There is a "social space of a commonly inhabited lifeworld that opens up in a conversation [which] provides the key to the communication-theoretical concept of society".[115] Not only democracy, but society—social systems and institutions, however formal or informal—are constituted by language and discourse. Husserl proposed the lifeworld as a scientific program that needed to be engaged, although he never undertook that engagement. Horster sees Habermas's theorization of the lifeworld as picking up the challenge laid down by Husserl, who wrote, "In opposition to all previously designed objective sciences, which are sciences on the ground of the world, this would be a science of

---

111 It is, in fact, a serious challenge to the Habermas interpreter as to how one can sufficiently describe and summarize his complex and polyvalent work within the limits of space demanded by an enterprise such as my project here. Indeed, I think the conversion of discourse ethics to democratic theory warrants book-length treatment. For a short but helpful explanation of this conversion, see Scott Bartlett, "Discursive Democracy and a Democratic Way of Life", in Hahn, 367–86.

112 *BFN*, 110.

113 Cf. Outhwaite, 369.

114 *Theory of Communicative Action*, 2, 35.

115 Habermas, "Entgegnung", *Kommunikates Handeln*, eds., Axel Honneth and Hans Joas (Frankfurt am Main: Campus, 1986), 334; cited in Horster, 21.

the universal how *of the pregiveness of the world*, i.e., of what makes it a universal ground for any sort of objectivity."[116] The lifeworld is context and setting, then, in an *a priori* way, there is a "givenness" to it, although it is not a metaphysical concept, but one of social construction.

The crisis of our time, according to Habermas, is that this lifeworld is under threat; indeed, it is being "colonized" by "systems imperatives", strategic rationality, bureaucratic authorities, systems, values, and ideas. This is a problem deeper than, and under the surface of, economic exploitation and totalitarian ideologies. The colonization of the lifeworld is a more radical problem that what Weber could have observed. The colonization of the lifeworld takes place through what Oakeshott calls Rationalism and Habermas calls, "strategic action". Only the normative theorization of communicative action, rationality, and freedom, coupled with discourse ethics and the radical democracy constituted by communicative action and discourse ethics can stave off this colonization, which is a kind of eating away at the soul of a society. Only communicative rationality, in which participants overcome their mere subjectivity, can "assure" us of "both the unity of the objective world and the intersubjectivity of the lifeworld".[117] In short, the distinction between "system" (an umbrella term Habermas uses for various of the dynamics that colonize the lifeworld, several mentioned above), and lifeworld defines a pathology, indeed, a colonizing pathology.[118]

Finally, then, a word about Habermas's use of the concept of the public sphere (*Öffentlichkeit*) is appropriate before I return to my summary of his democratic theory proper. This too is a fundamental and foundational theme in his larger program and certainly in respect to his theorization of democracy from *The Structural Transformation of the Public Sphere* (1962) to *Between Facts and Norms*. After his study with Horkheimer and Adorno, Habermas began an investigation of the ways that a new public sphere emerged during the Enlightenment and the American and French revolutions, and how political discussion and deliberation were promoted by these movements. This work was carried into *The Structural Transformation* where he came to elaborate the concept of the public sphere as a space containing the institutions and practices existing between private interests and the state. This space is, of course, referred to as civil society by various theorists. Habermas writes that "autonomous public spheres" (one can see

---

116 Edmund Husserl, *The Crisis of European Sciences and Transcendental Phenomenology*, trans. David Carr (Evanston: Northwestern University Press, 1970), 146–47 (emphasis, mine); cited in Horster, 23–4. Habermas's thorough theorization of this program taken up from Husserl is not confined to his conceptualization of the lifeworld, but extends to his ideas of "universal pragmatics". However, this latter theorization need not concern us here.

117 *A Theory of Communicative Action*, 1, 10.

118 See Rasmussen, 45–55, for an excellent discussion and critique of Habermas's system/lifeworld distinction.

these as components of the public sphere as a whole), are "anchored in the voluntary associations of civil society and embedded in the liberal patterns of political culture and socialization; in a word, they depend on a rationalized lifeworld". Further, he writes of the public sphere "as a communication structure rooted in the lifeworld through the associational network of civil society".[119] What should not be overlooked is that Habermas argues for the *transformation* of this sphere. He wants it to become, in a word, more democratic.[120]

Habermas also conceptualizes the public sphere as a "sounding board for problems that must be processed by the political system because they cannot be solved elsewhere". Thus, the public sphere is a kind of "warning system with sensors that ... are sensitive throughout society". He adds that as a part of his democratic theory, the public sphere must not only detect and identify, but also "amplify the pressure" and "convincingly and *influentially* thematize" and "dramatize" problems, yet furnish possible solutions as well. He warns, however, that the public sphere has a limited capacity to solve problems "*on its own*", needing state institutions for much of the work to be done.[121] As with the other Habermasian concepts I have introduced, much more can easily be written. *Between Facts and Norms* alone is saturated with references to the public sphere. Nonetheless, I have now defined communicative action, discourse ethics, the lifeworld, and the public sphere sufficiently so as to see the context these conceptions provide for his theorization of deliberative democracy. I can now, then, return to my summarization of his theory as it is presented in *Between Facts and Norms*.

The reader has already seen the procedural character of his theory, and how he converts his discourse ethics into democratic theory. I am now in a position to pull various strands together into a final synopsis. It is important to see the fundamental schematic of Habermas's theory, that the power of moral norms, democratic procedures and institutions, and law are all essentially related and foundational in modern and especially, contemporary societies. Further, that the meaning of morality, democracy, and law are not only socially constructed, but linguistically and communicatively constructed, and irreducibly so. One might say that given the logic of his own work as it has developed over his career, it was inevitable that his moral and social theory would turn to the democratic and legal theory that we find in *Between Facts and Norms*.

---

119 *BFN*, 358–59. Cf. Habermas's claim that the "forms of communication in a civil society" grow out of an intact private sphere, along with the communicative stream of a vital public sphere ... ", above.

120 Douglas Kellner, 259–70, 277.

121 *BFN*, 359.

Habermas articulates a two-track structure of politics, the informal and the formal. One has now encountered the informal sphere in respect to the lifeworld and civil society, wherein are found spontaneous as well as organized sources and systems of communication, even those which are "chaotic" and "anarchic". Important to his democratic theory is the conclusion that citizens undertake and undergo will-formation in the informal sphere through discourse and deliberation. He argues that healthy moral/political/democratic societies are porous in respect to the boundary between the informal and the formal tracks. The discourse in civil society needs to influence the discourse in the formal system of legislatures, and other institutions of formal politics. The will-formation of citizens should penetrate formal politics in any number of ways.

As can now be seen, the theoretical arguments as to how such a system — and political culture — is best developed so as to work in this thoroughly democratic way mandates a fusion of various republican/communitarian and liberal values and principles; the result, he theorizes, overcomes the shortcomings of republicanism and liberalism isolated from one another. Whereas the liberal autonomy he seeks to protect is fundamentally oriented to the proper *opportunities* persons should have, and their *rights* to pursue those opportunities, the republican/communitarian dimension of this theory seeks to adequately devise the means to *actualize* one's opportunities and rights. Formal rights mean little, as is well known, if they cannot be realized. The fusion might be accurately seen as fundamentally liberal but constructed so as to protect and promote republican/ communitarian values. In any case, it should be emphasized that both the liberal and republican features of the theory are subordinate and subservient to democracy itself. That is, the democratic proceduralism gives birth to liberal and republican features, rather than prior ideological commitments generating limited democratic structures.[122] His two-track system is related to the liberal/republican fusion: whereas the formal track is asymmetrically weighted toward the liberal dimensions, the infor-

---

122 Of course it is to be recognized that there is a chicken-or-egg problem here that is unavoidable in political, and especially liberal, theory: participants in discourse who get to choose the design of their political association "should not do so" in such a way as to limit certain rights or do harm to their fellows citizens, but if they have parameters to work within *before* they begin their deliberations, where can such parameters legitimately originate? Rawls works at this problem aggressively in respect to his theorization of the "original position", and it is, again, a pervasive problem. We need not explicate Habermas's work on the problem, but see the Introduction to Schomberg and Baynes, 1–11; Baynes, 15–30; and Bartlett, 367–86 as they address this problematic in a helpful manner.

In short, Habermas thinks that the best way to address this problem can only be found in the content of democratic procedures themselves (as he specifies them), and, like Rawls, the generative power of moral intuitions already widely held that persons would (or do) bring to such deliberation. Here is where Habermas's liberal commitments may be most important, as he thinks persons have prepolitical interests that they carry into deliberation, at least, given the chance.

mal track of civil society and lifeworld is imbalanced toward the republican dimension.[123]

It is well understood that liberal values, on the one hand, and republican
commitments, on the other, oscillate between conflict and healthy tension.
Habermas's democratic theory not only seeks to channel this fact into
moral and political stability, in its general respect; but the very function of
law, more particularly, is to mediate this conflict or tension. Law has the
function of aiding the social integration generated by communicative
action and moral discourse. Morality, on Habermasian terms, names the
ways that people seek to resolve conflicts of interest, coordinate actions,
and establish social order. Politics echoes, supports, protects, and stabi-
lizes morality, fundamentally, by transmitting it into law (which does not
mean, for Habermas, of course, that morality and law are inseparable.
Their separability is seen, for example, in moments of civil disobedi-
ence).[124]

The porousness that Habermas's system theorizes between the formal
and informal tracks, whereby will-formation in civil society penetrates
formal political institutions, includes the democratic influence on law. He
thinks that the input from citizens in civil society will tend to be rational
and that persons comply with law insofar as it is generated by them in
some respects, and conforms with their will. That is, law is valid when
generally endorsed, because it requires of people what they have independent, extra-legal reasons for doing. This Habermasian notion is found
elsewhere, of course, as I have shown above in respect to Oakeshott's theory of law, and it is not unlike Oakeshott's theory of "subscription". A
valid law, for Habermas, has both a normative and a factual dimension.
Here, one can recall the German title of *Between Facts and Norms* and the
tension he identifies in his title is between "facticity" and "validity". His
concern is about what makes for political, democratic, and legal *legitimacy*.
A law is legitimate when there are reasons for obeying it.[125] This basis of
legitimacy is necessary but not sufficient. A law must also be positive,
which is to say, imposed by legitimate (which is to say, recognized)
authority.[126]

To reiterate: Habermas is interested in political legitimacy. One recalls
that he summarized his theorization of discursive democracy into a principle of democracy, which is a specification of the discourse principle (D).
(D) specifies the validity of action-norms, that is, it holds for both moral

---

123 See James Gordon Finlayson, *Habermas: A Very Short Introduction* (New York: Oxford
    University Press, 2005), 109–13, for a brief and simple but helpful taxonomy of what Habermas
    rejects in liberalism and republicanism, and what the amalgam of the two consists in.

124 Cf. *ibid.*, 113.

125 That is, of course, reasons that are not circular, reasons that go beyond the fact that it is law (and
    concomitantly, that one might suffer unpleasant consequences for not obeying it).

126 A third, and obvious, necessity of legitimate law is that it is coercible; cf. Finlayson, 114–15.

and legal norms. He writes, "the principle of democracy already supposes the possibility of valid moral judgments. Indeed, it presupposes the possibility of *all* the types of practical judgments and discourses that supply laws with their legitimacy".[127] While the democratic principle also states that legitimate laws must have the assent of the legal community, he also specifies that the legal community is comprised of all those who are capable of lawful conduct and whose actions are governed by any given law in question at any given time. It can be seen that legitimate laws are also generated by citizens' discourse in civil society as that discourse penetrates formal political institutions, including the legal institutions. Further, laws must conform to the already-present system of legally constituted rights.[128] What Habermas theorizes then is a flow of discourse and deliberation that moves from society through civil society into formal political and legal institutions, the legal community broadly understood, and into the formation of law that wins the subscription of citizens. This organic and fluid process is generated and vitalized by discourse and deliberation that moves "up" and "down" the system. "Up" and "down" mischaracterize the flow, however, in that it is circular more than it is vertical. Habermas does not think, of course, that each citizen must endorse every law. His system is powered by discourse and interpentration of porous "boundaries" such that what *can* merit the subscription of citizens is not likely to be distant from what actually does merit their conscious and even conscientious assent. Of course, a democratic and legal system can ask nothing more than that which most probably and justifiably merits citizens' endorsements in respect to its laws. For Habermas, legitimate law not only "has a relation to morality inscribed within it",[129] but, as such (as summarized above), it also has an intrinsic relationship to the common good, which is much of what generates its legitimacy. In posttraditional societies, in which modern pluralism erodes the shared ethos of earlier times, law comes to the aid of a weakened moral culture, and provides a means by which "moral content can spread through a society".[130]

In conclusion, I want to reiterate succinctly: Habermas converts his discourse ethics into a theory of democracy. He builds a sophisticated system to do this work which is deeply procedural, seeks to guide discourse and deliberation along liberal and republican commitments, and ensures that the discourse and outcomes are reasonable. This procedural and discur-

---

127 *BFN*, 110. Habermas also writes that "Only those laws count as legitimate to which all members of the legal community can assent in a discursive process of legislation that has in turn been legally constituted", (*BFN*, 1996, 110). Here we see the principle of discourse extends to smaller units of political society, in this case, the legal community. The point is that at every level, we might say, micro to macro, discourse provides legitimacy.

128 Cf. Finlayson, 116.

129 *BFN*, 1996, 106.

130 *Ibid.*, 118. Finlayson, 119.

sive process secures the legitimacy of norms and decisions. "Specifically, the democratic principle states that only those statutes may claim legitimacy that can meet with the assent of all citizens in a discursive process of legislation that has in turn been legally constituted."[131]

The political sphere is not only formal, but also informal, with information exchange and other forms of discourse moving between the these two "tracks". Indeed, formal institutions give definitive form much needed in contrast to the effusive and even "subjectless" and "anonymous" communication that swirls about in the lifeworld and civil society, scattered across the public sphere. Lastly, Habermas understands his theory to be not only normative but descriptive. That is, he thinks it is the result of what can be known about the world, and practiced in societies as we have them (although clearly, no society is close to everything Habermas envisions; the claim here is only that any number of societies can approximate and move toward the realization of his vision). He realizes that his theory is an idealization, and so he works hard, particularly in *Between Facts and Norms*, to keep both the normative and descriptive features of his theory in constant and realistic relationship with one another.[132] It is hoped that this summary of Habermas indicates why he is considered by many to the "father of deliberative democracy".

Dryzek

Two of the reasons I include John Dryzek as a representative figure of deliberative democratic theory is because of the interpenetration of his *theory* with political *science* and, relatedly, his work in connecting discourse theory to practical problems, primarily, the problematic of environmental ethics and policy.[133] That is, Dryzek extends his reach beyond the usual philosophical and normative literature and seeks to demonstrate what deliberative democracy looks like in the context of concrete political demands. My consideration of Dryzek need not be, however, as detailed as that of Rawls and Habermas. I will simply summarize the argument of his 1990 text, *Discursive Democracy* and then turn to his argument made ten

---

131 *BFN*, 110.

132 Cf. Bartlett, 368–69, 372.

133 For example, see his *Rational Ecology: Environment and Political Economy* (New York: Basil Blackwell, 1987); "Green Reason: Communicative Ethics for the Biosphere", *Environmental Ethics*, 12, (1990), 195–210; "Ecology and Discursive Democracy: Beyond Liberal Capitalism and the Administrative State", *Capitalism, Nature, Socialism*, 3, no. 2, (1992), 18–44; "Foundations for Environmental Political Economy: The Search for Homo Ecologicus?" *New Political Economy*,1, (1996), 27–40; "Political and Ecological Communication", in Freya Mathews, ed., *Ecology and Democracy* (London: Frank Cass, 1996), 13–30; "Strategies of Ecological Democratization", in William M. Lafferty and James Meadowcroft, eds., *Democracy and the Environment: Problems and Prospects* (Cheltenham: Edward Elgar, 1996), 108– 23; *The Politics of the Earth: Environmental Discourses* (Oxford: Oxford University Press, 1997; and "Green Democracy" in Dryzek, *Deliberative Democracy and Beyond*, op. cit., 140–61.

years later in *Deliberative Democracy and Beyond*. Dryzek begins the Preface of *Discursive Democracy* with a wonderfully concise description of his project:

> Discursive democracy is woven here from threads supplied by a classical (Aristotelian) model of politics, participatory democracy, communicative action, practical reason, and critical theory. The product, or so I shall argue, is a coherent, integrative, and attractive program for politics, public policy, and political science. Ultimately, discursive democracy looks forward to a world of free and congenial political interaction where politics, properly understood, is returned to its Aristotelian primacy in the order of things. More immediately, discursive democracy charts escape from some contemporary impasses in political arrangements, public policy, and social science. Politics, policy, and science alike are currently beholden to instrumental and objectivist notions about rationality in human affairs. My case for discursively rational alternatives is constructed by the ruins of instrumental rationality and objectivism.[134]

One immediately sees the ambition and scope of this text and the promise of discursive democracy as claimed by Dryzek. My summary in the next few pages cannot unpack and explicate everything he has mentioned here, but this opening statement allows me to frame his project and my summarization of it. One can immediately see Habermasian and Oakeshottian resonances, and in the case of Habermas, this is no coincidence.[135]

Dryzek begins with a diagnosis of instrumental rationality and objectivism. The former has come to govern rational behavior, and the latter, rational belief and morality. Instrumental rationality destroys congenial, spontaneous, egalitarian, and intrinsically meaningful aspects of human association. It is undemocratic. It represses the freedom of the individual. It is ineffective when confronted with complex social problems, and it makes effective and appropriate policy analysis impossible. It also informs inappropriate and unfruitful social science instruments and methods (most particularly, the opinion survey). Objectivism is repressive; it *imposes* its own standards and practices upon traditions and ways of life that do not share its viewpoints (victims include, for example, indigenous cultures and dissenting epistemologies). Objectivism also, then, inhibits the progress of political science and politics.[136] This is the indictment explicated throughout the book which he thinks discursive democratic prac-

---

134 John S. Dryzek, *Discursive Democracy: Politics, Policy, and Political Science* (New York: Cambridge University Press, 1999), ix.

135 In respect to the claim that "Politics, policy, and science alike are currently beholden to instrumental and objectivist notions about rationality in human affairs", in addition to Habermas and Oakeshott (as well as Weber and Popper), see the sympathetic argument put forward by Ian Shapiro, *The Flight from Reality in the Human Sciences* (Princeton: Princeton University Press, 2006).

136 Dryzek, *Discursive Democracy*, 4–7.

tices overcome, which is, of course, the other part of the book's argument. Drawing on, and in the spirit of, the work of Aristotle, Popper, Arendt, MacIntyre, and Habermas, Dryzek argues discursive practices and science to be the cure. In a word, rationality itself needs to be *democratized*.

In response to instrumentalist rationality and objectivism, Dryzek argues a two-fold discursive direction. One part of this strategy focuses on the conclusion that valuing the views of others is impossible in the absence of shared commitments to the ultimate reasons *why* citizens pursue various actions, policies, and outcomes. Therefore, procedures must urge citizens toward consensus through deliberative means in respect to their reasons. The other strategic component is the one advanced by Habermas, wherein communicative action provides procedural criteria about how disputes and arguments might be resolved and discursive principles might be constructed. [137] The strategy, then, has both ends and means components, and it relies heavily upon critical theory. Yet, extending beyond the reach of the Frankfurt School, Dryzek writes,

> I seek not to defend the "lifeworld" from further colonization by the system but to conduct a counteroffensive by taking discursive rationality to the heart of the "enemy's" domain … . In short, what I offer is a constructive dimension that has so far been missing from the critical theory of society.[138]

Dryzek makes use of the Habermasian concepts of communicative action, the "ideal speech" situation (although Habermas has since modified this conception in an important way, as I indicated above), and the public sphere, to theorize "discursive designs" of democratic practices and institutions. He echoes Habermas in disallowing authority on any basis other than argument, recounting his phrase as to "the forceless force of the better argument". He also disallows all barriers to the participation of interested parties, as well as the existence of "autonomous formal constitutions or rules".[139] Dryzek is not an anarchist, but he emphasizes the power of discursive and deliberative democracy outside of the state:

> … complicity in state administration should be avoided. As long as a state is present, discursive designs should be located in, and help constitute, a public space within which citizens associate and *confront* the state. Within the discursive design, there should be no hierarchy or formal rules, though debate may be governed by informal canons of free discourse. A decision rule of consensus should obtain. Finally, all the features I have enumerated should be redeemable within the dis-

---

137 *Ibid.*, 17–18. Note that Dryzek thinks pure proceduralism to be incoherent.

138 *Ibid.*, 20, 21. His claim to offer a new "constructive dimension" may be an overstatement in respect to not fully appreciating the constructive dynamism of Habermas's work, but in another way, Dryzek's work is newly constructive: as I indicated in my opening remarks about Dryzek, his rigorous application of discourse theory to political *science* and policy is, in fact, a new "dimension".

139 *Ibid.*, 41.

cursive design itself. Participants should be free to reflectively and discursively override any of them.[140]

To flesh out his theory in concrete terms, Dryzek identifies features of this kind of discursive "design" he sees in various contemporary attempts to extend democracy and solve problems. These examples are found in response to civil, labor, international, and environmental disputes. He also indicates a number of organizations and movements as loci of concrete approximation of his theory, for example, Liberation Theology, the Quakers, the United Church of Christ, the feminist, and the green movement.[141] Further, Dryzek argues that "discursive action" facilitates the provision of public goods in decentralized and noncoercive ways; and in so doing, subsequent agreements are more likely because the parties involved will have reached previous agreements in such free and deliberative ways. Discursive designs are a less manipulative and more symbiotic means of problem solving. Additionally, such designs, "however incipient", expose deficiencies in established institutions (e.g., when mediation exposes weaknesses in litigation). Not being bound by constitutions and other formal rules, discursive procedures allow for their own supercession, so development can happen in ways participants think best. Lastly, the utilization and success of discourse in these ways erode the idea that it is legitimate to exercise authority on the basis of anything other than the better argument.[142]

As I write this my television blares a CNN program entitled "Broken Government", which documents serious problems in the United States at the moment, all of which U.S. citizens agree, it is government's responsibility to solve (e.g., the war in Iraq , the "war against terror", and border security).[143] Dryzek notes that "Spaces exist for the generation of discursive designs to the extent dominant political and economic institutions are crumbling under the weight of their contradictions". Can it be denied that the problems faced in Iraq, the congressional modification of the Geneva Conventions, and the recent revoking of *habeas corpus*, for example, are extant in no small measure because of a near absence of discourse and deliberation, not only in Congress and among the "chatting class" but at every level throughout civil society? Habermas's view, that (at least the capitalist) state is torn between legitimation and accumulation functions, is endorsed by Dryzek—and he sees the gap between legitimation and

---

140 *Ibid.*, 43 (emphasis, mine).

141 *Ibid.*, 43–50. For a statement about democracy as the insurgency of such groups, see Michael Walzer, "A Credo for this Moment", *Dissent*, 37, no. 2 (Spring 1990), 160. Also found in Philip Green, ed., *Democracy* (Atlantic Highlands, NJ: Humanities Press, 1994), 244–5.

142 *Ibid.*, 55–56.

143 Though I mention "the war on terror" here, I am aware, of course, that it is anyone's guess as to what this phrase means, or rather, that it means whatever anyone wants it to mean. It is just this propagandistic incoherency that helps me underscore the point I am making.

accumulation as presenting discursive and therefore, democratic opportunities.[144]

Dryzek thinks that given time

> a succession of discursive exercises held up to critical scrutiny could
> create and reinforce norms of free discourse, and the critical aspects of
> modern consciousness more generally. In so doing, such exercises
> would ... help constitute a world increasingly hospitable to truly dis-
> cursive designs and to the participatory *process* of discursive design.
> Institutional reconstruction would flourish in such a world.[145]

Democracy and rationality are two broad principles widely affirmed.
Dryzek argues that they have suffered an unnecessary and destructive
separation, and *Discursive Democracy* is an argument as to how healthy reconciliation can be achieved. Further, it is the misguided power of instrumental rationality that has eroded democracy and pushed the divide ever
farther apart. He notes how it is often "the authority claimed by expertise
that leads rationality to confront, corrupt, and perhaps even destroy
democracy". Only communicative rationality, he argues, can reconcile
rationality properly understood to democracy properly understood. The
result of such reconciliation is discursive democracy. In such democracy,
political *science* would not be diminished, but revived; and the destructive
(if not false) distinctions among political science, policy, and politics
would be eliminated.[146]

He seeks to establish the essential identity of political science, rationality, policy, and politics in a number of ways throughout the book. He
argues for "communicatively rational social science in the form of critical
oversight and discursive metadesign". He argues that the only defensible
(for both intrinsic/moral and instrumental reasons) kind of policy analysis proceeds in terms of contributions to, and facilitation of, free discourse
within the public sphere. He argues that political science instruments and
methods should be evaluated by the extent to which they embody discourses of uncoerced communication. Communicative rationality would
make our politics more felicitous, and enable better political science, disci-
pline, and polity and more effectively, harmoniously, and productively
solve complex social problems, improving international relations, democratic development, and social science.[147]

Dryzek's effort to analyze, penetrate, and reconcile rationality, political
science, policy, and politics makes his contribution to deliberative democracy important. In the interest of space, I have not dealt with the political
science, public policy, or international relations components of his argu-

---

144 Dryzek, *Discursive Democracy*, 77–78; cf. 78–89.
145 *Ibid.*, 87.
146 *Ibid.*, 217–18.
147 *Ibid.*, 218–19.

ment as much as his approach more generally. I turn now to *Deliberative Democracy and Beyond* which considers the deliberative turn more theoretically and in relationship to democratic theory more broadly. I might begin by simply noting his shift in language from "discourse" to "deliberation". Although he prefers "discursive democracy" to "deliberative democracy", the adoption of the latter terminology is a movement to coincide with the literature which more often than not uses it. He treats "deliberation" as the more inclusive category, but continued use of "discursive democracy" is employed for critical purposes.

In this latest book he takes a tour through the major theories of democracy as a means of determining "what the theory of democracy should look like in the wake of the deliberative turn". He rejects some of the directions deliberative theory has taken; and this criticism finds its primary nexus in what is probably the most important division in deliberative democratic theory: on one side, theorists have reached an easy accommodation to liberal and constitutional theory, while the other side is more insistently and consistently critical of liberal constitutionalism and its political economy.[148] He is to be found on the latter side of this debate. Above I emphasized his word "confront" as in what deliberative democrats should often do in respect to the state. In this latter text, he continues to argue that "a defensible theory of deliberative democracy must be critical in its orientation to established power structures, including those that operate beneath the constitutional surface of the liberal state, and so [be] insurgent in relation to established institutions".[149]

The liberal foundations of deliberative democracy emphasize "public reasons" as an important constitutive of democracy; this approach imposes limits on what constitutes authentic or allowable deliberation. Dryzek is critical of this perspective, thinking of the restrictions as limitations on democracy itself. He thinks democratic space is big enough for not only argument but rhetoric, humor, emotion, testimony, storytelling, and even gossip. He argues that the only condition for authentic democracy is that the communication "induce[s] reflection upon preferences in non-coercive fashion ... . Authentic *democracy* can then be said to exist to the degree that reflective preferences influence collective outcomes". Democracy should be, he argues, pluralistic, communicating across difference without erasing it, reflexive in its questioning orientation to established traditions, transnational, and extended to nature.[150]

Dryzek's democratic theory is an amalgam of sources from liberal and critical theory, but he clearly takes more from the latter tradition than the former. Indeed, he thinks that critical theory has itself become too compro-

148 *Deliberative Democracy and Beyond*, v.
149 *Ibid.*, 2.
150 *Ibid.*, 2–3.

mised by an ever-closer association with liberalism and the liberal state. One aspect of this book is to "resharpen" the critical edge of critical theory. As I have shown, part of this agenda is to ground his theory in communicative action and to "re-emphasize" civil society and public spheres as oppositional to the liberal state. This does not mean, for him, that democrats should give up on the state, nor think that democracy cannot be extended within the confines of the liberal state. "Sometimes it makes sense to highlight the state, sometimes civil society, and sometimes both." Nevertheless, "In today's world, control over issues increasingly eludes the state and its associated civil society." In respect to this fact, he turns to discussion of transnational deliberative democracy.[151]

In his last chapter Dryzek takes up the issue of intramural points of contention among deliberative democrats. Among the questions he addresses are these, Should deliberation be restricted to rational argument, or admit other kinds of communication? If it does admit other kinds, how should their relationships to rational argument be conceptualized? Are there some kinds of communication that should be ruled out in advance (e.g., bigoted or sectarian speech)? Are there particular values (e.g., impartiality, civility, and reciprocity) to which deliberators must be committed before they are admitted to the deliberative forum? Should deliberation be oriented toward consensus, or is it just a prelude to voting? Should deliberation be constrained by constitutional specifications that rule out in advance particular outcomes of deliberation? Is political equality central to the deliberative ideal, and if so, what deviations from that ideal are to be tolerated? Should we try to subject all decisions to extensive deliberation; if not, which ones? Is deliberation to be confined to members of a predefined community? Can it occur across boundaries? As is clearly seen, these concerns may be intramural, but they go to the heart of what constitutes any given deliberative theory; and as such one's answers to such questions create the relative strengths and weaknesses, feasibility and infeasibility of one's theory. Because of this, it is to be wished that Dryzek would have given more thorough answers to some of these (and other) questions.

In the first chapter of *Deliberative Democracy and Beyond*, Dryzek argues for ways that liberal theory and deliberative democracy are related in mutually reinforcing ways, and ways that liberalism is set against this more authentic democracy. He also argues for the value of critical theory, which he summarizes in this way: "In its broadest sense, critical theory is concerned with charting the progressive emancipation of individuals and society from oppressive forces. It follows that such forces are ideological contingencies rather than structural necessities." He adds that liberal democratic theory accepts the status quo which critical theories of democ-

---

151 *Ibid.*, 3–5. It is perhaps worth noting that Dryzek certainly does not think that the liberal state is the only kind of state against which democratic civil society should stand.

racy cannot accept. In fact, he simply conflates the program of critical theory with that of discursive democracy.[152]

In the second and third chapters, he engages the "minimal" democracy
of social choice theory, responds to the social choice critique of deeper
forms of democracy, and engages "difference democracy". In the fourth
chapter he addresses the relationship between the state and civil society
and refers to the latter space as one where "insurgent democracy" is possible, and sometimes extent. The fifth chapter considers transnational
democracy, and the sixth, green democracy. It is unsurprising that Dryzek
pushes for the extension of democracy in various ways in respect to both
the international realm and in relationship to nature.

In summary, Dryzek reiterates that

> Sometimes deliberative democracy can find a home in the state, but a
> vital civil society characterized by the contestation of discourses is
> *always* necessary ... both an orientation to the state and discursive
> mechanisms for the transmission of public opinion to the state are
> required, so long as the state is the main (though far from exclusive)
> locus of collective decision.[153]

The deliberative turn in democratic theory promises a renewed focus

> on the authenticity of democracy, thus deepening democracy. But that
> promise remains unfulfilled so long as deliberative democracy
> remains confined to the constitutional surface of political life. The
> assimilation to liberal constitutionalism must be resisted. A more criti-
> cal project of discursive democracy has to get beneath the surface to
> reveal and counteract the extra-constitutional factors that can prevent
> or distort political dialogue and its connection to collective decision
> making ... . While allowing that deliberation can occur within (or
> sometimes about) the structures of the liberal state, detaching discur-
> sive democracy from liberal constitutionalism also opens our eyes to a
> host of other democratic possibilities ... . Discursive democracy can
> embrace difference as well as consensus, the public sphere as well as
> the state, transnational as well as domestic politics, and nature as well
> as humanity.[154]

If not for my summarization of *Discursive Democracy*, I would have need
to report more about *Deliberative Democracy and Beyond*. As it is, one can,
sufficiently enough for present purposes, see how the theorization of the
two texts overlap and agree. Dryzek extends democratic theory and would
extend democracy, farther than Rawls, of course, but more importantly,
farther than Habermas. His democratic theory is radical by nearly any
measure. Part of his radicality is found in his work in the relationship
between deliberative democracy and environmental ethics and policy.
While his work in this literature is comparatively fecund, I will risk the

---

152 *Ibid.*, 20, 30.
153 *Ibid.*, 162.
154 *Ibid.*, 175.

impossible, and perhaps foolishly summarize its features most interesting to our purpose here, as briefly as follows.[155] I will simply draw from his sixth chapter in *Deliberative Democracy and Beyond*, "Green Democracy", as most of his important themes, found elsewhere in his thus-related work, are found there (rather undeveloped, of course).

Dryzek not only thinks that democracy should be extended to nature (many theorists agree), but it is *why* he thinks this that is interesting. He argues two provocative things: first, that nature participates in communicative action insofar as nature has its own ways of communicating. That is, various biota communicate, if nothing else, their needs, in various ways (verbal means constitute a small part of communication, after all, even among human beings). Second, he thinks that agency is to be found in nature, and agency deserves respect. Agency, he argues, is related to communication and not necessarily to subjectivity. Just as we disrespect and silence other persons by not listening to them, so too, we disrespect and silence nature in just the same way. Although Dryzek claims that nature cannot have votes, he indicates that nature can be represented by persons in voting contexts. He argues that any communication that allows domination merits condemnation, and this applies to otherkind as well as humankind. He also argues that mechanisms merit condemnation to the extent that their size and scope do not match the size and scope of ecosystems and/or ecological problems. This conviction disallows him from embracing ecoanarchism, because although "small is beautiful" in numerous respects, many of our environmental problems are quite large and thus we are driven toward bioregional and transnational democratic systems. Ecology will not lead us to privilege the state. The "spontaneous order" provided by both international environmental advocacy groups, and discursive "order," as opposed to reliance on the state, lead to democratic inclusion of nature.[156]

Gutmann and Thompson

Amy Gutmann and Dennis Thompson have coauthored a number of works in democratic theory, and have each published their respective con-

---

155 I have studiously avoided evaluation in this chapter, but in respect to Dryzek's work in democratic theory and environmental policy, see my unpublished "Beyond Rawls, Habermas, and Dryzek: Radical and Green Democratic Theory".

156 On the extension of democracy to nature, see, in addition to the relevant texts noted in footnote 133, Adolf G. Gundersen, *The Environmental Promise of Democratic Deliberation* (Madison: The University of Wisconsin, 1995); Brian Doherty and Marius de Geus, eds., *Democracy and Green Political Thought: Sustainability, Rights and Citizenship* (London: Routledge, 1996); Robert Goodin, "Enfranchising the Earth, and Its Alternatives", *Political Studies*, 44 (1996), 835–49; Douglas Torgerson, "Policy Professionalism and the Voice of Dissent: The Case of Environmentalism", *Polity*, 29 (1997), 345–74; John Barry and Marcel Wissenburg, eds., *Sustaining Liberal Democracy* (Basingstoke, England: Palgrave, 2001); and Ben A. Minteer and Bob Pepperman Taylor, eds., *Democracy and the Claims of Nature: Critical Perspectives for a New Century* (Lanham, MD: Rowman and Littlefield, 2002).

tributions as well. Yet two books more than adequately represent their views. In 1996 they published *Democracy and Disagreement* which created an immediate and wide response among political theorists, signified, for example, by a collection of essays written about their book, published in 1999. In 2004, they followed up with *Why Deliberative Democracy?* Here I will describe and summarize their argument in the 1996 text and, in minimal ways, report or employ reflections on this work found in the collection of responsive essays. I will then turn to the 2004 text, also describing and summarizing its argument.

Iris Marion Young writes of *Democracy and Disagreement* that it is "the most complete theory of deliberative democracy yet developed ... . Moreover, they use [the book's six principles] to analyze recent political discussion in the Untied States, more extensively and in greater detail than any other recent writing on deliberative democracy".[157] I am not at all certain about Young's first claim, but her second is certainly correct. Gutmann and Thompson begin *Democracy and Disagreement* with this signal of their purpose, "Of the challenges that American democracy faces today, none is more formidable than the problem of moral disagreement". They think that neither democratic theories or practices have been up to the challenge. They offer their own theory to address this shortcoming: "Along with a growing number of other political theorists, we call this conception deliberative democracy".[158] Gutmann and Thompson focus on and elaborate the six democratic principles of reciprocity (perhaps the heart of their theory),[159] publicity, and accountability—which are meant to constrain the *process* by which a political association deliberates upon content and liberty, basic opportunity, and fair opportunity—which is meant to define the *content* of deliberative democracy.[160] These guiding principles are built upon a theoretical foundation of citizens as free and equal who deserve respect and impartiality. They see their commitment to inclusivity as already incorporated in the principles of reciprocity, liberty, and opportunity.[161] They also think that the disposition to seek mutually justifiable reasons expresses the core of the process of deliberation (this disposition, they write, "implies" the principles of reciprocity, publicity, and accountability).[162] Gutmann and Thompson coin the term "middle democracy" to identify the territory of democratic deliberation; it is the space defined by the entirety of the political process—"virtually any setting in which citi-

---

157 Iris Marion Young, "Justice, Inclusion, and Deliberative Democracy", in Stephen Macedo, ed., *Deliberative Democracy: Essays on* Democracy and Disagreement (New York: Oxford University Press, 1999), 151.
158 *Democracy and Disagreement*, 1.
159 Macedo, Macedo, 7; and *Democracy and Disagreement*, 52.
160 *Democracy and Disagreement*, 12.
161 Gutmann and Thompson, "Reply to the Critics", in *ibid.*, 263.
162 *Democracy and Disagreement*, 52.

zens come together on a regular basis to reach collective decisions about public issues — governmental as well an nongovernmental institutions".[163]

As do Habermas and Dryzek, Gutmann and Thompson seek to offer a theory that avoids some of the pitfalls of liberalism, while embracing crucial liberal underpinnings. They argue against liberalism's preoccupation with basic rights and principles of justice at the expense of the moral disagreements which, in fact, are at the center of moral debate. That is, they are critical of the liberal strategy of preempting moral disagreement through constitutionalism and the courts. Nonetheless, their theory is grounded in liberal principles. They write, "Citizens and officials have to interpret and apply the principles of basic liberty, basic opportunity, and fair opportunity — in a process governed by the condition of deliberation" even while they "must also engage in deliberation to make morally justifiable decisions on questions that lie beyond the authority of the consitutional principles of liberty and opportunity".[164] Of course, they seek to steer democracy away from mere contestation between interests and preferences as well. Their theory also seeks to avoid mere proceduralism. While democratic discourse often bears a complementary relationship to legal recourse and to bargaining, the latter two phenomena often preempt, diminish, or eliminate discourse. To pretend, for example, that procedures are always absent of substantive values is unhelpful, insofar as in such cases, those whose values are embedded in the procedures are advantaged in the context of moral disagreement. Gutmann and Thompson think citizens' lives would go better if they allowed for, and perhaps even encouraged, a wider discussion of moral values by citizens (and their representatives). Of course, deliberation does not always bring agreement, but they argue that deliberation itself (at least on balance) contributes to the health of a democratic society.[165]

Macedo writes,

> Deliberative democrats often object to the constraints that liberals seem to impose on the kinds of reasons that are appropriate for citizens and public officials who are shaping fundamental principles of justice. Gutmann and Thompson, likewise, eschew much of the apparatus that Rawls uses to define what he calls "public reason". Nevertheless, Gutmann and Thompson allow that "in deliberative democracy the primary job of reciprocity is to regulate public reason, the terms in which citizens justify to one another their claims regard-

---

163   *Ibid.*, 12. Of course Rawls, Habermas, and Dryzek also, in their own ways, identify deliberative democracy as belonging to the same broad and inclusive territory as do Gutmann and Thompson. Each of these theorists has certain problems, in my view, as to the relationship of the various spheres of democracy with one another. Dryzek's theorization seems much less problematic than the others in this respect. While Gutmann and Thompson state their commitment to "middle democracy" in their Introduction, the rest of the book focuses overwhelmingly on official political actors, such as members of congress.

164   *Democracy and Disagreement*, 129.

165   Macedo in Macedo, 5–7.

ing all other goods" ....

In sum, Gutmann and Thompson may relax and reformulate, but they do not reject, the notion that public reason has a certain form ... .[166]

That form is one in which Gutmann and Thompson include all those who would seek fair terms for social cooperation to have the opportunity to do so in deliberative contexts where they are welcome to speak in their own ways and, for the most part, on their own terms. The qualification of this wide-open inclusivity lies just insofar as citizens are also encouraged in this model to "reason beyond their narrow self-interest" and consider "what can be justified to people who reasonably disagree with them".[167] Further, Gutmann and Thompson allow appeal to religious discourse and authority, while demanding that appeals to authority of any kind must be subject to critical assessment. Of course, practically, this demand is at times problematic, for it is not at all clear why religious persons should submit to the critical assessments of those who do not share their faith or what the authority of critical assessment means. In short, Gutmann and Thompson seek to extend the territory of deliberation as widely as possible, while valuing the importance of public reason (and thus critical assessment). The goal and idealization are important, but difficult to achieve.

Indeed, deliberative democracy is difficult in nearly all its aspects, it is the most demanding model of democracy, and many think it to be utopian. Are its difficulties and costs worth the effort? Gutmann and Thompson identify four principal benefits: first, that deliberative democracy helps promote the *legitimacy* of collective decisions; second, that it encourages the republican value of *public-spirited perspectives* on public issues; third, that it promotes *mutually respectful decision-making*; and, fourth, that it can help democracies *correct the mistakes of the past*.[168] It is a strength of Gutmann and Thompson's account that they explain the value of deliberative democracy in contradistinction to other conceptions and do so in a way that injects realism into their own view.[169] The mettle of their realism is tested not only in comparing their theory to other theories but in seeing how it meshes with the numerous concrete moral disagreements into which their theory is inserted.

These words from Gutmann and Thompson summarize the essence of their theory presented in *Democracy and Disagreement*,

Our theory of deliberative democracy expresses a set of principles that prescribe fair terms of cooperation. The most important principle is reciprocity, which says that citizens owe one another justifications for

---

166   *Ibid.*, 7; the quote is from *Democracy and Disagreement* (1996), 55.
167   *Ibid., Democracy and Disagreement* (1996), 55.
168   Macedo in Macedo, 9–10.
169   Cf. Jack Knight, "Constitutionalism and Deliberative Democracy", in Macedo, 159–60.

the laws they collectively enact. Other principles specify terms of cooperation that satisfy reciprocity. Theory is "deliberative" because the terms of cooperation take the form of reasons that citizens or their accountable representatives give to one another in an ongoing process of mutual justification.

The practice of deliberation also seeks to realize the root value of reciprocity that should prevail among democratic citizens .... passing the test of deliberation is no guarantee of justifiability; the policy may still not be right because deliberative democracy expresses a set of principles [*substance*], not only a practice [*procedures*].

The principles of deliberation are a powerful critical tool for challenging the actual practice of deliberation—both the substance of the policies and the process by which they are made.[170]

I can now engage Gutmann and Thompson's answers to the question "Why Deliberative Democracy?" in a way where their answers are not entirely framed by the problem of moral disagreement. *Why Deliberative Democracy?* is a collection of essays, all written after *Democracy and Disagreement* and *Deliberative Politics*. There are connections between Gutmann and Thompson's texts insofar as some themes presented and explicated in the first book are revisited in any number of essays in the second. I will here report conceptions that are additional to those we have already encountered in *Democracy and Disagreement*. Whereas the two texts dovetail, it will not be a feature of my summarization here to display this relationship between them (although occasionally it will be unavoidable or useful to summarize work in the second text which overlaps that of the first).

In the first third of their book Gutmann and Thompson present us with a number of questions and their answers to them. Here I simply repeat the questions and summarize their answers. To the question "What is Deliberative Democracy?" they answer that while it makes room for many other forms of decision making, its first and most important characteristic is its *reason-giving* requirement. The reasons it accepts and promotes are neither purely procedural or substantive. The second characteristic they offer is that the reasons given in deliberation should be *accessible* to all the citizens to whom they are addressed.[171] The third feature of deliberative democracy is that its process aims at producing a decision that is *binding* for some period of time. Fourth, they claim that the deliberative process is *dynamic*;

---

170 "Reply to the Critics", in Macedo, 244. Note the focus on "the laws" citizens "collectively enact". This narrow focus betrays their conceptualization of deliberation belonging to all of "middle democracy". Cf. footnote 163 above.

Although I am not undertaking an evaluation of the theories presented in this chapter, it is worth noting that while Gutmann and Thompson are deeply concerned to engage what they see as a grave problem of moral disagreement, they neither explain why moral disagreement is as problematic as they claim, nor do they offer any conceptualization, let alone theorization, of what they mean by morality.

171 Gutmann and Thompson do not explain why they argue that the reasons "should" be accessible rather than that they *must* be so.

it opens the possibility of continuing dialogue, decisions reached are pro-visional.[172] Oddly, given the importance of "middle democracy" in their previous book, now they claim these four characteristics constitute a "form of government", forgetting all the other kinds of democratic spaces and institutions they had earlier acknowledged.[173]

To the question "How Democratic is Deliberation?" they write that "the democratic element in deliberative democracy should not turn on how purely procedural the conception is but on how fully inclusive the process is … . What makes deliberative democracy democratic is an expansive def-inition of who is included in the process".[174] Of course, they see their own version of deliberative democracy as being as inclusive as possible. To the question "What Purposes Does Deliberative Democracy Serve?" they repeat the answers published earlier. It promotes legitimacy, encourages public-spirited perspectives on public issues, promotes mutually respect-ful processes of decision-making, and helps correct mistakes.[175] To the question "Why Is Deliberative Democracy Better Than Aggregative Democracy?" they answer that deliberative democracy is a "second-order theory" and such theories

> are *about* other theories in the sense that they provide ways of dealing with the claims of conflicting first-order theories. They make room for continuing moral conflict that first-order theories purport to eliminate … . Deliberative democracy's leading rivals among second-order theo-ries are what are known as aggregative conceptions of democracy.[176]

The primary reason why Gutmann and Thompson understand delibera-tion as superior to aggregation is that the expressed preferences which are aggregated need not be justified, and little or no attention is paid to the reasons that citizens or their representatives give or fail to give. Aggrega-tion, therefore, "cannot serve as a principled basis for democratic deci-sion-making … . [it] fundamentally accepts and may even reinforce existing distributions of power in society … [and aggregation does not] provide any process by which citizen's views about those distributions might be changed". Further, aggregation does not "provide any way for citizens to challenge the methods of aggregation … ".[177]

To the question "What Kind of Deliberative Democracy?" they answer that the best model is both "instrumental and expressive", that is, that it

---

172 Gutmann and Thompson do not engage the tension between their third and fourth features of deliberative democracy, i.e., that it both reaches binding decisions and its decisions are provisional.

173 *Why Deliberative Democracy?*, 3–7.

174 *Ibid.*, 9.

175 *Ibid.*, 10–12.

176 *Ibid.*, 13. Gutmann and Thompson also discuss deliberative democracy as a second- order theory in *Democracy and Disagreement*.

177 *Ibid.*, 15–16.

has both instrumental value and expresses intrinsic values. Noting that these values cannot be reconciled in every case where they are in tension, they argue that deliberative democracy has the capacity to both criticize unjust outcomes and to recognize its own limits; and in this way "it tends, over time, to reconcile its own instrumental and expressive values".[178] Quite relatedly, they also claim that deliberative democracy is both procedural and substantive and that if the moral and political authority of free and equal citizens is to be honored and safeguarded, then neither procedural or substantive principles of deliberative democracy can claim priority. They engage the tension and balance between the value of consensus, on the one hand, and pluralism, on the other. They even find a way to state a claim on which they think all deliberative democrats can agree: they "share a consensus that deliberation aims at least at a thin conception of the common good". One can note their agreement with one of the values both Mouffe and Soininen correctly see in Oakeshott, i.e., his understanding of civil association as a moral practice leading to republican and communitarian concerns about the "common good" in Soininen and "public spiritedness and ethico-political concern" in Mouffe. They write that pluralists agree that deliberation should both strive to justify as much agreement as possible, and seek ways of living well with disagreements. Deliberative democrats should, they continue, "economize" on moral disagreement, while noting that economizing does not mean eliminating. Citizens should try to clarify and narrow their disagreements without "giving up their core moral commitments". They affirm their liberal commitments in adding, "This is the pluralist hope. It is, in our view, both more charitable and more realistic than the pursuit of the comprehensive common good and consensus democrats favor."[179]

To the question "How Far Should Deliberative Democracy Reach?" they answer that deliberative democracy should take both participatory and representative forms (which, I would add, can be creatively mixed in numerous ways). They argue that deliberation should take place both in government and civil society (returning to their concern for "middle democracy" without using this term), noting that "because deliberative politics works best when citizens do not experience it as an alien activity, some substantial continuity between everyday and political life is desirable". In respect to whether such democracy must remain a domestic project or if it should be given international hope and structure, they argue that to the extent it is possible, "deliberative democracy should promote the globalization of deliberation".[180]

---

178   *Ibid.*, 23.
179   *Ibid.*, 23–29; cf. 126–27, 130–32.
180   *Ibid.*, 29–39.

To the question "How Can Deliberative Democrats Respond to Theoretical Objections?" they answer that deliberative democracy does not deny that sometimes justice should take priority over deliberation but add that deliberation is generally the best way to arrive at just decisions or, at least, the least unsatisfactory decisions. They admit a circularity in the explanation that deliberation determines justice but justice should determine deliberation. Yet they also see this circularity not as a problem so much as a virtue of deliberative democracy.[181]

To the question "How Can Deliberative Democrats Respond to Practical Objections?" they answer, foremost, that deliberative democracy is its own best critic. It has within it the best resources for addressing its deficiencies. For example, it calls for changes to eliminate biases in the political process, including deliberative forums, that derive from unequal wealth and entrenched power. To the charge that deliberation favors those who are best prepared, through educational experience, say, to engage in it, they respond that various forms of discourse are (or ought to be) welcome. Deliberation need not be designed so as to privilege those with skills in logic and argumentation. Gutmann and Thompson argue that "passionate rhetoric can be just as justifiable as logical demonstration".[182] To the charge that deliberation is biased against certain kinds of beliefs, they answer that while reasons offered in discourse must be mutually and generally acceptable, it is not a morally neutral condition — no standard of reasoning could be. To the charge that opening all principles and practices to challenge undermines political stability, they respond that deliberative democracy recognizes that constitutional rights should be more insulated than ordinary laws, not just completely isolated. Other critics worry that deliberation exacerbates cleavages and disagreements more than it heals them. Gutmann and Thompson admit that this often happens but note that such exacerbation is not inevitable, nor is all agreement desirable. "Convergence is not always to be preferred to polarization." One can, of course, imagine any number of cases in which they are right. Other critics simply think deliberation to be overrated, but in response Gutmann and Thompson allow that deliberative democrats do not deny the importance of many other kinds of political activities (although they insist deliberation is not just another activity on the list). They see a self-correcting capacity in deliberative democracy and a malleable and expansive character in it, which allows it to respond to all such criticisms.[183]

---

181 *Ibid.*, 40–43.
182 Other theorists specify various forms of communication that have a viable place in deliberation, e.g., testimony, protest, and everyday talk. See, e.g., Jane Mansbridge, "Everyday Talk in the Deliberative System," in Macedo, 211–39. Cf. Lynn M. Sanders, "Against Deliberation," *Political Theory*, 25 (1997), 347–76; and Dryzek, above.
183 *Why Deliberative Democracy?* 48–57.

Gutmann and Thompson articulate principles of accommodation that are a part of their theory of deliberative democracy. First, they argue that mutual respect manifests a distinctively democratic kind of character. It keeps open the possibility of resolving moral disputes about public policy and contributes not only to the social good but to individual virtue as well. Further, they write that citizens should espouse their moral positions independently of the circumstances in which they speak. Gutmann and Thompson do not refer here to a kind of neutral observer position, but rather that persons should demonstrate consistency as a sign of political sincerity. Third, they require that one act in a way consistent with the position one says one holds.[184] Fourth, they note that citizens should accept the broader implications of the principles presupposed by their moral positions. They call this the integrity principle.[185] Fifth, they call on citizens to acknowledge the moral status of the positions they oppose and believe doing so develops democratic character. Sixth, and paralleling the requirement of integrity, is the requirement to keep open the possibility that one could come to adopt and act on the position held by one's opponent(s). This requires a "disposition toward openness".[186] Gutmann and Thompson argue not only that deliberative democracy requires reciprocity, but that reciprocity requires deliberation. They add that while deliberative democracy accepts the provisionality of deliberation, it can never accept the provisionality of moral reasoning itself. Therefore all theories of democracy which allow the absence, in any respect, of moral justification are to be rejected. This is one reason theories of politics based on power alone must be rejected.[187]

The reader will recall that I sought to minimize the summarization of *Why Deliberative Democracy?* insofar as it presents material already discussed in respect to *Democracy and Disagreement*. Here, then, I can bring my summary of Gutmann and Thompson's democratic theory to a close. It is clear that they present robust thought in respect to the conditions, requirements, and limits of deliberative democracy. Perhaps the greatest virtue of their theory is the rather consistent concern for feasibility and practicality. Their theorization is not as philosophically rich as that of Rawls, Habermas, or Dryzek, but it gives one a large number of criteria to consider and guide one's democratic deliberations. These criteria strike balances between, for example, procedural and substantive concerns, between inclusivity and reasonableness, between constitutionalism and concerns about the common good. If one is to ask of a theory what practical

---

184 Gutmann and Thompson do not engage the problematic of how it is determined as to what actions best correlate with what positions.
185 As immediately above, it is not always clear what the broader implications of moral (or other) principles are.
186 *Ibid.*, 79–84.
187 *Ibid.*, 98–102, 115.

features, possibilities, and outcomes it may hold, Gutmann and Thompson offer one that may well be unsurpassed; and one can see why it has received the attention I have reported.

Conclusion

Near the beginning of this chapter I summarized the basic and widely agreed-upon features of deliberative democracy. After describing the theories of Rawls, Habermas, Dryzek, Gutmann and Thompson, one can see both the validity and densely condensed character of that early summarization. Recall that I chose to consider the work of these four "figures" because of the importance they hold in the deliberative democratic literature. At this point, one may now have a strong sense of the reason for their importance. If one were to schematize their respective theories she would find both tremendous agreement on many fundamental characteristics and criteria, and find considerable difference as well, each theory containing several unique and interesting features. It is hoped that the reader has a firm idea of both the similarities and the differences. Thus, this summary also shows something of not only the general agreement of deliberative democratic theory, but the fecund possibilities of its polyvalent dimensions.

I have only reported, described, and summarized the most relevant thought, for present purposes, of these theorists. I have not analyzed, examined, or evaluated their work. Occasionally I have made brief and simple comments as to where such interrogation is, in my view, welcome, but this book simply cannot contain a critique of the theorization described above. Moreover, and more importantly, such evaluation is not necessary for my purposes.

The reader has encountered and considered Michael Oakeshott's democratic theory and his political theory as it relates to democracy before *On Human Conduct* (Chapter Two), and in *On Human Conduct* and after it (Chapter Three). The question has been, Does Oakeshott have a democratic theory or a "democratic theory"? George Feaver, it seems, and Paul Franco and Nöel O'Sullivan, with certainty, would answer that his democratic theory is straightforward and that there is no need to complexify the matter by admitting ambiguity into the question. My own answer to this question comes in the following chapter. After considering the deliberative democratic theory presented in this chapter, I am now in a position to bring my argument to its culmination.

Chapter Five

Oakeshott's Discursive Democratic Theory[1]

I have presented no small amount of material that has described, summarized, and interrogated the thought of Michael Oakeshott as it bears directly and indirectly on democracy and democratic theory. This project has not only investigated and evaluated Oakeshott but nearly all of the secondary literature that considers Oakeshott in relevant ways. Further, using Rawls, Habermas, Dryzek, Gutmann and Thompson, I have presented a description and summary of deliberative democratic theory such that it is at this juncture understood sufficiently for my purposes. Here I add that the length and depth of my exegesis of these theorists is warranted because it is important to show that insofar as Oakeshott is a discursive democrat, he is a member of a significant movement in political theory. There is considerable theoretical energy in respect to deliberative democracy. Democratic theory is in a period of fecundity, and deliberative theory has nearly monopolized democratic theory. If Oakeshott's voice is added to the deliberative chorus, this is of justified interest to political (or at least, democratic) theorists.

Owing to the measure of the work done in Chapters One through Four, I can simply and briefly summarize the argument made to this point and draw the relevant conclusions. Chapter One forecast my argument and provided a simple map to the territory that followed in the subsequent chapters. Here the reader was oriented not only to Oakeshottian texts and conceptions, but to important moments in the secondary literature that invite, at a minimum, notice and, often, response. As my responses have unfolded, there have been matters of agreement, but more importantly, I have offered important disagreements, most significantly, with Gerencser. If the first chapter sets the reader on the right path, where does that path lead?

---

1   I have chosen to refer to Oakeshott as a discursive democrat because discourse is a broader concept than deliberation (Dryzek not withstanding). Nothing more is signified in this nomenclature.

In Chapter Two I considered Oakeshott's thought as it bears on democracy in his work before *On Human Conduct*. I began my interrogation with a look at what Oakeshott says about democracy explicitly, in part, because this had the effect of putting into context what he says about the other matters mentioned above. That is, insofar as one knows what Oakeshott thinks about democracy, one is in a favorable position to see how he conceptualizes other matters relating to democracy.

I demonstrated that Oakeshott gives considerable attention to democracy in his early career. He theorizes democracy as belonging to more than simply a manner of government, noting that it is also a matter of culture, society, and tradition. He also thinks that a more sophisticated theorization of democracy is needed.[2] The reader may recall that he sees democracy and liberalism as intrinsically related, such that the most natural term to be employed, he writes, would be "liberal democracy" (yet, he avoids this term because of the misunderstandings that attend to the word "liberal"). One will also recall that he understands democracy to be at odds with what he identifies as "rationalistic politics", and later comes to call "Rationalism".

Moreover, it is to be remembered that Oakeshott understands conversation as *inherent* in democracy. He writes of the "politics of conversation" as "the gist and meaning of democracy". "Politics alone", he adds, "belongs solely to the realm of conversation". Democracy "at its highest" is "the politics of conversation", and "politics is good for *nothing else*" but conversation.[3] He conceives of democracy as open-ended, pluralistic, nonfoundational, noninstrumental, and nonpurposive conversation. Indeed, he conceives of politics properly understood in just this manner, thus the unavoidable conclusion that he understands proper politics to be democratic in an intrinsic and robust sense. I demonstrated how this understanding of democratic politics cuts against elitism and is inherently tied to the great value he places on the agency, individuality, equality, and freedom of all persons. One is also reminded that Oakeshott thinks of individuality as "the pre-eminent event in modern European history";[4] and in "The Masses in Representative Democracy", he laments the emergence of

---

2   Oakeshott made the claim in 1939, that current conceptions of democracy were "by no means complete or ... satisfactory" and that there existed the need of "a radical restatement" of democracy. However, one can confidently assert that he found the available theorizations of democracy to be inadequate throughout most, if not all, of his career. Again, Franco and O'Sullivan would likely reply that *On Human Conduct* is a response to the need presented by this inadequacy. As I have indicated, they might very well be correct, but because Oakeshott does not label *On Human Conduct* a democratic theory, such a conclusion is, in one sense, overreaching. In respect to Franco, recall that he summarizes the fundamental themes in Oakeshott's work as consisting of "British democracy", "the diffusion of power", and "representative democracy or parliamentary government".

3   *What Is History? And Other Essays*, 194–95.

4   *Rationalism in Politics*, 370.

"mass man", the "anti-individual", and the "individual *manqué*" as anti
-democratic figures.

One sees in Oakeshott's earliest consideration of democracy a number of
gestures toward the deliberative, discursive democratic theory of the past
two decades. He emphasizes not only the contingent, noninstrumental,
nonpurposive, and egalitarian nature of democracy but also its discursive
essence. His robust valuation of individuals as free agents anticipates the
consideration of persons as free and equal which is foundational to recent
deliberative democratic theory. As a liberal, he is concerned about concentrations of power and endorses, therefore, the diffusion of power. It follows unsurprisingly, then, that democracy is important to him. Of course
discursive democratic theories are those *most* interested in the diffusion or
egalitarianism of power, and knowing of the importance of egalitarian
"conversational politics" to Oakeshott, one discovers another means to see
the discursive character of his political and democratic theory.[5] I have
demonstrated that he understands political activity as conversational and
deliberative engagement. Put differently, inasmuch as he values political
activity, he values discursive and, therefore, democratic forms of politics.
Again, one is reminded of the relationship between this connection, on one
hand, and contingency and nonpurposiveness, on the other. Just insofar as
political activity need not lead to some conclusion or outcome, conversation and deliberation are welcome and invited.[6] It is worth noting that
while Oakeshott is a nonelitist and does not construct boundaries in
respect to who can participate in political discourse, or what kind of discourse can be admitted, he does anticipate the "public reasons" criteria
elucidated by many recent theorists (as was shown in Chapter Four).

In sum, Chapter Two demonstrates that there is a significant body of
work in Oakeshott's early career relating to democracy and democratic
theory. There is a substantial amount of his writing which does so directly
and explicitly, and even more which does so indirectly and implicitly. I
have demonstrated that much of his thought endorses general notions of
discursive democracy. While this is most clearly seen in his discussion of
democracy and his theorization of "conversational politics" and "political
discourse", much of the other aspects of his thought pushes in this
direction as well.

---

5   This insight pushes in the direction of putting Oakeshott in sympathetic and complementary
     relationship with theorists such as Shapiro, Olson, Beitz, Foucault, Hardt and Negri, as well as
     Rawls, and Gutmann and Thompson, and especially Habermas and Dryzek.

6   The connection between political discourse and contingency is made strongly in "Political
     Discourse", found in *Rationalism in Politics* and "The Voice of Conversation in the Education of
     Mankind", found in *What is History? And Other Essays*.
     Recall that Soininen sees the discursive dimension of Oakeshott's theory of political activity
     as the key element of his mature thought about politics, and that she considers conversation to
     be his "master metaphor".

In Chapter Three I interrogated *On Human Conduct* in respect to its contribution to Oakeshottian democratic theory. I showed Oakeshott's theorization of the intrinsic relationship between deliberation, practice, and conduct, conduct is composed of conversation and deliberation. Conduct is constituted by "languages of self-disclosure and self-enactment" that are "the arts of agency".[7] Further, conduct is so basic for Oakeshott, that it takes the place of human *nature*, yet if conduct is comprised of discourse, then the most basic thing about being human is our discursive character. In this respect he is very close to Habermas and Dryzek. We are political animals because we are discursive animals.

I have demonstrated that civil association names Oakeshott's normative theorization of political association, which is the philosophically necessary embodiment and extension of the discourse and conduct which is basic to our humanity. This relationship of civility, which is inherently moral association, is his answer to the question of how human persons can be related in a way that constrains our conduct and respects our individuality. Therefore, it must be, in important ways, a theorization of democratic order. For, whatever else democracy is, it is a means to determine the way(s) to find the best relationship between these two values. No less than his earlier work, *On Human Conduct* demonstrates Oakeshott's valuation of agency, individuality, equality, and freedom. Civil association names a moral relationship in essential and important ways, as his exultation of agency, individuality, equality, and freedom indicates. Because morality *just is* our response to freedom and contingency, we are invited to explore and employ free and innovative energies and actions, such as those to which deliberative democrats invite us. The democratic dimensions of civil association have been recognized by Mapel and Mouffe, and even significantly, if not sufficiently, by Gerencser. Yet I have shown that Oakeshott's work is pregnant with democratic features and possibilities beyond those recognized by Mapel and Mouffe, and I have demonstrated the shortcomings of Gerencser's argument where he sees Oakeshott as inadequately democratic.

In Chapter Four I offered a brief summary of deliberative democratic theory and then turned to a considered summary of Rawls, Habermas, Dryzek, and Gutmann and Thompson, to both flesh out my summary and to reveal sufficient detail and nuance in the theories of these four important theorists.[8] What a careful consideration of their theories demonstrates is that discursive democracy is a large choir, allowing many voices room for expression. I have also shown that while there are any number of dif-

---

7   *OHC*, 59.

8   To repeat two simple ideas: (1) by "deliberative democracy", I am making no claims in
     contradistinction to "discursive democracy"; and (2) I am treating Amy Gutmann and Dennis
     Thompson as one "theorist".

ferences among deliberative theorists, there are many important agreements as well (which I summarized in the beginning of the chapter).

Having summarized the chapters above, it remains to bring my argument to conclusion. Primarily this will mean summarizing some of the ways in which deliberative theory and Oakeshott's theory overlap and interpenetrate. Of course, I have been noticing such overlap and interpenetration all along (and indeed have foregone mentioning instances of overlap in numerous places); thus I indicate the effort at this point as a summary. First, it cannot be overstated as to how important Oakeshott holds human agency, individuality, and freedom to be. As I cycled through numerous Oakeshottian texts above, I have noticed the paramount and unrivaled status these interconnected conceptions hold in his thought. It is noteworthy that so many Oakeshott scholars also notice the preeminence of these conceptions. Oakeshott is in his valuation of these characteristics and ideals as committed a liberal as is possible. What one notices in deliberative democratic theory, and this is particularly clear in Rawls, Gutmann and Thompson, is that the very basis of deliberation rests on this same liberal foundation. That is, the reason it is necessary to create societies, cultures, states, governments, and politics where discourse is pervasively encouraged and institutionalized is just because of the Kantian moral status of human beings. We are endowed with an agency, individuality, and freedom which deserve such respect that they deserve political institutionalization.

Of course, the philosophical and moral foundations for democracy as such are those just identified, but the logic of this moral foundation demanding democracy is simply extended in respect to deliberative theory. That is, if persons have a moral standing in relationship to other persons such that they *deserve* the opportunity, at least in principle, to be heard and to control their own lives as much as possible (recall Rawls's first principle of justice as fairness here), then the question becomes: How can any form of democracy which is less than deliberative and participatory be justified? Certainly the only reasons that can be offered in response to this question are of purely practical kinds, i.e., matters of feasibility. It follows, then, that just to the extent that one is committed to the importance of the agency, individuality, and freedom of persons, one would endorse as robust a democracy as one thinks feasible. Rousseau noted that representative democracy is an oxymoron.[9] In large modern and contemporary societies, representation may be to one degree or another unavoidable, but liberals, insofar as they are consistent with their liberalism, will always minimize representation and maximize deliberation and participation just as much as they conclude circumstances allow. Oakeshott was disillusioned with aggregative democracy for reasons not unlike those

9   See Chapter 15 of *The Social Contract*.

voiced by Rousseau. He saw insufficient authentic representation in "representative democracy"[10] and saw in place of such democratic authenticity, Rationalism, the mass-man (think here, among other things, of aggregation) and anti-individuality. His normative commitment, one recalls, was to "*liberal* democracy". Of course, as a tradition standing against other, nondemocratic traditions, Oakeshott valued "representative democracy" and parliamentary government. Yet we also recall that he thought current theorizations of democracy to be woefully inadequate and in need of "radical restatement".

In Rawls, Gutmann and Thompson, and other theorists, one often finds the conceptions I am here discussing clustered about the claim of persons as free and equal. I would be remiss to elide the egalitarianism of this moral foundation to deliberative democracy. As I have indicated, one finds a robust sense of egalitarian purchase to democratic participation in Oakeshott. Just insofar as persons are radically free, that freedom emerges from a fundamental equality. No one deserves to be freer than anyone else. Deliberative democrats are deeply concerned about notions of equality because democracy is authentic only to the extent that it recognizes, protects, and institutionalizes certain kinds of equality. This equality need not emit to forms of equal economic opportunities or outcomes, for example, but equality in respect to "negative" and other liberal rights are comprehensively endorsed.[11] Oakeshott is committed to the status of citizens as free and equal, and his abundant theorization of agency, individuality, freedom, discourse, and "conversational politics" makes this an unmistakable and unmistakably important dimension of his thought.

Second, as to his theorization of conversation, discourse, and deliberation, Oakeshott highly values reasons-giving criteria and what he called "argumentative" and *apodeictic* political discourse",[12] that is, the kinds of contributions that can be made to conversation, especially for political purposes, that bring rationality, empiricism, logic, and reasonableness to the fore. This valuation is, of course, entirely and importantly consonant with much of deliberative democratic theory. This is seen in Rawls, Habermas, Gutmann and Thompson, and it is found in many other deliberative theorists.

Moreover, Oakeshott values conversation. This is to say that the essentiality of our humanity being rooted in our conduct which is, in turn, essentially discursive and contingent, is far more foundational to political

---

10   For reasons that had everything to do with "Rationalism" and various forms of ideology. Recall that he thought that the Tories tended to do less harm than Labour.

11   Many democrats do think, however, that liberal, constitutional, and formal equality alone is sufficient and perhaps, vacuous, if radical economic equality is unachieved. See, e.g, Charles Beitz, *Political Equality: An Essay in Democratic Theory*; and Kevin Olson, *Reflexive Democracy: Political Equality and the Welfare State*, op. cit.

12   "Political Discourse", in *Rationalism in Politics*, 82.

association and "civility" than is the ability to make good arguments and offer acceptable reasons. In Oakeshott one finds a figure who has his feet in two camps. One camp in the deliberative community thinks that public reasons are crucial, and concomitantly, deliberation should be shaped by "the force of the better argument" to put it in Habermasian terms. Yet others occupy a different camp. They worry about how "the force of the better argument" is exclusionary, about how this kind of discourse is limited, and about how it devalues other forms of discourse such as everyday talk, testimony, narrative, poetry and protest.[13] Oakeshott's poetic near-adoration of conversation, in addition to his deep valuation of *poiesis*, presents a strong endorsement of the idea that there are important contributions to be made by those who do not use empirical, rational, logical, or argumentative discourse to make them. Again, this identifies a deep egalitarianism and respect for individuality and freedom in Oakeshott. He was famously unwilling to suffer fools gladly and quite willing to argue in the most sophisticated philosophical ways, so one has no reason to doubt his endorsement of that mode of discourse. What may be more surprising is his endorsement of the poetic and ordinary modes of discourse, beautifully articulated, especially (but not only) in his essays "On the Voice of *Conversation* in the Education of Mankind", and "The Voice of Poetry in the *Conversation* of Mankind".

This reflection on conversation and discourse brings one to the way Oakeshott understands the intrinsic relationship between discourse and contingency. After all, he invites us to have "nerve enough" to "abate contingency" while at the same time peacefully accepting the radical nature of our contingent world. Discourse is a person-making and a world-making tool for Oakeshott. It is the fundamental way we "enact" ourselves and "disclose" ourselves. The future lies open to us, and our conversations, deliberations, "self-enactment", and "self-disclosure" bring the futures we create. Of course, contingency means that our plans are interrupted, and, often enough, destroyed, and that persons pursue their plans at cross purposes with others' plans. Yet what is of fundamental importance to Oakeshott in respect to language and contingency is that nothing is determined. We live in a nonfoundational world, where we are agents who determine our futures, our political associations, our politics, and our lives.

What this means for democratic theory is that there are no *a priori* obstacles to democratic possibilities. His profound valuation of persons as agents, individuality, freedom, discourse, and contingency, are waves that

---

13 Again, members of this camp include, e.g., Lynn Sanders, "Against Deliberation", *Political Theory*, 25, 347–76; Jane Mansbridge, *Beyond Adversary Democracy* (Chicago: University of Chicago Press, 1983; "Everyday Talk in Deliberative System", in Macedo; Dryzek, as noted above; and Olson, 94.

rush toward robust participatory and deliberative democracy; and no Oakeshottian reasons exist to construct a levee against them. Deliberative democrats call for creative, optimistic, innovative, and even courageous forays into the future where all persons find their free and equal status honored. Convention and fear have little purchase on deliberative democrats. I find an Oakeshottian sensibility of hopefulness and nerve that resonates in deliberative democratic theory. There are wide-open possibilities in his theory that comport without reservation with the general thrust, ideas, and ideals of deliberative democracy, as both Mapel and Mouffe observe. Hilary Putnam writes that democracy is "a cognitive value in every area. Democracy is a requirement for experimental inquiry ... . To reject democracy is to reject the idea of being experimental".[14] I add "experimental" to the "hopefulness and nerve" that characterizes Oakeshott's theory.[15]

Oakeshott is a discursive democrat because of his unconditional commitment to what he called conversational politics. The importance of discourse and deliberation– of many kinds– shared among citizens who should enjoy robust freedom and flourish in their individuality is undeniable in his thought. The noninstrumental, nonpurposive, contingent character of politics, political association, and morality is rooted in, and calls for, the discursive nature of human conduct which is at the core of our humanness. Further, as a liberal committed to pluralism, to the idea that no one value, set of values, or way of life should dominate others, he has additional reasons to embrace discursive democracy. For, if society at its best is liberal in this sense, that is, full of diversity, then it follows that persons are encouraged to give voice to their various values and projects. Of course, I am not merely suggesting that he has reason to embrace deliberative democracy for these reasons, but that, in fact, one reason why he does embrace conversational politics is intrinsically linked to this kind of (classical) liberalism.

Sometimes, however, people want to diminish, resolve, or eliminate our differences as well. How is that best achieved? Deliberative democrats, including Michael Oakeshott, will answer that talking is the most promising strategy. Bruce Ackerman, for one, argues that dialogue is the load-bearing pillar in the project of maintaining peaceful coexistence and a

---

14 In G. Borradori, *The American Philosopher: Conversations with Quine, Davidson, Putnam, Nozick, Danto, Rorty, Cavell, MacIntyre, and Kuhn*, trans. R. Crocitto (Chicago: University of Chicago Press, 1994), 64. Cited in Misak, *Truth, Politics, Morality: Pragmatism and Deliberation* (New York: Routledge, 2000), 94. Note that the idea of democracy and experimentation implying one another, with the concomitant view that experimentation brings progress, goes back to Mill.

A value of Misak's book is in showing various consonances between Oakeshott, deliberative democratic theory more generally, and pragmatism. Indeed, an exploration in pragmatism as related to Oakeshott, and deliberative democracy warrants a project of its own.

15 Note that *poiesis* is not unrelated to experimentation. See Oakeshott's elegant valuation of *poiesis* in his "The Voice of Poetry in the Conversation of Mankind".

pluralistic (liberal) society. Among other distributions, the distribution of goods and power is best forwarded through conversation. Ackerman considers such discourse a "supreme pragmatic imperative",[16] and Oakeshott would hardly disagree, nor does Rawls, Habermas, Dryzek, Gutmann and Thompson, or the other deliberative democrats.

Third, and in respect to morality, Amy Gutmann and Dennis Thompson seize upon a truth: that democracy and morality are inherently related in many important ways, but before Gutmann and Thompson pursued the connection, Oakeshott had already offered original and robust theory about this relationship. As all deliberative democrats agree, moral disagreement necessitates conversation, and conversation has the best chance, all things considered, of ameliorating such disagreement. Of course, sometimes conversation identifies deeper moral disagreements than were previously noticed, and sometimes it even deepens our moral differences. Nevertheless, understanding is better than ignorance, talking is better than fighting, and persuasion is better than coercion. To think about the role and value of democracy is to think about how we negotiate difference. Conventional accounts of morality, such as the "standard account" I presented in Chapter Three have limited value in negotiating difficult differences.[17] Moral theories tend to run into one another and come to an impasse. In Wittgensteinian manner, one might say that the different theories are, in effect, different language games, and thus moral theorists end up talking past one another, neither understanding the language of the other.

However, Oakeshott's conception of morality as nonfoundational practice that is not reducible to rules, duties, or ideas, but rather, that which consists in all "intelligent" human behavior holds a kind of promise that conventional theories cannot hold. The adverbial, contingent nature of morality wherein these conceptions are used in, rather than applied to, conduct means that it is a matter of deliberation which brings morality to light and to bear upon problems and conversations. Conventional conceptions of morality hold that there are moral truths, principles, values, ideals, and rules to which our conduct must conform. As soon as we do not agree on these truths, principles, values, ideals, and rules, we have no way forward short of convincing one another of capitulating to moral conversions. Oakeshott's understanding of morality, moral practice, and civil association as moral association does not require that citizens find recourse only in seeking the conversion of others. His requirement is that citizens deliberate with one another, respecting each other's agency, indi-

16 Bruce Ackerman, "Why Dialogue?" *Journal of Philosophy*, 1989, 8–12; in Misak, 29–30.
17 The limits of this project disallow me from explicating why this is the case, but I have gestured toward some of the reasons in my discussion of moral theory and the "anti-theorists" in Chapter Three.

viduality, freedom, and equality. Conversation based upon these commitments holds the best possibility of tolerance, pluralism, and peace, all things considered, than does imposing moral theories upon our problems and disagreements.

Oakeshott is not the only person to recognize that problems should be resolved through dialogue, of course, but he may offer, from among all deliberative theorists, the richest theorization of morality consonant with this goal. In Rawls, Habermas, and Gutmann and Thompson, morality reduces to proceduralism. This means, in practical terms, that persons will often end up in just the Wittgensteinian impasses I mentioned above. Oakeshott offers a conception that understands morality as more fluid and undetermined in the first place than do conventional and rival theories. Although his view is closest to that of Habermas, his understanding of morality runs much deeper than it does in Habermas. For Oakeshott, we cannot get below morality; nothing is more basic. For Habermas, morality also ends up being the procedures we decide upon and, in the end, is no deeper than that.[18] Although an improvement over Rawls, and Gutmann and Thompson, given the rigorous theoretical treatment morality and ethics receive, morality, nevertheless, comes to be in Habermas, a negotiation tied to reason-giving discourse.[19] In an Oakeshottian civil association, persons would explore their moral commitments deeply yet without rigidity and intolerance. In a Habermasian democracy, persons would let "the force of the better argument win" and consider their moral convictions as indicators signifying the possibility of agreement or the danger of disagreement.

In the Conclusion of *Truth, Politics, Morality*, Misak writes:

> What I hope to have shown is that there are some good reasons for thinking that we can make assertions or have genuine beliefs about what is right and wrong, just and unjust, cruel and kind; that we can inquire about the correctness of those beliefs; that our moral deliberations aim at the truth. And I hope to have shown that if we are to make sense of this, we must conduct ourselves via democratic principles– ones that encourage tolerance, openness, and understanding the experiences of others … .
>
> Moral and political theory … . should perceive itself as articulating how it is possible for inquirers, immersed as they are in the contingent contexts of their lives and circumstances, to work out for themselves the details about what is right and wrong.[20]

---

18 Of course I am aware of the significant work Habermas does in moral theory, and his recognition of the depth it has had in traditional cultures. But my point goes to the role he thinks morality must now play in modern and contemporary societies, in which it is *merely* turned into a law-informing, negotiated, strategic discourse to handle disagreement.

19 I write of "morality and ethics" here because Habermas distinguishes between them, in ways partly similar to Hegel.

20 Misak, 155–56; cf. 123. Oakeshott's moral theory is close to that presented by Misak.

It is my view that Oakeshott's theorization of morality and democratic civil association incarnates Misak's hope better than all alternatives of which I am aware. Of course I have not shown that here, and as I wrote above, I think a book-length treatment devoted to doing so would be necessary and of value. Yet for our present purposes I do not need to demonstrate the viability of this argument, all I need to do is show that Oakeshott has a robust interest in deliberation and democracy in ways that are concerned with addressing the moral nature of being human and being in association with others. At the least, his theorization of morality, deliberation, and politics is close enough to Habermas, Dryzek, and Gutmann and Thompson to demonstrate his inclusion in the camp to which they belong.

Fourth and last, I conclude with a word about democracy and tradition. In his *Democracy and Tradition*, Jeffrey Stout laments a certain cultural impasse he argues has become current in American society. Without explaining the impasse, and only mentioning that he sees it as existing between traditionalism and democracy, I report his idea of how it is to be escaped.[21] He thinks that the way forward requires a form of "pragmatic expressivism that takes enduring democratic social practices as a tradition with which we have good reasons to identify". This means:

> —resolving the internal tensions in Rawls's political liberalism by discarding his notion of a freestanding conception of justice … while retaining the idea that we owe reasons to one another when we take stands on important political questions;

> —seeing our overlapping consensus on the legitimacy of constitutional democracy as involving a practical commitment to holding one another mutually responsible for our political arrangements and thus to keep a democratic discussion going across the boundaries … .;

> —working out an account of our discursive practices that takes seriously Rorty's ideal of conversation and MacIntyre's emphasis on the need to understand one's rivals on their own terms, while jettisoning the quest for principles that no reasonable person could reasonably reject;

> —developing a conception of tradition centered on enduring social practices, without begging the question in favor of traditions that are hierarchically organized and insistent on doctrinal conformity as a criterion of membership;

> —and redescribing modern democracy as a tradition of this looser sort by focusing attention primarily on the relatively freewheeling discursive practice it involves".[22]

---

21 I disagree with Stout's treatment of tradition in various respects, and in particular with his understanding that those he labels traditionalists are opposed to, or undervalue democracy. I think he misconceives MacIntyre and Hauerwas in egregious ways. Nonetheless, my disagreements with Stout are not relevant to my use of him here.

22 Jeffrey Stout, *Democracy and Tradition* (Princeton: Princeton University Press, 2004), 184–85.

I quote Stout at this length because his has been a much-discussed book, and this outline represents the heart of his argument, and I want to suggest that Oakeshott's theorization of discursive democracy comes close to fulfilling Stout's expectations. Stout seems unaware that Rorty's "ideal of conversation" is taken from Oakeshott, nor does he seem to be aware of Oakeshott's theorization over all. In any case, I will briefly summarize Oakeshott's understanding of democracy as a tradition, and then in addition to the conclusions I have already drawn, one can better see how his theory responds to Stout's hope.

Oakeshott refers to democracy as a tradition in several places, as I discussed in Chapter Two, and its existence as a tradition makes it superior to alternative conceptions because as a tradition, it is "capable of changing without perishing in the process".[23] Tradition is alive, fluid, and innovative. Rationalism, by contrast, shuts down the dynamism of traditions. Democracy is a tradition because it is an organic, unforced, development over time. It consists in "acquired habits", "ways of behaving", and the "abridgment of history". It is a conversation held across generations. Democracy is a tradition because it is "a story in which vicissitudes are recognized as the stuff and not the hindrances of change".[24] Democracy is a tradition because it emerged "where the impact of the aspirations of individuality upon medieval institutions of government was greatest".[25] Democracy is a tradition for a number of reasons in Oakeshott's thought, some which I have mentioned here. Just as practice shapes theory, more than the other way around; tradition shapes theory and ideology, because tradition is rooted in practice.

Franco finds Oakeshott's "valorization of habit, custom, and the unselfconsciousness of tradition" to be "profoundly anachronistic" and "irrelevant to modern democratic societies".[26] Franco undervalues the robustness and dynamism of tradition and, more importantly, seems to think that we can somehow live outside of traditions. The fact is, human beings and their narratives, societies, cultures, and communities are tradition-bound. The only questions are about what kind of traditions and how viable, fluid, dynamic, and changeable they are. Understanding democracy as a tradition is far from anachronistic, and as Stout acknowledges, seeing it as a tradition is a valuable insight.

---

23   *The Social and Political Doctrines of Contemporary Europe*, xviii. Cf. *Religion, Politics and the Moral Life*, 109.
24   "Democracy in England", in O'Sullivan, ed., 282.
25   "The Masses in Representative Democracy", in *Rationalism in Politics*, 368.
26   Franco, *An Introduction*, 96.

If democracy is understood as a tradition of a certain kind, it provides promise for us. Stout also thinks of democracy as a culture, and he is right in this.[27] He notes:

> Modern democratic culture ... does not have a single view of the grand scheme of things; it opens up space in which many ... views can be held and acted upon ... for the ethical life of democratic peoples clearly commits them to the importance of such matters as the people's survival and the decent treatment of others. It does not, however, entail the single ranking of the most important things ... ".[28]

One can think of democracy as a tradition of "openhandedness", and "unrhymed poetry" to use images from Whitman.[29] This again reminds us of the liberalism of Oakeshottian democracy.

Democracy is discursive all the way down, because traditions and cultures are discursive all the way down; they are "constructed" out of the narratives we create, employ, and change. Discursive democrats have a sense of this and in some cases, for example, in Habermas and Oakeshott, a very keen sense of it. Conventional, aggregative, majoritarian, polyarchic democrats fail to see this depth of discourse, but it is there. It is not created by deliberative theorists, it is recognized by them. Only after such recognition do they seek to theorize ways to institutionalize deliberation. This theorization makes democracy more authentic to its truest, deepest essence.

One of the things democratic cultures discuss is how power, authority, responsibility, and accountability will be distributed and maintained. Recall Oakeshott's theory of the legitimacy of the rules, or laws, of the moral association which is civil association, and how authority rests on the subscription of its members to those rules, and so, to that authority. I demonstrated, in my interrogation not only of Oakeshott but of Mapel, Mouffe, and Gerencser, that this idea of subscription and authority comports profoundly with discursive democratic tradition. Rules of authority in civil and moral association must be open to discourse and deliberation that may change them. Under such conditions, a democratic tradition is kept alive and strong. When discourse no longer has the opportunity to modify the structures of authority, that tradition is dying or dead.[30] Democratic tradition must, by definition, always be open to popular and discursive insurgency.

For Oakeshott, morality is a tradition too; it cannot be otherwise, just as democracy cannot be otherwise. Morality is a social *practice* (recall that

---

27 We do not have the space to explore the relationship between tradition(s) and culture(s), but it is clear these conceptions and phenomena are closely bound.

28 Stout, 199–200.

29 Walt Whitman, *Whitman: Complete Poetry and Collected Prose*, ed. Justin Kaplan (New York: Library of America), 6; in Stout, 207.

30 MacIntyre argues that this is part of the reason why a Burkean tradition is always in the process of decay, if not already dead; in *After Virtue*, 2d ed. (Notre Dame: University of Notre Dame Press), 222.

Oakeshott's language evolves such that he comes to write of "tradition" where he earlier wrote of "practice"). Democracy names the tradition which is simultaneously social, cultural, political, and moral in ways that are intrinsically related. What holds this constellation of phenomena together in a more-or-less coherent way? Our discursive powers which constitute our conduct. Morality and politics are, for Oakeshott, a discursive social practice, and this is why civil association is moral association, and why democracy is a tradition which holds a vitality and adaptability other political associations cannot hold. The irreducibility and importance of tradition do nothing, in Oakeshott, to diminish the power and value of our agency, individuality, and freedom. His discursive democratic theory is built from the ground up, as I have shown, on the happy embrace of these foundational conceptions and normative ideals.

John Dewey wrote that "Democracy is a form of government only because it is a form of moral and spiritual association".[31] This conviction resonates with Oakeshott's democratic theory. If I can here shed "spiritual" of religious connotations and take it to signify that which goes deepest in our humanity, Dewey surely makes an Oakeshottian claim.[32] Democracy is a living tradition just insofar as it is anchored in the contingent and discursive, deliberative, "politics of conversation". Democracy grows unforced from human conduct based upon the recognition of persons as individual agents who are free and equal. This conduct emerges from our discursive selves, persons who are at their essence "self-enacting" and "self-disclosing". To understand the thought of Michael Oakeshott, just insofar as this project has articulated it with accuracy, is to understand why his understated theory of discursive democracy responds to the hope expressed by Misak, Stout, and many others.

---

31   In "The Ethics of Democracy" (1885).

32   Oakeshott's writing about religion leads me to think that he would not, in fact, insist on shedding the concept of "spiritual" of religious connotations. My suggestion is meant only to make a simpler claim and avoid the enterprise of engaging in an exegesis of Oakeshott's understanding of religion in respect to its consonances with democracy.

Selected Bibliography

Abel, Corey. *Michael Oakeshott's Liberalism: The Epistemology of Experience and the Morality of Individualism*. University of Chicago, 1995.

Abel, Corey, and Timothy Fuller, eds. *The Intellectual Legacy of Michael Oakeshott*. Charlottesville, VA: Imprint Academic, 2005.

Ackerman, Bruce. "Why Dialogue?" *Journal of Philosophy* (1989): 8-12.

Alford, Fred C. *Science and the Revenge of Nature: Marcuse and Habermas*. Gainesville: University of Florida Press, 1985.

Anderson, Perry. "The Intransigent Right at the End of the Century." *London Review of Books* 14 (1992), 7-11.

Aquinas, Thomas. *Summa Theologica,* trans. The Fathers of the English Dominican Province. New York: Benziger Bros., 1948.

Baier, Annette. *Postures of the Mind*. Minneapolis: University of Minnesota Press, 1985.

Barber, Benjamin. *The Conquest of Politics: Liberal Philosophy in Democratic Times*. Princeton: Princeton University Press, 1988.

Barden, Garrett. *After Principles*. Notre Dame: University of Notre Dame Press, 1990.

Barry, Brian. *Democracy and Power: Essays in Political Theory I*. Oxford, UK: Clarendon Press, 1991.

Barry, John, and Marcel Wissenburg, eds. *Sustaining Liberal Democracy*. Basingstoke, England: Palgrave, 2001.

Bartlett, Scott. "Discursive Democracy and a Democratic Way of Life." In *Perspectives on Habermas,* ed. Lewis Edwin Hahn, 367-86. Chicago: Open Court, 2000.

Baynes, Kenneth. "Deliberative Democracy and the Limits of Liberalism." In *Discourse and Democracy: Essays on Habermas's* Between Facts and Norms, eds. René von Schomberg and Kenneth Baynes, 15-30. Albany: State University Press of New York, 2002.

Beiner, Ronald. *What's the Matter with Liberalism?* Berkeley: The University of California Press, 1982.

Beitz, Charles R. *Political Equality: An Essay in Democratic Theory*. Princeton: Princeton University Press, 1989.

Benhabib, Seyla. *Situating the Self: Gender, Community and Postmodernism in Contemporary Ethics*. New York: Routledge, 1992.

Berlin, Isaiah. *The Proper Study of Mankind: An Anthology of Essays,* eds. H. Hardy, and R. Hausheer. London: Pimlico, 1988.

_____. *The Crooked Timber of Humanity,* ed. Henry Hardy, New York: Knopf, 1991.

Borradori, G. *The American Philosopher: Conversations with Quine, Davidson, Putnam, Nozick, Danto, Rorty, Cavell, MacIntyre, and Kuhn,* trans. R. Crocitto, Chicago: University of Chicago Press, 1994.

Boucher, David. "Politics in a Different Mode: An Appreciation of Michael Oakeshott." *History of Political Thought* 12, no. 4 (1991): 717-28.

Cahoone, Lawrence E. *Civil Society: The Conservative Meaning of Liberal Politics*. Malden, MA: Blackwell, 2002.

Candreva, Debra. *The Enemies of Perfection: Oakeshott, Plato, and the Critique of Rationalism*. New York: Lexington Books, 2005.

Casey, John. "Philosopher of Practice." In *The Achievement of Michael Oakeshott*, ed. Jesse Norman, 58-66. London: Gerard Duckworth, 1993.

Chambers, Simone. *Reasonable Democracy*. Ithaca: Cornell University Press, 1996.

Coats, Wendell John, Jr. "Michael Oakeshott as Liberal Theorist." *Canadian Journal of Political Science* 18, no. 4 (1985): 773-87.

————. *A Theory of Republican Character and Related Essays*. Cranbury, NJ: Associated University Presses, 1994.

————. *Oakeshott and His Contemporaries: Montaigne, St. Augustine, Hegel, et al.* Selinsgrove: Susquehanna University Press, 2000.

————. *Political Theory and Practice: Eight Essays on a Theme*, Selinsgrove, PA: Susquehanna University Press, 2003.

Cohen, Joshua. "Deliberation and Democratic Legitimacy." In *Deliberative Democracy: Essays on Reason and Politics*, eds. James Bohman and William Rehg, 67-92. Cambridge: MIT Press, 1997.

————. "For a Democratic Society." In *The Cambridge Companion to Rawls*, ed. Samuel Freeman, 86-138. New York: Cambridge University Press, 2003.

Connolly, William E. *Identity/Difference: Democratic Negotiations of Political Paradox*. Ithaca: Cornell University Press, 1991.

Constant, Benjamin. *Political Writings*. Cambridge: Cambridge University Press, 1988.

Covell, Charles. *The Redefinition of Conservatism: Politics and Doctrine*. London: Macmillan, 1986.

Dagger, Richard. *Civic Virtues: Rights, Citizenship, and Republican Liberalism*. New York: Oxford University Press, 1997.

Dallmayr, Fred. *Polis and Praxis: Exercises in Contemporary Political Theory*. Cambridge: MIT Press, 1984.

Deen, Patrick J. *Democratic Faith*. Princeton: Princeton University Press, 2005.

Digeser, Peter. *Our Politics, Our Selves?: Liberalism, Identity, and Harm*. Princeton: Princeton University Press, 1995.

Doherty, Brian, and Marius de Geus, eds. *Democracy and Green Political Thought: Sustainability, Rights and Citizenship*. London: Routledge, 1996.

Dryzek, John. *Rational Ecology: Environment and Political Ecology*. New York: Basil Blackwell, 1987.

————. "Green Reason: Communicative Ethics for the Biosphere." *Environmental Ethics* 12 (1990): 195-210.

————. "Ecology and Discursive Democracy: Beyond Liberal Capitalism and the Administrative State." *Capitalism, Nature, Socialism* 3, no. 2 (1992): 18-44.

————. "Foundations for Environmental Political Economy: The Search for Homo Ecologicus?" *New Political Economy* 1 (1996): 27-40.

————. "Political and Ecological Communication." In *Ecology and Democracy*, ed. Freya Mathews, 13-30. London: Frank Cass, 1996.

————. "Strategies of Ecological Democratization." In *Democracy and the Environment: Problems and Prospects*, eds. William M. Lafferty and James Meadowcroft, 108-23. Cheltenham: Edward Elger, 1996.

————. *The Politics of the Earth: Environmental Discourses*. Oxford: Oxford University Press, 1997.

————. *Discursive Democracy: Politics, Policy, and Political Science*. New York: Cambridge University Press, 1999.

————. *Deliberative Democracy and Beyond: Liberals, Critics, and Contestations*. New York: Oxford University Press, 2002.

Dworkin, Ronald. "Liberalism." In *Public and Private Morality*, ed. Stuart Hampshire, 113-43. Cambridge: Cambridge University Press, 1978.

Eccleshall, Robert. "Michael Oakeshott and Sceptical Conservatism." In *Policial Science Since 1945: Philosophy, Science, Ideology*, eds. Leonard Tivey and Anthony Wrights, 173-95. Brookfield, VT: Ashgate, 1992.

Ellul, Jacques. *The Ethics of Freedom*, trans. Geoffrey W. Bromiley, Grand Rapids: Eerdmans, 1976.

Farr, Anthony. *Sartre's Radicalism and Oakeshott's Conservatism: The Duplicity of Freedom.* London: Macmillan, 1998.

Feaver, George. "Regimes of Liberty: Michael Oakeshott on Representative Democracy." In *The Intellectual Legacy of Michael Oakeshott,* eds. Corey Abel and Timothy Fuller, 132-59. Charlottesville, VA: Imprint Academic, 2005.

Finlayson, James Gordon. *Habermas: A Very Short Introduction.* New York: Oxford University Press, 2005.

Flack, Colin. "Romanticism in Politics." *New Left Review* 18 (1963): 60-72.

Flathman, Richard E. *The Practice of Political Authority: Authority and the Authoritative.* Chicago: University of Chicago Press, 1980.

_____. *Willful Liberalism: Voluntarism and Individuality in Political Theory and Practice.* Ithaca: Cornell University Press, 1992.

_____. *Reflections of a Would-Be Anarchist: Ideals and Institutions of Liberalism.* Minneapolis: University of Minnesota Press, 1998.

Fox, Richard M. and Joseph P. DeMarco. *Moral Reasoning: A Philosophic Approach,* 2d ed. New York: Harcourt, 2001.

Franco, Paul. "Michael Oakeshott as Liberal Theorist." *Political Theory* 18, no. 3 (1990): 411-36.

_____. *The Political Philosophy of Michael Oakeshott.* New Haven: Yale University Press, 1990.

_____. "Oakeshott's Critique of Rationalism Revisited." *Political Science Reviewer* 21, no .3 (1992):15-43.

_____. *Michael Oakeshott: An Introduction.* New Haven: Yale University Press, 2004.

Fukuyama, Francis. "Identity, Immigration, and Liberal Democracy." *Journal of Democracy* 17, no. 2 (2006): 5-20.

Fuller, Lon. *The Morality of Law.* New Haven: Yale Press, 1963.

Fuller, Timothy. "The Poetics of the Civil Life." In *The Achievement of Michael Oakeshott,* ed. Jesse Norman, 67-81. London: Gerard Duckworth, 1993.

Gerencser, Steven Anthony. "A Democratic Oakeshott?" *Political Research Quarterly* 52, no. 4 (1999): 845-65.

_____. *The Skeptic's Oakeshott.* New York: St. Martin's Press, 2000.

Goodin, Robert. "Enfranchising the Earth, and Its Alternatives." *Political Studies* 44 (1996): 835-49

Grant, Robert. *Oakeshott,* London: The Claridge Press, 1990.

_____. *The Politics of Sex and Other Essays: On Conservatism, Culture, and Imagination.* New York: St. Martin's Press, 2000.

Gray, John. "Michael Oakeshott and the Political Economy of Freedom." *The World and I* 3 (1988): 607-17.

_____. *Liberalisms: Essays in Political Philosophy.* London: Routledge, 1989.

_____. *Post-Liberalism: Studies in Political Thought.* London: Routledge, 1993.

Greenleaf, W.H. *Oakeshott's Philosophical Politics.* New York: Barnes and Noble, 1966.

Gutmann, Amy. "Rawls on the Relationship Between Liberalism and Democracy." In *The Cambridge Companion to Rawls,* ed. Samuel Freeman, 168-99. New York: Cambridge University Press, 2003.

Gunderson, Adolf. G. *The Environmental Promise of Democratic Deliberation.* Madison: University of Wisconsin Press, 1995.

Gutmann, Amy, and Dennis Thompson. *Democracy and Disagreement.* Cambridge: Belknap/Harvard University Press, 1997.

_____. "Reply to the Critics." In *Deliberative Democracy: Essays on Democracy and Disagreement,* ed. Stephen Macedo, 243-79. New York: Oxford University Press, 1999.

_____. *Why Deliberative Democracy?* Princeton: Princeton University Press, 2004.

Habermas, Jürgen. *Legitimation Crisis,* trans. Thomas McCarthy. Boston: Beacon Press, 1975.

_____. *A Berlin Republic: Writings on Germany,* trans. Steven Rendall. Lincoln: University of Nebraska Press, 1977.

_____. *The Theory of Communicative Action. Volume 1: Reason and the Rationalization of Society,* trans. Thomas McCarthy. Boston: Beacon Press, 1984.

_____. *Die neue Unübersichtllichkeit.* Frankfurt am Main: Suhrkamp, 1985.

_____. "Entegung." In *Kommimikates Handlen*, eds. Axel Honneth, and Hans Joas. Frankfurt am Main: Campus, 1986.

_____. *Between Facts and Norms: Contributions to Discourse Theory of Law and Democracy,* trans. William Rehg. Cambridge: MIT Press, 1998.

_____. *The Structural Transformation of the Public Sphere,* trans.Thomas Burger. Cambridge: MIT Press, 1989.

_____. *The Theory of Communicative Action,* Volume 2: *Lifeworld and System: A Critique of Functionalist Reason,* trans. Thomas McCarthy. Boston: Beacon Press, 1989.

_____. *Moral Consciousness and Communicative Action,* trans. Christian Lenhardt and Sherry Weber Nicholson. Cambridge: MIT Press, 1990.

_____. "Reconciliation Through the Public Use of Reason: Remarks on John Rawl's Political Liberalism." *Journal of Philosophy* 92 (1995): 109-31.

_____. *The Inclusion of the Other.* Cambridge: MIT Press, 1998.

_____. *Justification and Application: Remarks on a Discourse Ethics,* trans. Ciaran P. Cronin. Cambridge: MIT Press, 2001.

Hahn, Lewis Edwin, ed. *Perspectives on Habermas.* Chicago: Open Court, 2000.

Hardt, Michael, and Antonio Negri. *Multitude: War and Democracy in the Age of Empire.* New York: The Penguin Press, 2004.

Hart, H.L.A. *The Concept of Law.* Oxford: Clarendon Press, 1961.

Hauerwas, Stanley with David B. Burrell. *Truthfulness and Tragedy: Further Investigations into Christian Ethics.* Notre Dame: University of Notre Dame Press, 1977.

Held, Virginia. *Rights and Goals.* Chicago: University of Chicago Press, 1984.

Honig, Bonnie. *Political Theory and the Displacement of Politics.* Ithaca: Cornell University Press, 1993.

Horkheimer, Max, and Theodor Adorno. *Dialectic of Enlightenment.* New York: Seabury Press, 1972.

Horster, Detlef. *Habermas,* trans. Heidi Thompson. Philadelphia: Pennbridge, 1992.

Howard, Dick. *The Spectre of Democracy.* New York: Columbia University Press, 2002.

Howe, Leslie. *On Habermas.* Belmont, CA: Wadsworth, 2000.

Husserl, Edmund. *The Crisis of European Sciences and the Transcendental Phenomenology,* trans. David Carr. Evanston: Northwest University Press, 1970.

Jonsen, Albert R. and Stephen Toulmin. *The Abuse of Casuistry: A History of Moral Reasoning.* Berkeley: University of California Press, 1988.

Kellner, Douglas. "Habermas the Public Sphere, and Democracy: A Critical Intervention." In *Perspectives on Habermas,* ed. Lewis Edwin Hahn, 259-87. Chicago: Open Court, 2000.

Kirk, Russell. *The Conservative Mind.* London: Faber and Faber, 1954.

Knight, Jack. "Constitutionalism and Deliberative Democracy." In *Deliberative Democracy: Essays on Democracy and Disagreement,* ed. Stephen Macedo. New York: Oxford University Press, 1999.

Koerner, Kirk F. *Liberalism and Its Critics.* London: Croom Helm, 1985.

Kovesi, Julius. *Moral Notions.* London: Routledge and Kegan Paul, 1967.

Kupperman, Joel. *Character.* New York: Oxford University Press, 1991.

Kymlicka, Will. *Contemporary Political Philosophy: An Introduction,* 2d ed. New York: Oxford University Press, 2002.

Lasch, Christopher. *The Revolt of the Elites and the Betrayal of Democracy.* New York: Norton, 1995.

Leib, Nathan. *Deliberative Democracy in America: A Proposal for a Popular Branch of Government.* University Park: The Pennsylvania State University Press, 2004.

Liddington, John. "Oakeshott: Freedom in a Modern European State." In *Conceptions of Liberty in Political Philosophy,* eds. Zibiginew Pelczynski and John Gray, 289- 319. New York: St. Martin's Press, 1984.

Lomasky, Loren. "Liberal Obituary?" In *Liberty for the Twenty-First Century: Contemprorary Libertarian Thought,* eds. Tibor R. Machan and Douglass B. Rasmussen, 243-58. Lanham, MD: Rowman and Littlefield, 1995.

Macedo, Stephen, ed. *Deliberative Democracy: Essays on* Democracy and Disagreement. New York: Oxford University Press, 1999.

MacIntyre, Alasdair. *A Short History of Ethics.* New York: Macmillan, 1966.

_____. *After Virtue: A Study in Moral Theory.* Notre Dame: The University of Notre Dame Press, 1981.

_____. "Does Applied Ethics Rest on a Mistake?" *Monist* 67 (1984): 498-513.

_____. *Whose Justice? Which Rationality?* Notre Dame: University of Notre Dame Press, 1988.

_____. "The Privatization of the Good." *The Review of Politics* 52, no. 3 (1990): 344-61.

_____. *Three Rival Versions of Moral Inquiry: Encyclopedia, Genealogy and Tradition.* Notre Dame: University of Notre Dame Press, 1990.

_____. *Dependent Rational Animals: Why Human Beings Need the Virtues.* Chicago: Open Court, 1999.

Manning, D. "The Philosophical Foundations of Liberal Ideology." *Journal of Political Ideologies* 2 (1997), 137-58.

Mansbridge, Jane. *Beyond Adversary Democracy.* Chicago: University of Chicago Press, 1983.

_____. "Everyday Talk in the Deliberative System." In *Deliberative Democracy: Essays on* Democracy and Disagreement, ed. Stephen Macedo, *Deliberative Democracy: Essays on* Democracy and Disagreement. New York: Oxford University Press, 1999.

Mapel, David. "Civil Association and the Idea of Contingency." *Political Theory* 18, no. 3 (1990): 392-410.

_____. "Purpose and Politics: Can There be a Non-Instrumental Civil Association?" *Political Science Reviewer* 21 (1992): 63-80.

McCarthy, Thomas. *The Critical Theory of Jürgen Habermas,* Cambridge: MIT Press, 1994.

McDowell, John. "Virtue and Reason." *Monist* 62 (1979): 331-50.

McIntyre, Kenneth B. *The Limits of Political Theory: Oakeshott's Philosophy of Civil Association.* Charlottesville, VA: Imprint Academic, 2004.

McKinnon, Christine. *Character, Virtue Theories, and the Vices.* Orchard Park, NY: Broadview Press, 1999.

Mewes, Horst. "Modern Individualism: Reflections on Oakeshott, Arendt, and Strauss." *Political Science Reviewer* 21 (1992): 116-47.

Minch, Michael. "Authority and the Rule of Law as Contingent Moral Practice in Michael Oakeshott's Civil Association." In *Law, Justice, and Civic Virtue,* ed. David Keller, 79-88. Orem, UT: Utah Valley State College, 2005.

Minoque, Kenneth. "On Identifying Ideology." In *Ideology and Politics,* eds. Maurice Cranston and P. Mair, 27-42. Firenze: Bdia Fiesolana, 1980.

Minteer, Ben A. and Bob Pepperman Taylor, eds. *Democracy and the Claims of Nature: Critical Perspectives for a New Century.* Lanham, MD: Rowman and Littlefield, 2002.

Misak, Cheryl. *Truth, Politics, Morality: Pragmatism and Deliberation.* New York: Routledge, 2000.

Mouffe, Chantal. "Democratic Citizenship and the Political Community." In *Dimensions of Radical Democracy: Pluralism, Citizenship, and Democracy,* ed., Chantal Mouffe. London: Verso, 1992.

_____. *The Return of the Political.* London: Verso, 1993.

Nardin, Terry. *The Philosophy of Michael Oakeshott.* University Park: The Pennsylvania Sate University Press, 2001.

Nietzsche, Friedrich. *The Gay Science,* ed. Bernard Williams. New York: Cambridge University Press, 2001.

Norman, Jesse, ed. *The Achievement of Michael Oakehsott.* London: Gerard Duckworth, 1993.

Nussbaum, Martha. *The Fragility of Goodness.* New York: Cambridge University Press, 1985.

Oakeshott, Michael. "The Conception of a Philosophical Jurisprudence." *Politica* 3 (two parts: September and December, 1938): 203-22, 345-60.

_____. ed. *The Social and Political Doctrines of Contemporary Europe.* Cambridge: Cambridge University Press, 1939.

_____. "Contemporary British Politics." *The Cambridge Journal* 1 (1947): 474- 90.

_____. *A Letter to Karl Popper.*
www.michael_oakeshott_association.org/lifeworkspopper.pdf

_____. Introduction to *The Essentials of Parliamentary Democracy,* 2d ed., Reginald Bassett, xxi-xxiv. London: Frank Cass, 1964.

_____. *Hobbes on Civil Association.* Indianapolis: Liberty Fund, 1975.

_____. "On Misunderstanding Human Conduct: A Reply to My Critics." *Political Theory* 4, no. 3 (1976): 353-67.

_____. *Rationalism in Politics and Other Essays.* Indianapolis: Liberty Fund, 1991.

_____. *Religion, Politics and the Moral Life,* ed. Timothy Fuller. New Haven: Yale University Press, 1993.

_____. *Morality and Politics in Modern Europe: The Harvard Lectures,* ed. Shirley Robin Letwin. New Haven: Yale University Press, 1993.

_____. *Experience and Its Modes.* New York: Cambridge University Press, 1994 (first published, 1933).

_____. *The Politics of Faith and the Politics of Scepticism,* ed. Timothy Fuller, New Haven: Yale University, 1996.

_____. *On Human Conduct.* New York: Oxford University Press, 1996 (first published 1975).

_____. *On History and Other Essays.* Indianapolis: Liberty Fund, 1999.

_____. *The Voice of Liberal Learning.* Indianapolis: Liberty Fund, 2001.

_____. *What is History? And Other Essays,* ed. Luke O'Sullivan. Charlottesville, VA: Imprint Academic, 2004.

Olson, Kevin. *Reflexive Democracy: Political Equality and the Welfare State.* Cambridge: MIT Press, 2006.

Orr, Robert. "A Double Agent in the Dream of Michael Oakeshott." *Political Science Reviewer* 20 (1992):44-62.

O'Sullivan, Luke. *Oakeshott on History.* Charlottesville, VA: Imprint Academic, 2003.

O'Sullivan, Noël. "Michael Oakeshott in the Perspective of Western Thought." In *The Achievement of Michael Oakeshott,* ed. Jesse Norman, 101-06. London: Gerard Duckworth, 1993.

Outhwaite, William, ed. *The Habermas Reader.* Cambrdige: Polity Press, 1996.

Palon, Kari. "Das 'Webersche Moment'." *Zur Kontingenz des Politischen.* Opladen/Weisbaden: Westdeustscher Verlag, 1998.

Parekh, Bhikhu. "The Philosophy of Michael Oakeshott," *British Journal of Political Science* 9, no. 3 (1979): 487-95.

_____. "Michael Oakeshott." In *Contemporary Political Thinkers,* 100-23. Oxford: Martin Robertson & Co., 1982.

Pilbeam, Bruce. "Conservatism and Postmodernism: Consanguineous Relations or 'Different' Voices?" *Journal of Political Ideologies* 6, no. 1 (2001): 33-54.

Pinches, Charles R. *Theology and Action: After Theory in Christian Ethics.* Grand Rapids, MI: Eerdmans, 2002.

Pincoffs, Edmund L. "Quandary Ethics." *Mind* 80 (1971): 498-513.

_____. *Quandaries and Virtues: Against Reductivism in Ethics.* Lawrence: University of Kansas Press, 1986.

Pitkin, Hanna. "The Roots of Conservatism: Michael Oakeshott and the Denial of Politics." *Dissent* 20 (1973): 496-525.

_____. "Inhuman Conduct and Political Theory." *Political Theory* 4, no. 3 (1976): 301-20.

Pocock, J.G.A. *The Machiavellian Moment.* Princeton: Princeton University Press, 1975.

Podoksik, Efraim. *In Defense of Modernity: Vision and Philosophy in Michael Oakeshott.* Charlottesville, VA: Imprint Academic, 2003.

Porter, Jean. *Moral Action and Christian Ethics.* New York: Cambrdige University Press, 1999.

Quinton, Anthony. *The Politics of Imperfection: The Religious and Secular Traditions of Conservative Thought in England from Hooker to Oakeshott.* London: Faber and Faber, 1978.

Rasmussen, David M. *Reading Habermas.* Cambridge, MA: Basil Blackwell, 1990.

Rawls, John. *A Theory of Justice*. Cambridge: Harvard University Press, 1971. Revised, 1999.
_____. "Justice as Fairness: Political Not Metaphysical." *Philosophy and Public Affairs* 14 (1985): 223-52.
_____. *Political Liberalism*. New York: Columbia University Press, 1993. Revised 1996.
_____. "Political Liberalism: Reply to Habermas." *Journal o f Philosophy* 92 (1995): 132-80.
_____. *Collected Papers*, ed. Samuel Freeman. Cambridge: Harvard University Press, 1996.
_____. *Justice as Fairness: A Restatement*. Cambridge: The Belknap Press of Harvard University Press, 2001.
Rayner, Jeremy. "The Legend of Oakeshott's Conservatism: Sceptical Philosophy and Limited Politics." *Canadian Journal of Political Science* 18, no. 2(1985): 313-39.
Raz, Joseph. *The Morality of Freedom*. Oxford: Clarendon Press, 1986.
Rehg, William. *Insight and Solidarity: A Study in the Discourse Ethics of Jürgen Habermas*. Berkeley: University of California Press, 1994.
Richardson, Henry S. "Specifying Norms as a Way to Resolve Concrete Ethical Problems." *Philosophy and Public Affairs* 19, no. 4 (1990): 270-310.
Riley, Patrick. "Michael Oakeshott: Philosopher of Individuality." *The Review of Politics* 54, no. 4 (1992): 649-64.
Rorty, Richard. *Mind in Action: Essays in the Philosophy of Mind*. Boston: Beacon Press, 1988.
_____. *Objectivity, Relativism, and Truth: Philosophical Papers 1*. New York: Cambrdige Universtiy Press, 1991.
_____. *Contingency, Irony, and Solidarity*. New York: Cambridge University of Press, 1993.
Rousseau, Jeans-Jacques. *The Social Contact and Other Later Political Writings*, ed. and trans. Victor Gourevitch. New York: Cambridge University Press, 1997.
Sandel, Michael. *Liberalism and the Limits of Justice*. New York: Cambridge University Press, 1982.
Sanders, Lynn M. "Against Deliberation." *Political Theory* 25 (1997): 347-76.
Segal, Jacob. "A Storm in Paradise: Liberalism and the Problem of Time." *Critical Review* 8, no. 1 (1994): 23-48.
Shapiro, Ian. *The State of Democratic Theory*. Princeton: Princeton University Press, 2003.
_____. *The Flight from Reality in the Human Sciences*. Princeton: Princeton University Press, 2003.
Singh, Randhir. *Reason, Revolution, and Political Theory: Notes on Oakeshott's* Rationalism in Politics. New Delhi: People's Publishing House, 1967.
Skinner, Quentin. "The Idea of Negative Liberty: Philosophical and Historical Perspective." In *Philosophy in History*, eds. Richard Rorty, J.B. Schneewind, and Quentin Skinner, 193-221. New York: Cambridge University Press, 1984.
Soininen, Suvi. *From a "Necessary Evil" to an Art of Contingency: Michael Oakeshott's Conception of Political Authority*. Charlottesville, VA: Imprint Academic, 2005.
Spitz, David. "A Rationalist *Malrgé Lui*: The Perplexities of Being Michael Oakeshott." *Political Theory* 4 (1976): 335-52
Stout, Jeffrey. *Ethics After Babel*. Boston: Beacon Press, 1988.
_____. *Democracy and Tradition*. Princeton: Princeton University Press, 2004.
Taylor, Charles. *Philosophy and the Human Sciences: Philosophical Papers* Vol. 2. New York: Cambridge University Press, 1985.
_____. *Sources of the Self: The Making of the Modern Identity*. Cambridge: Harvard University Press, 1989.
_____. *The Ethics of Authenticity*. Cambridge: Harvard University Press, 1991.
_____. *Multiculturalism and the Politics of Recognition*. Princeton: Princeton University Press, 1992.
Thomas, D.A. Loyd. "Review of *On Human Conduct*." *Mind* 86, no. 343 (1977): 453- 56.
Thompson, Martyn. "Intimations of Poetry in the Practical Life." In *The Intellectual Legacy of Michael Oakeshott*, eds. Corey Abel and Timothy Fuller, 281-92. Charlottesville, VA: Imprint Academic, 2005.

Torgerson, Douglas. "Policy Professionalism and the Voice of Dissent: The Case of Environmentalism." *Polity* 29 (1997): 345-74.

Tregenza, Ian. *Michael Oakeshott on Hobbes: A Study in the Renewal of Philosophical Ideas.* Charlottesville, VA: Imprint Academic, 2003.

Tseng, Roy. *The Sceptical Idealist: Michael Oakeshott as a Critic of the Enlightenment.* Charlottesville, VA: Imprint Academic, 2003.

Walsh, David. *The Growth of the Liberal Soul.* Columbia: The University of Missouri Press, 1997.

Wallach, John. "Liberals, Communitarians, and the Tasks of Political Theory." *Political Theory* 15, no. 4 (1987):581-611.

Walzer, Michael. "The Communitarian Critique of Liberalism." *Political Theory* 18, no.1 (1990): 6-23.

_____. "A Credo for this Moment." *Dissent* 37:2(1990): 159-60.

Warnke, Georgia. "Communicative Rationality and Cultural Values." In *The Cambridge Companion to Habermas,* ed. Stephen K. White, 120-42. New York: Cambridge University Press, 1999.

White, James Boyd. "Law as Rhetoric, Rhetoric as Law." In *The Social Organization of Law,* ed. Austin Sarat, 62-67. Los Angeles: Roxburg, 2004.

White, Stephen K. *The Recent Work of Jürgen Habermas: Reason, Justice, and Modernity.* New York: Cambridge University Press, 1988.

_____. "Reason, Modernity, and Democracy." In *The Cambridge Companion to Habermas,* ed. Stephen K. White, 3-16. New York: Cambridge University Press, 1999.

Whitman, Walt. *Whitman: Complete Poetry and Collected Prose,* ed. Justin Kaplan. New York: Library of America, 1982.

Williams, Bernard. *Morality: An Introduction to Ethics.* New York: Harper and Row, 1972.

_____. *Ethics and the Limits of Philosophy.* Cambridge: Harvard University Press, 1985.

Williams, Michael. "Liberalism and Two Conceptions of the State." In *Liberalism Reconsidered,* eds. D. MacLean and C. Mills, 117-29. Totowa, NJ: Rowman and Allanheld, 1983.

Wolin, Sheldon S. "The Politics of Self-Disclosure." *Political Theory* 4, no. 3 (1976): 321-34.

Wood, Neal. "A Guide to the Classics: The Skepticism of Professor Oakeshott." *The Journal of Politics* 21:4 (1959): 647-62.

Worthington, Glenn. "Michael Oakeshott on Waiting for Godot." *History of Poltiical Thought* 16, no. 1 (1995): 105-19.

_____. *Religious and Poetic Experience in the Thought of Michael Oakeshott.* Charlottesville, VA: Imprint Academic, 2005.

Young, Iris Marion. "Justice, Inclusion, and Deliberative Democracy," In *Deliberative Democracy: Essays on Democracy and Disagreement,* ed. Stephen Macedo, 151- 58. New York: Oxford University, 1999.

Index